Black Queer Girlhood on the Musical Theatre Stage

Black Queer Girlhood on the Musical Theatre Stage

LA DONNA L. FORSGREN

OXFORD
UNIVERSITY PRESS

OXFORD
UNIVERSITY PRESS

Oxford University Press is a department of the University of Oxford.
It furthers the University's objective of excellence in research, scholarship,
and education by publishing worldwide. Oxford is a registered trade mark of
Oxford University Press in the UK and in certain other countries.

Published in the United States of America by Oxford University Press
198 Madison Avenue, New York, NY 10016, United States of America.

CIP data is on file at the Library of Congress

ISBN 9780197661413 (pbk.)
ISBN 9780197661406 (hbk.)

DOI: 10.1093/9780197661444.001.0001

Paperback printed by Marquis Book Printing, Canada
Hardback printed by Lightning Source, Inc., United States of America

The manufacturer's authorized representative in the EU for product safety is
Oxford University Press España S.A. of Parque Empresarial San Fernando de Henares,
Avenida de Castilla, 2 – 28830 Madrid (www.oup.es/en or product.safety@oup.com).
OUP España S.A. also acts as importer into Spain of products made by the manufacturer.

FSC www.fsc.org MIX Paper | Supporting responsible forestry FSC® C103567

For my daughters and all the young and gifted Blackgirls

Contents

Figures

Introduction

Chapter 1

Chapter 2

Chapter 3

Chapter 4

Chapter 5

Chapter 6

Acknowledgments

Many hours spent in the company of brilliant artists, colleagues, friends, and family made this book possible. I want to thank Aduke Aremu for generously sharing a copy of her original musical, *The Liberation of Mother Goose*, from her personal archives. Aduke, Kirsten Childs, J. e. Franklin, Micki Grant, Christiani Pitts, Jeff Sugg, Jackie Taylor, Schele Williams, and Jayla Williams-Craig graciously gave of their time and shared their keen insights with me. Giovanna, a staff member in the Permissions and Reproduction Services, helped me secure and digitize so many images at the New York Public Library. A dozen photographers (named throughout this manuscript) granted me permission to use their production photographs and I am surely in your debt as well. Shelby Lunderman, thank you for encouraging me to go see *King Kong* and for connecting me to Christiani. You are the realist.

I am blessed with really great colleagues: Christine Becker, Terrance Brown, Tarryn Chun, Jim Collins, Anne García-Romero, Matt Hawkins, Peter Holland, Michael Kackman, Mary Celeste Kearney, Olivier Morel, Susan Ohmer, Matthew Payne, and Pamela Robertson Wojcik. I will be forever grateful for your expertise, encouragement, and genuine interest in my work. A special thank you to Kevin Dreyer for asking the question that gave me perfect clarity.

I have a fantastic writing group. Each week I have the pleasure of checking in with Marisa Exeter, Toyosi Onwuemene, and Wanda Wright. Thank you for your support and friendship. I could not imagine how much trouble I would get into without you.

Thank you, Cayley Robinson, for your research assistance, for introducing me to Starbucks chocolate croissants, and for your incredible enthusiasm for musical theatre. I don't know how I could have ever taken archival trips to New York without you!

Daniel Banks and Kyson Smith: thank you for your help and support.

Lundeana Thomas has been a mentor and wonderful friend to me since my early days in graduate school. Thank you for laying the groundwork for my research, introducing me to some of the artists who appear in this study, and providing unfailing encouragement. I hope to be as kind and brilliant as you one day.

I would like to thank the University of Notre Dame for their generous support of my research. Receiving the Institute for Scholarship in the Liberal Arts, College of Arts and Letters Small Grant, and Faculty Research Support Program Initiation Grant allowed me to complete preliminary archival research, conduct interviews, and hire AAA Transcription, LLC. Notre Dame's Resilience and Recovery Grant provided course reduction which gave me the time I needed to conduct preliminary research during and immediately following the COVID-19 pandemic.

Karin Arnold and AAA Transcription, LLC transcribed thousands of hours of audio for my last two book projects. Michael Gnat edited an early draft of Chapter Five and Shelby Brewster created the fabulous index. You were my first "readers" and I am so grateful for your genuine interest in the project, incredible attention to detail, and outstanding work.

I have the most supportive family I could have ever asked for. Thank you, Layne, for providing me with an endless supply of Dr. Pepper Zero and dark chocolate, reading my ROUGH drafts, and helping me talk through my writing blocks. Jacoby, you defy all odds and your incredible achievements continue to inspire me. Piper, I'll admit that your book is better than mine. Cruser, let's be real: math homework only gets worse in high school. Emmett, thank you for your patience as I work off the treasure-hunting games I still owe you. Phoebe, I will always cherish the gift of hearing your giggles and receiving your sticky kisses. Jacoby, Piper, Cruser, Emmett, Phoebe, and Penelope: you are my dream come true. *I'll love you forever.*

Introduction

To Be a Young and Gifted Blackgirl

Elizabeth Davenport (1926–1979) isn't a name that most musical theatre lovers would ever recognize. Yet, my earliest memories are of listening to my mother tell stories about her musical talent, her drive, and the racial barriers that effectively limited her theatrical career. Under the tutelage of her mother, Helen Thomas, she and her younger sisters Naomi, Beverly, and Dorothy formed The Thomas Sisters' Violin and Vocal Quartet and performed at Black churches and events throughout the Mahoning Valley (see Figure I.1). During the 1960s, Elizabeth began a solo career on the musical stage, performing in numerous productions at The Youngstown Playhouse (1924–present), one of the oldest continuously running community theatres in the United States. Although her beauty and melodious soprano voice filled auditoriums, she could not breach institutional white racism and remained confined to supporting roles throughout her career. She financially supported herself, her daughter, and her mother by single-handedly running a convent kitchen. During the day, as she prepared food for nuns, Richard Rodgers and Oscar Hammerstein II's masterpieces were never too far from her lips. In the evenings, she attended audition after audition to make her vision of a life on Broadway a reality. When she died in an automobile accident at the age of fifty-two, she had never given up on her dream. Today, when I remember my great aunt Elizabeth's legacy, I think of Lorraine Hansberry who famously wrote: "though it be a thrilling and marvelous thing to be merely young and gifted in such times, it is doubly so, doubly dynamic—to be young, gifted and black."[1] My great aunt Elizabeth stands among countless numbers of unheralded young and gifted Black girls who contributed to the proliferation of musical theatre.

While I did not inherit much vocal talent, I grew up with a deep appreciation for Black women's musical genius and continue to share this knowledge with my twelve-year-old daughter Piper. Their works became even

Black Queer Girlhood on the Musical Theatre Stage. La Donna L. Forsgren, Oxford University Press.
 DOI: 10.1093/9780197661444.003.0001

Figure I.1 The Thomas Sisters' Violin and Vocal Quartet: Naomi Ruth, Elizabeth Alice, Beverly Agnes, and Dorothy Rebecca, Youngstown, Ohio, c. 1938. Courtesy of the author.

more meaningful to us as a global pandemic raged on, and the call to value and protect Black life reached our doorsteps in rural Indiana. As public schools and universities pivoted to online instruction during the spring and fall of 2020, any semblance of normalcy in my household evaporated.

Musical theatre "showdowns" became our "new normal." The showdowns were simple; Piper would blast a song from one of her favorite musicals at any point in a given day. We would then sing along. Loudly. Badly. After our screeching concluded, we debated the song's merits: lyrical composition, tempo, and emotional resonance. Finally, I would try to best my daughter's choice, blasting a song drawn from this very study. The battles abruptly ended when I would have to log in to teach my online course or when her virtual class began. These seemingly inconsequential musical theatre interludes brought much-needed joy and laughter into my daughter's day as feelings of fear, anxiety, and uncertainty encircled our lives.

Our lively showdowns also provided an opportunity to enrich my daughter's understanding of how our family history relates to broader discussions of Black women's performance and activist traditions. Prior to our showdowns, Piper's knowledge of musical theatre consisted of canonical musicals and more recent megahits such as *Hamilton* (2015), *Dear Evan Hansen* (2015), and *Beetlejuice* (2018). As I shared our musical theatre heritage with my daughter, I also discussed how the institutional barriers that prevented great aunt Elizabeth from achieving her dream persist today. Yet, despite these challenges, contemporary Black women theatre artists continue to create works that speak to the realities of Black life. Indeed, they continue the longstanding tradition of using the seemingly escapist platform of musical theatre to foster a more just and equitable society. By "contemporary," I refer to a periodization following the Civil Rights Act of 1964, spanning from 1970 to today. While the US government has extended some civil liberties since the 1960s—with the passage of the Americans with Disabilities Act of 1990, the Marriage (Same Sex) Act of 2013, etc.—we have yet to eradicate systemic racism, sexism, ableism, and heterosexism from our stages or society.

When Piper's eyes would begin to glaze over—I find that every Black girl enjoys a long-winded history lesson—I introduced her to the Off-Broadway musical *The Bubbly Black Girl Sheds Her Chameleon Skin* (2000). Piper's immediate response to the song "Sweet Chitty Chatty" was, "Wait. What? Did a girl just die?!" The seemingly innocuous upbeat song, sung by an elementary school-aged Black girl and her talking dolls, delves into the 1963 bombing of the Birmingham 16th Street Baptist Church. This act of white supremacist terrorism killed four Black girls: Addie Mae Collins, Cynthia Wesley, Carole Robertson, and Carol Denise McNair. After we analyzed the song's engagement with Black girlhood and the history of white terrorism,

Piper summarized Kirsten Childs's award-winning musical with the age-old wisdom of a Generation Zer: "Deep meanings but happy tunes." Indeed, Childs crafted *The Bubbly Black Girl Sheds Her Chameleon Skin* to provide three-dimensional images of Black people—especially Black girls—onstage. "The most important thing I wanted was to truly see *me* in the mirror. Maybe some of those other little girls that I knew and others like them throughout the country that were growing up at that time could also see themselves in the mirror and realize that the mirror that was being held up to them was false and reflected somebody else's reality of who they were. I knew I had to bear witness to my own truths," remembers Childs.[2] The genre of musical theatre—with its ability to communicate storytelling and emotional depth through words, music, movement, and spectacle—provided the means by which Childs could bear witness to the perils and possibilities of Black girlhood and further the cause of social justice. This study celebrates these efforts and the longer tradition from which it emerged.

Just as Black girlhood intersects multiple fields of intellectual query, so too must this study. *Black Queer Girlhood on the Musical Theatre Stage* examines the critical tension between Black women's representation of Black girlhood, social activism, spectatorship, and popular entertainment. Throughout the study, I ask: How have Black women theatremakers contributed to the development of politically engaged popular entertainment on the contemporary musical theatre stage? How does their work represent Black girlhood? Does their artistry contradict, complicate, or critique dominant society's representations of Black girlhood? Finally, how might Black queer feminist spectators engage with musical theatre productions created by Black women artists?

My methodology relies heavily upon Black queer feminist criticism. As both political theory and praxis, Black queer feminist criticism serves as a vital but underresearched area of critical thought located at the intersections of intellectual, popular, and Black women's cultures. The literary critic and theorist Laura Alexandra Harris conceptualizes personal narrative, politics, and the pursuit of pleasure as central components of Black queer feminist models.[3] Harris writes:

> Queer black feminism can best be understood to take up sexuality in ways that make it simultaneously about race, class, and gender—in ways that

> politicize pleasure—not just personalize it as a politics of being. The constituency for queer black feminism may alter daily, may be organized differently around class or race, and may carry agendas from welfare activism to academic cultural analysis. It should exhibit the methods for a changing agenda by changing the concept of the feminist body and its pleasure and its history.[4]

In other words, Black queer feminist criticism illuminates the gaps and silences within queer and feminist histories and theories by reclaiming and writing Black queer feminist subjectivity into history.[5] Applying Black queer feminist theories to my performance analyses and close readings of nearly twenty musical productions allows a more nuanced understanding of how Black women's identity politics and their pursuit of pleasure converges with the contemporary Black freedom struggle.

Black Queer Girlhood on the Musical Theatre Stage enters into dialogue with musical theatre scholarship, Black girlhood studies, film and television studies, Black queer feminist criticism, and reception studies, critiquing the gaps and silences within these fields. I invite musical theatre scholars to consider the importance of Blackgirl representation and to explore significant works of Black women musical theatre artists produced off-Broadway and on the popular Contemporary Chitlin Circuit. I ask Black girlhood studies scholars to consider the potential Black musical productions have to resist pathological images of Black girlhood, center their stories, and produce politically engaged Black popular entertainment. My analysis considers "live" televised musical events—a form of camp in its own right. I invite film and television studies to decentralize camp spectatorship from white urban gay male subjectivity and situate Black girls as *subjects* of camp. Finally, my use of Black queer feminist criticism encourages reception studies to engage with the importance of intersectionality and situate Black queer feminists as ideal spectators. In so doing, I apply "resistant readership" to understand what *meaning* and *pleasure* Black queer spectators might derive from engaging with popular musical performances created by Black women. At times, this means "reading" heteronormative works as Black lesbian narratives. Other times, this entails considering how Black queer feminist spectators might "read" special meaning within heteronormative narratives. Regardless of the "reading," both approaches *theorize* spectatorship and do not include actual interviews with spectators.

Black Women, Girlhood, and Contemporary Musical Theatre

Within the past fifty years, only a select few Black women have been granted entrée into elite white male circles of Broadway and break (albeit briefly) racial and gender barriers. For example, Urban Arts Corps (1967–1983) founder Vinnette Carroll became the first Black woman to direct a Broadway musical with Micki Grant's revue, *Don't Bother Me, I Can't Cope* (1972). Carroll would also receive two Tony Award nominations for Best Direction of a Musical (*Don't Bother Me*, 1973; *Your Arms Too Short to Box with God*, 1977), the first Black woman to do so. Producer and theatre founder Rosetta LeNoire championed diversifying casting on Broadway stages, providing space for talented actors, regardless of their race, to cultivate their talents at her Amas Repertory Theatre Company (1968–present). Perhaps most notably, her collaboration with playwright Loften Mitchell resulted in a Broadway run and a 1976 Tony Award for their musical revue, *Bubbling Brown Sugar*. In terms of acting, Audra McDonald helped usher in nontraditional casting by performing in the historically white role of Carrie Pipperidge in the 1994 Broadway revival of Rodgers and Hammerstein's *Carousel*. McDonald's breakout role garnered her first (of six) Tony Award for Best Featured Actress in a Musical. Other legendary Black Broadway actresses include performers Jennifer Holliday, Debbie Allen, Loretta Devine, Leslie Uggams, Sheryl Lee Ralph, Micki Grant, Phylicia Rashad, LaChanze, and countless others. More recently, popular Black women singers and entertainers such as Keke Palmer, Nene Leakes, Raven-Symoné, Toni Braxton, Deborah Cox, Vanessa Williams, Viola Davis, and Fantasia Barrino have also found opportunities to perform on Broadway stages.

However, Black women's greater visibility on Broadway stages does not extend to increased leadership opportunities offstage. In most cases, creative control remains out of reach for Black women artists working on Broadway. This truth is perhaps best exemplified by the fact that after Carroll received a Tony nomination for Best Direction, it would take nearly forty years for a Black woman director to receive a similar nomination.[6]

Despite the commercial success of a select few Black women musical theatre artists, most Black women achieve creative control of musical productions and acquire leadership positions in Off-Broadway, regional and community theatres, or with touring companies. Challenged by sexism and racism, Black women musical theatre artists are all too often excluded from elite Broadway spaces and opt to showcase their talents in alternative spaces. In fact, some of the most successful contemporary Black women musical theatre artists have never written, composed, directed, produced, or performed on a Broadway stage. Yet, artists such as Jackie Taylor, Aduke Aremu, and Vy Higginsen are well-respected within their communities and have garnered national and international reputations for their work. For example, Higginsen and her husband Ken Wydro remember being rejected by New York producers, who doubted there was an audience for their gospel-based musical *Mama, I Want to Sing!* (1983). Rather than accept defeat, they used their own funds to produce and tour the musical across the United States, Japan, and Europe. Within three years of its debut, *Mama, I Want to Sing!* garnered three million spectators and grossed 62.3 million dollars in ticket sales.[7] In addition to this long-celebrated musical which continues to tour, Taylor's *The Other Cinderella* (1976) and Aremu's *The Liberation of Mother Goose* (1972) remain a popular draw for predominately Black audiences throughout Chicago and New York, respectively.

Unfortunately, musicals created by Black women are rarely, if ever, included in musical theatre scholarship. For example, Allen Woll's *Black Musical Theatre: From Coontown to Dreamgirls* (1989), one of the most comprehensive histories of Black musical theatre, does not even reference the hit, *Mama, I Want to Sing!*. Instead, he positions "the smashing success" of shows such as *Purlie* (1970), *Raisin* (1973), *The Wiz* (1975), *Bubbling Brown Sugar* (1976), *Eubie!* (1978), *Ain't Misbehavin'* (1978), *Sophisticated Ladies* (1981), *Dreamgirls* (1981), and *The Tap Dance Kid* (1983) as the "culmination of ninety years of blacks' experience on Broadway."[8] While Woll recovers the presence of early Black talent on the Great White Way, his Broadway-centric study cannot attend to the wealth of Black artistry created beyond Broadway. Nonetheless, my study owes a debt to Woll's recuperative efforts to reclaim early Black musical theatre artists.

More recently, musical theatre scholars have begun questioning Broadway-focused scholarship, which in turn has created space to explore Black women's artistry. Stacy Wolf's aptly titled book, *Beyond Broadway: The Pleasure and Promise of Musical Theatre Across America* (2020), for example, explores how local musical theatre productions—often hidden from the purview of academia and theatre critics—sustain the field and bring pleasure to people's lives. "I intended to document an aspect of musical theatre production history that seldom garners attention, much less sustained appreciation. My purpose was to shine light on places and practices that have touched and shaped many of us (places and practices, in fact, fundamental to who we are) but to which scholars, critics, and ethnographers have not paid proper attention," writes Wolf.[9] Rashida Z. Shaw McMahon's *The Black Circuit: Race, Performance, and Spectatorship in Black Popular Theatre* (2020) similarly considers the local, providing much-needed insight into the Contemporary Chitlin Circuit, a popular form of entertainment that blends gospel and R&B music, Christian faith, comedy, melodrama, and Black cultural expression for predominately Black audiences. McMahon concludes that the Contemporary Chitlin Circuit "produce[s] safe meeting and testing grounds in which Black artistic, cultural, ideological, and spiritual thoughts and imaginings can be expressed, confirmed, and/or rejected by and among African American practitioners and audiences with shared priorities and interests."[10] Perhaps most importantly, McMahon situates Higginsen and Wydro as early pioneers of this commercially successful touring circuit.[11] *Black Queer Girlhood on the Musical Theatre Stage* builds on these efforts to privilege the local, Black popular entertainment, and audience reception within musical theatre studies. Yet, this study also departs by centering Black women's artistry.

Black Queer Girlhood on the Musical Theatre Stage enters into dialogue with more recent studies that explore constructions of race and women's contributions on musical theatre stages. Grace Barnes's *Her Turn on Stage: the Role of Women in Musical* (2015); Bud Coleman and Judith A. Sebesta's collection *Women in American Musical Theatre: Essays on Composers, Lyricists, Librettists, Arrangers, Choreographers, Designers, Directors, Producers and Performance Artists* (2008); and Sara Whitfield's collection *Reframing the Musical: Race, Culture and Identity* (2019) exemplify these corrective efforts. These studies examine the disconnect between women's creative agency and contributions to the musical stage and their (often) marginalized position within musical theatre scholarship. However, Whitfield's collection also considers how previous approaches to understanding constructions of race, culture, and identity ignore the artistic contributions of Black, Indigenous, and People of Color (BIPOC). Whitfield writes that "race and identity studies in musical theatre have tended to be relegated to sections of whole collections rather than placed at the centre of the discussion."[12] Within these histories, whiteness and maleness become normative; the integration of BIPOC artists on Broadway results from benign white male patriarchy.[13] Rather than recirculate these false narratives, Whitfield issues a call for musical theatre scholars to include a more rigorous examination of intersectional identities and *respond* to the work done to historicize Black musical theatre artists within the fields of African American and Black diaspora studies.

Ryan Donovan's *Queer Approaches in Musical Theatre* (2023) also acknowledges this concern, noting that "it still took decades for musicals to include queer characters beyond the white male roles, which were often in drag, before newer ways of categorizing gender (e.g., cis, trans, non-binary) became common. Roles for queer performers who aren't white are still relatively scarce; for every Celie in *The Color Purple* (2005) or Usher in *A Strange Loop* (2022)—two of a handful of leading roles both Black and queer—there are dozens of roles for white gay men."[14] *Black Queer Girlhood on the Musical Theatre Stage* builds on Donovan's critique and answers Whitfield's call by attending to Black women's artistry and the Black queer feminist spectators who derive meaning from their works.

Black Queer Girlhood on the Musical Theatre Stage privileges the artistry of contemporary Black women musical theatre artists, all of whom contribute to the creation and dissemination of complex, multidimensional images of Black girlhood. Ruth Nicole Brown defines Black girlhood as "the representations, memories, and lived experiences of being and becoming in a body marked as youthful, Black, and female. Black girlhood is not dependent, then, on age, physical maturity, or any essential category of identity."[15] Brown conceptualizes the transition from Black girlhood to womanhood as a complex, fluid, and liminal site of possibilities. Building on Brown's scholarship, Dominique C. Hill also recognizes Black girlhood's transgressive possibilities. As an advocate of Black girlhood and Black queer resistance, Hill re-envisions a transgressive approach to Black girlhood studies that values the wholeness of identity. "Blackgirl one word rejects compartmentalization of Blackgirls' lives, stories, and bodies and serves as a symbolic transgression to see them/us as complex and whole."[16] According to Hill, welding the phrase "Black girl" into one word allows the symbolic resistance to the fracturing of race and gender and the celebration of every aspect of Blackgirls' lives. In the spirit of resistance, I hereafter use the term "Blackgirl" to signal my linguistic transgression, "to see them/us as complex and whole."[17]

In keeping with Brown and Hill's formulations of Black girlhood, this study directly contradicts stereotypes found within popular culture, the media, and political spheres, which render Blackgirls pathologized, fractured, and devoid of any humanity. Indeed, society is replete with images of Blackgirls as loud, angry, disrespectful, aggressive, ignorant, hypersexual, and unattractive. Moreover, scholars and politicians have given more credence to these stereotypes by ignoring Blackgirl resiliency and promoting "research" and dog-whistle politics that fetishize behaviors such as promiscuity and delinquency to support their own agendas.[18] Keenly aware of the multidimensional lives of Blackgirls, the importance of representation, and the need to exorcise these wrong-headed notions of Black girlhood, Black women musical theatre artists have crafted a body of work that reclaims the sanctity of Black girlhood.

Staking a claim to Black girlhood is not an innocuous exercise for Black women musical theatre artists; it is an act of resistance to white-authored violence. Childs, for example, compares her experiences of Black girlhood with navigating a minefield. "You navigated it with the conscious understanding that if you miscalculated even one step, it was going to be over for you. *And* you also understood that sooner or later, you were going to miscalculate a step. So, all the little Black girls that I knew were like soldiers in that army. That is what Black girlhood was to me," remembers Childs.[19] Using war and minefields as a metaphor for Black girlhood, Childs reinforces the reality that white-authored violence—including poverty, mass incarceration, sexual assault, and white cultural hegemony—can harm Blackgirls at any moment. Whether negotiated with great care or not, these unforeseen hazards will result in psychological harm, physical injury, or actual death. Contemporary Black women musical theatre artists center these concerns and, in so doing, articulate the joys and painful truths about Black girlhood in the United States.

The musical theatre artists who appear in this study follow the long tradition of Black women writers who privileged the interiority of Blackgirls' lives. The Black girlhood studies scholar Nazera Sadiq Wright writes that nineteenth-century Black women writers "wrote about their inner thought, their plans, their dreams and aspirations. They emphasized the determination and grit black girls exhibited as they formed successful strategies for fighting and rejecting oppression."[20] Following in the footsteps of Harriet Wilson, Harriet Jacobs, Frances E. W. Harper, and other foremothers, contemporary Black women musical theatre artists situate Black girlhood as a site worthy of intellectual query and celebration. I read the trials and triumphs of the Blackgirl protagonists who populate their musicals as a symbol of Black queer experiences in the United States and the pressing need to value *all* Black life. Perhaps more importantly, my Black queer feminist reading enriches ongoing efforts to amplify Black queer visibility and liberate the Black queer feminist gaze.

Black Queer Feminist Spectatorship, Resistant Readership, and Pleasure

The Black gaze has always been political, steeped in racialized discourse between the subject and the object, the empowered and the oppressed. Just as white slaveowners denied Black people the right to gaze, their act of looking served as a site of opposition to white domination. bell hooks writes that "all attempts to repress our/Black people's right to gaze had produced in us an overwhelming longing to look, a rebellious desire, an oppositional gaze."[21] hooks remembers that as a Black queer girl spectator, the gaze served as a source of her empowerment. "I remembered being punished as a child for staring, for those hard, intense, direct looks children would give grown-ups, looks that were seen as confrontational, as gestures of resistance, challenging authority. . . . Imagine the terror felt by the child who has come to understand through repeated punishments that one's gaze can be dangerous. . . .There is power in looking," writes hooks.[22] Since Black women—queer, trans, or otherwise—often experience marginalization within Black communities and greater society, the gaze offers a possible means to experience pleasure and resistance.

Regardless of their (at times) tenuous relationship with the Black community, Black queer women activists continuously demonstrate a deep commitment to the well-being of *all* Black people, regardless of gender, sexuality, age, class, and so forth. In her book, *Unapologetic: A Black, Queer, and Feminist Mandate For Radical Movements* (2018), the Black queer feminist activist Charlene A. Carruthers celebrates this tradition and negates erroneous mythology that positions Black lesbians as a threat to Black masculinity or a detriment to the cause of Black liberation. Carruthers writes that "regardless of the risk, however, we Black queer and trans women have been on the front lines of anti-police and Black liberation organizing in the United States. We have been there after Black men and boys have been slain by police officers and vigilantes. We have shown up, even when masses have not, after a Black woman, girl, or trans, or queer, or gender-nonconforming person has been killed. And we will continue to show up."[23] In contrast to many other queer folx, most Black lesbians live within Black communities, not in isolation with other gay populations.[24] As such, Black women's culture and Black political thought heavily influence Black queer women's subjectivity and political activism. This unique subject position enables Black queer women to simultaneously attend to and critique Black culture, Black women's culture, and Black queer culture.

While I locate Black queer women within Black communities, I do not assume that all Black queer women spectators identify with the contemporary Black freedom struggle or embody a Black queer feminist gaze. Rather, I contend that those who embrace Black queer feminist praxis have an appreciation for the longstanding Black political belief that *none of us are free until all of us are free*. Black queer women embody this political thought by standing at the forefront of the contemporary Black freedom struggle, from founding the Black Lives Matter movement to leading its local chapters. Their oppositional gaze allows them to read hypocrisies within and outside of the Black community, correcting homophobia and other harmful ideologies that weaken the movement for Black lives. *Black Queer Girlhood on the Musical Theatre Stage* suggests that Black queer feminists can also level their oppositional gaze on and off musical theatre stages.

Despite their contributions to the development of musical theatre, Black queer women artists and spectators are often rendered invisible within discussions of women on Broadway and audience reception theories of popular culture.[25] For example, in her investigation of women's historical representation on Broadway stages, Barnes writes that "one thing we all recognize but rarely discuss openly: that musical theatre is dominated, onstage, behind the scenes, and in the audience by gay men. This is not a criticism; it is merely a fact."[26] She further notes that musical theatre has long-functioned as a safe space for gay men—creative artists and spectators—to commune with one another. Before the 1969 Stonewall uprising and subsequent gay rights movement, gay artists and spectators used coded language, embodiment, and resistant readership to allow them to take pleasure in heterosexual love stories presented onstage, even as laws prohibited any outward display of queer identity. However, Barnes writes that this same level of inclusiveness did not extend to women, who were celebrated onstage but not given any control of the creative process.[27] While Barnes makes a compelling argument about (white) gay male spectatorship and the need to attend to women's contributions to musical theatre, her analysis does not fully attend to the intersections of women's identity. In so doing, Barnes misses an opportunity to explore Black women's artistry and the meaning garnered through Black queer women's spectatorship.

Invariably, when conversations do arise about the relationship between queer identity and spectatorship, "queer" often becomes synonymous with *gay men,* and "lesbian" does not reach beyond the borders of *white women.* The scholar of queer musical theatre David Savran writes that "musical theater, in particular, has in popular mythology been adjudged a sacred preserve of gay men, who have been among its most important producers."[28] Such mythology situates gay white men as musical theatre's "most visible devotees."[29] In reality, Black queer women have also contributed profoundly to the creation and dissemination of musical performance. Stacy Wolf, for example, acknowledges the influence early Black women blues singers—many of whom identified as or were rumored to be lesbians—had on writers during the Golden Age of musical theatre. "The strength, singularity, and passionate expressiveness of the Broadway musical's female star are reminiscent of women blues singers; these qualities are not found elsewhere in mid-twentieth-century American culture," writes Wolf.[30] While we understand that musicals have "long offered personal, emotional, and cultural validation for gay men," we have yet to fully appreciate how musicals have afforded Black queer feminist spectators, as the blueswomen before them, opportunities to reaffirm or challenge the status quo.[31] *Black Queer Girlhood on the Musical Theatre Stage* centers Black queer feminist spectators, positioning them as ideal spectators.

The pervasiveness of sexism, racism, and heterosexism has meant that Black women—queer, trans, or otherwise—rarely make the cut as the ideal spectator. By suggesting that Black queer feminist spectators might draw special meaning from within heteronormative narratives or interpret contemporary musicals as Black lesbian narratives (despite the original intent), I continue the tradition of "exposing the ways in which dominant ideology is naturalized by the performance's address to the *ideal* spectator."[32] In other words, Black queer feminists and their representation—on the stage, behind the scenes, and in the audience—matters. In situating Black queer feminists as ideal spectators, I offer multiple entry points into understanding how they might engage with works created by Black women musical theatre artists.

As ideal spectators, Black queer feminists *can* and *do* wield resistant readership as a tool of empowerment. Coined by the literary scholar Judith

Fetterly in *The Resisting Reader: A Feminist Approach to American Fiction* (1978), "resistant reading" originally referred to a feminist critique of the politics of literature. Fetterly writes:

> The first act of the feminist critic must be to become resisting rather than an assenting reader and, by this refusal to assent, to begin the process of exorcizing the male mind that has implanted in us. The consequence of this exorcism is the capacity for what Adrienne Rich describes as re-vision—'the act of looking back, of seeing with fresh eyes, of entering an old text from a new critical direction.'[33]

In other words, Fetterly conceptualizes resistant reading as a weapon, allowing women "the power of naming reality they do reflect and so change literary criticism from a closed conversation to an active dialogue."[34] Applying Fetterly's theorization to performance criticism, the feminist theatre scholar Jill Dolan considers how feminist critics can "read" performances as political interventions.[35] Dolan encourages feminist critics to "analyze a performance's meaning by reading against the grain of stereotypes and resisting the manipulation of both the performance text and the cultural text that it helps to shape."[36] Furthering Fetterly's and Dolan's feminist interventions, I demonstrate how resistant readership fosters active dialogue between the experiential knowledge of Black queer feminist spectators, the performance text, and the cultural text from which a performance emerges.

Black Queer Girlhood on the Musical Theatre Stage not only reclaims Black queer feminist subjectivity and Black queer imagery and culture but also celebrates the *pleasure* Black queer feminist spectators might experience through their resistant readership. As intellectuals in their own right, Black women do not spend the entirety of their lives combatting sexism, heterosexism, and institutional white racism. Black women also experience the complexities of life and feel a spectrum of human emotions that range from joy to the erotic to fear. As resistant readers, Black queer feminist spectators affirm this profound truth through their pursuit of pleasure. Indeed, Black queer feminist spectators can and do draw special meaning from the critical moments wherein heterocentrism, sexism, and white cultural hegemony (whether intentionally or not) are subverted. They also experience pleasure through reading lesbian narratives into the performance text.

Mapping the Minefield Of Black Girlhood

The structure of this book mirrors the transgressive nature of Black girlhood and Black queer feminist identity. In addition to the linguistic transgression of the term "Blackgirl," I recall the pioneering efforts of second-wave feminists to acknowledge that the personal is *always* political. I follow the tradition of Black women intellectuals—from Harriet Jacobs' *Incidents in the Life of a Slave Girl* (1861) to Emily Bernard's *Black is the Body: Stories from My Grandmother's Time, My Mother's Time, and Mine* (2019)—who explore Black girlhood through their own experiences. As such, each thematically-linked chapter begins with my memories of navigating the minefield that is Black girlhood. Inspired by the form and content of bell hooks' *Bone Black: Memories of Girlhood* (1996), June Jordan's *Soldier: A Poet's Childhood* (2000), and Aishah Rahman's *Chewed Water: A Memoir* (2001), my creative first-person narratives serve as entry points into the inner lives of Blackgirls. My narratives include memories of childhood poverty and parentification, my sibling "coming out," witnessing childhood sexual abuse, performing as Snow White in a devised musical, watching *The Wiz* with my sisters, and navigating "colorblind" casting in educational theatre. Thus, I answer hooks' call to explore the experiences of Blackgirls more fully.[37]

Chapter 1, "Blackgirl Worker Bees and Resiliency," analyzes how risk factors and protective factors impact Blackgirls' identity formation and resiliency. By "resiliency," I refer to the process Blackgirls use to form a positive sense of self despite hostile external forces. The mental and behavioral practices by which Blackgirls navigate pressures from their families, communities, schools, and greater society significantly influence how they view themselves and are deserving of further critical attention. Drawing from musicals adapted from popular novels, I consider how *The Color Purple* (2005; 2015 revival) and Lynn Nottage's Off-Broadway masterpiece, *The Secret Life of Bees* (2019), represent the interiority of Blackgirls. These musicals demonstrate that while adversity, trauma, and stress are not the exclusive domain of Blackgirls, their marginalized identities, coupled with experiences of poverty and abuse, make them particularly vulnerable to low self-esteem, poor health, and maladaptive behaviors, such as overworking and self-silencing. However, these performances also reveal that the social construction of family, spirituality, "Black Girl Magic," and sisterhood provide powerful protective factors that foster Blackgirl agency and resiliency.

In so doing, I examine how Black queer feminist spectators might experience pleasure in bearing witness to this transgression.

Chapter 2, "Blackgirls, the Black Church, and Gospel Music," examines the relationship between the Black Church, sexual deviancy mythologies, and Black girlhood. By "the Black Church," I refer to both Black Christian churches in the United States and Black Christians who worship within predominantly Black congregations. The sociologist Patricia Hill Collins writes that the Black Church has "incorporated dominant ideas about the dangers of promiscuity and homosexuality into its practices" and, in so doing, "failed to challenge arguments about sexual deviancy."[38] Burdened with the need to protect the Black community's image from dominant society's assault, the Black Church has historically "resisted *any* hints of Black sexual deviance, straight and gay alike" by adopting a conservative stance regarding sexuality.[39] As a result, churchgoers often perceive Blackgirls who defy heteropatriarchy by rejecting marriage, having children out of wedlock, or partnering with other women, as a threat to the Black community. Meanwhile, the hypocrisies of Black Church practices—including publicly shaming pregnant teenage girls, ignoring the behavior of predatory men, and justifying the oppression of Black queer folx—remain unexamined. J. e. Franklin's *Prodigal Sister* (1974), Micki Grant's *Your Arms Too Short to Box With God* (1976), Higginsen and Wydro's *Mama, I Want to Sing* (1983), and Angela Barrow-Dunlap's *Church Girl* (2010) confront these concerns and, in so doing, allow spectators to reject mythologies that stigmatize the sexual practices of Blackgirls.

Chapter 3, "Blackgirl Wit and Imagination," considers the relationship between white-authored violence, Black imagination, and Black liberation. Building on Carruthers's assertion that "the black imagination lives . . . in our ability to create alternatives," I position Blackgirl imagination as a powerful force of pleasure and resistance to the violence in their lives.[40] Through an analysis of Childs's *The Bubbly Black Girl Sheds Her Chameleon Skin* (2000), *Bella: An American Tall Tale* (2017), and Aishah Rahman's *The Tale of Madame Zora* (1986), I demonstrate how Black women musical theatre artists use their agency to celebrate Blackgirl storytelling and dance. In so doing, these works create space for Black queer feminist spectators to engage with the long history of normalizing violence against Blackgirls, consider how violence continues to disproportionately harm Black queer and trans girls, and imagine new forms of activism for the contemporary Black freedom struggle.

Chapter 4, "Blackgirl Fairy Tales," explores the impact of fairy tales within the lives of Blackgirls. During the 1970s, feminists launched vigorous critical debates about the influence of fairy tales, positioning the promise of "happily ever after" within the larger cultural and political struggle for gender equality. Unfortunately, these studies and those that followed rarely, if ever, considered the works created by Black women writers, the Blackgirl protagonists who populate their fairy tales, or how intersectionality impacts meaning-making for Black queer feminist spectators who enjoy their transgressive works. My analysis of the Tony Award-winning *Once on this Island* (1990) and the less-studied but popular musicals *The Liberation of Mother Goose* (1972) and *The Other Cinderella* (1976) intervene within these ongoing conversations, and in so doing, demonstrate how fairy tales socialize Black queer feminist spectators to navigate a society that does not always recognize their humanity.

Chapter 5, "Blackgirl Fantasy," explores four major productions of *The Wiz* throughout its forty-year history in the theatre, television, and film industries. I read Dorothy's journey through Oz as a Black lesbian fantasy, and in so doing, demonstrate how Black queer feminist spectators *can* and *do* create meaning from within politically engaged popular entertainment.

Chapter 6, "Blackgirls Navigate Show Business," investigates the relationship between identity politics, popular culture, and social justice. My analysis includes Aishah Rahman's *Lady Day: A Musical Tragedy* (1972), Katori Hall's *Tina: The Tina Turner Musical* (2019), and *King Kong* (2019), all of which feature the struggles and triumphs of Blackgirl protagonists navigating the theatre and music industries. I enrich my discussion of the barriers that have historically marginalized Blackgirl performers with original interviews with Black women musical theatre artists who actively promote racial justice both on and off musical theatre stages. The Broadway director Schele Williams, for example, remembers co-founding Black Theatre United (2020–present) "to protect Black bodies on our streets and on our stages."[41] Interviews with artists such as Williams reveal how artistic stages do not offer protection from white-authored violence. Black women musical theatre artists understand this profound truth and use their artistry to reveal how anti-Blackness, heterosexism, and sexism permeate every facet of society, including musical theatre stages.

The Conclusion discusses the pressing need to foster diversity, equity, and inclusion on our stages and within our greater society. I issue a call for

BIPOC artists and their allies to continue to fight for large-scale systemic change and realize the anti-racist statements expressed in the wake of the COVID-19 global pandemic. Finally, in light of a second Trump administration, I urge BIPOC artists and their allies to continue to do the work of theatre: to dream, to create, and to build community.

1
Black Girl Worker Bees and Resiliency

I'm five years old and stand on a chair so I can reach the hot stovetop. I've already spent hours slicing potatoes into perfect rectangles. I've only cut my finger once. I can still feel the sting of the potato juice on my thumb. I'm in pain but I'm also excited. I love cooking. It's my turn to make dinner for my sisters and Mom. Even though I'm alone in the kitchen it's difficult to stay focused. If I start daydreaming and forget to flick roaches off the vent hood, they'll drop into the hot grease. I hate finding crisp roaches nestled in with my French fries. I'm not allowed to throw the French fries out so I have to pick the roaches out and eat the fries anyway. Sometimes I don't find any fried roaches but then Mom ruins my joy by telling me she already picked them out.

Hmm, we eat French fries a lot.

Mom says potatoes are all we can afford. I love that we eat French fries for dinner nearly every night. My only wish is that I could have a glass of strawberry milk with dinner. But I can't. Only one cup of milk with cereal a day.

Milk does not grow on trees.

What does milk grow on? I've lost focus. A roach drops into the hot grease, wedged in between the nearly golden fries. I use a metal spoon to scope the plump brown roach out. I try to be careful but the grease pops on my arm. I want to stop cooking but I need to make three more batches of French fries.

You are a hard worker.

I blink back my tears and continue my watch.

A few years later, I teach my four-year-old niece how to peel and slice potatoes. We're hungry. Her mom is gone. My mom is at work. I watch her all day long. Just me and her. Every day feels like an eternity. I look at the old scars on my arm. I don't let her touch the stovetop. I carefully season and fry the potatoes. I use the spatula to inspect my work. No roaches. When we finish eating, I take her on a walk to the library. We check out more books than we could ever possibly read within the two-week limit. On the way home, I let

Black Queer Girlhood on the Musical Theatre Stage. La Donna L. Forsgren, Oxford University Press.
 DOI: 10.1093/9780197661444.003.0002

her steal her favorite rocks from yards. She fills her backpack to the brim. She chats nonstop about how she'll add these to her collection. I squeeze her hand with affection. Silently, I count down the days until she can go to kindergarten.

If you work hard, you'll get to go back to high school. But I never return. Instead, I take the G.E.D. test when I'm sixteen. I earn a Diversity Achievement Scholarship to attend college and work hard. I study, study, study. I graduate and then continue my education, becoming one of the 4.4% of Blackgirls who earn a doctorate degree in the United States.[1]

I am a hard worker. I am a worker bee.

All too often, when I share memories of my girlhood, I am mistakenly lauded as a poster child for Blackgirl resiliency. The American Psychological Association defines resilience as the "process and outcome of successfully adapting to difficult or challenging life experiences, especially through mental, emotional, and behavioral flexibility and adjustment to external and internal demands."[2] In their studies of resiliency, social workers, psychologists, and health professionals have found that certain factors put some people more at risk of encountering difficult or challenging life experiences than they do others. These factors include "poverty, abuse and victimization, neighborhood disorganization, and, marginalization due to race/ethnicity, gender, sexuality, and other aspects of identity."[3] Unfortunately, resiliency is often measured primarily by positive outcomes as defined by dominant (i.e., middle-class, white, male, heteronormative) values.[4] This outcomes-based approach socializes Blackgirls to think that by following the rules, working hard, and ignoring mistreatment, they will be able to "overcome" adversity, trauma, and stress, and find "success," such as securing a college education or prestigious occupation.[5] However, by heralding the few overachievers who adapt to and "overcome" adversity and blaming the vast majority of those who do not, undue pressure is put on individual Blackgirls. Furthermore, this erroneous thought rarely considers the following questions: *Why do Blackgirls have to be resilient in the first place? Why do Blackgirls bear disproportionate risk factors on their shoulders? How can we, as a society, work to eradicate the systems that create such difficulties and challenging life experiences?*

In their study of Blackgirls and empowerment programming, the psychologists and social workers Sara Goodkind, Britney G. Brinkman, and Kathi Elliott found that individual and outcomes-based approaches to resiliency put Blackgirls in an unfair predicament. "Recent research shows that many individual level, adaptive behaviors through which people strive to achieve success in which are defined as resilient (e.g., plan self-control, unwavering persistence) have harmful effects on the health of people who are experiencing marginalization. . . . However, when they resist oppression in ways that may protect their health but do not conform to dominant values (e.g., by protesting or challenging injustice), they are frequently labeled defiant or delinquent and experience disciplinary consequences," writes Goodkind et al.[6] The pressure to mask injustice, show outward strength, and demonstrate a "successful" outcome, despite lacking the same opportunities as others, not only harms Blackgirls and fails to promote collective action but also allows institutional white racism to continue unnoticed.[7] For these reasons, there is a vital need to redefine resiliency as a process that attends to individual agency and critical consciousness, as well as a collective identity/action to *change* systems of oppression, rather than simply adapt to them.[8]

Scholarship and media coverage contribute to the "individual overcoming adversity" narrative by often noting the risk factors that harm Blackgirls, but rarely studying or reporting the protective factors that foster resilience in Blackgirls. The educational studies scholar and social worker Venus E. Evans-Winters writes that "politicians, the media, social service personnel, religious groups, and researchers tend to focus on teenage pregnancy and high school dropout rates among urban African American adolescent girls. Very rarely do we hear discussions about the majority of black girls from urban and inner-city communities who graduate high school and college. The generalized depressing statistics about poor minority girls erase the role of discriminatory practices in education and other structures."[9] Simply put, Black girlhood is fraught with both peril and possibility as Blackgirls traverse home, school, church, and greater society. Navigating the waters of Black girlhood entails battling a constant bombardment of negative imagery that depicts them as unintelligent, aggressive, hypersexual, unattractive, and incapable of leading black communities. Myths of Black girlhood—that their behaviors, attitudes, and sexual practices perpetuate cycles of poverty within Black communities—create a pathology that is used to explain and justify their mistreatment.

Despite these perils, Blackgirls continue to carve out a sense of self and imagine new possibilities for the future. In their 2022 study on the resilience of Blackgirls, Zinobia Bennefield and Taylor Jackson found that while the media and white systems of oppression do cause harm, Blackgirls are by no means "perpetual victims of white racism."[10] "Black girls are healthy, confident, and full of the belief in themselves, their beauty, and their power," write Bennefield and Jackson.[11] Several vital support systems allow Blackgirls to develop a positive self-concept: the Black family, spirituality, "Black Girl Magic," and building a sisterhood with peers and elders who support self-love.[12]

Black women musical theatre artists engage with resiliency discourse by dramatizing the process of acquiring individual critical consciousness, as well as collective action to change systems of oppression. This often involves creating counternarratives that privilege the support systems and journeys Blackgirls take to discover the power of self-definition. The Broadway director Schele Williams offers perhaps the best explanation as to why Black women musical theatre artists often focus on Blackgirl resiliency. Williams remembers:

> When I think about Black girlhood, immediately I think of my daughters and I think of how to both protect and prepare them—which has very different requirements and are very specific for Black girls. I think about protecting them from the world that is always doubting them and their intuition and their greatness. How do I protect them from having any preconceptions about their beauty, their bodies, and their value and how do I prepare them to be resilient? I don't want to prescribe for them what I know is coming because I am working very hard to change the world for them, but I am smart enough to know we will not have arrived where I wish the world would be for my daughters. Maybe for my great-granddaughters. So, I do have to teach them how to be resilient and how to continue to rise.[13]

For many Black women musical theatre artists, depicting Blackgirl resiliency is both a deeply personal and politically charged endeavor. Williams's experiential knowledge of Blackgirls' beauty, intelligence, and greatness, as well as the risk factors that harm them, gives her the ability to provide support systems for her daughters and create art that empowers countless Blackgirls. As *The Color Purple* (2005; 2015 revival) and *The Secret Life of Bees* (2019) musicals can attest, musical theatre provides an important platform for Black women artists to craft tales that honor the "magic" of Blackgirls, meaning their ability to recognize their worth, engage in self-definition, and take collective action to dismantle the oppressive forces within their lives.

The Color Purple and *The Secret Life of Bees* are both based on best-selling novels, include interracial artistic collaboration, and perhaps most importantly, use the metaphor of the honey bee to celebrate Southern Blackgirl history, queer culture, and resiliency. In nature, honey bee colonies consist of several thousand female "worker bees" or foragers that gather resources (i.e., pollen, nectar, tree resin, and water) and produce honey to sustain their female-dominated community. The colony also includes a queen bee whose sole purpose is to lay thousands of eggs per day to replenish the colony. A small number of "drones" or male bees compete to mate with the queen and die following copulation. Female drones are selected to work as "nurse bees" to care for their offspring.[14] In other words, honey bees create an efficient community built on reciprocity and productivity. Many comparisons have been made between female honey bees and Black women's history. For example, former editor in chief of *The Black Panther* newspaper Judy Juanita remembers Black women playing a pivotal role in the success of the Black Panther Party. "We innovated, ran, and serviced many of the programs, including: free breakfast for children, all of the free health clinics, the food giveaways, the shoe giveaways. If the party was two-thirds women, all you could see were those guys holding the bayonets and rifles but behind the scenes: there we were. Just working away. Worker bees. Worker bees!"[15] Scholars also use the metaphor of the worker bee to discuss Black women's history and queer culture. For example, in his book *Honeypot: Black Southern Women Who Love Women* (2019), the performance studies scholar E. Patrick Johnson writes:

> Given the history of slave labor in the South in particular, where women worked both in the fields and in the plantation home, bore and nursed her master's children and her own, and did so with dignity pride, it is not a stretch to make an analogy to the work of female bees. . . And, according to one group of scientists, it is likely that honeybees all had one common ancestor in Africa. Thus, the connection between the history of black women—of any sexual orientation—and bees abounds. Even the designation of 'bee charmer' is a southern slang term for lesbians who are particularly adept at seducing other lesbians![16]

In *The Color Purple*, Blackgirl protagonist Celie labors away as an essential slave to her abusive husband and does not form a sense of self until she encounters "the Queen Honeybee" or blueswoman, Shug Avery. As a bee charmer, Shug Avery helps Celie gain a sense of agency and value as a Black queer Southern girl. In *The Secret Life of Bees*, honey bees act as a source of food, a spiritual connection to the ancestors, and a livelihood for the

Boatwright sisters, who build a business out of beekeeping. Their female-dominated household offers a respite from the oppressive forces within the lives of Rosaleen Daise, a domestic servant, and her fourteen-year-old white charge, Lily Owens. As the Boatwright sisters use ritual to introduce Rosaleen to the magic of Blackgirls, she begins to define herself, rather than be defined by others.

While *The Color Purple* and *The Secret Life of Bees* musicals can (and have) been read as tales of individual Blackgirls "overcoming" adversity, trauma, and stress related to experiences of poverty, abuse, and victimization, this chapter considers how Black queer feminist spectators might read against the grain of traditional resiliency narratives while also celebrating the erotic as a powerful resource for Blackgirls. The Black queer feminist poet and activist Audre Lorde refers to the erotic "as an assertion of the lifeforce of women; of that creative energy empowered, the knowledge and use of which we are now reclaiming in our language, our history, our dancing, our loving, our work, our lives."[17] Rather than view adaptations of *The Color Purple* and *The Secret Life of Bees* as "individual overcoming adversity" tales, Black queer feminist spectators may understand these musicals as revaluations of the *process* of resiliency and a celebration of the collective efforts of Blackgirls to use their creative energy to empower themselves and their communities. Moreover, these musical productions provide space for Black queer feminist spectators to witness how Black families (including fictive kin), spirituality, "Black Girl Magic," and sisterhood support the development of Blackgirls' critical consciousness. In addition, these musicals provide opportunities for Black queer feminist spectators to experience *pleasure* in identifying Blackgirl history and queer possibilities embedded within the honey bee metaphor as they witness Blackgirls negotiate their interests at home, school, church, and greater society. Finally, my focus on the lives of Southern Blackgirls is not a fortuitous exercise. Blackgirls exist beyond the bounds of the urban North. In sum, the collective resiliency of Southern Blackgirls—whether queer, trans, or otherwise—deserves more critical attention.

The Color Purple: The Musical

Alice Walker's Pulitzer Prize-winning novel, *The Color Purple* (1982), is, without a doubt, the most iconic Black lesbian love story ever told. Walker's novel uses journal entries to chronicle the life of Celie, an adolescent Blackgirl living in rural Georgia during the turn of the twentieth century. Celie acts as a voiceless worker bee, silently caring for everyone else's needs and working her Pa and husband Mister's farms while experiencing rape, teenage pregnancies, a forced marriage, and familial separation, only to transform—through the support of her lover, the "queen bee" and blueswoman, Shug Avery—into a confident, independent, and joyful middle-aged woman. Charged with the task of retelling this decades-long tale, white book writer Marsha Norman brought Celie's story to Broadway audiences with the help of a trio of pop songwriters, including Black singer-songwriter Brenda Russell, Black composer and lyricist Stephen Bray, and white songwriter Allee Willis. Using Walker's novel and director Steven Spielberg's 1985 film adaptation as source material, Norman, Russell, Bray, and Willis managed to transform Celie's lesbian love story into a sanitized musical palpable for both white liberals and conservative-leaning Broadway audiences.

Although the 2005 musical adaptation removes much of the novel's Black lesbian eroticism, Black queer feminist spectators do have the ability to "read" moments of Celie and Shug's love story through the production modes, including four musical numbers: "Dear God—Shug," "Too Beautiful for Words," "What About Love?," and "What About Love? (Reprise)." Indeed, Celie's use of song and direct address to the audience—these moments act as journal entries—allow her to express her innermost thoughts. These moments provide spectators with glimpses into how protective factors, including her chosen family, sisterhood, and spirituality, help Celie develop the critical consciousness and erotic power she needs to build collective resistance to abuse and exploitation. While traditional resiliency narratives may focus on Celie's outcome (i.e., against the odds, she establishes a successful business), *how* she gets there and *with whom* she shares this success with are just as important. In addition to depicting Celie's resiliency journey, *The Color Purple* musical also uses Blackgirl characters such as Shug and the Church Ladies to engage with other liberatory and problematic aspects of Black women's culture, including the blueswoman tradition, Superwoman mythology, and spirituality.

While adaptations of *The Color Purple* rely heavily on Blackgirl talent, onstage and onscreen, the critically acclaimed works have not, for the most part, included Black women on the senior design or storytelling teams. Even Walker's writing talent was excluded from the first realized adaptation of *The Color Purple*. Walker had written a treatment for a film adaptation of her novel but the Academy Award-winning director Steven

Spielberg opted to film the Dutch screenwriter Menno Meyjes's version instead. The Spielberg-Meyjes collaboration garnered eleven Academy Award nominations, including Best Picture, Best Actress (Whoopi Goldberg), Best Supporting Actress (Margaret Avery and Oprah Winfrey), and Best Adapted Screenplay (Meyjes) (see Figure 1.1). Two decades later, Norman, Russell, Bray, and Willis transformed Walker's novel into a Broadway hit, earning eleven Tony Award nominations. The 2005 all-Black cast included LaChanze (Celie), Renée Elise Goldsberry (Nettie), Brandon Victor Dixon (Harpo), Felicia P. Fields (Sofia), Kingsley Leggs (Mister), Krisha Marcano (Squeak), Elisabeth Withers-Mendes (Shug Avery), Kimberly Ann Harris (Church Lady/Doris), Maia Nkenge Wilson (Church Lady/Jarene), Virginia Ann Woodruff (Church Lady/ Darlene), and J. C. Montgomery (Pa / Ensemble). The 2005 design and storytelling team included white artists Gary Griffin (director), John Lee Beatty (set), Paul Tazewell (costumes), Brian MacDevitt (lighting), Jon Weston (sound), and Donald Byrd (choreography). The next adaptation, a 2016 revival of the musical, earned two Tony Awards, including Best Revival of a Musical. Again, Black women performers appeared onstage in these more recent adaptations, but other than Russell, they did not serve on the senior design or storytelling team.

Figure 1.1 Whoopi Goldberg (Celie) in *The Color Purple* (1985) film directed by Stephen Spielberg. Still image courtesy of the author.

The Color Purple returned to the big screen again in 2023—this time, in musical form based on the successful Broadway production. This more recent musical adaption included greater Black representation offscreen, with Ghanaian filmmaker Blitz Bazawule directing the film and the Black queer poet and playwright Marcus Gardley providing the screenplay. Bazawule's musical film features talented Black women performers from the film, television, and theatre industries, including Fantasia Barrino, Danielle Brooks, Halle Bailey, Ciara, Taraji P. Henson, Whoopi Goldberg, H.E.R., and Aunjanue Ellis-Taylor (see Figure 1.2). Thus, while the source material for all the aforementioned adaptations draws from the creative genius of a Black queer woman writer, features outstanding award-winning performances by Black women performers, and includes the work of Black songwriters and financial backing of Black celebrity co-producers Oprah Winfrey and Quincy Jones, Black women artists—queer, trans, or otherwise—have been largely absent from the creative storytelling team.

For these reasons, I contend that adaptations of *The Color Purple* do not signal a shift toward greater racial inclusivity on Broadway stages or in the Hollywood industry. Rather, the production history signals minimal inroads. Showcasing Black bodies onstage merely creates the illusion of diversity,

Figure 1.2 Phylicia Pearl Mpasi (Young Celie) and Halle Bailey (Nettie) in *The Color Purple* (2023) film directed by Blitz Bazawule. Still image courtesy of the author.

equity, and inclusion in the entertainment industry while maintaining white-led and male-led power structures. In other words, it is not enough to represent Black (queer) women and girls on Broadway stages and in film. Black women musical theatre artists must be visible and lead at every level of production—onstage, onscreen, and off. The openly bisexual actress Aunjanue Ellis-Taylor, who performs the role of Celie's mother in the recent musical adaptation, addresses similar concerns in her 2023 interview with the LGBTQ online newspaper, PinkNews. "I want people to walk away from *The Color Purple* thinking: 'I just saw a movie about Black lesbians.' I don't think that has happened. . . . Somebody has to be brave. Alice Walker wrote a book about Black lesbians, and we're still telling that story today. *The Color Purple* is one of the most important books in the canon of world literature. Also, you have to have Black women and Black queer women in the making of it. . . the first one was directed by a white man. The remake was directed by a Black man," remembers Ellis-Taylor.[18] Simply put, it may feel like a gut punch when spectators realize that a major theme within the musical—that of (queer) Blackgirl empowerment—was not realized in the artistic leadership of the production.

Despite the near absence of Black women artists—queer, trans, or otherwise—leading adaptations of *The Color Purple* in the theatre and film industries, the original source material does derive from the perspective of a Black queer womanist author. Walker coined the term "womanist" in her 1979 short story, "Coming Apart" and more fully developed the term in her 1983 book, *In Search of Our Mother's Gardens: Womanist Prose*. Walker conceptualizes a womanist as "a woman who loves other women, sexually and/or non-sexually. Appreciates and prefers women's culture, women's emotional flexibility (values tears as natural counterbalance of laughter), and women's strength. Sometimes loves individual men, sexually and/or nonsexually. Committed to survival and wholeness of entire people, male *and* female. Not a separatist, except periodically, for health."[19] She later adds that a womanist "loves music. Loves dance. Loves the moon. *Loves* the Spirit. Loves love and food and roundness. Loves struggle. *Loves* the Folk. Loves herself. *Regardless*."[20] As a womanist, Walker wanted *The Color Purple* to chronicle not only the emotional complexities, strength, and resilience of Blackgirls but also the sexual and/or nonsexual love between them. It was her hope that by sharing Celie's journey, she might help destigmatize Black lesbian love and be *seen* by her own family and within her community. Walker addresses this desire in her 1996 book, *The Same River Twice: Honoring the Difficult*.

"I wanted to give my family and friends an opportunity to see women-loving women: lesbian, heterosexual, bi-sexual, 'two-spirited' womanist women in a recognizable context. I wanted them, I suppose, to see me."[21] Starting from the desire to make herself and other Black queer women visible, Walker turned to her personal family history for inspiration.

Writing *The Color Purple* provided the space for Walker to reflect on her family history of domestic violence and expose a painful truth: that Blackgirls are just as susceptible to violence from *within* than outside of their own communities. More recently, Walker revealed that her characterizations of Celie, her abusive husband Mister/Albert, and his lover Shug Avery were inspired by her actual paternal grandmother Rachel Little, paternal grandfather Henry Clay Walker, and his lover Estella "Shug" Perry. Walker remembers:

> It is safe to say, after a frightful life serving and obeying abusive men, who raped in place of 'making love,' my grandmother, like Celie, was not attracted to men. She was, in fact, very drawn to my grandfather's lover, a beautiful woman who was kind to her, the only grown person who ever seemed to notice how remarkable and creative she was. . . . In giving Celie the love of this woman, in every way love can be expressed, I was clear in my intention to demonstrate that she too, like all of us, deserved to be seen, appreciated, and deeply loved by someone who saw her as whole and worthy.[22]

While all Blackgirls—queer, trans, or otherwise—are deserving of being seen and worthy of love and protection from their partners and the Black community, the sad reality is that they are not. Rather, Blackgirls are more vulnerable to becoming victims of violence. The sociologist Patricia Hill Collins writes that "much of this violence occurs within the context of Black heterosexual love relationships, Black family life, and within African American social institutions. Such violence takes many forms, including verbally berating Black women, hitting them, ridiculing their appearance, grabbing their body parts, pressuring them to have sex, beating them, and murdering them. . . . Black girls are especially vulnerable to childhood sexual assault."[23] At the time Walker wrote *The Color Purple*, there was very little public discussion about the victimization and abuse of Black women and girls.

Sadly, this situation continues today as public discussions celebrate the so-called strength of Blackgirls who endure the emotional and physical harm inflicted upon them. In her book *Pushout: The Criminalization of Black Girls in Schools* (2016), the social justice scholar Monique W. Morris writes that "Black women, and other women of color bear scars that are both visible and invisible. . . . The assumption that Black women and girls should be able to 'handle it all' dominates our consciousness. But in doing so, we mistake the resiliency of our sisters for the absence of harm, and we miss girls . . . who then blame themselves when their actions fall short of this unrealistic and contrived ideal."[24] For these reasons, spectators should not mistake Celie's ability to silently endure decades of abuse and exploitation as the embodiment of Superwoman strength. Rather, Black queer feminist spectators might note that it is through acceptance of Shug's sexual and nonsexual love for Celie that allows her to truly see and love herself completely (see Figure 1.3). Love liberates Celie, freeing her to express her thoughts, feelings, and erotic power regardless of what others think.

Despite her efforts to provide greater visibility to Black queer women and girls, Walker faced harsh criticism for not intervening in the erasure of the lesbian love story in Spielberg's 1985 film adaptation. Spielberg limits the physical elements of Celie's lesbian relationship to just one scene wherein Shug (Margaret Avery) tells Celie (Whoopi Goldberg) that she is "beautiful" and loves her, and kisses her on her forehead, cheeks, and lips. In a 2011 interview, Spielberg justified this radical departure by citing his personal

Figure 1.3 Whoopi Goldberg (Celie) and Margaret Avery (Shug Avery) in *The Color Purple* (1985) film directed by Stephen Spielberg. Still image courtesy of the author.

hesitations and concern that the novel's erotic lesbian romance would not lend itself to a PG-13 rating. Spielberg remembers:

> I made the movie I wanted to make from Alice Walker's book. Alice was on the set a lot of the time and could have always stepped forward to say, 'You know, this is too Disney. This is not the way I envisioned the scene going down.' She was very supportive during filmmaking, and so I felt that we were doing a good job adapting her novel. There were certain things in relationship between Shug Avery and Celie that were finely detailed in Alice's book that I didn't feel could get a [PG-13] rating. And I was shy about it. In that sense, perhaps I was the wrong director to acquit some of the more sexually honest encounters between Shug and Celie, because I did soften those. I basically took something that was extremely erotic and very intentional, and reduced it to a simple kiss. I got a lot of criticism for that.[25]

While I agree that Spielberg, as an artist, has the right to create the film he wants to make, I find it incredibly disheartening that he was too "shy" to depict sexual love between two Black women but completely capable of depicting gratuitous violence against Blackgirls, including the graphic rape of an adolescent Blackgirl by the man she believes to be her father. In addition, Spielberg puts the onus on Walker—not on the director (i.e., himself)—to ensure the film captures the "very intentional" sexual love between Black women in the novel. When asked if he, with the advantage of hindsight, would change his direction now, Spielberg responded: "I wouldn't, no. That kiss is consistent with the tonality, from beginning to end, of *The Color Purple* that I adapted."[26] What becomes even more demoralizing is the knowledge that Walker did write a screenplay that captured the erotic love between Shug and Celie but Spielberg rejected the script.

Walker's 1984 screenplay, "Watch For Me in the Sunset, or The Color Purple," offers an unapologetic depiction of sexual love between Black women. While Spielberg declined her incomplete treatment, she later published her adaptation in *The Same River Twice: Honoring the Difficult.* "It was quieter than the one by Menno Meyjes, which was filmed, and which I was happy to find I liked a lot. There was not so much music in mine. It was clear the women loved each other. It was clear that Shug is, like me, bisexual. That Celie is lesbian. Do I regret my version of my book was not filmed? I have accepted that it wasn't. But to balance this experience, I have felt a need to share what I did attempt," writes Walker.[27] She later compares her adaptation to Spielberg's film, noting her dissatisfaction with Shug's characterization and erasure of Celie's newfound spiritual belief system. Walker writes:

> What I have kept [from the novel], which the film avoided entirely, is Shug's completely unapologetic self-acceptance as outlaw, renegade, rebel, and pagan; her zest in loving both women and men, younger and older. When Shug says in the book *The Color Purple* "I believe God is everything that is, ever was, or ever will be," she is saying what I too believe; she is also quoting Isis, the ancient African goddess, a precursor of the Virgin Mary, mother of Christ, although I did not know this at the time. I have also kept Celie's grasp of the concept that what is holy is the whole thing, not something above it or beyond it, not something separate from herself; as well as her complete bafflement that there could be anything wrong with loving another woman. Especially a woman so loving, brave, and sweet-smelling as Shug.[28]

Thus, Shug and Celie embody Walker's own womanist belief that sexual love between Black women can be a source of strength and "extraordinarily holy" experience.[29]

Ironically, at the time of filming *The Color Purple*, Walker was unable to voice her concerns with Spielberg's direction due to her poor mental and physical health. According to Walker, she was battling emotional pain of staying with an unfaithful partner, her mother's fading health (Walker believed her mother was dying), and her own (undiagnosed) case of Lyme disease. "For even though I was present on the set every moment I could drag myself up from my couch, I was also not there. As I watched each scene unfold I felt more like a spirit than a person," writes Walker.[30] Struggling with the debilitating side-effects of Lyme disease led Walker to experience what she identifies as "soul-deep exhaustion."[31] Walker remembers: "I was unequal to the task of pointing out to Steven [Spielberg] every 'error' I saw about to be made, as my critics later assumed I should have, or even of praising the exquisite things he constantly thought up, which moved me to tears each evening as we watched 'dailies.' This pained me; I felt it an unexplainable and quite personal failing."[32] Among her concerns, Walker identifies three major errors, which she felt undermined the message of her novel. To begin, in the opening scenes of the film Celie discloses that she was raped and impregnated by her "daddy" which was not only "a horrible shock" to Walker, but also "effectively obscure[es] the fact that her biological father was forcefully heroic."[33] Walker also found it "disturbing to see Shug pretend not to know why Celie can't 'speak up' after Shug leaves her alone with Mister to go back on the road."[34] Finally, Walker admits that more than a decade later, Spielberg's depiction of Mister/Albert's stunted growth and the erasure of Shug and Celie's erotic and sensuous relationship, continue to cause her "regret."[35] Perhaps Walker's regret stems from the pushback from Black activists who attempted to ban the film. While Black organizations such as the National Association for the Advancement of Colored People (NAACP), the Nation of Islam, and the Coalition Against Black Exploitation decried the film's representation of Black men as violent abusers and lesbian relationships as an assault on traditional Black family values, Black lesbians also criticized the film for obscuring Black lesbian sexuality.[36] Pleasing neither conservative Black organizations nor radical feminists, Walker was forced to cross the picket line for the film's premiere screening.[37]

Despite early backlash to the 1985 film, the white and openly gay television, film, and theatre producer Scott Sanders, with the help of co-producers Oprah Winfrey and Quincy Jones, used the film and Walker's novel as source material for the 2005 Broadway musical. The 2005 cast album liner notes discuss the unique nature of the musical adaptation. "The novel, which won the Pulitzer Prize in 1983, is a series of letters, which give us Celie's *voice*, convey her discoveries as they happen, and let her describe her own life day after day. The movie gives us a powerful *visual* understanding of Celie's world—the sky, the dirt roads, her porch, her bedroom, the fields, the town. It lets us see the world that she saw."[38] The Broadway musical, however, uses song and Celie's "letters" (i.e., direct addresses to the audience) to convey her world to spectators. "Characters sing to express their secret thoughts, the things they cannot say even in print. The whole town comes to life as we hear the voices of the Church Ladies, the Choir, the fieldhands, the women who shop at Celie's store, and the townsfolk who anticipate Shug's arrival. And the changing style of the music, from the beginning of the show to the end, makes it clear that forty years are going by (with a visual aid of hemlines and wigs, of course)."[39] Thus, the musical form lends itself to the incorporation of a variety of musical genres—including spirituals, blues, jazz, and contemporary-sounding pop music—which not only help convey the passage of time but also the otherwise unutterable thoughts and feelings of characters. While the musical production does replicate Spielberg's reduction of physical intimacy between Celie and Shug to one stage kiss, the production's incorporation of music allows them to also express their innermost thoughts, including their physical desire, creative passion, and love for one another. Contemporary Black queer feminist spectators may view these changes as compromising the integrity of Walker's lesbian love story. However, directing a Black lesbian kiss on a Broadway stage was (and still is) considered "daring."

Celie's first solo, "Somebody Gonna Love You," conveys her innermost desire to love and nurture her children. When spectators first meet a motherless fourteen-year-old Celie (LaChanze), she feels trapped within the depths of extreme abuse and parentification. Pa (J.C. Montgomery), the man she believes to be her biological father, repeatedly rapes and beats her while also forcing her to take on adult responsibility, including caring for the home, family farm, and her younger sister Nettie (Renée Elise Goldsberry). Despite the emotional, physical, and mental abuse, Celie finds moments to experience joy and love with Nettie, whom she nurtures and protects. The pair is inseparable as spectators see them sit side by side on a barren Wisteria tree, singing children's rhymes and clapping together.[40] Their bond continues strong, even in the worst of times as they again sit side by side during Celie's hour of need. Having just given birth, Celie—now dressed in a modest white nightgown that only emphasizes her youthful appearance—sits on a stack of burlap sacks and croons a brief and hauntingly beautiful lullaby to her second baby, Adam. Knowing that Pa will force her to relinquish Adam, she gently cradles him and, through song, expresses her inability to give him material possessions, her hope that God will provide for him, and her abiding love for him. Celie concludes: "Sleep baby, sleep / 'Cause somebody gonna love you / Oh, I'm always gonna love you."[41] This loving vision of Madonna and child comes to an abrupt end as Pa enters, demanding Celie give Adam to him. Nettie tries to intervene and convince Pa to let Celie keep Adam, stating, "I'll help Celie, Pa." Unfortunately, Pa perceives Nettie's promise as backtalk, which only fuels his wrath. Pa jerks Nettie roughly by the arm and bellows, "You give me that baby!" Upon seeing Pa's violence towards Nettie, Celie relinquishes Adam. At this moment, spectators not only witness domestic violence from within Black families but also Celie's compassion and love for her sister.

Having experienced parentification, Celie's love for Nettie surpasses a typical sisterly bond and becomes more akin to that of a mother/child relationship. Unwilling to cause her "daughter" of sorts pain, Celie obediently relinquishes one of the greatest loves of her life to protect Nettie. Later, Celie continues to take on the role of a self-sacrificing mother by agreeing to an arranged marriage to an older farmer and widower named Mister/Albert (Kingsley Leggs). When Nettie encourages Celie to refuse the marriage, she explains, "If I don't go with him, he'll take you and you'll never finish school." Above all, Celie wants Nettie to accomplish her dream of becoming a school teacher and believes that life with Mister/Albert will effectively doom her to life on the farm. Finally, when Nettie refuses Mister's sexual advances and he kicks her out of his home, spectators witness Celie comes to Nettie's aid. As Mister pulls Nettie by the hair, shoves her to the ground, and kicks dirt on her, Celie pleads with him not to hurt Nettie. When combined, Celie's lullaby and protective actions not only demonstrate her incredible maternal instincts but also her inner beauty.

Blind to Celie's inner beauty—she loves and nurtures others unconditionally—the abusive men in her life deem her "ugly," and therefore undeserving of respect and protection. Pa and Mister/Albert link her physical ugliness with her lack of womanly curves. In their eyes, Celie's masculine build makes her capable of doing both the domestic labor of a woman and the masculine work of a fieldhand. Pa expresses these sentiments when he refuses to let Mister/Albert marry Nettie. Pa advises, "You lookin' for a new Shug Avery, you better go to Memphis. All we got here is one pretty girl you can't never have, and one ugly girl . . . " Together, the two men complete Pa's sentence, stating: "Can work like a man." Undaunted, Mister/Albert still considers Celie a marriage prospect and inspects her as one would an enslaved person or livestock. After finding her appearance and demeanor repulsive—Celie (LaChanze) walks with a quick shuffle, stiffened back, and pelvis thrust forward—Mister/Albert tries to backtrack from his offer of marriage, stating, "She worse than I thought. She don't even look like kin to Nettie." Pa then reminds Mister/Albert that Celie could tend to his children and offers an additional cow if he takes her off of his hands. Mister/Albert grudgingly agrees but never actually proposes to Celie, nor does Pa ever ask Celie about her desires because, again, her "ugliness" makes her undeserving of basic human rights. While a bit hesitant to leave her home, Celie meekly follows after Mister/Albert, who whips her with his riding crop and pulls her along until they are both offstage. Unfortunately, any concern for Celie's fate quickly abates upon the arrival of the "hyper-lively" trio of Church Ladies who enter singing, "That Fine Mister."[42]

Black queer feminist spectators, however, cannot ignore the fact that Celie is treated like an animal, further cemented in the blues song "Big Dog," performed by Mister/Albert and his fieldhands. During the song, Celie

(LaChanze) appears overwhelmed and frightened as she scrubs the floors and chases after Mister's son Harpo and three unnamed daughters (one of the girls even climbs on Celie's back as she tries to style her hair). Meanwhile, the fieldhands stand in a line and "dig" holes in the ground while singing/ordering Celie to make Mister/Albert's hamhocks hot and his lemonade cold, pluck chickens, scrub dishes, and churn butter until her "hands cramp." Afterward, Mister/Albert joins in, singing/ordering Celie to mop the floor, sweep the barn, milk the cow, get water from the well, brush his horse, feed his pig, prepare firewood, dig a ditch, gather eggs, pitch hay, patch the fence, tend to the garden, feed, the baby goats, etc. At the conclusion of the song and Celie's workday, an even worse fate awaits her as Mister/Albert guides her into the bedroom. Before Mister/Albert banishes Nettie from his home, Celie confides that, "If I really buried [in that house] it be better. I not have to work. But I finish most nights by ten. Then while he on top of me, I lay there, think bout you. Wonder if you safe." Celie survives Mister/Albert's abuse by turning inward, using disassociation for psychic relief. However, by disconnecting her actual thoughts, feelings, and sense of identity from her reality, she stifles her development of critical consciousness. Resiliency experts have found that "like adolescent identity development, the development of a critical consciousness is dependent upon context: one's local social environment, individual experiences, and the presence (or lack of a presence) of adult allies who nurture seeds of critical consciousness. Similarly, like all developmental competencies, the mediating competency of critical consciousness evolves and develops."[43] Rather than nurture Celie's critical consciousness, the adults in her life exploit her in every possible way, providing her with no time, support, or space for further development. Indeed, whether under the "care" of Pa or married to Mister/Albert, Celie must labor as a worker bee from sunup to sundown, ending her workday with a ritual of sexual violence. Marital or spousal rape, however, would not have been considered a crime during the early twentieth century. In fact, marital or spousal rape was not illegal in every US state until 1993. Thus, as horrific as it sounds, even at the time of the film premiere, Mister/Albert's rape of Celie could have been both morally and legal justified through the use of the Bible and marital rape exemptions.

Black queer feminist spectators might understand that Pa and Mister/Albert's rape, abuse, and exploitation of Celie reflects the unfortunate reality for many Blackgirls who suffer spiritual and domestic violence. Walker witnessed and heard stories about domestic violence as a child and as such, conceptualized the Black family and spirituality as potential sources of strength and oppression within the lives of Blackgirls. Walker's experiential knowledge influenced her depiction of Black families and organized religion in *The Color Purple*. Walker writes:

> Ever since I was a child, I had been aware of a high rate of domestic violence in our town, among our people; wives shot or stabbed to death, children sometimes abused and beaten. Miserable men who seemed unable not to ruin their lives; who seemed born with the prison door stretched wide before them. Men who had been taught from the Bible that women are the cause of all evil in the world, and were not, simply as female with human beings, to be trusted and certainly not be honored, respected, loved, or held in reverence as the center of human life. The Bible had been the only reading matter black people were permitted during our long enslavement; for 300 years they were not even allowed to read it for themselves. This was indoctrination at its most relentless; naïve to think it would not leave a deadly, self-despising mark. One might be expected to love one's neighbor as one's self—such a beautiful sentiment—but never one's wife, one's mother, one's mate. We needed to see how we looked, I thought, behaving as if still under the spell of a religion that made it nearly impossible to love the female body that was our source.[44]

In addition to identifying how early religious violence poisoned Black men and harmed the most vulnerable within Black communities during US chattel slavery, Walker suggests that loving the original life source—the Black female body—provides a powerful antidote. In the musical, Celie constructs a similar womanist theology as she develops her own critical consciousness through the use of song, journaling, and romantic love with Shug (see Figure 1.4). The musical then juxtaposes Celie's spiritual journey with that of traditional conservative views regarding gender and sexuality through the trio of Church Ladies—Jarene (Maia Nkenge Wilson), Darlene (Virginia Ann Woodruff), and Doris (Kimberly Ann Harris)—who position themselves as a moral compass for the Black community.

The Church Ladies, who represent some of the worst aspects of the Black church, act as a problematic storytelling device within Celie's narrative of trauma. Clothed in modest floor-length dresses in yellow, pink, and green, the trio of Church Ladies present themselves as models of temperance, charity, and purity. However, in reality, they imbibe alcohol (Doris secretly

Figure 1.4 LaChanze (Celie) center, in the musical *The Color Purple* (2005), directed by Gary Griffin. Photo Sara Krulwich, courtesy of *The New York Times*/ Redux.

grabs a flask from a homeless man on the street and drinks), gossip about the problems of their neighbors, and sing about the attractiveness of a married man (i.e., Mister/Albert). The Church Ladies also function as a chorus, providing spectators with important exposition, commentary on the action of the musical, and comic relief from Celie's traumatic experiences. "I think the Church Ladies are Greek chorus slash comic relief slash everywoman—people we know who are busybodies and are very interested in what's going on in the town. There was no television back then, so you had to be amused in some way and this was a good, scandalous way," remembers actress Kimberly Ann Harris.[45] Unfortunately, their quest for amusement, coupled with their articulation of traditional views regarding gender and sexuality, often comes at Celie's expense. For example, when a very pregnant Celie enters the church at the beginning of the musical, the Church Ladies smile to her face, ask her what she's planning to name her child, and as soon as she walks away, they malign her name. Using direct address to draw spectators into their gossip circle, the Church Ladies sing/chant the following exposition:

JARENE: Livin' with that man what killed their mother. Now it gon kill them too.
DORIS: I heard about po' chile Celie Heard about po'
JARENE: Already ruint
DORIS: Chile Celie
JARENE: Two times!
DORIS: Heard about po'
JARENE: Already ruint
DORIS: Chile Celie
JARENE: Two times!
DARLENE: She only 14 Years old![46]

The Church Ladies conclude by turning their heads, one by one, to face the audience as they ask, "Who de daddy?" Afterward, the Church Ladies continue to repeat their question, turning into a cacophony (i.e., a harsh discordant mixture of sounds). The women answer their own question together, with a robust "Nobody know!" Rather than report the abuse that "killed" Celie and Nettie's mother or the continued sexual abuse that "kills" Celie's spirit, the Church Ladies place the blame on the victim. They feign concern about Celie's "ruined" state, using her suffering as a source for their enjoyment. Perhaps even worse, their upbeat and humorous delivery encourages spectators to laugh along with them. However, this was not the intention of director Gary Griffin, who wanted the Church Ladies to serve as a storytelling device. "They're a great device if they reveal humanity. They're a bad device if they're there just to get laughs. Because then it looks like we're making fun of those women, and I never wanted to make fun of them," remembers Griffin.[47] Black queer feminist spectators who understand the history of Black churchwomen's social justice efforts, including their (at times) problematic endorsement of respectability politics, might at best read the Church Ladies' performance as satirical. At worse, their performance distracts from Celie's narrative and makes light of deeply important issues such as the rape and exploitation of Blackgirls.

Shug Avery, also known as the Queen Honeybee, offers an alternative vision of spirituality, one that is rooted in nature, the blues tradition, and the divinity of the Black female body. Walker originally conceived of Shug as pagan, which she defines as "people whose primary spiritual relationship is with Nature and the earth; people who have traditionally been oppressed or destroyed by patriarchal religions."[48] Shug's pre-Christian spirituality allows her to embrace all that nature has to offer, including love and sexual pleasure with both men and women. Her work as a blues artist allows her to then convey these liberatory systems to a much broader audience. However, as a bisexual Blackgirl living in the rural South at the turn of the twentieth century, Shug's spiritual thought constantly runs afoul of patriarchy and Christianity. Angela Y. Davis discusses the critical tension between the blues, sexuality, and Christianity in her book, *Blues Legacy and Black Feminism: Gertrude "Ma" Rainey, Bessie Smith, and Billy Holiday* (1998). "The blues were part of a cultural continuum that disputed the binary constructions associated with Christianity. . . . Blues singers were (and to a certain extent still are) associated with the Devil because they celebrated those dimensions of human existence considered evil and immoral according to the tenets of Christianity. But precisely because they offer enlightenment on love and sexuality, blues singers often have been treated as secular counterparts to Christian ministers, recognized by their constituencies as no less important authorities in their respective realms," writes Davis.[49] Before audiences even meet Shug, the Church Ladies perform a blues song of their own, casting Shug as the epitome of sin. In "All We've Got to Say," Church Lady Doris questions if Shug has "got dem heebies and jeebies" from moonshine and reefer, while Church Lady Darlene speculates that Shug caught a venereal disease from "the nasty relations." Regardless of whether or not these rumors are true, the Church Ladies imply that Shug's health has suffered because of her moral decay. Mister/Albert and Pa, who represent violent patriarchy, both desire Shug and repudiate her alternative lifestyle as immoral. For example, when discussing why he could not possibly form a heteronormative marriage with Shug, Mister/Albert states, "Shug Avery not a child-raisin' woman, you know that. She the Queen Honeybee," to which Pa responds, "She a low-down whore is what everybody say." As the Queen Honeybee, Shug surrounds herself with a hive of worker bees—a group of drinking and dancing patrons who adore her. While she does not perform any manual or domestic labor (including tending to her own children), Shug does what no one else in her colony can do: sing and flaunt her beautiful Black body.

Shug "preaches" about the joys of nature and the divinity of the Black female body in her performance of "Push Da Button." Like honey, Shug's blues song "Push Da Button" oozes with sexuality, inviting both men and women to dip their fingers into her "honeypot," as well as discover their own sexual pleasure. By "honeypot," I refer to the Black lesbian vernacular term for a woman's vagina. In his interviews with contemporary Black queer Southern women, Johnson found that Black women's "honeypot" does not just act as "a receptacle," but also "a space where sexual expression, desire, and power reside."[50] Shug similarly embraces her sexual power, using song and dance to express her desires. In creating "Push Da Button," Russell remembers: "We got that concept from Alice's book, of course, and we just wanted it to be a really raunchy, fun song for Shug, just to have a real good time."[51] The song's concept derives from a moment in the novel wherein Walker's Celie reveals that she does not enjoy sex with Mister, and Shug teaches her how to masturbate. "Listen, [Shug] say, right down there in your pussy is a little button that gits real hot when you do you know what with somebody. It git hotter and hotter and then it melt. That the good part. But other parts good too, she say. Lot of sucking going on, here and there, she say. Lot of finger and tongue work. Button? Finger and *tongue*? My face hot enough to melt itself" remembers Celie.[52] Walker's Shug then gives Celie a mirror and encourages her to examine her vagina and discover her "button" while she keeps a lookout to make sure no one enters the bedroom. In contrast, the musical transforms the novel's original masturbation lesson into an upbeat blues number performed at Celie's stepson Harpo's juke joint. During her performance, Shug (Withers-Mendes) advises heterosexual couples, teaching women how to sexually excite their men (i.e., "Watch the juice begin to flow") and encouraging men to let women take charge of sexual acts (i.e., "Give her the stick / she do the rest"). Afterward, Shug shares her spiritual knowledge, creating a moment of call-and-response with her colony or "congregation" of band members and drinking/dancing patrons. Shug sings/preaches, "To let your baby know / It ain't no sin," to which her congregation responds, "Push da button!" Throughout the performance, Shug (Withers-Mendes) confidently and joyfully spreads her legs, thrusts her hips back and forth, pushes a man's head near her vagina, grinds with male dancers, and shakes her buttocks at the theatre audience. Celie witnesses Shug's entire musical number—which contradicts the conservative Christian values she has been taught her entire life—and becomes curious about the notion of unbridled sexuality.

Before meeting Shug, Celie spent her early life trying to adhere to the Black church's conservative views regarding gender and sexuality, but doing so only fostered her subjugation. Like many Southern Blackgirls at the turn of the twentieth century, Celie attends church with her family regularly and appears to have blind faith in the power of a white patriarchal God. Before the curtains open, spectators catch a glimpse of her religious indoctrination through her journal entry, which appears larger than life across a scrim on the stage. In contrast to the novel, which employs Black English, the musical presents her short entry in standard English. The scrim reads: "Dear God, I am fourteen years old. ~~I am~~ I have always been a good girl. Maybe you can give me a sign letting me know what is happening to me." Celie follows the teachings of the Bible by silently obeying her Pa. Yet, this obedience or being "a good girl" has come at a hefty price. As an innocent child, even she does not fully understand the depths of her abuse and exploitation. Spectators witness Celie continue to turn to God for comfort and direction throughout her childhood as she performs musical numbers such as "Our Prayer." Performed as a duet with her sister Nettie, the uptempo song "Our Prayer" functions as Celie's "I want" song. As spectators watch Celie pick up presumably heavy burlap sacks with ease—Nettie struggles to do so—Celie sings: "Wanna sit and do nothing / Make you a new dress / Hope my babies are happy / Some place God will bless." They end the song together, sweetly harmonizing: "No matter what life bring / Us in God's hands." Celie dreams of a life of leisure and the ability to pursue her creative passions—making clothing for her beloved Nettie. With this dream comes the hope that God will protect her, Nettie, and her children and ensure their happiness. However, this hopeful optimism comes to an abrupt halt when Mister/Albert kicks Nettie out and hides her correspondence from Celie, effectively separating the sisters. Celie returns to prayer with "Lily of the Field," a blues-inspired song that refers to the Gospels of Matthew and Luke. The Biblical account recites the Sermon on the Mount, wherein Jesus teaches his followers that the lilies, the grass, and the owls do not worry about material needs such as food and shelter, and yet God provides for them. Celie begins "Lily of the Field" by likening herself to a lily, praying that God will also provide for her. However, as she performs she begins to question God, singing: "Dear God / What you done with my sister? / How this play in your plan?" She then pleads with God to bring her sister back and by the end of the song, questions the nature of the Biblical God. "If I really a lily of the field / You will answer my prayers / Or you're no God at all!" Celie sings. This moment of prayer/song provides the first crack in Celie's belief that a patriarchal God answers prayers and is all-knowing and all-powerful. By age twenty-two, Celie confirms out loud to herself (and to spectators) that Nettie "must be dead" and asks "What kind of God are you?" At this point, Celie has no use for a white male deity and begins removing Christian indoctrination from her identity.

Celie begins removing what Walker refers to as the "spell of a religion" when she falls in love with Shug's naked body and expresses the joy that this newfound knowledge brings her in the song, "Dear God—Shug." Celie does not actually meet Shug until 1922—or about half of the way through Act I of the musical—after having suffered more than a decade of abuse at the hands of her husband, Mister/Albert. When Celie meets Shug (Withers-Mendes), she appears sickly but beautifully cloaked in a black sequined gown on her doorstep. Shug, however, does not immediately see Celie's inner beauty and declares: "You sho is ugly!" After insulting her twenty-seven-year-old rival, Shug commands Celie to wash her while she soaks in a clawfoot bathtub. Rather than view Shug as a rival for Mister/Albert's attention, Celie's (LaChanze) eyes grow large as she abruptly stops and examines the length of Shug's body in the bathtub. Annoyed at her delay, Shug asks, "What you lookin' at? You never seen a naked woman before?" Celie answers her through her inner prayer/song, "Dear God—Shug," an uptempo number that allows Celie to express her sexual desire for Shug. A spotlight frames the couple and Celie sings: "Got about a million tingles / Sneakin' on up my spine / I wash her body and it feel like I'm prayin'." Celie cannot find words to express her arousal but knows the feeling is nothing like she has ever felt for her sister, her daughter-in-law Sofia, or any other person. As she sings, Celie dips her hand into the bathtub and Shug returns this action with a knowing smile. Shug then spreads her legs wide, dangling one over the lip of the bathtub to allow Celie greater access to touch/bathe her vagina. When Shug gets out of the bathtub, the spotlight focuses on Celie, casting Shug's naked body in a silhouette. With her back to the audience, a naked Shug faces Celie with her hands on her hips, a vision of beauty and erotic possibilities that Celie does not yet understand. By "erotic," I refer to Lorde's assertion that "the erotic is a resource within each of us that lies in a deeply female and spiritual plane, firmly rooted in the power of our unexpressed or unrecognized feeling. In order to perpetuate itself, every oppression must corrupt or distort those various sources of power within the culture of the oppressed that can provide energy for change. For women, this has meant a suppression of the erotic as a considered source of power and information within our lives."[53] The erotic, then, functions as an expression of joy and spectators can witness Celie discover this feeling through her wide-eyed gaze upon Shug's body, which exudes the confidence, self-knowledge, and unencumbered sexual freedom Celie has never known before. This moment of pleasure shakes Celie out of her numbed, detached state (which has heretofore helped her survive unimaginable abuse), allowing her to begin the journey of self-actualization.

Experiencing Shug's love allows Celie to begin to see her inner beauty and worth, *regardless*. As with many people in her life, Shug does not originally *see* Celie. After all, Shug's first words to Celie declared her "ugly." However, after the bathtub scene, Shug and Celie establish an intimacy with one another that opens Shug's eyes, allowing her to actually see the depth of Celie's beauty and compassion for others. The next scene begins in Shug's bedroom, with Celie sitting upright on the bed combing a red robe-clad Shug's hair. When Shug asks Celie to hurry, Celie responds: "I'm gonna work on your head like you were my own little girl, Olivia." Celie's gentle touch works its magic and Shug shifts from impatient to joyful as she admits how wonderful it feels to be cared for, even stating that the experience "feels like my grandma used to do." Shug then sighs, leans back into the comfort of Celie's lap, and begins asking Celie questions about her life. Later, after Shug performs the bawdy blues number "Push Da Button," the pair return to Shug's bedroom for another heart-to-heart. Concerned that Celie might despise her for sleeping with her husband, Shug asks her how she feels about their living situation. Rather than answer her question, Celie asks Shug if she "likes" sleeping with Mister/Albert and the two have the following exchange:

SHUG: I just love it. Don't you?

CELIE: I don't like it at all. Most times I pretend I ain't there. He never know the difference. Just do his business, get off, go to sleep.

SHUG (*laughs*): Do his business? You make it sound like he going to the toilet on you.

CELIE: That what it feel like.

SHUG: You never enjoy it ever?

CELIE: No, never. He think I'm ugly. It all right.

Celie's candor—her simple words reveal the depth of sexual and psychological abuse she has endured—appears to surprise and sadden Shug. Celie responds to Shug's distress by trying to comfort her, telling her "It all right" while gently caressing Shug. Following this emotional moment, Shug tries to lighten the mood with humor, revealing that she only receives attention through outrageous behavior such as "shakin' [her] titties" and "waving [her] ass." When the joke does not land, a visible change occurs and Shug abruptly stops talking and abandons her blueswoman act. Shug gently guides Celie to a bench, stands with her arms wrapped around Celie's shoulders, and sings the contemporary soulful pop ballad, "Too Beautiful for Words," as the pair gaze into an unseen mirror (see Figure 1.5). A projection of a moon shines down on the lovers as Shug sings: "I danced with dukes, crooned with counts / Been courted like a queen / But when I see what's in your heart / All the rest is blurred / The grace you bring into this world's / Too beautiful for words." At last, Shug finally sees the beautiful spirit inside Celie and acknowledges how her quiet, fragile beauty has changed her for the better. Songwriter Allee Willis remembers that "we felt Celie was this little wounded bird, and Shug really recognized that. Shug did see her beauty, because Celie was the first person who did anything for her without wanting anything [so this performance] would be the deepest most real that Shug had ever gotten with a song."[54] Celie responds to Shug's vulnerability with an embrace, and from that moment on, the pair becomes inseparable.

Celie and Shug's performance of the soulful pop ballad "What About Love?" becomes a defining moment in their love story, as well as a rare moment for Black queer feminist spectators to witness physical intimacy between Blackgirls on a Broadway stage. Despite their obvious chemistry, Celie and Shug do not shift from friends to lovers until Celie gains the

Figure 1.5 LaChanze (Celie) and Elisabeth Withers (Shug Avery) in a scene from *The Color Purple* (2005), directed by Gary Griffin, NBC News "Oprah Comes Full Circle," May 16, 2006, still image courtesy of the author.

confidence to express her innermost feelings about Shug's departure. Within the safety of Shug's bedroom, Celie tries to convince Shug to stay. "You gone an hour it feel like a year to me" Celie admits, to which Shug responds, "I'll be back. Nobody ever love me like you." The two pause, staring at each other until Shug says, "Damn, girl!" and kisses Celie on the mouth. In the filmed recording of the performance, the audience responds with a loud, audible "Ooh!" Shug (Withers-Mendes) then puts her arm around Celie's (LaChanze) neck and kisses her more deeply, effectively blocking this moment from the view of spectators. When Shug ends the kiss and leans back, she reveals Celie's response to this moment as the "Too Beautiful for Words" instrumental plays. Celie displays the biggest, sweetest smile on her face while Shug also appears overcome with emotion. Shug takes deep breaths, closes her eyes, and smiles as Celie performs "What About Love?" As Celie sings about feeling as if she is "floating away" for the first time, Shug appears bashful and joins Celie in song, asking "Is that me I don't recognize?" As the duet continues and they sing about the importance of trust, tenderness, love, hope, and joy, Shug appears vulnerable as she leans close to Celie, gently caresses her hair, and holds her hand to her breast. Celie returns Shug's affection by gently caressing Shug's face and breast as she asks/sings "What about love?" Towards the end of their ballad, the lovers hug, giggle, and Shug offers Celie her bangled bracelet as a token of her love. This romantic interlude concludes with the lovers hugging one final time before Shug's departure.

While this staging of Black lesbian desire may appear as a diluted version of the sexually erotic moments in Walker's novel, this scene was considered radical for its time. Songwriter Stephen Bray, for example, remembers the following response from spectators when "What About Love?" was performed for the first time as a workshop at Alliance Theatre in Atlanta, Georgia in 2004:

> Right after the song ended I saw a woman with tears coming down her face get up and go make a phone call, and we imagined, Somebody has made a life decision change based on that song. Something just became okay for this woman. I love that. I really do believe it does that to people. You would always hear the applause start slow, like, Let me look around and see if everyone's applauding this lesbian stuff. Is this okay? Sure enough, it started softly and got louder and then the whoops and whistles and everybody was totally into it. But it would always start off like, Hmmm, I don't know if it's okay if people see me clapping. So I just love that we were brave

> enough to have a lesbian love song, to put it on the stage and not shy away from it. I'm really proud of that.[55]

Having Blackgirls kiss and sing a love song to each other on a Broadway stage was considered "brave" and unheard of in the mid-2000s (and perhaps still today). However, I surmise that Bray, Willis, and Russell's use of contemporary-sounding lyrics and instruments—"What About Love?" sounds like a top 100 pop song—helped make the lesbian love song more familiar and easily consumable for a wide range of spectators along the political spectrum, from the progressively "woke" to the more conservative-leaning. Willis even admits that "we needed a song that was going to sound like it belonged in the show, but that if you had to pick a song to go on the radio, this would be it."[56] Regardless of its broad appeal, "What About Love?" remains an important song for Black queer spectators who rarely, if ever, see Black love stories presented on the musical theatre stage.

Having established a relationship built on trust, love, and a myriad of other positive and affirming feelings, Shug teaches Celie how to embrace the liberatory nature of Black women's spirituality through the titular song, "The Color Purple." Akasha Gloria Hull writes that spirituality "involves a conscious relationship with the realm of spirit, with the invisibly permeating, ultimately positive, divine, and evolutionary energies that give rise to and sustain all that exists."[57] Shug fully embraces spirituality as a means of understanding humanity's relationship with nature. When an older, forty-two-year-old Celie expresses her bitterness towards God for destroying her life, she argues: "If God ever listen to a poor colored woman the world would be a different place" and gently corrects her vision of God. Building on her belief that nature is sacred, Shug counters Celie's argument with her belief that God provides Black women laughter, song, and sex, as well as the sky, the fields, and birds singing. When Celie refuses to change her mind, stating that "God just another man as far as I'm concerned. He triflin' and low down—" Shug interjects, stating, "No, Celie! God not some gloomy old man like the pictures you've seen of him. God not a man at all."[58] Shug then breaks into the contemporary-sounding soulful pop ballad, "The Color Purple," teaching Celie that "God is inside you" in every living thing, including honey bees, flowers, waterfalls, the moonlight light, and even a blade of corn. From this moment on, Celie abandons the psychological vestiges of slavery, including the emotional impact of religious violence, and embraces a new, liberatory spirituality based on womanist thought which begins to heal her spirit.

Walker, in fact, wanted her novel to act as a healing balm for all those negatively impacted by religious violence. "*The Color Purple* is basically about helping to heal people in their relationships with each other, with themselves, and with the earth, the planet. It's also to help them reconsider their inherited gods. . . . So what I think of as my greatest gift is this possibility of re-examining religion and also seeking to decolonize the spirit. We need to decolonize our spirits the same way that we try to decolonize our thoughts. Our brains. This is a very long journey," writes Walker.[59] Scholars such as Porshé R. Garner have suggested that Walker signifies Celie's spiritual transformation in the novel through the use of letters. "Through the life of Celie, Walker is able to disentangle spirituality from this mystery figure, which readers see through the use of 'Dear God' in many of her written letters, to later entangle spirituality within the community of those who help her break free from domination. . . . At this turning point, we see Celie's letters go from being addressed to God, to herself, or to her sister Nettie," writes Garner.[60] *The Color Purple* attempts to reveal this spiritual journey through the incorporation of "letters" spoken in direct address (i.e., Celie shifts from "Dear God" to "Dear Nettie") and through songs such as "The Color Purple." In so doing, the production creates space for Black queer feminist spectators to also question their relationship to a white patriarchal deity and perhaps even embrace a newfound love of nature (including the divinity of the Black female body) as the ultimate life source.

After embracing Shug's love and decolonizing her thoughts and spirit, Celie develops a critical consciousness that allows her to form a sisterhood with other Blackgirls in her community. In her 2017 article, "Why Black Sisterhood is The Unshakable Bond that Keeps Us Going," the journalist Ashley McDonough describes Black sisterhood as a powerful connection built on generations of love, support, affirmation, and celebration among Black women and girls. "Black sisterhood is an unexplainable bond that includes love and respect for one another that we were forced to support early on. After all, if we didn't support each other, who would? This bond has been passed down throughout generations. Success after success, failure after failure, our sisters are there to cheer us on or wipe our tears. An unbreakable bond like no other," writes McDonough.[61] While Shug affirms her beauty, offers her unconditional love, and helps her heal from spiritual and sexual violence, Celie remains inward-focused. Celie does not move towards collective empowerment until she inherits a business from her deceased father, who was lynched by white business owners in Memphis. With Shug's encouragement, Celie accepts her inheritance and uses her creative energy to start a pants business. At this point, the musical undergoes a tonal shift, as the jazz/swing musical number, "Miss Celie's Pants" unfolds. Reminiscent of Cab Calloway, Frank Froeba, and Jack Palmer's 1939 "Jumping Jive," the upbeat and colorful performance includes an ensemble of Blackgirl dancers sporting vibrant pants. For the first time, spectators witness Celie surrounded by a sisterhood of caring Blackgirls who support Celie's dream and appreciate her creative talent. No longer performing backbreaking labor under the threat of Mister/Albert's whip, Celie sits in her shop, smiles, and chats with her customers as she fulfills her dream of helping other Blackgirls look and feel confident in their own skin.

While the image of Black sisterhood is commendable, the abrupt tonal shift between news of Celie's biological father's lynching and the spectacular "Miss Celie's Pants" musical number obscure a painful historical truth. During the Jim Crow era, white mobs lynched thousands of Black men and women, and systematically destroyed thriving Black businesses to eliminate perceived threats to white supremacy. The destruction of Black Wall Street and the murder of hundreds of prosperous Black community members during the 1921 Tulsa Race Massacre is but one example of this history of white-authored violence. Black queer feminist spectators who know this history will understand that even in the 1940s, Celie's decision to establish a business in the South—especially one that caters to the beauty and comfort of Blackgirls—would have been seen as a revolutionary act and in keeping with her father's legacy.

Today, Black queer feminist spectators might read Celie's decision to build her own business—despite the threat of white-authored violence—as a form of Black Girl Magic. The Black feminist studies scholar Janell Hobson writes that while hashtag Black Girl Magic has become "a shorthand description for any Black woman stylishly posing for Instagram selfies or fabulously dominating her profession if she happens to be a public figure in entertainment, sports, politics, activism, or the academy," the expression also celebrates "the articulation of the resolve and persistence of Black women and girls to triumph in the face of intersectional oppressions."[62] Celie perhaps best articulates the sentiments of Black Girl Magic near the end of the musical in her anthem ballad, "I'm Here." After ending her romantic relationship with Shug when she refuses to end her affair with a young man in their duet "What About Love? (Reprise)," Celie expresses her innermost thoughts in the song, "I'm Here." Celie sings: "I don't need you to love me / I don't need you to love me." She then reminds herself—and the spectators who witness her heartbreak—that she has her sister Nettie, her home, her hands, and her eyes. Determined to practice emotional resilience, Celie (LaChanze) tears up as she sings: "I'll stand as tall as the tallest tree / And I'm thankful for every day that I'm given / Both the easy and the hard ones I'm livin' / But most of all I'm thankful for / Knowing who I really am / I'm beautiful/ Yes, I'm beautiful / And I'm here." Having once been ostracized, silenced, and defined by others, Celie now acts as the heartbeat of the community, speaks her truth, and defines herself as proud, beautiful, and resilient. In so doing, Celie follows a tradition of Blackgirls "who dare to see themselves as beautiful and desirable in a culture that undermines their sex appeal, who dare to recognize their own brilliance in a society that constantly refutes their intellectual abilities, and who dare to revere their own communities, knowledge systems, and cultural practices in a nation that is determined to only view these entities through the lens of dysfunction."[63] This truth is perhaps best exemplified at the conclusion of the musical, wherein a now fifty-year-old Celie hosts a picnic in the front yard of her restored childhood home surrounded by her chosen family, including Shug, Nettie, and her adult children. However, the "magic" of this moment only comes about through Celie's efforts to abandon the spell of religion and fully embrace Black womanist thought, spirituality, and sisterhood.

While Black queer feminist spectators can certainly find meaning in *The Color Purple*, theatre critics gave the 2005 musical production a blend of responses ranging from mixed to negative reviews, citing poor characterization, the depiction of the lesbian love story, the fast pacing, and theatrical excess as artistic missteps. In terms of characterization, David Rooney of *Variety* writes that "A chief weakness is the failure to give Celie (LaChanze) decisive ownership of the story."[64] According to Rooney, "it's not until the penultimate song, 'I'm Here,' that [Celie] gets to stake her claim on the center-stage position."[65] The theatre critic Jeremy McCarter of *New York Magazine* found Norman, Russell, Willis, and Bray's musical adaptation an unfaithful retelling of Walker's lesbian love story. "Amid all this faith-based dramaturgy, it's no surprise that the lesbian element and Celie's story gets swept aside. The love she shares with Shug in Walker's book is dispatched here with a couple of timid kisses and some platitudinous lyrics. Hollywood has gay cowboys, and a Broadway musical gets nervous about an awkward hug? Who's responsible for this madness?"[66] Indeed, some critics argued that remaining faithful to the vast majority of Walker's tale actually hindered the pacing of the production. For example, *The New York Times* theatre critic Ben Brantley writes that "watching this beat-the-clock production summons the frustrations of riding through a picturesque stretch of country in a supertrain like the TGV. . . . It never slows down long enough for you to embrace it."[67] In addition to creating a "plot-crammed" production to remain faithful to the novel, the musical also took liberties with the visual elements of Walker's story. "As for the rest of the production, there's a sumptuousness throughout that, while hardly true to the harrowing bleakness of the early chapters of Ms. Walker's novel, does bring to mind the enjoyable hokey cinematic ravishments of Steven Spielberg's 1985 film version," writes Brantley.[68] In other words, John Lee Beatty's "fairy-tale sense of wonder" sets, Brian MacDevitt's "sunset-and-starshine lighting," and Paul Tazewell's beautiful period costumes presented a romanticized view of rural poverty in Georgia.[69] After receiving these less-than-stellar endorsements from theatre critics, the production garnered only one Tony Award; LaChanze's performance as Celie securing the Best Performance by a Leading Actress.

However harsh, criticism of the 2005 production remains valuable as it continues to raise important questions regarding storytelling, Black women's artistic agency, and Black queer visibility. Some of these questions include: How can artists depict Celie's silent subjugation while also allowing her to maintain a dominant presence within her story? What do spectators lose when artists remain faithful to the majority of Walker's story but choose to diminish the most important aspects of her writing (i.e., Black lesbian love)? Finally, what barriers prevent storytellers from embracing stories of Black queer love?

The 2015 revival of *The Color Purple*, starring Cynthia Erivo (Celie), Danielle Brooks (Sofia), and Jennifer Hudson (Shug), attempted to alleviate most of the problems of the original production by stripping the musical down to its bones, and focusing on characterization, storytelling, and authenticity. The musical theatre director and scholar Aaron Brown encapsulates the issues that the revival would seek to overcome. Brown writes:

> The original production allowed little time to absorb the harrowing tale of Celie's life. Events of rape, assault, and abuse were quickly glossed over as audience members moved into the next production number. The production was concerned with making this dark African-American story accessible to the typical Broadway consumer—a middle age or older white consumer with disposable income—while also attempting to honor Walker's story.

> In order to be competitive, the production attempted to function like the elaborate, high-energy, fast-paced Broadway musical adaptations of the time: *Hairspray*, *Wicked*, and *The Producers*. The plan worked. The musical was a box-office success, yet an element was missing: genuineness.[70]

In order to present a more "genuine" African American story—note that "lesbian love story" does not factor in here—the Scottish stage director John Doyle removed all of the "glamour" from the original production, which became "a key component to the overall success of the revival."[71] Rather than have a fully realized set, Doyle's scaled-down production relied on a few dozen wooden chairs, woven baskets, and props to recreate the starkness of Celie's life. In addition, Doyle made the decision to place an often-silent Celie onstage throughout the musical, allowing her to witness all aspects of the production as if she is controlling the unfolding of the narrative. Finally, Brown credits Doyle for attending to the "vocal stylization associated with the black church" which "create[d] a phenomenon more closely correlated with the African-American experience."[72] The theatre critic Charles McNulty writes that revival functioned "more like a church service than a traditional book musical [with] the force and fluidity of a Gospel service."[73] Doyle's vision proved successful, with the revival receiving positive critical reviews and theatrical awards, including a 2016 Tony Award for Best Revival of a Musical, 2016 Dreama League Award for Outstanding Revival of a Musical, and 2017 Grammy Award for Best Musical Theatre Album. Sadly, these changes within the production modes did not include efforts to recover more of Walker's original lesbian narrative.

Many LGBTQ spectators hoped that the 2023 release of *The Color Purple* musical film starring Fantasia Barrino (Celie), Danielle Brooks (Sofia), and Taraji P. Henson (Shug) might fully realize the novel's lesbian love story. For example, the trans Latina lesbian entertainment journalist Mey Rude expressed her eagerness to *finally* see a film capture the sexual eroticism within Celie and Shug's love story. "One aspect of the story that fans have been hoping will be prominently featured in the new movie is the lesbian love story between Celie and blues singer Shug Avery (Henson), which was present in the book, but was relegated to subtext in the 1985 film," writes Rude.[74] Perhaps part of this excitement was due, in part, to the presence of a Black and openly gay screenwriter on the production team. Having previously worked on LGBTQ projects, fallen in love with Walker's novel at age thirteen, and watched the 1985 film, screenwriter Marcus Gardley discussed his desire to restore the lesbian love story with *Out Magazine* and other major LGBTQ media outlets. "That's part of the reason I got the job. My pitch led off with, 'This is a love story between two women.' It was the most important thing to Alice Walker. . . . In the original film, there was not enough of the romantic love between Celie and Shug. I wanted the love story to be prominent and didn't want to brush over that these two women are in love," remembers Gardley.[75] The film's Black director Blitz Bazawule, similarly, discussed the importance of *The Color Purple* within queer communities. "Celie is a queer icon, and Alice Walker has been very vocal about that. . . . Our job was to just lean into it harder, and give a little bit more context and a little more beauty to her coming-out moment," remembers Bazawule.[76] Despite this commitment, the hopes for a restoration of queer thematics were crushed for many fans, including members of the more recent film cast.

Rather than center the lesbian love story within the reality of Celie's daily life, the 2023 musical film adaptation opted to present much of her romance with Shug within surrealist fantasy sequences. For example, after Shug's (Henson) performance of "Push Da Button," she takes Celie (Barrino) by the hand, and the two watch a film together. As they enjoy the film, Celie's mind wanders, and viewers witness her romantic fantasy unfold in black and white (see Figure 1.6). Celie's dream sequence begins with her and Shug entering an art deco-style performance hall and walking down two large white

Figure 1.6 Fantasia Barrino (Celie) and Taraji P. Henson (Shug Avery) in *The Color Purple* (2023) film directed by Blitz Bazawule. Still image courtesy of the author.

staircases (an homage to the music hall staircases in the 1943 musical comedy *Stormy Weather*). As Celie begins singing the ballad "What About Love?," the film slowly changes back to color, and the camera pans back to reveal a pianist and an all-Black orchestra. Shug then joins Celie in song; the lovers slow dance and end their musical number with a passionate kiss that slowly transitions them back into their original seats in the movie theatre. In the next scene, Shug and Celie wake up in the same bed together, suggesting that the lovers have consummated their relationship.[77] Bazawule explains this artistic choice as follows: "Celie's mind goes into this incredible place of what she believes love is, and when she comes back into reality, it has happened for her."[78] However, in so doing, Bazawule runs the risk of obscuring the realities of Black queer love.

Black queer performers and critics have criticized Bazawule's artistic vision for failing to center the lives and love of queer Blackgirls. For example, the bisexual actress Aunjanue Ellis-Taylor, who stars in the role of "Mama," remembers that "the book is about Black lesbians. Whether the choice was made to focus on that or not in the cinematic iterations of *The Color Purple*, it's still a movie about Black lesbians. . . . People can try to say the story is about sisterhood, but it's a story about Black lesbians. Period. What is hard for me is that when we have those spaces where we can honour the truth of that, we walk away from it. We suppress it. We hide it. We sanitize it. . . . Someone like me, knowing that the book is about Black lesbians, look at that and thinks: 'You're sanitising [sic] me and my friends, and other people who I live and adore.'"[79] In her review of the musical film, the Black Puerto Rican feminist writer Carmen Phillips also criticized the production team—and perhaps spectators as well—for dishonoring the lives of Black queer women and a seminal Black queer text. Philips writes:

> As a Pulitzer Prize winning, Tony winning testament to the strength of Black womanhood, spirituality, self-actualization, and resilient sisterhood, everyone seems to get on board. As a [sic] incredibly important, purposeful Black queer text by a Black queer woman author? Less so. [. . .] There's almost an air of discomfort, an unspoken agreement: "OK we'll finally say Celie and Shug were gay for each other—but not too much now on our (straight) Sisterhood icons." As if Celie and Shug's queerness isn't at the root of the very sisterhood we proclaim to be honoring. *The Color Purple* has never been only about Black women saving each other. It's about Black women finding beauty and worth in each other, in all aspects of who we

> are, and on this Alice Walker could not be more clear: that means in our bedrooms, too.[80]

However, Phillips's biting remarks become even more concerning when one knows that Alice Walker and her daughter Rebecca Walker served as executive producers of the musical film adaptation. *What role did Alice Walker have in executing the film?* Regardless of the answer, *The Color Purple* musical remains culturally significant to Black queer feminist spectators.

For better or for worse, *The Color Purple* remains one of the only Black musicals on Broadway to attempt to center the lives of queer Blackgirls. Why? Why are there so few representations of queer Blackgirls on Broadway when we know that Black queer girls exist? If we want to see greater representation, we must do more to foster Black queer women playwrights. Chisa Hutchinson, C. A. Johnson, Aziza Barnes, Carmen LoBue, Donnetta Lavinia Grays, Erika Dickerson-Despenza, Patricia Ione Lloyd, and Staceyann Chin have made some inroads regarding the representation of queer Blackgirls in "straight" plays, but they have not received the recognition that they deserve, nor have they delved into musical theatre. If we truly value diversity of thought and experience on the musical theatre stage, more action must be taken to cultivate the rising generation of Black queer feminist artists and their allies.

The Secret Life of Bees

As with *The Color Purple*, Lynn Nottage's musical adaptation *The Secret Life of Bees* takes place in the rural South and privileges the lives of Blackgirls. Set against the backdrop of the Long Civil Rights Movement (1930s–1960s), conflict arises in the segregated town of Sylvan, South Carolina, when local Black ministers host voting rallies to encourage Black community members to register to vote following the passage of the Civil Rights Act (July 2, 1964).[81] While on her way to register to vote and with Lily in tow, Rosaleen is accosted by two white men on a country road. The white men call her a "nigger" and demand to know where she is going. Rosaleen retaliates by boldly declaring her mission and tossing her tobacco juice on their shoes. The white men demand that she clean the spittle off their shoes, and when she refuses, they grab her by the neck, throw her down on the road, and stomp on her abdomen until blood gushes from her mouth. Afterward, police officers arrest

Rosaleen for assaulting the white men and disturbing the peace and take her to a hospital to recover before her trial. Meanwhile, Lily, having just had a heated argument with her abusive father T-Ray, decides to run away from home and "rescue" Rosaleen from a sure death at the hands of white vigilantes. While Rosaleen lies injured on her hospital bed, Lily convinces her to join her on her quest to discover more information about her late mother. With only the clue "Tiburon, South Carolina" written on a card with a Black Madonna of Breznichar image, the pair eventually stumble upon a store with jars of honey, made by the Boatwright sisters, with a label with the exact image. While Lily does not reveal why she arrived at their doorstep, August Boatwright instantly recognizes her as her former employer's granddaughter. August also suspects there is more to Rosaleen's injuries than meets the eye but does not press them. Instead, she allows the travelers to work in exchange for their room and board, teaches them about The Daughters of Mary spiritual practices, and offers them a safe space to heal from their emotional and physical scars. By the end of the musical, all secrets are revealed, T-Ray allows Lily to remain with the Boatwright sisters, and Rosaleen is welcomed into a sisterhood of resilient Blackgirls.

The Secret Life of Bees received its world premiere at the Atlantic Theatre Company's Linda Gross Theater in New York, New York, on May 12, 2019. Nottage, a two-time Pulitzer Prize-winning playwright, provided the book which she adapted from white author Sue Monk Kidd's best-selling novel, *The Secret Life of Bees* (2001). The Off-Broadway production included music by Tony and Grammy Award-winning composer Duncan Sheik, lyrics by Drama Desk winner and two-time Tony Award nominee Susan Birkenhead, and direction by Tony Award winner Sam Gold. The predominantly Black cast included Broadway legend LaChanze (August), Saycon Sengbloh (Rosaleen), Elizabeth Teeter (Lily), Manoel Felciano/Chris Stack (T-Ray), Eisa Davis (June), Anastacia McClesky (May), Nathanial Stampley (Neal), Brett Gray (Zachary), Romelda Teron Benjamin (Queenie), Jai'Len Josey (Sugar Girl), Vita E. Cleveland (Violet), Joe Cassidy (Clayton, Radio Announcer & others), and Matt DeAngelis (Silas & others) (see Figure 1.7). *The Secret Life of Bees,* with its powerful performances and variety of music—ranging from country, to rock and roll, to 1960s pop and funk—garnered much critical success. The production won five Drama Desk Awards, including Outstanding Musical, Outstanding Book (Nottage), Outstanding Lyrics (Birkenhead), Outstanding Music (Sheik), and Outstanding Lighting Design for a Musical (Jane Cox). *The Secret Life of Bees* also won

Figure 1.7 LaChanze, Jai'len Christine Li Josey, Vit E. Cleveland, Elizabeth Teeter, and Romelda Teron Benjamin in Atlantic Theatre Company's World Premiere Musical of *The Secret Life of Bees* directed by Sam Gold. Photo Sara Krulwich, courtesy of *The New York Times*/Redux.

the Drama League Awards' Outstanding Production of a Musical and four Outer Critics Circle Awards for Outstanding New Off-Broadway Musical, Outstanding Book of a Musical (Nottage), Outstanding New Score (Sheik), and Outstanding Orchestrations (Sheik). With such a successful premiere, *The Secret Life of Bees* was poised for a Broadway debut but could not find its footing in the wake of the COVID-19 global pandemic.

While the creative leadership of the musical was white-dominated—the composer, lyricist, director, and original author are white—Nottage still managed to do what the 2001 novel and 2008 film adaptation starring Dakota Fanning and Queen Latifah failed to do: that is, center the experiences of Blackgirls. The theatre critic Frank Rizzo celebrates this and other changes to the narrative in his review. Rizzo writes:

> Indeed, in Lynn Nottage's nuanced script that efficiently distills the novel to its theatrical essence, the shift and focus is now towards this community of black women to whom Lily and Rosaleen journey and where they find refuge—and more. [. . .] But here it is Rosaleen's journey of discovery as much as Lily's. At this spiritual sanctuary where sweetness lives with

stings, redemption, growth and discovery eventually come to most all the characters. Note to fans of the book: Nottage makes one major change to one of the characters that strengthens the theme of resiliency and healing.[82]

Nottage's adaptation honors Kidd's novel but also makes important critical departures. The most radical changes, aside from centering the lives and spiritual practices of Blackgirls within the narrative, include: omitting much of Rosaleen and Lily's travel; crafting three-dimensional Black characters that exist beyond the purview of the white gaze and racial trauma; elevating the importance of the Long Civil Rights Struggle and its continued relevance; allowing Blackgirls to challenge Lily's white privilege and White Savior complex; empowering May to live, rather than commit suicide; and having police officers beat Zachary, rather than everyday white vigilantes. These changes make the musical—produced on the eve of the 2020 Black Lives Matter protests—even more relevant to Black queer feminist spectators.

By compressing Rosaleen and Lily's journey to Tiburon into only a moment in the musical, Nottage effectively sidesteps white voyeurism as found within Kidd's novel. Perhaps the most blatant scene of white voyeurism occurs in Kidd's depiction of the pair traveling at night near a creek. A disgruntled Rosaleen complains that Lily did not ask her if she wanted to escape jail. Flabbergasted that Rosaleen does not understand that she helped her escape impending white-authored violence, Kidd's Lily responds by calling Rosaleen "dumb."[83] Immediately following the argument, the pair part ways. Unbeknownst to Rosaleen, Kidd's Lily lurks in the shadows, following the sound of Rosaleen humming a gospel-like tune. "I followed the sound and found Rosaleen in the middle of the creek, not a stitch of clothes on her body. Water beaded across her shoulders, shining like drops of milk, and her breasts swayed in the currents. It was the kind of vision you never really get over. I couldn't help it, I wanted to go and lick the milk beads from her shoulders. [. . .] I opened my mouth. I wanted something. Something, I didn't know what," Kidd's Lily remembers.[84] Prior to this passage, Kidd's Lily does not sexually objectify Rosaleen. Rather, Kidd's Lily describes Rosaleen as ignorant, obese, and a "stand-in mother" between the ages of forty-five and fifty-five years old.[85] Lily tells readers: "She had a big round face and a body that sloped out from her neck like a pup tent, and she was so black that night seemed to seep from her skin."[86] In the novel, readers only envision Rosaleen through the perspective of Lily, and this mammy-like description continues throughout the novel, with Lily constantly referencing

Figure 1.8 Nate Parker (Neil), Alicia Keys (June), Jennifer Hudson (Rosaleen), Sophie Okonedo (May), Dakota Fanning (Lily), and Queen Latifah (August) in *The Secret Life of Bees* (2008) film directed by Gina Prince-Bythewood. Still image courtesy of the author.

her intellectual superiority and embarrassment of Rosaleen's childlike behavior. Indeed, Rosaleen's lack of manners, social etiquette, and inability to take action to save herself gives readers the impression that *Lily* is actually the caretaker of *Rosaleen*. Thus, within this complicated relationship, Kidd's Lily both loathes and desires Rosaleen sexually and nonsexually. However, Nottage avoids crafting Rosaleen as an object of white desire and a constant victim in need of a White Savior by telling the story through the eyes of Blackgirls, rather than a Southern white girl (see Figure 1.8).

The production modes amplify Nottage's critical departures, providing spectators with an intimate view of Blackgirl labor, rituals, relationships, and journey to self-recognition. *The Secret Life of Bees* was produced at the Linda Gross Theater, a former nineteenth-century church-turned-theatre. Originally built following the US Civil War in 1871, the Linda Gross Theater seats up to 193 patrons. The small number of spectators, coupled with director Sam Gold's intimate staging within a church-like space, allows a feeling of togetherness to permeate the atmosphere. In the Atlantic Theatre Company production, Gold directed the full cast and musicians to remain on the small stage throughout the entire performance. In so doing, the audience literally never loses sight of the Blackgirls who populate the narrative. Set designer Mimi Lien's sparse set created the visual world of the play through simple props, allowing spectators' imaginations to fill in the blanks. For example, when the set shifts from Rosaleen's hospital room, Blackgirl ensemble members act as worker bees, moving a table (i.e., "hospital bed") a few feet away and place a case of chewing tobacco and two small crates of honey on top to act as a store. Gold's decision to cast Blackgirls as the "bees" not only complimented the simplicity of the scenic design but also reinforced the metaphor of Blackgirls as worker bees. Throughout the musical, three Blackgirl ensemble members act as puppeteers, holding rods with "bees" dangling on wires as the sound of the piano creates the "buzz" of bees. While these puppeteers are "unseen" by the other characters onstage, they nonetheless embody the emotions of the bees. For example, during the opening scene where Rosaleen swats the bees away from her face, one puppeteer looks at the audience and contorts her face as if offended. In other words, the metaphor of Blackgirls as worker bees permeate every aspect of the production.

Rosaleen and August represent the countless number of Blackgirls throughout history who have had to take on a tremendous amount of labor as worker bees to support their families and the greater Black community. In contrast to white women, many of whom had to fight for the right to work outside of the home, Blackgirls have *always* labored outside of the domestic sphere to provide for their families. During chattel slavery, they worked in white slavers' homes, performing domestic duties such as wet nurses to white babies, cooks, and laundresses, as well as laboring outside in the fields by sowing, planting, and harvesting crops. In fact, domestic, service, and agricultural labor were the few employment opportunities afforded to Black women and adolescent girls well into the 1960s and 1970s, a direct outgrowth of chattel slavery. Black women's history of laboring within close proximity to whites informs Nottage's characterization of Rosaleen and August. The sociologist Patricia Hill Collins writes that "African-American women domestics are exposed to all the intimate details of the lives of their white employers. . . . In some cases domestic workers form close, long-lasting relationships with their employers. But domestic workers also encounter some of the harshest exploitation confronting women of color. The work is low paid, has few benefits, and exposes women to the threat and reality of sexual harassment."[87] In *The Secret Life of Bees*, exposition reveals that Rosaleen was removed from the hot fields picking peaches into the Owens home as cook and caretaker when she was only an adolescent. August, too, was forced to put her educational ambitions on hold and become a domestic worker to financially provide for her family. Both Rosaleen's and August's experiences reveal how her close proximity to white families causes fraught relationships between them, their white charges, and their actual families.

While many Blackgirls today have found employment opportunities beyond domestic and agricultural labor, they continue to experience occupational segregation and exploitation. Jocelyn Frye, the former Deputy Assistant to the President (Barack Obama) and President of the National Partnership for Women and Families, writes that "occupational segregation occurs when people are unevenly represented in different jobs with very different wages, benefits, and working conditions in part based on their race, gender, and other identities. Black women are overrepresented in occupations with lower wages and inadequate benefits, making them more vulnerable to economic precarity and resulting in billions of lost wages."[88] Frye then offers a quantitative breakdown of how occupational segregation negatively impacts Black women:

> Research by the National Partnership for Women and Families has found that Black women make up almost a third of all nursing assistants and home health aides, and are also disproportionately employed as personal care aides; the average wage across the top ten most common occupations for Black women was $30,200 compared to $80,500 for white, non-Hispanic men's ten most common occupations. Black women lose nearly $36 billion annually compared to white, non-Hispanic men when considering the wage gap in the ten occupations in which they are most likely to work."[89]

Continuing the practice of confining the majority of Black women and girls to devalued occupations with low wages is intentional, allowing white-led and male-dominated systems of oppression to flourish socially and economically. In other words, Black queer feminist spectators are not too far removed from the worker bees of the past. Nottage helps bridge the connection between the past and present by allowing spectators to see a bit of themselves and their economic circumstances through Rosaleen.

Rather than present Rosaleen as a mammy-like stereotype and sidekick to Lily, Nottage's Rosaleen embodies the complex and multidimensional lives of Blackgirls. In the Atlantic Theatre Company production, Rosaleen (Saycon Sengbloh) appears as a beautiful, young, and spirited twenty-two-year-old who uses her agency to actively participate in the democratic process. She continues on her quest to register to vote, despite Lily's warning that she "heard a man in Mississippi got himself killed trying to register."[90] Rosaleen, however, is not naive to the consequences of such a decision, nor unaware of the tactics used to suppress Black votes. She even reveals that she practices her cursive so that her registration cannot be denied "on account of nothing, even my signature." Rosaleen shares her innermost thoughts about this brave action in the upbeat, funk-sounding song, "Sign My Name." Accompanied by drums, electric guitar, and tambourine, Rosaleen sings about a "beautiful" new law that allows even a poor Southern Blackgirl to cast her vote for president. Rosaleen understands the magnitude of her participation in the democratic process, a basic right of citizenship that her mother and grandmother were never afforded. "For mama and/ her mama too / and what they never / got to do / gonna sign my name," Rosaleen sings. She concludes her declaratory song with the statement, "Cuz Miss Rosaleen she matters." Mirroring the contemporary "Black Lives Matter" anthem, Rosaleen asserts her basic right to exist. Black queer feminist spectators then discover that her self-confidence is formed by the support of her Black community. As she sings, everyday Black men and women from the laboring class greet her by name, smile, and offer encouragement along her journey into town. Unfortunately, when alone and cornered by two racist middle-aged white men, even her confidence cannot save her from a brutal attack.

Figure 1.9 LaChanze (August) and Elizabeth Teeter (Lily) in Atlantic Theatre Company's World Premiere Musical of *The Secret Life of Bees* (2019) directed by Sam Gold. Photo by Ahron R. Foster, courtesy of Ahron R. Foster.

Black queer feminist spectators might read Rosaleen's experience with white-authored violence as a part of a larger history (and ever-present reality) of Black voter suppression in the United States. After the brutal attack, the police conduct a so-called investigation. In this moment, the white assailants face the audience (who take on the role of the police) and justify their actions, demanding that the police make Rosaleen apologize for destroying their property. Afterward, both men turn to Rosaleen, who lies crumpled on the ground, and await her apology. Rosaleen responds by simply singing, "I'm gonna go vote / I'm gonna go vote" while holding a white handkerchief to her bloodied mouth. This everyday act of resistance to voter suppression, a gesture performed just months after the controversial 2018 Georgia gubernatorial election, might prove particularly powerful for Black queer feminist spectators to behold. Indeed, the narrow defeat of the Democratic nominee Stacey Abrams—the first African American woman major-party gubernatorial nominee—to the Republican candidate Brian Kemp continue to raise questions regarding the long history of Black voter suppression. Abrams's refusal to concede to Kemp, who served as Georgia Secretary of State and presided over the counting and certification of votes, stemmed from her accusation of voter suppression impacting the election results. Although Abrams ultimately lost her 2018 and 2022 bid for governor of Georgia, her very act of running and challenging systems of oppression emboldened Black activists across the United States. In her book, *Minority Leader: How to Lead from the Outside and Make Real Change* (2018), Abrams writes that "for every success—becoming deputy city attorney, running for office, and rising in less than four years to serve as the minority leader of the Georgia House of Representatives—I have consistently confronted racism, sexism, ageism, and other phobias about my otherness."[91] Despite the fictional Rosaleen's optimism about the Civil Rights Bill leading to a future of equality, Abram's contemporary experiences of racism, sexism, and other social ills stand as a testament that much more work needs to be done. In other words, individual effort and new legislation is not enough to foster large-scale social change. Collective action and the more difficult task of seeing each other's humanity is needed to realize a truly liberatory politics.

Nottage amplifies the danger that awaits Rosaleen and those engaged in the Black liberation struggle through the use of Radio Announcer, a white broadcaster who shares actual accounts of white-authored violence during the Long Civil Rights Movement. Radio Announcer appears four times throughout the musical and speaks directly to the audience, relaying historical events as if they have just occurred. This artistic choice creates a heightened sense of immediacy and connection to the Long Civil Rights Movement. As the past becomes the present, Radio Announcer tells spectators that "local activists vow to test the new provisions" of the Civil Rights Bill, which has just been signed into law by President Lyndon B. Johnson. In his second appearance, Radio Announcer continues his account, explaining that three Civil Rights movement workers—Chaney, Goodman, and Schwerner—have "gone missing in Mississippi," and their "burned out car was found on a marshy road off the highway." August's sister May responds to this news with some naivete, wondering out loud if the missing activists might still be alive. Of course, spectators in the know would understand this moment as a reference to the disappearance and murder of Black activist James Chaney and his Jewish colleagues, Andrew Goodman and Michael Schwerner on June 21, 1964. Their remains were discovered seven weeks later and received national attention as it was eventually revealed that members of the local Ku Klux Klan, the Neshoba County Sheriff's Office, and the Philadelphia, Mississippi Police Department were involved in the crime. This information only cements the long-held suspicion that white vigilantes and the police force are often one and the same. Radio Announcer's third appearance at the beginning of Act II departs from the Civil Rights movement and announces the creation of The Ranger 7. While seemingly disjointed, the topic of a space voyage allow Rosaleen, August, and May to ponder and dream about the larger wonders of the world without the threat of white-authored violence. Blackgirls, after all, do spend the majority of their days discussing matters not related to white-authored violence. During his fourth and final appearance, Radio Announcer returns to the movement, stating: "Despite threats, Negro ministers at Mount Zion Baptist church have vowed to keep their doors open for today's voter registration. The police chief has encouraged people to stay away, fearing the agitators will use the opportunity to ignite racial disharmony." While this announcement does not refer to a specific event within the Civil Rights movement, spectators in the know might understand this moment as a celebration of the work to register Black voters. Although leading Black ministers often stand in the center of these stories, this campaign would be nothing without the support of everyday Blackgirls. August's sister June encourages Rosaleen to make a second attempt to register, stating: "Those poor men in Mississippi gave their lives for folks like us to vote. We back away now, what's that gonna say?" June's use of the collective "we" places Rosaleen within a Black sisterhood, offering her a sense of protection and togetherness that she has not experienced during her travels with Lily.

While Rosaleen always believed that her life and vote matter, she doesn't gain the confidence to critique Lily's expressions of internalized racial superiority until she befriends the Boatwright sisters. When Rosaleen first arrives at the Boatwright sisters' home, she shows deference to Lily, who expects her to continue to meet her every need, despite her abdominal injury and the fact that she no longer works for Lily's father. For example, the morning after their arrival, as the two prepare to start their day, Lily commands: "Gimme my shoes." In the Atlantic Theatre Company production, Lily's shoes are within her arm's reach. Rosaleen silently crosses to the shoes and hands them to Lily who does not utter a "thank you." Lily assumes it is her right to order Blackgirls about and that Rosaleen should make her life more comfortable. While Black queer feminist spectators may empathize with Lily's plight—her father does, after all, abuse her and blame her for accidentally killing her mother—her behavior is far from excusable. Lily may perceive herself as a liberal ally but she also benefits from white privilege and assumes Blackgirls only exist to do her bidding (see Figure 1.9). Emboldened by the Boatwright sisters—she has never encountered educated and financially independent Blackgirls before—Rosaleen begins to critique Lily's behavior. For example, when Lily charges into the kitchen, tosses her satchel on the table, and demands Rosaleen make her food, Rosaleen tells her that dinner isn't ready. Lily, completely unaware that she has interrupted June's heartbreaking story about her sister April's suicide, dismissively states, "Whatcha you been doing all day? Lazy bones! Winter'll be here before you finish." Nottage describes Rosaleen as being "embarrassed" by Lily's behavior.[92] In the Atlantic Theatre Company production, Rosaleen (Sengbloh) and June (Eisa Davis) exchange a knowing look, June abruptly leaves the kitchen, and Lily (Elizabeth Teeter) appears genuinely confused about why they are upset. Afterward, Rosaleen and Lily have the following exchange:

ROSALEEN: You didn't have to talk to me like that in front of June.

LILY: Like how?!

ROSALEEN: Like I'm just a pair of serving hands. I may not be educated like these folks, but I ain't ignorant, and I ain't stupid. We both guests in this house, and that's how I wanna be treated.

LILY: Whatcha getting so mad about!

ROSALEEN: I'm sick and tired of being talked through, who do you think you are?

Rosaleen expresses her awareness of and disdain for Lily's air of racial superiority, unearned privilege, and inflated self-image. Rosaleen's speech suggests that even though Lily may refer to her as a "stand-in mother," she actually treats her as less than human.

Once her mask of subservience has been lifted, Rosaleen boldly articulates her innermost thoughts through her upbeat ballad, "All About You." Rosaleen begins her song by expressing her displeasure with Lily ordering her around and "draggin'" her along on her journey. She sings: "You got ideas? / Well I do too / It ain't always about you." In colloquial terms: *Lily is not the main character of Rosaleen's story*. Instead of blindly following Lily and being deceived by her feigned altruism, Nottage's Rosaleen relies on her own rational thinking to decide to escape the hospital. Furthermore, throughout her song, Rosaleen insists that she has experienced pain and sorrow too. She reveals her hardships in life, including abandonment by her mother. Without parental support, Rosaleen had to drop out of school so she could find employment and not starve to death. While Rosaleen does not provide her exact age when this happened, spectators can piece together that she has provided housekeeping and child care for the Owens family since Lily's mother Deborah died ten years ago. If Rosaleen is only twenty-two, this places her around age twelve when she began serving the Owens family and even younger when she worked in Owens's peach orchard. This timeline suggests that, at best, Rosaleen received a seventh-grade education before taking on the demands of a full-time job while a child herself. Rosaleen survived these hardships as the generations of Black domestic workers did before her: through cultivating a culture of dissemblance. The historian Darlene Clark Hine writes that "the dynamics of dissemblance involved creating the appearance of disclosure, or openness about themselves and their feelings, while actually remaining enigmatic."[93] Creating a culture of dissemblance allowed domestic workers to retain a sense of self and avail themselves of psychic relief from oppressive forces by fostering the appearance of openness with their white employers while keeping their innermost lives private. In addition to appearing "open" with whites, Rosaleen uses self-deprecating humor to shield herself from further pain. Rosaleen has done this so effectively that her white employers see her as disembodied: just a pair of serving hands that can be "talked through." Rosaleen, however, understands that her value does not lie in performing manual labor for white people, and The Daughters of Mary help her along her path of self-discovery.

The Daughters of Mary welcome Rosaleen into their sisterhood, offering her love, respect, and friendship. Rosaleen is initially bewildered by The Daughters of Mary and their unexplainable bond. After witnessing their first ritual, a look of wonderment appears on Rosaleen's face and she later confides to Lily: "I just hope they ain't witches or nothing." Rosaleen has never met Blackgirls who are college-educated, homeowners, business intrapreneurs, fully independent of men, and grounded in alternative Black religious practices. While initially hesitant, Rosaleen eventually turns to the older Blackgirls for guidance and support. After the ritual, the Boatwright sisters begin to advise Rosaleen and build her self-confidence. For example, May admonishes Rosaleen to break her "nasty habit" of chewing tobacco, with August explaining: "You're too beautiful a gal to have the spitting habits of a mule. You won't have but one tooth left by the time you get to my age." When Rosaleen apologizes for not being "refined" like them, August corrects her, and the two have the following exchange:

AUGUST: Please. I paid some dues taking care of white folks babies, so I could get where I am. And I'm not ashamed to say it.
ROSALEEN: And you've done good. But, me and you is different.
AUGUST: Not as much as you think.

August's experience as a former domestic-turned-business woman highlights the fact that given the opportunity and resources, Rosaleen could be just as educated and business savvy as August. Unfortunately, structural racism precludes opportunities and resources for many Blackgirls. Instead, Rosaleen and the vast majority of Blackgirls are often deemed "de mule uh de world."[94] As such, they must rely on their physical strength, taking on backbreaking jobs with low pay to provide food and shelter for themselves and their families. Rather than internalize racist imagery that dehumanizes Black women and girls, August affirms the younger girl's beauty and intelligence. At the conclusion of their conversation, August insists that Rosaleen borrow her copy of Jane Austen's *Jane Eyre* (1847) and states: "And I look forward to your opinion." August's pronouncement produces a look of startlement on Rosaleen's face, leaving spectators to suspect that Rosaleen is rarely treated as if she has worthwhile thoughts and opinions. The care given by The Daughters of Mary becomes a protective factor that allows Rosaleen to see herself as much more than just a pair of serving hands.

Figure 1.10 Atlantic Theatre's World Premiere Musical of *The Secret Life of Bees* (2019) directed by Sam Gold. Photo by Ahron R. Foster, courtesy of Ahron R. Foster.

The Daughters of Mary use ritual performance to affirm their divine identity, cultural heritage, and collective strength. The Daughters of Mary worship the "Our Lady of Chains," which Nottage describes as "a three-foot high masthead carving of a beautiful black woman twisted like driftwood."[95] The Daughters of Mary find meaning in the masthead, revering its resemblance to the Virgin Mary, and its connection to their ancestors (see Figure 1.10). When Rosaleen and Lily arrive at the Boatwright sisters' home, they witness The Daughters of Mary perform their sacred ritual. In the Atlantic Theatre Company production, "Our Lady of Chains" rises from a trapdoor on the stage, appearing larger than life. Afterward, The Daughters of Mary sing a soulful supplication prayer, "Tek A Hol A My Soul" to the upbeat tempo of the Congo drums. As Violet plays the drum, August, June, May, Sugar Girl, and Queenie sing verses of the song in Gullah Geechee dialect. In the second verse, Sugar Girl celebrates her cultural heritage, referring to herself as a "Geechee daa'tuh" who remembers the "story Geechee Grammy / done told." June affirms the importance of this ritual in the next verse. As she plays the cello, June sings: "Hail Mary / the journey is long / bind us tuhgedduh for / tuhgedduh we strong." Similar to worker bees, June understands that they are stronger when working together. June's supplication addresses the vital need for Blackgirls to unite as sisters. The ritual increases in intensity as The Daughters of Mary chant for Mary to give them strength and take part in a call-and-response. As this happens, the Blackgirls embrace one another, lift their arms in prayer to "Our Lady of Chains" statue, spin in circles around the Mary masthead, and touch the statue's heart. Neil, the only Son of Mary, observes the ritual but does not actively participate until this moment and joins the women in laying his hand on the statue's heart. The religious excitement abruptly stops when June calls attention to outsiders intruding on their sacred communion. Despite the interruption, The Daughters of Mary still manage to use spiritual practices—including song, chant, call-and-response, and movement—to affirm their identity, culture, and inner strength.

Ritual performance has always played a vital role in affirming Black humanity and fostering our well-being, strength, and collective identity. In her essay, "The Sense of Self in Ritualizing New Performance Spaces for Survival" (2002), Beverly J. Robinson defines ritual as "a recurring pattern of action that represents the desire to begin life anew, and the need to find some way of expressing that desire."[96] Robinson writes that long before African Americans took a step on the proscenium stage, ritual performance—including dance (movement) and storytelling (oral tradition)—provided early African Americans the psychic space needed to retain a sense of self despite their bondage on slave ships and in the fields and plantations.[97] Robinson writes:

> These rituals, sacred and secular, would include knowing the names of your gods, your ancestors, and yourself, and knowing your community and clan affiliation. You would also know your native language and social prerequisites that prevailed in your home community; and you would understand your place in a culture where oral traditions prevailed over written ones. An awareness of communal traditions—language (including gestures), tales, games, humor, music, dance, religion, riddles, food, and other forms of folklore—was part of the human knowledge carried by the men and women transported across the Atlantic.[98]

The rituals performed by The Daughters of Mary help them remember and draw strength from this ancestral legacy. Their use of storytelling, Geechee language, dance, and the Congo drum allow the women to preserve the oral traditions passed down from their enslaved ancestors who also used ritual performances to maintain a sense of self and community despite their bondage. Black queer feminist spectators who understand the importance of ritual performance might gain pleasure from witnessing a Black empowerment celebrated on an off-Broadway stage.

Black queer feminist spectators might also read the worship of "Our Lady of the Chains" statue as a proxy for the Yoruba deity, Osun. When Africans set foot on the American continent, they maintained many of their spiritual practices—even while seemingly adopting Christianity—resulting in an amalgamation of belief systems. The Daughters of Mary represent this transformative spirit, with August performing as a "pastor" and The Daughters of Mary acting as her congregation. August discusses her beliefs with Lily, stating: "when in doubt I got the statue of Our Lady in our parlor, I can reach for her heart when I need help. It reminds me, that everybody needs to see God in their own image." While the musical does not detail August's religious heritage, in the novel she describes her mother as a "good Catholic," her father as "Orthodox Eclectic," and that she and her sisters "take our mother's Catholicism and mix in our own ingredients."[99] While neither the novel nor the musical reference "mixing" attributes of Osun into their worship of Mary, the major symbol of honey nonetheless resonates with the African goddess. Johnson notes the connection between honey and Osun in his study on Black queer women of the South. "It is no coincidence, then, that honey is also one of the proprieties of the Yoruba deity of love and beauty, Osun. . . . Osun is the patron deity of the Osun River in Nigeria, which bears her namesake, and is why she is associated with fresh water. She also symbolizes sensuality, divine beauty, fertility, luxury, and abundance of all kinds."[100] The second ritual performed by The Daughters of Mary embraces the attributes of Osun as they coat "Our Lady of the Chains" statue with honey, share a Black oral history rooted in the power of water, and express their love for one another.

The Daughters of Mary's second ritual provides an oral history, which helps Rosaleen to recognize her power and love herself, *regardless*. In the Atlantic Theatre Company production, May takes a hesitant Rosaleen by the hand, drawing her into the circle of women. Clothed in their Sunday best—in vibrant orange, yellow, red, and blue dresses—The Daughters of Mary transform the Boatwright's parlor into what Sugar Girl and Queenie call a "praise house." As August sings "Our Lady of the Chains" and recounts the story of an enslaved man named Obadiah, the women surround her and periodically interject "Amen" to affirm the oral history of their people. Clothed in a blue floral dress with African print along the border, August moves about the stage revealing that when Obadiah discovered the statue while working by the waterside, he took this as a sign from Mary that she would free him. August recounts that when Obadiah's community also turned to Our Lady for hope and the slave master discovered her power over the enslaved people, he chained her to the carriage house. When the statue returned to the praise house the next day, the slave master repeated his action. August reminds The Daughters of Mary that this happened fifty times before the slave master gave up. At this point, the ritual rises in energy, with August invoking traditional call-and-response with the women. As all join in the singing, they place honey on the statue; press their fingers, palms, and foreheads on her heart; and embrace one another. Nottage describes this moment of transformation as follows: "They kiss each other in a gesture of solidarity. May takes Rosaleen's hand and leads her to Mary. Rosaleen touches Mary, she is emotionally overcome with a spirit and weeps. August comforts Rosaleen."[101] The ritual concludes with Rosaleen singing the chorus, acapella: "Raise me up / Like Our Lady of Chains, Lord / Bring me safe to shore / Raise me up like / Our Lady of Chains, / And I'll be a slave no more." The lyrics suggest that even though chattel slavery has ended, the chains of bondage continue to harm Blackgirls. With this prayer/song, spectators witness a visible change in Rosaleen as she begins to heal her mind, body, and spirit from the chains of white oppression.

Rosaleen's newfound network of sisters offer her the emotional and material support she needs to embrace her magic. After communing with August and May, Rosaleen nearly spits tobacco juice into the Boatwright sisters' flower bed but abruptly stops herself mid-action. Rather than continue her old behaviors, Rosaleen shares her new self-awareness and thoughts on life in the musical number, "Who Knew." During this R&B song, Rosaleen gazes longingly at May, June, and August (who sit motionless on their front porch) and expresses her wonderment that three Southern Blackgirls like her could own a home, start a business with nothing more than honey bees, acquire college educations, and "do fine without men." In her fourth and final verse, Rosaleen sings: "Who knew / I could speak my own mind / and them that don't like it / can kiss my behind / but I mean what I say / and I say what I mean / cuz I'm learnin' from them / to love Rosaleen." Rather than hide who she is behind a culture of dissemblance, Rosaleen celebrates her new ability to speak truth to power and love herself. She concludes her soul-stirring, powerful song with her declaration to read *Jane Eyre* and become liberated like the Boatwright sisters.

Invigorated by the ritual, Rosaleen later shares her innermost thoughts and feelings—including her desire for love and sexual autonomy—with August and May. As they commune with one another on the front porch, far beyond the purview of the white gaze, Rosaleen ponders Neil's love for June, stating, "Must be something to be loved like that." She then ponders aloud about the lives of the women around her, asking August if she's ever fallen in love. When August admits that she nearly got married, Rosaleen presses to find out why this never happened and they have the following exchange:

AUGUST: I loved my freedom too much.
ROSALEEN: Amen to that. But, I don't understand it, if there was a man like Neil chasing me, Lord, you wouldn't ever see me outside the bedroom.

Rosaleen's "Amen" uses Black church practices to affirm the importance of Black women's autonomy. Rosaleen and August equate heterosexual marriage as another form of bondage for Blackgirls, making them subject to the demands of a husband. Rather, Rosaleen envisions having sexual agency outside the bonds of matrimony as a liberatory. This conversation does not occur in the novel. Nottage alone imagines an autonomous life filled with sexual possibilities for Southern Blackgirls.

Nottage takes great care to humanize June, allowing her to vocalize her innermost thoughts and express a depth of emotions not present in the novel. Again, since the novel only provides Lily's perspective of the Black community, readers are not privy to the inner lives of the Boatwright sisters. The musical, however, allows the Boatwright sisters to exist beyond the purview of the white gaze, adding additional scenes that explain their perspectives of the world. One of these additional scenes occurs at the beginning of the musical, immediately after Rosaleen and Lily spin a fictional to explain about why they are traveling together. August reveals to June that she is not taken in by their lies and suspects that Lily is the offspring of her former employer's daughter, Deborah. August allows the travelers to stay in their home because she suspects they are "in real trouble." While the novel only presents June opposing Lily's stay, the musical allows June to explain her reasoning. June tells August: "Don't forget, caring for Deborah took a toll on all of us." Later, June elaborates and reveals that while she does not begrudge August for becoming a housekeeper, she does resent how this decision impacted August's life. After all, August's income provided the means to pay for June's college education and keep their grandfather's home which they inherited. June further clarifies: "I resent how that sick child took the better years of your life. [. . .] If you hadn't been tending to someone else's children, then maybe April wouldn't be—." In other words, Lily's entrance into the Boatwright home triggers June's feelings of sadness for August's sacrifice had grief over April's suicide. While June does not blame August for April's death, June continues to believe that April's suicide could have been prevented if August had been present and not caring for Deborah. While June never outright says why she rejects Neil's proposal of marriage—he has previously proposed nearly two dozen times—spectators can surmise that the weight of this past falls heavy on June's shoulders, preventing her from moving forward with her own life. For these reasons, June loves Neil from afar, playing her cello to ease her pain.

Nottage makes another major critical departure from the novel in her characterization of May, allowing her to live rather than compounding Blackgirl suffering with the ritual of Black death. Within the safety of the kitchen, June reveals to Rosaleen how girlhood trauma—in this case, white-authored violence—fueled April's suicide and triggered May's mental health issues:

> When April was about Lily's age she wandered alone into town to buy some ice cream. She knew she wasn't supposed to go through the front door of the parlor, but she did so anyway. Cuz' that's the kinda girl she was. Spirited. The white soda jerk didn't like her gumption, so he spat on her ice cream cone, dropped it at her feet and then laughed . . . as a crowd of White men made her lick it up like a dog. [. . .] April couldn't get that humiliation outta her head, so she blew it out with a shotgun. [. . .] Since, May feels things more deeply, as if she's taking on the burden of her twin. That's why she leans on Mary so often.

While April understood her worth, racist white men did their best to beat her into submission. Alone, and unprotected from her kinfolk, April experienced an everyday act of degradation that continued to haunt her until she felt that she could not continue on. Since April's suicide, May has lived with crippling anxiety, which she seemingly downplays for survival. For example, when May and her sisters introduce themselves to their uninvited houseguests, Lily tries to lighten the mood by teasing them about their names. "What about April and July?" Lily asks, to which May responds, "April was my twin. She died." Of course, April did not simply "die," she committed suicide. Nottage's stage directions state: "Tears form in May's eyes. Anxiety sweeps over her body."[102] In the Atlantic Theatre Company production, The Daughters of Mary immediately surround May, touching her gently and murmuring comforting words to her. Unfortunately, May's anxiety only increases as she begins listing the names of murdered Black children and freedom fighters who have also been killed. "Emmett Till. Medgar Evers. Birmingham, four little angels dead," whispers May. By uttering April's name alongside better-known historical victims of white-authored violence, May makes the Black freedom struggle—and the psychological harm caused by the carnage of Black lives lost—more immediate and potent for spectators to witness. May works through this pain through ritual performance, singing a reprisal of "Tek A Hol A My Soul," with gospel singer Queenie and The Daughters of Mary. This act of solidarity comforts May in her hour of need. May's anxiety returns when their hired beekeeper Zachary is arrested and sent to prison. May tells the Daughter of Mary: "When I heard what happened, I thought about joining April, but there are too many people lost to the river of sadness and I knew Mary would bring you home." However, rather than drown herself (as she does in the novel), Nottage's May instead makes the powerful decision to live.[103] It is all too easy for spectators today to witness the ritual of Black death from the comfort of their cell phones. What the world has not seen enough of is Blackgirls living, loving, and creating community together.

The Boatwright sisters serve as "othermothers" to Zachary, who in many ways embodies the future of Black America. Nottage describes Zachary as "a handsome athletic teenager."[104] Zachary plays high school football but has aspirations to become a lawyer. When he is not working for the Boatwright sisters or playing football, he listens to musicians such as the legendary Muddy Waters and reads old law books given to him by a local lawyer, Mr. Forrest. Zachary also stays attuned to Black political radicalism of his day, carrying around a copy of the Black queer icon James Baldwin's *The Fire Next Time* (1963). While Zachary has a blood mother in his life, the Boatwright sisters provide additional support as othermothers, helping him achieve his educational goals despite oppressive forces that would render him powerless. As the daughters of a college-educated Black dentist, the Boatwright sisters see education as an important tool to combat systemic racism. However, their belief in the value of education is not unique. Collins writes that "education has long served as a powerful symbol for connections among self, change, and empowerment in African-American communities."[105] The Boatwright sisters believe in Zachary's potential to be a force for good in the community, so much so that August matches every penny Zachary saves for his college education. Knowing the cost of tuition, Zachary works hard to achieve his dreams and does not abandon his plan to deliver honey to customers even when Neil warns him racial tension in town (i.e., a rumor has started that a white actor named Jack Palance is coming to town and taking his Black girlfriend to the cinema). When Zachary discovers Lily has snuck in his car to catch a ride into town, he again doesn't turn back to the relative safety of the Boatwright's home. However, like many youth, Zachary does make time for romance. He and Lily stop along the way to sing a reprise of their pop/rock ballad "What Do I Love?" At the end of the song, with their voices harmonizing beautifully, Zachary leans in to kiss Lily. Unfortunately the innocent kiss never happens as Zachary abruptly pulls away as he hears the sound of a siren and sees the flash of red lights against the darkness of the stage. Two white police officers appear onstage, obscured in darkness while their "flashlights" (i.e., two spotlights) remain focused on Zachary and Lily. The officers immediately ask Lily: "You all right, this boy giving you trouble?" Lily assures them that she is fine and Zachary tries to explain before the officers order him to step out of the car. "Don't he fit the description of that boy who assaulted Mary Clemmonds," Police Officer asks his partner. When Lily interjects that Zachary was with her all day, Police Officer ignores her, stating: "Don't be scared, you can tell me if he touched you." Again, Lily denies any assault but the police handcuff and beat Zachary with their flashlights before arresting him. When the Boatwright sisters hear of Zachary's arrest, they do everything within their power to save him, even hiring a white lawyer, Mr. Forrest, to represent him.

Zachary's experience of police brutality, on the eve of the passage of the Civil Rights Bill, taps into the long history of criminalizing, over-policing, and killing Black men and women. When August expresses her fear that Zachary will go to jail, Mr. Forrest counsels her that this would be the best outcome for Zachary. "If he's lucky! I'm gonna do what I can.[. . .] Hang tight. The sheriff owes me a favor, and I'm gonna go back to the station, and see what more I can do," states Mr. Forrest. The accusation that a Black man has assaulted a white woman has been used as an excuse to justify white vigilante justice since enslavement began in the United States. That Mr. Forrest cannot guarantee Zachary's safe transfer to jail speaks to the long history of officers of the law *allowing* or *taking part in* white vigilante justice. Mr. Forrest's assurance that the sheriff "owes [him] a favor" further suggests a corrupt, "good 'ole boys" justice system. Zachary, of course, will not be given a fair trial under these circumstances. Furthermore, Mr. Forrest's advice that the women "hang tight" suggests that they should do nothing and rely solely on him, a "white Savior," to deliver them. Instead, the women channel the spirits of their foremothers, performing the musical number, "Hold This House Together." May begins the song acapella, offering a plea to end their suffering. "When will the misery end? / I got no more patience / for that kind of pain / I got no more tears I can spend," sings Mary. August and June join May in song, slamming their palms against the kitchen table to create a beat. August sings: "Got to be a pillar up strength / for Zach / Holdin up each other till we get him back / so that this house and all it means / will still be standing." June joins, testifying of their struggles fighting "demons." Eventually, Neil and Rosaleen join their song, creating a rhythm to the beat. The cast end the song with repetition of a call-and-response of "Hold this house together." Rather than wait on Mr. Forrest to deliver them, The Daughters of Mary perform a third and final ritual to protect Zachary, offering supplication to Mary/Osun to guide his safe return. Near the end of the ritual, Zachary arrives in Boatwright parlor with his once-beautiful face now marred by angry black stitches. Despite his disfigurement, the women rejoice in his safe return. In this moment, spectators might also rejoice and understand Blackgirl spirituality as a powerful tool to protect and empower their community.

The truth is that Blackgirls have always actively fought—whether in the foreground like former Georgia State Representative Stacey Abrams, or in the background as "worker bees"—to ensure the collective well-being of *all* Black people. During enslavement, freedom fighters such as Sojourner Truth, Harriet Tubman, and countless other unnamed Blackgirls helped Black folx escape the bonds of slavery and demand basic rights as citizens. Black women continued to fight, even when the dream of true freedom was deferred following Reconstruction (1865–1877) and the Jim Crow era of the late 19th and early 20th centuries. As Black communities continued to experience disenfranchisement under Jim Crow laws, as well as white vigilante justice from both mobs and officers of the law, Blackgirls such as Ida B. Wells demanded gender equality while also pressing elected officials to establish anti-lynching laws to protect Black America. Indeed, Blackgirl activists such as Septima Poinsette Clark, Ella Baker, Fannie Lou Hamer, Dorothy I. Height, and many others continued the fight for Black liberation during the Long Civil Rights Movement. In their 2017 report, "The Status of Black Women in the United States," the social policy and economic analysts Asha DuMonthier, Chandra Childers, and Jessica Milli celebrate the legacy of these trailblazers. "Black women were instrumental in passing the Voting Rights Act of 1965 and today are engaged in activism to change restrictive voter identification laws that have passed in many states, making it more difficult for some individuals—especially Black and Latino voters, women and men with low incomes, and young and older individuals—to vote. . . . As of 2016, Black women were one of the most active groups of voters in the country," writes DuMonthier et al.[106] However, despite the passage of the Civil Rights Act (1964) and Voting Rights Act (1965), Black folx have yet to receive basic rights as citizens of the United States. Black queer feminist spectators understand that the fight to end white-authored violence and discrimination against Black folx remains just as pressing today.

The Secret Life of Bees premiered during a particularly volatile period of race relations in the United States. Social media exploded with video footage of unarmed Black folx experiencing violence and death at the hands of police and white vigilantes who act as judges, jurors, and executioners of the law. For the first time in history, the world could bear witness to these horrific crimes against humanity. The Black Lives Matter movement (2013–present) emerged as one of the many movements during this era to protest the extrajudicial murders of Black people. Founded by community organizer Opal Tometi, queer artist Patrisse Khan-Cullors, and queer activist Alicia Garza after the acquittal of Trayvon Martin's murderer, the Black Lives Matter movement began as a social media hashtag but is now a global organization "whose mission is to eradicate white supremacy and build local power to intervene in violence inflicted upon Black communities by the state and vigilantes."[107] The name itself speaks to a fundamental truth: Black Americans have yet to be recognized as human. Khan-Cullors and Asha Bandele address this heartbreaking reality in the memoir *When They Call You A Terrorist: A Black Lives Matter Memoir* (2020). Khan-Cullors and Bandele write:

> We know that if we can get the nation to see, say, and understand that Black Lives Matter, then every life would stand a chance. Black people are the only humans in this nation ever legally designated, after all, as not human. Which is not to erase any group's harm or ongoing pain, in particular, the genocide carried out against First Nations peoples. But it is to say that there is something quite basic that has to be addressed in the culture, in the hearts and minds of the people who have benefited from, and were raised up on, the notion that Black people are not fully human.[108]

Recognizing Black humanity is just the first step. The Black Lives Matter organization believes that "by combating and countering acts of violence, creating space for Black imagination and innovation, and centering Black joy we are winning immediate improvements in our lives."[109] *The Secret Life of Bees* embodies these ideals by providing opportunities for spectators to bear witness to Black love and joy through representations of ritual, sisterhood, and community activism.

In conclusion, Blackgirl resiliency is not an individual achievement, but a *process* whereby an individual gains a sense of self by working collectively with her sisters for the betterment of her entire community. Just as the Black poet and queer activist Audre Lorde stated that poetry is not a luxury for Black women; so too is resiliency.[110] Harkening back to Lorde, Abrams articulates this important truth in her memoir. Abrams writes:

> No one born into the minority has the luxury of giving up, even if we do not win enough of the time. When I am standing before groups of activists of color, leading a dialogue with women, or sitting in intimate conversation with the young people who work with me, I want them to understand the urgency of self-confidence coupled with self-awareness. Our obligation is to trust our capacity to lead and gather the tools and training necessary to do it well. We'll make mistakes, as everyone does, and ours will likely be judged more harshly. Yet our triumphs will also resound, and they will show the way for those who also doubt their calling.[111]

If anything else, musicals such as *The Color Purple* and *The Secret Life of Bees* reify the sentiment that Blackgirls *can* and *should* lead the Black freedom struggle. However, they must possess self-confidence and self-awareness, have the support of the Black community, and acquire the resources necessary to make their dreams a reality.

The following chapter, "Blackgirls and the Black Church," continues the exploration of spirituality, taking a deep dive into the impact of organized religion in the lives of Blackgirls. Popular Black musicals such as *Your Arms Too Short to Box With God* (1976), *Mama, I Want to Sing* (1983), *The Prodigal Sister* (1974), and *Church Girl* (2010) reveal how the Black Church has both fostered the works of Black women musical theatre artists and caused spiritual violence in the lives of queer Blackgirls.

2

Blackgirls, the Black Church, and Gospel Musicals

My sister and I are born in the same year. January 1981. November 1981. We like to imagine we are identical twins but that's impossible because we have different fathers. She's been my protector since we started kindergarten together. We're now in the eighth grade and the only Blackgirls in our middle school. I grow tired of white kids asking me why my palms are white and my skin is brown. My sister has an idea: we can educate everyone by celebrating Black History Month. We find our principal and demand Black history be taught in our school.

If you want to celebrate Black History Month, you can make posters and put them in the display case outside the main office.

No help from teachers. No art supplies. Our white friends shrug off our righteous anger. So, we get down to business. She makes beautiful posters and I am her sidekick. We are two proud Blackgirls. We can do anything together.

Later, when she tells me she likes girls, I am frightened for her.

The Bible tells us that God hates homosexuals. You have to repent or you're going to be burned in the Lake of Fire.

She doesn't repent. Instead, she gets kicked out of our house because God can't abide sin. She's thirteen and homeless. Our faith community does nothing. We are no longer together. I can no longer be her sidekick. I start to question everything I have been taught but am left with no clear answer. If everything God makes is perfect and He made her, isn't she perfect as well?

Decades later, I continue to think about the spiritual violence heaped upon my sister and the challenges she faced as a young Blackgirl left to wander alone without the protection of faith, family, or community . . . simply because of her refusal to "repent" of her queer identity. By "spiritual violence," I refer to the church or individual Christian using religion "to make people think God hates them or wants them to suffer, or to diminish their capacity to participate in religious life."[1] Black Americans have a long history of being on the

Black Queer Girlhood on the Musical Theatre Stage. La Donna L. Forsgren, Oxford University Press.
 DOI: 10.1093/9780197661444.003.0003

receiving end of spiritual violence. During enslavement, white supremacists used the Bible to justify chattel slavery and the degradation of Black people. While the Black Church has historically offered Black communities protection against racialized violence, it has all too often failed to advocate for the most vulnerable congregants, including Blackgirls and LGBTQ members of their congregations.

Historically, the Black Church has functioned as the cornerstone of Black communities, fostering radical Black activism to combat systemic racism. During enslavement, the church provided one of the few opportunities for Black people to commune with one another without the white gaze present. Black preachers could use the teachings of the Bible to promote a spectrum of Black politics, ranging from the fostering of hope for an eternal reward in the afterlife, to a more open condemnation of slavery as irreconcilable with Christianity, to concrete revolutionary action (i.e., helping the enslaved escape capture). In other words, church services and practices provided one of the few opportunities for enslaved persons to openly commune with their God and their community and strategize ways to survive and/or dismantle chattel slavery. After emancipation, the Black Church continued to offer congregations spiritual guidance, messages of resistance from the pulpit, and a sense of community. Patricia Hill Collins writes that "the Black Church remains the linchpin of African American communal life, and its effects can be seen in Black music, fraternal organizations, neighborhood associations, and politics."[2] Although Black women do not often hold senior leadership positions in the Black Church, they do dominate churchgoing membership and have had a major influence on shaping its more conservative gender ideologies.[3] The Black women musical theatre artists discussed in this chapter carry the legacy of Black churchwomen's development of sacred music, spirituality, and activism.

Black churchwomen greatly shaped the values of the Black Church, including its endorsement of conservative sexual politics within Black communities. During the early twentieth century, for example, Black churchwomen promoted a politics of respectability for Black women and girls. By "politics of respectability," I refer to the term coined by the historian Evelyn Brooks Higginbotham, who writes that "the politics of respectability emphasized reform of individual behavior and attitudes both as a goal in itself and as a strategy for reform of the entire structural system of American race relations. . . Through the discourse of respectability, the Baptist women emphasized manners and morals while simultaneously asserting traditional forms of protest, such as petitions, boycotts, and verbal appeals to justice."[4] Black women who used their agency to claim respectability essentially weaponized their morals and behavior against white assault on the Black community. While the Black Church created space for Black women to develop and voice an oppositional stance against systemic racism, these same women were also influenced by the society in which they lived. In other words, the politics of respectability reinforced social norms regarding gender, class, and sexuality. The works of contemporary Black women musical theatre artists demonstrate a continued interest in respectability politics—whether reinforcing these social norms or encouraging spectators to take a decided break from them.

The works of contemporary Black women musical theatre artists engage with the cultural dichotomy of "the church" versus "the street," a concept fully embraced by the Black Church's promotion of respectability politics. Within this dichotomy, which was formulated during the Great Migration of the early twentieth century, the notion of "the church" and "the street" distinguishes the "respectable" and "non-respectable" behavior of working-class Blacks. Higginbotham describes this dichotomy and the normative values promoted by the Black Church as follows:

> As both physical and discursive space, the church and the street constituted opposing sides of assembly, with gender-laden and class-laden meanings. The street signified male turf, a public space of worldly dangers and forbidden pleasures. Churches and households, both rejecting the worldly attractions of male social space, signified fame and also sacred space. Women who strolled the streets or attended dance halls and cheap theaters promiscuously blurred the boundaries of gender.[5]

This codified notion of the sanctity of the church and the dangers of the street encouraged poor Blackgirls to embrace cleanliness, temperance, etiquette, and sexual purity as a means of resistance to racial stereotypes.[6] Moreover, Blackgirls who accept church doctrine—including their role within the domestic sphere, male authority, and traditional family structures—could find a source of protection against white assault. However, those who did not comply with heterosexual marriage and male authority could experience censure from the Black Church.[7] Contemporary Black women musical theatre artists explore this age-old dichotomy through their depiction of Blackgirl protagonists who wander through the forbidden pleasures of "the street" in isolation, only to discover (or re-discover) the protective power of "the church" community. Thus, the politics of respectability remains just as relevant today as it was a hundred years ago as the Black Church continues its efforts to combat systemic racism.

Although well into the twenty-first century, Blackgirls—queer, trans, or otherwise—remain particularly vulnerable to censorship, as the Black Church continues to resist societal stigmatization of Black people through the castigation of those deemed sexually deviant. For example, the Black Church has been accused of double standards regarding its condemnation of unwed pregnant teenage girls. Collins writes that "teenage girls are condemned for out-of-wedlock pregnancies but . . . the men who fathered the children escape censure. The girls are often required to confess their sins and ask for forgiveness in front of the entire congregation whereas the usually older men who impregnate them are excused."[8] The Black Church's emphasis on traditional heteronormative family structures has not only reaped spiritual violence upon unwed teen mothers, but also other vulnerable populations, including Black queer folx. Collins writes that "holding fast to dominant ideology, many African American ministers believe that homosexuality is unnatural for Blacks and is actually a 'white disease.' As a result, out LGBT African Americans are seen as being disloyal to the race."[9] This wrong-headed doctrine can cause Black LGBTQ folk to experience feelings of shame, ostracism, and victimization within their religious communities. Yet, despite this pressure to conform, Blackgirls—queer, trans, or otherwise—continue to form relationships and build families with other women and battle sexism, homophobia, and alienation within the Black Church.

While twenty-first-century attitudes regarding sexuality remain steadfastly conservative, there is growing support for eliminating sexist practices within Black Church practices. The 2021 study "Faith Among Black Americans," published by the Pew Research Center, reports that Black Americans tend to be more conservative regarding sexuality than the general public does. "[R]oughly six-in-ten Black Americans say that homosexuality should be accepted in society, compared with seven-in-ten in the larger public. And half of Black Americans say religious leaders should not perform same-sex marriage ceremonies, a slightly higher share than in the larger public," writes Mohamed et al.[10] In other words, more than half of Black Americans believe that queer folx should be granted basic rights within the public sphere. However, this paltry "acceptance" is not enough and has not translated into social change. This same study does report a decline in traditional attitudes regarding premarital sex, as, "three-in-ten religiously affiliated Black adults say avoiding sex before marriage is essential to their faith, while an additional 44% say it is 'important, but not essential.'"[11] In addition, the Pew Research Center found that seven-in-ten Black Christians believed that opposing sexism as "essential to their faith" and most Blacks Americans felt that Black women "should be able to serve as senior leaders of congregations."[12] Yet, the same respondents note that their *belief* in gender equality has not translated into *action*. "Much smaller shares say they have actually heard recent sermons on sexism at their houses of worship. They are more like to hear messages on racial inequality, criminal justice reform, voting and protesting."[13] Furthermore, despite their dominance in congregational participation, Black women senior pastors remain a rarity among Black churches.[14]

Black queer folx have used sacred music and the church choir to help navigate homophobic sentiments expressed on the pulpit. The performance studies scholar E. Patrick Johnson describes the Black Church as "a contradictory space, one that exploits the creative talents of its gay members, even as it condemns their gayness, while also providing a nurturing space to hold those same talents."[15] This contradiction can perhaps best be understood by delving deeper into the stereotype of Southern Black gay men as the flamboyant musical director, soloist, or musician within the church choir. "Participation in the church choir provides a way to adhere to the religiosity of southern culture, but also build a sense of community within what can sometimes be a hostile space. . . . [T]he choir [also] provides a medium to express one's sexuality through the theatricality already built into the church service," writes Johnson.[16] However, Johnson's study finds that Black queer Southern women have not found a similar sense of belonging within the Black church. "Because the notion of 'God' was tied to a male figure or because the male leadership of the church upheld sexist interpretations of the Bible, these women sought out forms of worship that were more woman centered or turned inward to a self-discovery of a communion with a higher power," writes Johnson.[17] Thus, while the church choir can function as a space of acceptance, community, and even refuge for many Black gay men, Black queer women have often had to create alternative spaces and spiritual practices to find a similar sense of belonging.

Black queer women have cultivated alternative spiritual beliefs known as "womanist theology" to navigate sexism and homophobia within the Black Church. In her seminal book, *Sisters in the Wilderness: The Challenge of*

Womanist God-Talk (1995), Delores S. Williams writes that "womanist theology challenges all oppressive forces impeding black women's struggle for survival and for the development of a positive, productive quality of life conducive to women's and the family's freedom and well-being. Womanist theology opposes all oppression based on race, sex, class, sexual preference, physical ability, and caste."[18] Well before the term was coined in the 1990s, the concept of womanist theology emerged out of "black women's experiences of relation, loss, gain, faith, hope, celebration, and defiance."[19] The works of Black women musical theatre artists celebrate the power of womanist theology, sacred music, and the church choir in Black girls' lives.

Musical theatre artists such as J. e. Franklin, Micki Grant, Vinnette Carroll, Vy Higginsen, and Angela Barrow-Dunlap—in varying degrees—present sacred music as the Lord's language, a healing balm, and a platform for individual self-expression. In addition, they imagine the church choir as a safe space (in an otherwise oppressive world) that can help forge a sense of community among Blackgirls and churchwomen. The didactic "message" within their musicals articulates a womanist theology that stresses the importance of faith, freedom, and well-being in the lives of Black women, men, and children. Many of these spiritual beliefs were forged during childhood, as church pageantry and sacred music shaped their consciousness and nurtured their creative talents. Grant, the accomplished actress, singer, and Obie-award-winning lyricist and composer remembers: "We started in churches. Usually, that's where programs began for you as a kid. When you would do your Easter recitation or your Christmas recitation. Yes, the combination of the music and the spirituality—all of that—came together. By the time I was fourteen, I was directing the youth choir at the church. Then when I was about seventeen, I was directing the young adults."[20] Nora Cole, a singer, actress, director, and former member of Carroll's Urban Arts Corps (1967–1983), also recalls the Black Church being a "very big" influence on her early life, providing a catalyst for her future career in theatre. Cole remembers:

> One of the things about the church that I know—is a part of my attraction to theatre—was the pageantry of communion. This church has a beautiful altar and the altar would be—still is—all dressed in white for communion Sunday and there's a whole liturgy. You didn't have to learn it by heart but I did because I was just in love with the language. [*Chants*] 'Therefore with angels and archangels and all the company of heaven. We laud and magnify

> Thy glorious name. Evermore praising the ends.' The choir was just singing this so beautifully, the organ played, and everything was in white and so ceremonial. I just fell in love with that.[21]

While the works of Black women musical theatre artists express faith in a higher power, love of sacred music, and other celebratory sentiments, they also provide space to critique detrimental practices—within and outside of the Black Church—that harm Black women, men, and children.

This chapter explores how contemporary Black women artists have used musical theatre as a vehicle to examine the relationship between Blackgirls, sexuality, music, and the Black Church. I begin my analysis with Franklin and Grant's *The Prodigal Sister* (1974), a musical comedy that transforms the Parable of the Prodigal Son into a contemporary tale about the struggles of an unwed and pregnant Blackgirl named Jackie. Black queer feminist spectators can read Jackie's genderqueer identity, deviant sexuality, feelings of ostracism from her family and church community, and ultimate homelessness as a metaphor for the real-life struggles of queer Blackgirls. I then turn to Carroll, Grant, and Alex Bradford's award-winning gospel musical, *Your Arms Too Short to Box With God* (1976). Using a play-within-a-play structure, *Your Arms Too Short* presents a Black Church congregation performing the birth, ministry, and death of Jesus Christ. However, unlike traditional narratives, Blackgirls take center stage, performing as Singing Mary, Pilate's Wife, and disciples of Jesus Christ all the while bearing their testimonies of His divinity through gospel song. My analysis also highlights the theatrical depiction of Judas, who uses dance to portray his betrayal of Jesus, expression of shame, and eventual suicide. I surmise that this subplot might offer Black queer feminist spectators the communal space to mourn a generation of Black queer youth who have committed suicide after experiencing shame and other forms of spiritual violence for their sexuality. Next, I turn to Higginsen and Ken Wydro's *Mama, I Want to Sing* (1983), which marks a shift away from plots based on the Gospel and the ushering in of the Contemporary Chitlin Circuit. *Mama, I Want to Sing* allows spectators to witness the sexual freedom of song and the healing power of sacred music through the experiences of Blackgirl protagonist Doris Winter. I conclude with an investigation of Barrow-Dunlap's *Church Girl* (2010), a more recent musical that presents gospel music as the Lord's language, as well as an expressive power Black churchwomen can wield to invite Jesus into the hearts of wounded Blackgirls.

The aforementioned musicals reveal not only the complex and multidimensional lives of Blackgirls but also why the Black Church must protect Blackgirls. In other words, within these unique visions of Black girlhood comes a call for the Black Church to protect Blackgirls by cultivating feelings of love, acceptance, and community within its practices. Similar to the Parable of the Lost Sheep as found in the Gospels of Matthew (18:12–14) and Luke (15:3–7), these works invite the one lost sheep (i.e., spectators) through music, song, dance, and the recitation of scripture passages, to gain a personal relationship with Jesus and return to the flock of ninety-nine sheep (i.e., the Black Church). While none of the musicals expressly use the terms "lesbian," "gay," "bisexual," "transgender," or "queer" to describe the Blackgirl protagonists, Black queer feminist spectators can read their spiritual journeys and pursuit of freedom as metaphors for the ongoing struggles of Black queer folx.

The Prodigal Sister

J. e. Franklin and Micki Grant's *The Prodigal Sister* (1974) uses the structure of a traditional musical comedy while also engaging with elements of the Black Church—its music, values, and sacred text. The plot derives from the Parable of the Prodigal Son, as told by Jesus and recounted in the Gospel of Luke (15:11–32) but updates the story for contemporary audiences. Franklin's book incorporates rhymed dialogue, song, dance, a chorus of DoWahs, and eight "beats," rather than scenes, to tell Jackie's story.[22] Jackie, a 17-year-old high school senior from a small Southern town, runs away from home to escape her father's censure due to her impending status as an unwed mother. Having been raised as a boy, Jackie takes her inheritance, travels to Big City, and tries (without success) to find employment in traditionally male occupations. Lacking the protection of her family or church community, a madam/business woman named Baltimore Bessie tricks Jackie into working her debt off in her casket factory/house of ill repute. Jackie escapes this situation with the help of Lucille, a former domestic servant-turned-casket factory worker, who ships her home in a coffin to her family. As with the Parable of the Prodigal Son, when Jackie makes a miraculous appearance, her father accepts her and her older sibling learns to rejoice in her return. However, unlike the original Biblical message of repentance and forgiveness, Jackie never repents of her pursuit of forbidden pleasures. Instead, it is a womanist theology espoused by the Reverend Wynn that convinces her parents to repent of *their* actions and love their daughter unconditionally. In addition to womanist theology, the use of song—including gospel, jazz, rock, 1950s doo-wop, ballads, and blues—becomes a vehicle for this change of heart, creating space for the articulation of moral values, feelings, and self-expression. Ultimately, Black queer feminist spectators may read this musical as a coming-of-age tale of a genderqueer Blackgirl who finds love, acceptance, and community from her family and the Black Church through womanist theology.

The Prodigal Sister premiered at Woodie King Jr.'s New Federal Theatre (1970–) under the direction of Shauneille Perry at Henry Street Settlement in New York, New York.[23] The production marked the New Federal Theater's initial foray into musical theatre and Grant's first musical composition since the hit Broadway musical, *Don't Bother Me, I Can't Cope*. By this point, Perry had also established herself as a seasoned artist, having directed the Negro Ensemble Company's 1969 production of Franklin's *Mau Mau Room*, the 1971 production of Barbara and Carlton Molette's *Rosalee Pritchett*, the 1971 Off-Broadway production of Franklin's *Black Girl*, and many more. *The Prodigal Sister* production team included musical arranger/director Neal Tate, choreographer Rod Rodgers, lighting designer Shirley Prendergast, scenic designer C. Richard Mills, and costume designer/ New Federal Theatre company member Judy Dearing, who also danced in the production. The original production included four musicians, dancer Ronald Dunham, and a cast of thirteen, including Paula Desmond (Jackie), Victor Willis (Jackie's Boyfriend/ Hot Pants' Man/Dr. Patton), Francis Salisbury (Mother), Esther Brown (Miz Johnson), Ethel Beatty (Sissy), Leonard Jackson (Father), Louise Stubbs (Essie/Baltimore Bessie), Saundra McClain (DoWahs/Lucille), Kirk Kirksey (Slick/Pallbearer), Frank Carey (Reverend Wynn/Employment Man), Ronald Dunham (2nd Policeman), Joyce Griffen (DoWah/Hot Pants Harriet/Dancer), and Larry Lowe (DoWahs/1st Policeman/Dancer). These performers played to packed houses, with reviewers praising Grant's superb musical composition, the dedicated cast, and Perry's clever direction (see Figure 2.1). Production reviews reveal that the production had aspirations to transition to a Broadway stage and record the twenty musical numbers into a cast album, but neither dream came true.[24]

Critical reviews of the time suggest that despite support from Black audiences, *The Prodigal Sister* could not make the transition to Broadway because the musical lacked a strong book. *New York Amsterdam News* critic

Jessica B. Harris, for example, found Franklin's writing "weak," yet praised the musical's ability to connect with Black audiences through music. "This [music] lends a kind of familiarity that gives the audience, and particularly the Black audience, easy accessibility to the material," writes Harris.[25] She continues to commend the cast for performing in the exaggerated stylings of the musical comedy tradition, writing that "Shauneille Perry's direction fills the stage with activity at all times makes 'The Prodigal Sister' an immensely entertaining production."[26] Mel Gussow of the *New York Times* also found *The Prodigal Sister* entertaining but concluded that Franklin's book needed more refining. "Miss Grant is a sophisticated composer who has chosen to work 'down home,' with songs that run from the gospel 'Bless My Soul' to the bluesy 'The World Is Hard on a Woman-Child,'" writes Gussow.[27] Yet, the plot and dialogue needed further attention. "This is a slapdash cartoon. The emotions are as basic as the set, and the plot is a series of contrivances. The dialogue is, unwisely, written in sing-songy, rhymed couplets," writes Gussow.[28] While the majority of reviews support Gussow's criticism of the rhyming couplets, theatre critics of the historically Black newspaper, *New York Amsterdam News*, found some merit in Franklin's creative endeavors. For example, Harris found the writing "unfortunate" because the language "at times creates comic moments as the audience anticipates the rhyme."[29]However, the critic Angela E. Smith provides a stronger endorsement for Franklin's book, writing that "the dialogue is often funny and witty and is written in a poetic form that flows in rhythmical and offbeat style of slangish phrases.... *The Prodigal Sister* should make it to Broadway, because it definitely could survive with an improved plot."[30] Despite these mixed reviews, critics agree that the production was popular with Black audiences and played to packed houses.[31]

Production reviews offer insights into why *The Prodigal Sister* garnered support from its original audience—especially Black women spectators. Gussow describes the expectations and typical behavior of Henry Street Settlement audiences as: "Cheer the hero, hiss the villain, recognize the stereotype."[32] He then provides an account of the audience's reception of *The Prodigal Sister*. "At the performance that I attended every seat was taken (with several infants in mothers' arms). The play indulged the audience, and the audience, readily, indulged the play. Its members were demonstrative and appreciative of the evening's entertainment to the point of freely making contributions at the door on their way home (admissions free)."[33] Gussow describes an engaged, yet unsophisticated, audience that enjoys formulaic

Figure 2.1 Frances Salisbury and Louise Stubbs in J. e. Franklin and Micki Grant's *The Prodigal Sister* (1974) directed by Shauneille Perry. Photo by Bert Andrews. ©Billy Rose Theatre Division, The New York Public Library for the Performing Arts. Permission granted by the Estate of Bert Andrews and the Claudia Menza Literary Agency.

plots and characters, and lack even basic theatre etiquette (i.e., bringing infants to the theatre). In reality, Black spectators—including Black women—can ascertain what is meaningful to them. Whereas Gussow sees the celebration of an entertaining melodrama, the Black Arts Movement critic and playwright Ed Bullins articulates the production's cultural relevance and its popular appeal with Black women spectators. Bullins begins his review by considering the types of spectators who might enjoy *The Prodigal Sister*, beginning with his own holiday guests, including his mother, churchgoing Aunt Bea, and family members who want to see "the best entertainment value in town" that will also "goose their spirits, offer them a reinforcement of their collective attitudes and folkways, and provide them with the will to live through the coming uncertain year."[34] *The Prodigal Sister*, Bullins argues, fulfills these criteria. "It is a Black folks play. It reaches those in our deepest cultural recesses with its sincerity, group recognition, downright cuteness, dash and purposefulness of its Black family message. . . . And check this – you can even take your mama or Aunt Bea and give them a real Black treat," writes Bullins.[35] For Bullins, *The Prodigal Sister* did not merely entertain; the musical reflected Black culture at its finest, offering Black women (including churchwomen) an opportunity to see their values, concerns, and spiritual practices represented on the stage.[36]

The Prodigal Sister centers the inner desires of Blackgirls through Jackie's "I want" song entitled "Slip Away." "Slip Away" not only provides spectators an entry point into the musical (i.e., exposition) but also a Blackgirl's desire to experience unconditional love and sexual freedom. In this first beat, Jackie and her unnamed boyfriend enter the stage and he kisses her, hands her a suitcase, and exits. Despite taking part in the conception, this is the first and only time the unnamed boyfriend makes an appearance onstage, leaving Jackie to single-handedly bear the brunt of her father's and church community's ire. The first lines of "Slip Away" reveal that Jackie has spent her entire life obeying her father, but used her agency to break her father's rule and give in to forbidden sexual pleasures. Jackie sings: "When I was just a little girl about so high / my papa used to say things that made me cry / he told me he would drown me in the bay / if I should come up in a family way. / . . . I used to dream of the day that I could slip away."[37] From an early age, Jackie learned that her father's love was not unconditional, but predicated upon her maintaining her virginity. The threat of violence—in this case, death by drowning—caused Jackie to experience emotional trauma. Jackie survived this toxic household by dreaming of her escape to the city. She explains that finally, as a sophomore in high school, she escaped her sister Sissy's watchful eye and begins to secretly see a boy. Curiously, Jackie never mentions sexual intercourse but instead, self-censors her unborn child's conception story, singing: "There I met a boy who took my hand, / he said to me, 'You woman, me man.' / So I put Papa's warning upon the shelf / and only thought of *that* boy and my own self/ and now I find I'm in the family way / but this girl won't be drowning in nobody's bay" (6). Even the threat of death could not stop Jackie from experiencing the delights of physical touch, leading to her pregnancy. Rather than become a victim of a patriarchal structure that does not allow girls to experience sexual autonomy, Jackie runs away from home.

Jackie's escape from the country allows her to not only escape physical death at the hands of her father but also the social death of unwed pregnancy within the Black Church. The stigma of unwed pregnancy becomes clear when Miz Johnson, the neighborhood gossip and conservative churchwoman, "outs" Jackie by confronting Mother with the rumor that one of her daughters is expecting. Publicly, Mother defends her daughters' virtue and refuses to listen to any gossip. However, once Miz Johnson leaves her home, Mother's defense quickly dissipates and she tells Jackie: "Two months 'fore you due to graduate and done ruint yourself!" (10). In Mother's eyes, Jackie's lack of virginity and impending childbirth have irreparably harmed her chances of earning a high school diploma and damaged her future marriage prospects. However, it is Jackie's lack of remorse that truly confounds Mother, who laments: "They must'a gave me the wrong baby at the hospital where I got you. Cause ain't no way in the world I could'a birthed the likes of you!" (10). Mother continues to disavow her maternal connection to Jackie by interjecting, "Ain't no woman on my side of the family ever been this fast. . . . Why, it's a wonder you didn't try to get rid of it" (11). A defiant Jackie responds, "Oh, I know what to do. But I ain't going to" (11). Clearly, Mother represents the conservative values of the Black Church, deeming a Blackgirl's sexual desires with moral deficiency. Jackie, on the other hand, embodies the values of the sexual revolution of the 1960s and 1970s. Her more radical attitude regarding sexuality includes the belief that single Blackgirls have sexual desires and should have the same freedoms as men. Franklin's decision to include dialogue about the possibility of Jackie having an abortion reflects the discourse of the times, as politicians and activists debated how the increased sexual freedom for women and girls might impact the risks of unwanted pregnancies. In fact, *The Prodigal Sister* premiered just one year after the US Supreme Court's landmark *Roe vs. Wade* decision which decriminalized abortion. While Franklin's book does not vilify unwed pregnant teenage girls, neither does the musical support abortion as the "solution." In any case, Jackie's lack of shame, coupled with her knowledge of abortion, causes further distress to Mother, who says, "We won't even be able to show our faces in public no more. Or set our feet outside the door. . . . Where did I go wrong, Lord?"(11–12). Unfortunately, Mother cares more about the *appearance* of respectability—or what the church will think of her and her family—than supporting her daughter through this challenging time.

Black queer feminist spectators who have experienced pressure to feel shame and repent of their "sexual sin" might experience pleasure in witnessing Jackie's refusal to perform any outward display of shame for her "deviant" sexuality. Unfortunately, the Black Church's desire to protect the

Black community from the onslaught of sexual stereotypes can perpetuate an unspoken "sacramental shame" in the lives of everyday Black LGBTQ Christians. Theresa W. Tobin and Dawne Moon consider sacramental shame a form of spiritual violence leveled against LGBTQ people in general, but with an added layer of stigmatization for people of color who deviate from white sexual norms.[38] "Shame is an emotion in which one feels exposed as defective to important others—in this case to God and the church—in ways that threaten belonging and worthiness. . . . Shame feelings indicate both a desire to turn away or hide the defective self from others and a longing to re-establish connection and belonging. . . . Shame's ambivalence has led some to consider it an important moral emotion, an affective cue that one's behaviour or character harm or threaten to damage important relationships," write Tobin and Moon.[39] Thus, if a Black LGBTQ Christian "struggles" with same-sex attraction or is "confused" about their gender identity, feelings of shame can motivate them to repent and find redemption.[40] However, sacramental shame does not lead to redemptive outcomes for LGBTQ Christians. Tobin and Moon write that "being LGBTQ does not generally respond to acts of will, which makes the shame perpetual, and that these characteristics do not in themselves break relationship as sins do, but constitute a person's capacity to relate to others. Thus the shaming in these cases perpetually attacks not a person's ability to break relationships, but their ability to form them."[41] Furthermore, Tobin and Moon find that even if LGBTQ Christians remain celibate and follow their church's guidelines regarding sexual conduct, they "often remain under constant suspicion and scrutiny and are deemed unfit to serve."[42] Black LGBTQ Christians who internalize sacramental shame come to the understanding that their relationships are "sinful," damaged, and harmful to the Black community. LGBTQ Christians survive this spiritual violence by compartmentalizing their life, suffering in silence, and isolating themselves with the knowledge that their queer identity makes them unworthy of protection from the Black community. Still, other LGBTQ Christians may resist sacramental shame by "distinguishing between people's teachings and God's will and cultivating a personal relationship with God.[43]

Black queer feminist spectators who resist heterosexual marriage as the "cure" for their "immoral state" might also experience pleasure witnessing Jackie's refusal to accept marriage as the solution to her so-called "problem." After Mother and Sissy confront Jackie about how her actions have harmed the entire family's reputation, Jackie refuses to name her boyfriend, express shame for her sexuality, or accept Sissy's narrative that she's "in trouble."

Jackie boldly declares: "I ain't marrying nobody!" and breaks into the aptly titled song, "Ain't Marrying Nobody" (12). Throughout the musical number, Jackie shares her perspective of heterosexual marriage, explaining why she refuses to become a wife. Having witnessed her parents' marriage, she understands that the role of "wife" means becoming a "washer woman," "pants patcher," "maid," "cleaning lady," "slipper bringer," "back scratcher," and "slave" (12–13). *The Prodigal Sister* allows Black women spectators—queer, trans, or otherwise—to have the opportunity to bear witness to Jackie's truth as they watch Jack fulfill his role of slave master. For example, when Jack comes home from work, he commands Sissy to take his hat and lunch pail, Jackie to take off his shoes, and Mother to draw his bath water, and they respond by "running around in circles trying to do as Papa says" (15). Rather than view heterosexual marriage through the conservative Christian doctrine of complementary genders, Jackie understands the relationship as *anything but* mutually beneficial. Backed up by the DoWahs, who repeat the refrain, "Ain't gonna be," Jackie sings: "I was born a free bird / and a free bird has to fly" (12). As such, Jackie's belief system has more in common with Cheryl Clarke's "Lesbianism: An Act of Resistance" (1981) than Mother's religious dogma. Clarke writes:

> For a woman to be a lesbian in a male-supremacist, capitalist, misogynist, racist, homophobic, imperialist culture, such as that of North America, is an active resistance. (A resistance that should be championed throughout the world by all the forces struggling for liberation from the same slave master.) No matter how a woman lives out her lesbianism—in the closet, in the state legislature, in the bedroom—she has rebelled against becoming the slave master's concubine, viz., the male-dependent female, the female heterosexual.[44]

While Jackie does not form a romantic relationship with another Blackgirl, her decision to enjoy her sexual freedom, assert her autonomy, and embrace her genderqueer identity embodies radical Black queer feminist sentiments of the time. Mother deems Jackie's "Ain't Marrying Nobody" song as "foolish talk" and warns: "Why, you're papa'll beat you so you won't even be able to walk"(13). The parental pressure to conform to heterosexual unions and the threat of violence for not acquiescing would be particularly potent for Black queer feminist spectators. They, too, might experience joy by witnessing Jackie grab a pair of scissors for protection, boldly declare her intentions of metaphorically freeing herself from her father's restraint, and demand money before her departure.

Rather than view Jackie as "fast" or "foolish," she can be read as a genderqueer Blackgirl who works hard to navigate her interests within a male-supremacist, capitalist, racist, and homophobic society. While there are multiple definitions of "genderqueer," I use the term to refer to the subversion and resistance to normative constructions of gender binaries *male* and *female*. Julian Honkasalo writes that the origins of the term emerged from Black and Latinx activists of the 1960s "such as Marsha P. Johnson, Sylvia Rivera, and Miss Major Griffin-Gracy (and many more whose names have not been recorded in written history) [who] used terms, such as "gay," "street queen," and "sister" to signify resistance against gender binary, class oppression, US imperialism, and violence against sex workers."[45] Furthermore, the contemporary meaning of the term genderqueer is "a potentially powerful, performative concept that exposes techniques, methods, and structures of power that regulate both gender and sexuality. The term also calls for recognition and respect of lives regarded as unintelligible in the cisheteronormative and neoliberal matrix of emergent far-right and neo-fascist mobilization" writes Honkasalo.[46] In *The Prodigal Sister*, Jackie navigates the world as both male and female, thus complicating strict gender constructs. Spectators learn that since Jack lacked a son, he decided to raise Jackie "as a boy." Mother reminds Jack: "You was kinda disappointed when you saw it wasn't a son. But then you said, 'Don't make no nevermind, I'll make this 'on one'" (19). Jack's ability to "make" Jackie a son works so well that her pregnancy shocks Mother, who believes boys would find her masculine behavior unattractive. Mother states: "The way she used to climb them trees / And shoot them marbles down on her knees, / Wearing them old, dirty blue jeans everyday, / I didn't think no boy would ever look at her in that certain way" (19). However, boys do find Jackie's masculine behavior—climbing trees, shooting marbles, and unkempt appearance—physically attractive. Jackie also takes pride in her gender nonconformity. After running away from home and arriving in Big City, Jackie addresses her upbringing in the song, "If You Know What's Good For You." Jackie sings: "But my Papa taught me how to be tough. And I'm made of sterner stuff./ So I know that I'm gonna get through" (18). Later, in her song, "Gonna Get Through," Jackie reveals her high hopes of finding a job painting houses, cutting grass, or fixing cars—traditionally male occupations that her father taught her. Unfortunately, Big City, much like the real world, does not allow Jackie entry into male-dominated spaces, which forces her to choose work as a low-paid domestic servant, factory worker, or sex worker.

The Prodigal Sister engages with "the church" versus "the street" dichotomy through the representation of Big City. As with too many queer Blackgirls, the lack of support pushes Jackie to run away from the protection of her home, church, and community and into the dangers of the street. After Mother watches Jackie leave, she realizes the horrors that await Jackie on the streets of Big City and has an emotional breakdown. Mother states: "Young girls found in gulleys and alleyways everywhere. . . . Somebody done kilt'em for nothing at all" (17). Jack responds to her emotional concerns with a terse: "Better dead than unwed" (17). Inconsolable, Mother deals with her grief by turning to prayer and music. Mother sings the bluesy song, "The World is Hard on a Woman Child" in which she acknowledges, "They won't treat you like they should / They'll make you think that you're no good" (24). She then challenges Black women spectators to care for Blackgirls and welcome them back into the fold. Mother sings: "Now all you women folk out there, / All y'all that's gathered in the square, / When my Jackie's home to stay, / Who'll make her wish she'd stay'd away? / Who's gonna be so hard on my woman child? / Who'll be so hard on my woman child?" (25). Meanwhile, a vulnerable Jackie does fall prey to the dangers of the streets. She meets a hustler named Slick who convinces her through his song "Sister Love," to deliver a package to Baltimore Bessie's Casket Factory/ house of ill repute. Too late, Jackie realizes that the package contains drugs and she is apprehended by the police officers who pinch her breasts and drag her offstage. Eventually, Jackie realizes that Baltimore Bessie's goons have tricked other Blackgirls by giving them a package of drugs to deliver, paying their bail in exchange, and then forcing them to work off their debt in her casket factory or her house of ill repute. Jackie's decision to live on the streets, rather than face her father's physical wrath for her "sexual deviancy," is an all too common outcome for Black LGBTQ youth. In their study of LGBTQ youth and homelessness in the United States, Matthew Morton, Amy Dworsky, and Sonali Patel found that LGBTQ young adults are "twice as likely to experience homelessness as their peers" with "both LGBTQ and black or multiracial ha[ving] some of the highest rates of homelessness."[47] Some of the adverse risks while homeless include exchanging sex for basic needs, being forced to have sex, and being physically harmed by others.[48] Black LGBTQ youth—especially runaways—are among the most vulnerable within our society. Although fictional, Jackie's tale mirrors the unfortunate danger awaiting many Black LGBTQ youth.

Reverend Wynn's articulation of womanist theology causes Jack to repent of *his* sins and allow Jackie to return to her family and the Black Church. While Mother attends church, prays for Jackie's safe return, and shares the Parable of the Lost Sheep and testimony of the Savior with Jack, he remains unmoved. Instead, Jack continues to spew hatred for Jackie, use profanity, and express irritation with Mother's religious convictions. Jack does not experience a change of heart until the Reverend Wynn admonishes him in Beat 7, near the end of the musical. Reverend Wynn admonishes Jack, stating: "I believe the Lord is trying to say something to you" (46). Reverend Wynn then calls Jack to repentance, counseling him to return to church with his wife and take better care of his daughters. "You done thou-sholt-notted one-a of your girls to death / About this motherhood situation. / I heard you practically had 'em in prison / And you been acting like the warden. / Why, girls been getting in the family way ever' since / Adam ate that apple in the Garden. . . . / Better unwed than dead, Brother, Jack. / Better unwed than dead," states Reverend Wynn (47). This expression of care, rather than ostracism of Blackgirls, stuns Miz Johnson, who upholds conservative values. However, Reverend Wynn's speech provides the moral and spiritual grounds for forgiveness and reconciliation to happen. Of course, they express their joy at discovering Jackie alive through song. Mother sings "That's My Baby" and the gospel song, "Bless My Soul." Jackie follows these musical numbers with her solo, "I Been Up in Hell," which details the hardships she suffered being estranged from her family and community for three long weeks. Jackie sings: "I fled from my home / hell bent on freedom, / only to find--/ that the world's full of jails" (50). Afterward, Reverend Wynn praises the miracle of Jackie's return in the song, "Thank You, Lord." The musical ends in the spirited number, "Celebratin'," performed by the entire cast to celebrate Jackie's safe return. While Jackie does not "repent" of her deviant sexuality, she does learn to appreciate her family and community. Jack's repentance allows the community to welcome Jackie and her unborn child into the fold.

Curiously, there is an alternative ending and "message" to the musical which calls on spectators to make peace and forgive others in their own lives. The Alexander Street Press version omits Jackie's song "I Been Up in Hell" and, instead, Reverend Wynn delivers a sermon before breaking out into the song "Thank You, Lord." As Reverend Wynn delivers the following sermon, the cast ad-libs "Amen" and other responses throughout:

> Lord, we hear you talking to us today. We feel you moving in your mysterious way. And we know what you're trying to say. Tell me if I'm wrong, Lord. But it sounds like you're sending us a warning to get our business straight. Sound like you're telling us to make peace with one another. To renew our love for our neighbor and our children and our sister and our brother before it's too late. . . . I got a feeling Brother Jack is gonna' set his soul in order cause he's grateful to you, Lord, for giving him back his daughter. . . . When we all leave this occasion, Lord, where your miracle has gone on, we gonna call our loved ones on the telephone and we gonna talk to 'em, Lord. . . . We gonna to ask 'em to forgive us for doing 'em wrong. We know they can't hear us after they're dead and gone. . . . Yes, Lord, we hear you talking to us. And we gonna to let thy will be done.[49]

This alternation detracts from the plot, taking focus from Jackie's experiences of adversity while homeless, and replacing it with a more didactic spiritual lesson for spectators. In addition, Reverend Wynn's thinly veiled admonition for the audience to take action after the conclusion of the musical would not be lost by spectators. His call to love one another is similarly expressed by Clarke. "So, all of us would do well to stop fighting each other for our space at the bottom, because there ain't no more room. We have spent so much time hating ourselves. Time to love ourselves spectators would," advises Clarke.[50] Black queer feminist spectators would do well to remember that loving oneself is not just a revolutionary act; it is essential to their humanity.

Whereas *The Prodigal Sister* uses gospel music, Black Church values, and sacred text within the conventions of musical comedy, *Your Arms Too Short to Box With God* (1976) fully embraces gospel music as *the* driving force behind the musical. Indeed, gospel music functions as a form of prayer, an expression of Black political thought, and a healing force within the lives of Blackgirls.

Your Arm's Too Short to Box With God

Your Arm's Too Short to Box With God is much more than "entertainment." The gospel musical encourages spectators—regardless of their religious affiliations—to invite Jesus into their everyday lives. As spectators witness a fictional congregation share their testimonies of the birth, ministry trials, death, and resurrection of Jesus through sermons, more than two dozen musical numbers, live music, and dance, they're encouraged to leave the theatre space feeling empowered and having a renewed desire to draw closer to the Savior. The title of the gospel musical, which Carroll drew from James Weldon Johnson's *The Autobiography of an Ex-Colored Man* (1912), mirrors this religious message. In the novel, Johnson describes a Black preacher who uses his gift with words to deliver striking sermons that stir the hearts of his congregation. Johnson writes:

> John Brown's powers in describing the delights of heaven were no greater than those in depicting the horrors of hell. I saw great, strapping fellows,[*sic*] trembling and weeping like children at the 'mourners' bench. His warnings to sinners were truly terrible. I shall never forget one expression that he used, which for originality and aptness could not be excelled. . . . He struck the attitude of a pugilist and thundered out, 'Young man, yo' arm's too short to box wid God!' "[51]

John Brown's thunderous performance commands congregants to recognize that they, as sinners, are too weak to fight the strength of the Lord. Inspired by this message, Carroll combined the teachings of Saint Matthew and the musical talents of the Reverend Alex Bradford and Urban Arts Corps resident artist, Micki Grant, to create a two-act gospel musical that celebrates these religious truths. However, *Your Arm's Too Short* remains unique by centering Black women's discipleship and depicting Jesus as a Black radical thinker; a trailblazer who could not be conquered in life nor death.

Carroll developed and directed *Your Arm's Too Short* at the Urban Arts Corps, which she founded in 1967. Her decision to found a theater and direct/adapt her own works was nearly unheard of at the time. Carroll famously stated: "They told me that I had one-third less chance because I was a woman; they told me I had a third less chance again because I was black, but I tell you, I did one hell of a lot with that remaining one-third."[52] Yet, Carroll stood among a small circle of Black women who defied the odds in New York. These trailblazers include Barbara Teer (founder of National Black Theatre, 1968–present), Hazel Bryant (founder of Richard Allen Center for Culture and Art, 1968–present), Rosetta Le Noire (founder of AMAS, 1968–present), and Aduke Aremu (founder of Harlem Children's Theater Company, 1971–1990), and Marjorie Moon (executive director of the Billie Holiday Theatre, 1972–present). Carroll's Urban Arts Corps provided training for emerging Black and brown talent and as such, she instilled an incredible work ethic with her company of actors. She became known for lengthy rehearsals in her small, sixty-seat black box theatre located at 26 West and 20th Street.[53] By the time she mounted *Your Arm's Too Short* at the Festival of Two Worlds in Spoleto, Italy in 1975, she had already held the distinction as the first African American woman to direct a musical on Broadway; received a Tony Award nomination for her direction of Grant's musical revue, *Don't Bother Me, I Can't Cope* (1971); and established a reputation as an innovative director.[54] For example, Carroll played a major role in the development of the gospel song-play—a precursor to what today is known as gospel musicals, urban musicals, or Chitlin Circuit theatre. Carroll directed Langston Hughes's *Black Nativity* (1961), the first gospel song-play, which told the story of Jesus's humble birth through the combination of text, music, dance, and mime.[55] According to Calvin A. McClinton, Carroll incorporated gospel music into her craft because she believed the genre embodied the spirit, history, and culture of Black America. McClinton writes:

> Carroll was especially interested in the new 'gospel' music that had begun to emerge in the African American church. This new music was alive and vibrant, fully rhythmical and drawing from an ancestral spirit. She felt this music expressed the basic qualities of Black life, its sorrows, its joys, and most of all, the magnificent wonder in being one of God's creatures. Carroll understood the gospel roots to be germane to the African American experience in America. The use of gospel music in the theater, however, was a new concept which Carroll incorporated easily and early in her career.[56]

Carroll's use of gospel music in *Your Arm's Too Short* invited Black spectators to not only embrace their ancestral spirit but also their divinity as children of God.

Your Arm's Too Short made a total of three Broadway appearances, garnering awards and honors along the way. The musical first appeared at the Lyceum Theatre in 1976 and featured soloists Salome Bey, Clinton Derricks-Carroll, Sheila Ellis, Delores Hall, William Hardy Jr., Hector Jaime Mercado, Mabel Robinson, William Thomas Jr., and Derek Williams (see Figure 2.2). Other company members included Adrian Bailey, Deborah Lynn Bridges, Sharon Brooks, Thomas Jefferson Fouse Jr., Michael Gray, Cardell Hall, Bobby Hill, Edna M. Krider, Leone Washington, and Marilynn Winbush. Carroll's production team included William Schroder (sets and costumes), Gilbert V. Hemsley Jr. (lighting), Talley Beatty (choreography),

Figure 2.2 swope_259479. Swope, Martha. A scene from the Broadway production of the musical *Your Arms Too Short To Box With God*. 1982. Photo by Martha Swope. ©Billy Rose Theatre Division, The New York Public Library for the Performing Arts.

Chapman Roberts (choral arrangements and direction), and H. B. Barnum (orchestrations and dance music). *Your Arm's Too Short* made a second appearance on Broadway at the Ambassador Theatre on June 2, 1980. Company members included Jennifer Holliday (who would later star as Effie White in the 1981 Broadway production of *Dreamgirls*), Julius Richard Brown, Cleavant Derricks, Sheila Ellis, Ralph Farrington, Jamil K. Garland, Elijah Gill, William-Keebler Hardy Jr., Garry Q. Lewis, Linda Morton, Jai Oscar St. John, Kiki Shepard, Leslie Hardesty Sisson, Ray Stephens, Quincella Swyningan, Faruma S. Williams, Marilynn Winbush, Linda E. Young, Adrian Bailey, and Linda James. Most of the original production team returned, except Richard Winkler designed lights, Michael Powell provided musical direction, and Abe Jacob provided sound design. *Your Arm's Too Short* was revived a final time at the Alvin Theatre on September 9, 1982, with gospel singers Patti LaBelle and Al Green as headliners. Company members included Nora Cole, Julius Richard Brown, Jamil K. Garland, Elijah Gill, L. Michael Gray, Ralf Paul Haze, Cynthia Henry, The Bobby Hill, Rufus E. Jackson, Elmore James, Linda James, Tommi Johnson, Janice Nunn Nelson, Dwayne Phelps, Quincella, KiKi Shepard, Leslie Hardesty Sisson, and Marilynn Winbush. Again, nearly all of the original production team returned except Talley Beatty's choreography was restaged by Ralf Paul Haze, and R. Shepard and J. Esher provided sound design. The original and revival productions received overwhelmingly positive reviews, garnering Tony Award nominations for Best Musical, Best Direction of a Musical, and Best Choreography, with Delores Hall winning a 1977 Tony Award for Best Featured Actress in a Musical. The success of *Your Arm's Too Short* set the standard for future gospel musicals and helped usher in an "explosion" of Black musicals during the 1970s and early 1980s.[57]

Your Arm's Too Short attempts to elicit emotional responses from spectators through a blending of sacred text, gospel music, and religious "excitement." This process begins as soon as spectators arrive, as the set welcomes them into a church-like atmosphere. The theatre critic Emory Lewis writes: "The set resembles a church, with segments of stained glass windows at the rear. The entire action takes place around the chapel, which is represented by a series of raised platforms at various heights."[58] In contrast to this sparse set, the choir-cast wears choir robes described as "colorful capes of orange, coral, and red" which draw attention to their movements and compliment their high-energy performance.[59] Clinton Turner Davis praised Carroll's ability to create the spirit of religious revivals during her productions. "Her work's transcendent quality often placed it at the center of a religious experience, in not ecstasy, that elicited calls and responses many associate with the black church. ("Can I get a witness?" "Amen!!")" writes Davis.[60] Carroll's use of Black Church practices begins during the ensemble's spirited opening number, "The Beatitudes." Recorded in the Gospel of Matthew (5:3–12) and Gospel of Luke (6:20–26), Jesus delivered his instructions on how to treat each other during his opening for the Sermon on the Mount and Sermon on the Plain. Known from the fifteenth century onward as the Beatitudes (from the Latin word "beatus," meaning 'blessed"), Jesus is said to have taught eight blessings in the Gospel of Matthew and four blessings and woes in the Gospel of Luke. Rather than read from the Bible directly, the ensemble employs gospel music to stir the hearts and minds of spectators. "The Beatitudes" share this doctrine text through the lyrics: "Blessed are . . . the poor in spirit . . . they that mourn . . . the meek . . . they which do hunger and thirst after righteousness . . . the merciful . . . the pure in heart . . . the peacemakers."[61] The song concludes with: "Blessed are the peacemakers; Blessed are the peacemakers . . . for they shall be called the children of God." The repetition of "for they shall be called the children of God" sends an important message to Black spectators: namely, that their Black identity is irrevocably linked to their divine origins and faith. Carroll delivers this message through religious "excitement," utilizing call-and-response, movement, and live musical accompaniment (i.e., the piano, organ, bass, drum, and guitar) to emotionally "move" spectators. Theatre critic John Beaufort describes this opening number as a "rich compilation of melody, harmony, and movement" that sets the stage for later performances that include "an outpouring of musical expression that ranges from deepest grief to exaltation."[62] Spectators responded in kind, with the theatre critic Lucile M. Scott describing a May 13, 1979 production as "a hand-clapping a foot padding evening . . . everyone had a real good time [and] was caught up in the spirit that imbues the entire case."[63] Needless to say, gospel music's use of religious excitement provided a powerful means of eliciting audience participation.

Your Arm's Too Short uses gospel music as a vehicle for both ensemble members and spectators to "witness" and "testify" of the divinity of Jesus Christ. After "The Beatitudes," the energy builds to a frenzy of religious excitement through the musical number "We're Gonna Have A Good Time." This song was performed by a soloist with the accompaniment of the ensemble cast (acting as a congregation). The premiere and revival performances of "We're Gonna Have A Good Time" showcased the talents of gospel singers Clinton Derricks-Carroll (prod. 1976), Julius Richard Brown/Cleavant Derricks (alternated roles, prod. 1980), and Patti LaBelle (prod. 1982). Most notably, the lyrics repeat the phrase "We're gonna have a good time" sixteen times, "Let's have a good time" twenty-one times, and "Have a good time" six times—suggesting a desire for an entertaining and communal relationship between performer and audience. The lyrics encourage spectators to witness, testify, and participate throughout the performance: "Don't be afraid to raise your voice/let's have a good time./ The Lord said make a joy-ful noise/ let's have a good time." The musical number establishes song as a form of testimony, with the soloist singing: "When you hear me sing and shout/ What's inside me must come out/ When the Lord told me to testify/ That's what he meant cause the Lord don't lie." "We're Gonna Have A Good Time" also includes a special "Women's Verse," which essentially repeats the same sentiments, but in so doing, reinforces the importance of Black women's testimonies. Indeed, throughout the production, Black women bear witness of Jesus's teachings and miracles.

Your Arm's Too Short celebrates Blackgirl soloists within church choirs, providing ample opportunities for them to use gospel music to bear their testimonies and provoke spectators to invite Jesus into their everyday lives. For example, after Preacher's first sermon, a soloist performs "There's A Stranger in Town." Originally performed by Sheila Ellis in 1976, with later performances by Linda E. Young (prod. 1980) and the Reverend Al Green (prod. 1982), "There's A Stranger in Town" includes lyrics that testify of Jesus performing miracles—namely, giving sight to the blind with His mere touch. Later, when a mob decides to crucify Jesus, a female soloist (Salome Bey, prod. 1976; Sheila Ellis, prod. 1980; Nora Cole, prod. 1982) performs the gospel song, "See How They Done My Lord." As she describes the pain Jesus suffered during His crucifixion, her soulful voice repeats the phrase "my Lord," concluding the song with: "On Friday He died for you and me / He died for you and me." The gospel blues song, "I Love You So Much Jesus," provides another opportunity for a Black woman soloist. Performed by Delores Hall (prod. 1976), Jennifer Holliday (prod. 1980), and Patti LaBelle (prod. 1982), "I Love You So Much Jesus" combines evangelist lyrics with blues instrumentation. The simplicity of lyrics—which include repetition of "I love You Jesus"—does not capture the incredible vocal range, belting technique, and emotional tonality needed to perform this musical number. Spectators, however, fully appreciated the vocal prowess of the soloist. The theatre critic Lucile M. Scott, for example, captures audience responses to what is essentially a love song to Jesus. "The singing of "I Love You So Much Jesus" by Jennifer Yvette Holliday was really the high point of the last act. . . . She was given a standing ovation and the audience asked for more and more. While she sang you imagine the things that she sang about had really happened to you and what a wonderful feeling it is to know that someone has done something wonderful for you," writes Scott.[64] Thus, Black women soloists provided vicarious pleasure for spectators, who could experience the love of Jesus from their musical testimonies. In addition to solo performances, Black women performers take center stage within the narrative of *Your Arms Too Short,* acting as key figures in Jesus's life.

Despite their limited portrayal in the Bible, Carroll conceptualized Blackgirls—especially Jesus' young mother, the Virgin Mary—as central to His earthly ministry. In Carroll's production, the Virgin Mary is portrayed by two "Singing Mary" ensemble members: Salome Bey and Mabel Robinson (prod. 1976), Sheila Ellis and Quincella Swyningan (prod. 1980), and Nora Cole and Quincella (prod. 1982). Accompanied by a choir of cast members, the Singing Marys perform "Something is Wrong in Jerusalem," an uptempo song set to funk music. In the song, Singing Mary shares a premonition that trouble awaits Jesus and advises Him, singing: "Be careful whom You talk with, / Consider what You say / For there are those who will twist Your words / To get their way / Be careful whom You walk with / For, my Darling, there are those / Who'll betray Your trust if You let them get too close." This moment of maternal concern presents the very human side of Jesus which might resonate with Black mothers in the audience who likewise desire to protect their children. Black mothers often bear the responsibility of socializing their children to navigate a society that does not recognize their humanity. Knowing these dangers, Black mothers teach their children similar "rules" of survival: be careful when choosing your words, your friends, and the places you visit. The reality is that even one ill-advised word to a police officer, for example, or being "in the wrong place at the wrong time," could result in death. Unfortunately, as with the case of Singing Mary, Black mothers cannot make these choices for their children and are forced to watch these trials unfold. Singing Mary knows this and sings: "When You were a boy I could hold You and protect You / But when a boy becomes a man / What's a mother to do?" Rather than allow officers of the law to capture her son, she decides to travel to Jerusalem to save him. In Singing Mary's second and final appearance in the musical, she performs a duet with an offstage Jesus in the song, "I Know I've Got to Leave Here." In her song, she laments, "Wish I could tell You what I feel and see / But I can't prevent what's certain to be" and later reveals "His name is Judas / He's tryin' to steal Your life." As with Singing Mary's knowledge of what will come to pass, spectators so too know the fate that awaits Jesus but cannot save Him. They, like Singing Mary, can only watch in agony as Jesus is wrongfully put on trial, sentenced, and crucified as in the account of the Gospel of St. Matthew.

Your Arm's Too Short celebrates the wisdom of the seemingly unremarkable and unnamed Blackgirls from the Bible, including Pontius Pilate's wife. While Pilate, the fifth governor of the Roman province of Judaea, only appears onstage as the voice of the chorus, his wife, aptly named "Pilate's Wife," takes center stage, singing the musical's titular song. Performed by Delores Hall with lead dancer Cardell Hall (prod. 1976), Jennifer Holliday and company (prod. 1980), and Patti La Belle (prod. 1982), Pilate's Wife offers Pilate advice through song. She begins the first verse of "Your Arm's Too Short to Box with God" following the rhythms of traditional gospel music, telling Pilate that a voice in her dream told her that Jesus is innocent. Her second verse provides a break from her somber tone and slow tempo. With excitement and jubilee, Pilate's Wife repeats the phrase "You don't know what the Lord told me" and sings/warns: "Pilate, you better keep your hands clean / Your arms are too short to box with God." Afterward, two choruses perform a dance number as they join Pilate's Wife in song. Rather than have a male preacher deliver a sermon, it is Pilate's Wife who testifies of the Lord's strength: "God is bigger than you, yeah / God is bigger than you, yeah / Taller than the trees / Wider than the seas / Deeper than the river that's flowin." Moved by her performance, Pilate listens to his wife and allows the crowd of cast members to choose to either release Barrabas or Jesus from their death sentence. As with the Biblical tale, the crowd chooses to spare Barrabas, Jesus is crucified, and the earth quakes (which Carroll depicted through the "Veil of the Temple – Ballet" performance).[65] Despite the doomed outcome, Pilate's Wife's attempt to thwart Jesus's enemies provides a powerful example of Black women's longstanding wisdom, faith, and advocacy (see Figure 2.3).

Carroll interweaves three powerful sermons in between soul-stirring gospel musical numbers, creating a narrative structure that connects Jesus's trials to the contemporary Black freedom struggle. In the original production and subsequent revivals, sermons are delivered by male cast members in the role of Preacher who engages spectators by moving "down the aisles 'working' the audience."[66] Brian Granger writes that the preacher "is a central figure in Carroll's gospel musicals, helping the audience connect the space of the spiritual with the space of secular theater through performance."[67] Most notably, the Reverend Al Green, a famous gospel conductor, performed the role of Preacher in 1982. In the first of three sermons, Preacher invites spectators to travel back in time with him and introduces them to a more radical vision of Jesus. During his short but impassioned speech, Preacher states: "I want to tell you a story about a man / Who lived a long time ago, / Some called him a troublemaker / Because he disturbed the status quo, / If he were around today / They'd probably called him a radical, / A revolutionary, a malcontent, / A thorn in the side of the establishment." By comparing Jesus's leadership to that of contemporary Black leaders, Preacher positions Black political thought and struggle as a just cause. This becomes further evident when the priests and elders gather townspeople to search for witnesses to conspire against Jesus. The script notes that a company member sings: "He's a heretic and dangerous, / He wants to change the law, / He must be stopped before he goes too far." The "law" has a twofold meaning. At face value, the priests and elders refer to the Law of Moses but a deeper meaning could also refer to the history of Black leaders (often ministers), who likewise questioned unjust laws of the land and galvanized the Black community into action. Many tried to halt the work of these trailblazers, stooping so low as to assassinate their character or through literal assassination. After the ensemble has shared the

Figure 2.3 swope_259475. Swope, Martha. A scene from the Broadway production of the musical *Your Arms Too Short To Box With God*. 1982. Photo by Martha Swope ©Billy Rose Theatre Division, The New York Public Library for the Performing Arts.

ministry, crucifixion, and resurrection of Jesus, Preacher returns at the beginning of Act II and continues to draw parallels between Jesus's trials and contemporary Black life. Speaking directly to the audience, Preacher takes on the rhythmic pattern of Black preachers and tells the audience the "message" of the musical. Preacher states that the story they witnessed is "a story about power, that's right, power / I'm talking about the power of faith." He then encourages spectators to take action in their own lives, regardless of their religious background, stating: "Faith is the power to change your life." This sermon reveals that the audience has attended a performance at the Church of Good Faith and extends an invitation for all to go forth and make positive changes in their lives. Some spectators might interpret this as a call to follow the example of Jesus and become agents of change.

In addition to centering Blackgirls in the Bible and presenting Jesus as a Black radical, Carroll makes a third critical departure from standard Biblical interpretations by humanizing Judas and his "sin" through dance. To begin, Judas is often seen as the "villain" of the Biblical tale. As one of the twelve disciples, Judas should have protected Jesus from the priests and Pharisees, but instead, he betrays Him to authorities. The Book of Matthew (27:3–5) describes Judas and his fate as follows:

> Then Judas, which had betrayed him, when he saw that he was condemned, repented himself, and brought again the thirty pieces of silver to the chief priests and elders,
>
> Saying, I have sinned in that I have betrayed the innocent blood. And they said, What *is that* to us? see thou *to that*.
>
> And he cast down the pieces of silver in the temple, and departed, and went and hanged himself.

In *Your Arms Too Short*, Judas appears immediately following Jesus's trial and performs "Judas Dance," a modern dance set to upbeat funk music. While there are no filmed recordings of the dance, we do know that dance was used to convey Judas's feelings of guilt, his attempt to repent of his sin, and his ultimate suicide. The lack of words—only quick movements of the body set to funk music—provided an optimal means of allowing spectators to understand Judas's immense grief and regret. Theatre critics of the time report that spectators were moved by the dance, which was originally performed by Hector Jaime Mercado in 1976, with revival performances by Ralph Farrington (prod. 1980) and Ralf Paul Haze (prod. 1982). The theatre critic John Beaufort writes that Beatty's Tony-nominated choreography "is occasionally spectacular—notably in the dances by Stanley Perryman as Jesus and Hector Jaime Mercado as Judas."[68] In addition, Scott reports that "the trial and the Judas dance by Ralph [Farrington] seemed almost unbelievable . . . at times the audience seemed loathe to allow the performers to stop."[69] Judas's decision to commit suicide, rather than face ostracism from church leaders for his "sin," would undoubtedly resonate with Black queer spectators today, who, we know, are disproportionately impacted by high suicide rates. The Trevor Project, for example, reports that in 2022 "50% of Black LGBTQ youth had considered suicide within the past year and about

20% attempted suicide in the past year."[70] If one adds spiritual violence to this equation, is it any wonder that the United States is on the verge of losing an entire generation of Black queer youth to suicide?

Carroll concludes *Your Arms Too Short* by abandoning the narrative altogether, shifting focus on celebrating the legacies of Blackgirl gospel singers, many of whom have yet to receive the recognition that they deserve. Preacher ushers in this celebration during his final sermon, delivered during the musical finale, "The Band." Preacher explains that during his travels spreading the gospel, he's noticed that singers and musicians have left the Church bands and choirs. This experience prompts Preacher to "call the roll" and honor legendary gospel singer Mahalia Jackson (1911–1971), and lesser-known (today) LGBTQ luminaries and gospel singers Clara Ward (1924–1973) and Sister Rosetta Tharpe (1915–1973). These singers defied the limitations placed on Blackgirls during this era, making a career in an industry not readily open to Blackgirls.[71] The journalist and gospel music scholar Robert Darden describes their legacy as follows:

> Into this lily-white boys-only club barged three strong, black women, gifted, indefatigable, undeniable: Sister Rosetta Tharpe, Clara Ward, and Mahalia Jackson. Together, they changed not only gospel music but they helped transform American popular music as well. Gospel music was one of the few places an African-American female could command respect in the face of a double whammy: endemic male sexism and a Jim Crow world.[72]

Jackson, Ward, and Tharpe passed away within a year and a half of each other, delivering a heavy blow to gospel music enthusiasts. By saying their names, Preacher honors their legacy and provides an opportunity for spectators to mourn their passing. However, this "mourning" takes the form of a jubilee as Preacher and the choir-cast perform "The Band" and invite spectators to experience religious excitement. The theatre critic Robert Jones of the *New York Daily News* perhaps best describes this joyful experience. "The show is about gospel singing and it's as close to euphoria as I ever expect. . . . Before seeing the play I wonder[ed] how the stars would be able to hold the attention of the audience, young, small, old and teenagers for about 2 hours . . . now I know - they made you a part of the musical."[73] Indeed, the critical and commercial success of *Your Arms Are Too Short* paved the way for a new crop of gospel-based secular musicals, including *Mama, I Want to Sing.*

Mama, I Want to Sing

In *Mama, I Want to Sing*, music functions as a healing force, an expression of burgeoning sexuality, an act of defiance, a tool to educate, and a source of freedom for Blackgirls. The semibiographical gospel musical is based on the life of Doris Troy, a pop star who rose to fame with the 1963 pop-soul song, "Just One Look." *Mama, I Want to Sing* tells the story of Doris Winter, a young Blackgirl, who loses her spirit after the death of her beloved father, the Reverend Winter of Mt. Calvary Church in Harlem. With the encouragement of Sister Carrie, a former blueswoman and current star soloist in the church choir, Doris (and spectators) discover the power of song as a healing force in her life (see Figure 2.4). The gospel musical then jumps ahead a few years to depict a seventeen-and-a-half-year-old Doris. She now sings in her late father's Pentecostal church choir but dreams of becoming a commercial star like her idols Lena Horne, Sarah Vaughan, and Billie Holiday. Unbeknownst to Geraldine "Mama" Winter, Doris and her three church friends form a girl's pop group called The Halos and perform a successful musical act at "Amateur Night" at the Apollo Theater. Afterward, The Halos receive a contract to tour the United States and Doris has to convince Mama to let her sign the agreement and jump-start her career in the professional music industry. Tensions run high as Mama refuses to let Doris go on tour but eventually, with the help of Miss Carrie and didactic lessons taught in powerful gospel musical numbers, Mama relents. The Narrator/Disc Jockey then tells the audience that Doris used her newfound freedom to travel and perform in small towns and it was during a long bus ride that she penned "Just One Look." The musical concludes with the Narrator/DJ recounting Doris's successful career and her philanthropic enterprises, assuring spectators that despite Doris's commercial success, she remained a moral pillar within the Black community.

The production history of *Mama, I Want to Sing* has humble beginnings. After completing a draft of their first musical, Higginsen and Wydro workshopped the piece at Rosetta LeNoire's Amas Repertory Company in 1980. The couple then rewrote the script and produced the musical at Fordham University in New York as a benefit for the Black student group, Molimo Players. The theatre critic Peter Bailey writes that the success of this university production, which ran for six performances, "convinced [Higginsen and Wydro] that their 'story in concert' deserved an opportunity to reach out to a larger audience."[74] Higginsen and Wydro eventually

Figure 2.4 Desiree Coleman Jackson (Doris Winter) in *Mama, I Want to Sing* (1983). Mama Foundation production trailer, directed by Ken Wydro, still courtesy of the author. https://www.youtube.com/watch?v = M_yc2ANAjeU

used their $35,000 in savings to refurbish and produce *Mama, I Want to Sing* at the Heckscher Theatre, an Off-Broadway theatre located in the East Harlem neighborhood. Unfortunately, the Heckscher Theater, which formerly housed Joseph Papp's New York Shakespeare Festival, required extensive cleaning and renovations because it had sat empty for fifteen years.[75] Higginsen and Wydro put in the time, money, and effort to prepare the space for the premiere on March 23, 1983. The original cast included a fourteen-year-old Tisha Campbell (Doris Winter), legendary gospel singer Queen Esther Marrow (Mama Winter), singer Carol Dennis (Sister Carrie), Higginsen (Narrator/Disc Jockey), and musical artist Benny Diggs and his New York City Community Choir. The production featured performances of classic gospel and spirituals, including: "On Christ/Traveling Shoes," "We Come This Far by Faith," "Faith Can Move a Mountain," "My Faith Looks Up to Thee," "He'll Be Your Strength," "Precious Lord," and "His Eye Is on the Sparrow." *Mama, I Want to Sing* also includes secular songs and introduces spectators to new gospel songs composed by musical director, Grenoldo Frazier. These secular songs and new gospel renditions include "Just One Look" and "The Treasure of Love," as well as original songs "You Are My

Child," "Gifted Is," "The One Who Will Love Me," and "Mama, I Want To Sing." Higginsen and Wydro originally envisioned running the musical for three or four weekends, or at least long enough to justify their financial investment.[76] However, the overwhelming audience support has allowed continued revival, with Doris Troy joining the cast for a ten-year run as Mama Winter, beginning in 1984.

Higginsen and Wydro used unconventional means to market the musical, garnering strong audience support from Black churchgoers. Bailey writes: "Since 'Mama's' opening was greeted with a loud silence by the theatre press and the theatre community, creative ways were designed to attract the attention of prospective audiences. Cast members visited churches on Sunday mornings and sang at various community events. Rev. Wyatt Tee Walker, senior pastor of Harlem's Canaan Baptist Church, contributed by playing the role of Rev. Randolph Winter for several performances."[77] Indeed, churchgoers accepted cast invitations by forming "theatre parties," traveling on buses from the city, and from places such as Washington, D.C., to attend the production.[78] "We were keeping things moving until 'word of mouth' had a chance to work its magic," Higginsen explains.[79] Word-of-mouth eventually snowballed into more traditional means of publicity, including reviews in *Time* magazine, *Washington Post*, National Public Radio, USA Today, etc. For example, *Time* magazine selected *Mama* as one of the Top 10 theatrical productions of 1984.[80] "By the end of 1987, 'Mama' had secured its place in history as one of the major theatre successes of the decade and as the longest-running Black production in theatre history. Over one million people are estimated to have seen either the New York City production or the road show which, since opening in Washington D.C. in March 1986, has been performed in major cities around the U.S. and around the world."[81] The show surpassed expectations, running for eight years before undertaking a national tour, followed by an international tour across Europe and Japan.

The financial success of *Mama, I Want to Sing* provided greater opportunities for Black artists, both on and offstage. In the first five years alone, *Mama, I Want to Sing* grossed more than $20 million, providing steady employment for dozens of Black performers, designers, and staff.[82] In addition, the lead role of Doris Winter has become an important breakout role for several Blackgirl ingénues. The role of Doris requires an actress to perform as a young girl in pigtails and a young contemporary diva onstage. For example, Richard Harrington of *The Washington Post* praises eighteen-year-old Deitra "D'atra" Hicks's 1986 performance as Doris, writing that she "transformed from a mousy minister's daughter to a Whitney Houston-like diva. And when you remember Houston's mother is a gospel singer Cissy Houston, it makes this exploration of family/church musical tensions—a theatrical refrain at least as old as 'The Jazz Singer'—seem all the more current."[83] Throughout the production's forty-year history, the role of Doris has launched the careers of Hicks, Tisha Campbell, Desiree Coleman, Noreen Clayton, and Ramon Keller. In addition to acting, the role demands incredible talent and singing technique—a soprano voice capable of hitting the whistle register, or the highest register of the human voice (think Minnie Riperton's high note in "Lovin' You" or Mariah Carey's "Emotions"). In fact, the theatre critic Peter writes that the role of "Doris" is for aspiring Black singer-actresses what "Annie" is for white girl performers.[84] More recently, Higginsen and Wydro's daughter Ahmaya Knoelle Higginsen, has performed the vocally challenging role. The theatre critic Kalia Richardson writes that Higginson "first appeared onstage before she was ever born" as her mother was pregnant with her while performing as the Narrator/Disc Jockey in the premiere production.[85] "When Higginson was a toddler, she waddled backstage during the musical's international tours, and at the age of 10 she joined its choir for performances at Madison Square Garden. Then as a teenager, she stepped into the lead role of Doris Winter."[86] Now a talented gospel choir director in her own right, in 2023 Higginson took on the role of director for the fortieth anniversary production of *Mama, I Want to Sing.*

Higginsen and Wydro's use of Black church service practices, the celebration of gospel music, and the use of celebrity help explain why *Mama, I Want to Sing* remains a popular choice among Black theatregoers. To begin, *Mama I Want to Sing*'s use of gospel music and simple set convey a strong sense of place. In the 2020 production, Higginsen and Wydro used a minimalist set to transform El Museo's El Teatro (formerly Heckscher Theatre) into a sacred space.[87] The production began with a choir singing on risers and an oversized white cross and stained glass window were projected in the background. As the Minister of Music (Elijah Ahmad Lewis) led the choir through their practices, Reverend Winter (Tyrone Flowers) delivered his sermon, and Sister Carrie (Sandra Huff) performed her solo, the predominantly Black audience clapped, laughed, wept, and shouted "Amen!" along with their performances of Black Church service.[88] Early production reviews suggest that the energy and spirit found within these performances have always been an integral component of the musical's success with audiences. In a 1986 review, the theatre critic V. Williams writes: "The cast of 'Mama, I Want To Sing' and its audience connected in an emotionally charged service that was like a Sunday Morning service."[89] Decades later, the theatre critic Linda Armstrong would commend Kathleen Murphy's performance as Sister Carrie and the musical's ability to maintain audience engagement during the 2003 production. "[Kathleen Murphy's] versatile, phenomenal voice takes everyone to church as she sings gospel songs including 'He'll Be Your Strength' and 'Faith.' As she performed 'Faith' the show's gospel choir, the New York Reach Ensemble, danced while doing backup vocals. The music was incredible. You could feel the spirit of the Lord and an energy in the church. The audience seemed to get into the music as they stomped their feet, clapped their hands and put their hands in the air, waving in testimony to God's power," writes Armstrong.[90] Even if spectators did not have this strong religious experience while in attendance, they certainly could experience celebrity sightings both on and off the stage. Major celebrities and leaders in the Black community attended the production, including Eddie Murphy, Diana Ross, Patti La Belle, Dionne Warwick, Cissy Houston, Berry Gordy Jr., Reverend Jesse Jackson, and the Nation of Islam leader Minister Louis Farrakhan, who reportedly "was so inspired that he joined the cast on stage after the show and personally thanked and congratulated them."[91] In addition to offstage celebrities, *Mama, I Want to Sing* incorporated major Black singers of the day. The 1995 West End production at Cambridge Theatre, for example, showcased the "Queen of Funk" (i.e., Chaka Khan), who performed the role of Sister Carrie alongside singer Stacy Frances's Doris. The inclusion of Black divas onstage only enhances the plot and further justifies Doris's desire to break into the music industry.

The act of singing initially allows Doris a chance to express grief and heal her wounded spirit, and in so doing, creates space for Black queer feminist spectators to reflect on their girlhood, as well as feelings of grief and pleasure. In the 2020 production, the Narrator/Disc Jockey (Higginsen) stands in a booth high above the action of the play as if she were an omnipotent god, she reads Ephesians 4:1 from the Bible before announcing the Reverend Winter's funeral. While she never utters the word "depression," clearly Doris (Higginson) is experiencing a mental health crisis as a result of her father's premature death. Narrator/Disc Jockey states:

> Death is not easy to accept or to understand at any age. But for young Doris Winter, the loss of her love was simply devastating. She said it took one full year for her to begin to recover and it was only when she was convinced to get up out of his favorite chair, to come out of the bed, to come out of the house, to return to the church . . . and to the music.

Doris eventually returns to the land of the living but remains a shell of her former self.

Sister Carrie (Sandra Huff) intuitively understands Doris's pain and tries to reach her through song. Sister Carrie sings a gospel number with the choir and ends with an improvised "run" that encourages Doris to begin singing, "I Don't Worry About Tomorrow." This moment of encouragement and love from Sister Carrie helps Doris find her voice again. Mama (Tara Bramble) offers additional support when Doris becomes sad that she cannot belt notes like Sister Carrie. "You don't have to sing like that. Sing in your own sweet way," Mama advises. Doris responds by performing a run in her iconic whistle note, shaking her hips like Sister Carrie, and laughing at her antics. As to not leave any doubt in the audience's minds about Doris's newfound happiness, the Narrator/Disc Jockey states: "Doris said after that Sunday afternoon service at Mount Calvary that's when she began to open up and communicate and blossom." Singing and dancing allow Doris to finally express her emotions, move beyond the pain of death, and acknowledge her burgeoning sexuality. Witnessing Doris's transformation invites spectators to remember or vicariously experience girlhood and the healing power of song.

Mama, I Want to Sing refashions "the church" versus "the street" dichotomy through Doris's desire to break free from the church choir and embrace the sensual nature of secular music. At the beginning of the 2020 production of *Mama, I Want to Sing*, Doris (Higginson) appears as a child wearing her Sunday best. She sports pigtails and wears a modest light pink dress (in an exaggerated children's silhouette), white ankle socks with ruffles, and shiny black shoes. However, as she listens to secular music on the radio, she transforms into an independent young woman before the audience's very eyes. Narrator/Disc Jockey explains:

> Now, the teenage daughter wanted something more than to just sing at church her whole life. She wanted the glamor, and the travel, and the life of a professional singer. Now she knew that she would always have a message in her music and the church in her heart, but she thought it was time for her to spread her wings and fly on her own... and that's when she heard a different kind of music. The music outside of the church. She began to tap into the messages and music that she heard from the popular singers of that time.

In one of the most memorable moments of the musical, Narrator/Disc Jockey calls the names of legendary Black women performers whom Doris listens to on the radio: Dinah Washington, Lena Horne, Sarah Vaughan, and Billie Holiday. As ensemble cast members step off the risers to embody these blueswomen, they perform a few bars from their famous songs, including "God Blessed the Child Who's Got His Own." Afterward, Washington, Horne, Vaughan, and Holiday help Doris out of her children's clothes and replace them with black gloves, high-heeled shoes, and a poodle skirt. This moment creates a lineage, a passing of the baton from blueswomen of the past to a new generation of pop stars. This theatrical moment also marks a fracture in Doris's psyche. While she cherishes her gospel music foundation, she also desires freedom, mobility, and financial independence. For these reasons, she secretly forms "The Halos," puts on a fitted red gown, and performs "I'll Do Anything," an upbeat doo-wop style song a la The Supremes about loving a guy and being willing to do "anything he wants me to do because I love him" at the Apollo. Doris's new look, new sound, and the suggestive lyrics of her song mark her decision to fully embrace her sexuality.

Singing also becomes a means for Doris to defy her mother and take control of her own destiny. In many ways, Mama Winter embodies the values of the Black Church. When her husband was alive, she served as First Lady of Mt. Calvary Church and devoted her time and talents to cleaning the building and supporting her husband. His death not only causes the loss of a husband but also a means of providing for the Winter family. However, parishioners allow Mama to continue to perform the services she has always done for the church but now pay her an actual wage. Mama does not assume the ecclesiastical role of her husband but instead supports the deacons and new male reverend. She embraces a politics of respectability, raising Doris to present herself as morally and physically clean before the world. Mama also clearly loves Doris and supports her desire to sing gospel music but believes that secular music will destroy Doris. Their conflicting views come to a head when Mama discovers that Doris performed at the Apollo and wants to sign a contract to tour. After Doris performs the titular song, she has the following conversation with Mama:

MAMA: Doris, you better not sing another note.
Doris hits a high note with some hesitation.
MAMA: Doris, what did I say?
Doris hits a whistle note with confidence. Audience laughs.
MAMA: Not another note.

Doris hits a series of whistle notes that bring down the house. She exits to her bedroom.[92]

Later, Mama responds to Doris's defiance by using a series of questions to simultaneously emotionally manipulate and threaten her. Mama asks: "What are you trying to do, Doris?! Give me a heart attack? And another thing: I brought you into this world, Doris, and I will take you out!" Mama then shakes a rolled-up newspaper at Doris, threatening to whop her behind. When Doris reveals that her father encouraged her to follow her dreams and asks Mama for her blessing, Mama uses religious guilt to sway her, performing an emotionally charged rendition of the gospel classic, "Precious Lord (Take My Hand)." Doris then counters Mama's heartbreaking performance with another gospel classic, "His Eye Is on the Sparrow." In contrast to Mama's robust style of singing, Doris uses her gentle, angelic-sounding voice to sing the refrain: "I sing because I'm happy, / I sing because I'm free; / For his eye is on the sparrow, / And I know He watches me."[93] The theatre critic Richard Harrington writes that at this moment, Doris is "reminding her mother that she sings not for money but 'because I'm so happy and because my spirit is free'" and by the end of the performance, "mother and daughter are singing in counterpoint, connected even in their distance."[94] Doris's performance also reminds Mama that her ability to sing is a gift from God and that He will watch over her and protect her while she pursues her dream. Ultimately, singing becomes the means of freeing Doris from her mother's control of her life, allowing her to travel and experience the world. However, Mama cannot let Doris experience "freedom" without knowing how to navigate the dangers that await her outside the safety of the Black Church.

In keeping with the blueswoman tradition, Sister Carrie uses song to teach Doris how to navigate the negative influences of "the street" (i.e., the secular music industry). After Doris confides that The Halos have "won" a touring contract, Sister Carrie counters her naivete with a question of her own, asking: "What do you 'win' when you win Doris?" In other words, Sister Carrie urges Doris to think beyond her childish understanding of the "glamor" of touring to consider where her musical career could take her. After reminding Mama to be strong and assuring her that Doris will return home, Sister Carrie turns her attention back to Doris. "She needs to know some stuff. She's still wet behind the ears," Sister Carrie tells Mama. Sister Carrie then promises to tell Doris "things about life" and performs, "Know When to Leave the Party," an upbeat, catchy bluesy song. As she sings about the fun of parties but the importance of knowing when to leave, a group of ensemble members enter the stage and dance as if at a party. Intermixed within her song, Sister Carrie warns: "Now, Doris, after the concert, there'll be parties, gatherings, receptions, that kind of thing. Now, you can go to the party but you never, never let the party go to you." Later in the song, Sister Carrie continues to advise, stating: "Doris, there's another side of the party." With these words, a Black male actor begins to dance suggestively, performing pelvic-like thrusts against a lone female ensemble member, and Sister Carrie warns: "This.... He ain't never seen a paycheck." The female ensemble member then takes off her wig and hits the man dancing suggestively and Sister Carrie warns: "Don't you ever go to a party and end up last." While this comical moment certainly provides much-needed levity after the previously contentious scene between Mama and Doris, Sister Carrie's advice is no laughing matter, especially in light of the MeToo movement (2017–), which has helped bring greater awareness to sexual harassment and sexual abuse within the television, theatre, film, and music industries. These efforts have brought many of the sexual abusers to justice for their crimes committed against Blackgirls, including the singer, songwriter, and record producer R. Kelly.[95] Thus, the need to protect talented Blackgirls from predatory businessmen remains just as essential today as when *Mama, I Want to Sing* premiered forty years ago.

Higginsen and Wydro may show Doris choosing "the street" (i.e., the secular music industry), but they also take great pains to assure the audience that Doris maintains the values instilled by "the church." Higginsen and Wydro use Narrator/Disc Jockey as a vehicle to deliver this moral message. During the final moments of the musical, Narrator/Disc Jockey shares the fate of Doris with the audience:

> Doris began to write, arrange, and produce all her own albums. Her next album was entitled "High Standards" and indeed, Doris did set high standards, especially in herself and her career in the performing arts. Doris was rewarded handsomely for her gifts, her talents, and many years of hard work. On her walls were six gold records, four platinum albums, and three Grammys but more than that, she had a dream and a vision just as Sister Carrie predicted that she would. Doris Winter went back home to 126th Street in Harlem, USA and there she began to build and to rebuild. She started with a daycare center for working mothers, a recreation home for senior citizens, and a music school for gifted children. So, it really is Doris's

> courage, her conviction, her gifts, her talents, her generosity that we here tonight at this radio station, WVHW reach out to salute Miss Doris Winter.

Narrator/Disc Jockey's monologue praises Doris for upholding a politics of respectability. Despite the temptations of "the street," Doris maintains her spiritual morality, work ethic, family values, and commitment to the Black community of Harlem. Furthermore, her financial success allows her to cultivate young talent and help the most vulnerable within the Black community, namely working mothers, the elderly, and children.

Mama, I Want to Sing celebrates the music, the history, and spirit of Black America, and in so doing, demonstrates how popular music is an *outgrowth* of Black Church music. While the actual Doris Troy did not achieve the level of critical success as the fictional Doris Winter, she did become known by her fans as the "Mama of Soul" and enjoyed a long and successful career in the music industry until her death in 2004.[96] Her career serves as a reminder of the important role the Black Church has had in cultivating the talents of Black singers—especially women. In his review of *Mama I Want to Sing*, Harrington writes that "Black church music has been a breeding and proving ground for countless singers. Many have chosen to remain in the tradition, but popular music has also been blessed by those who have crossed over, from Sam Cooke, Ray Charles and Aretha Franklin to Jennifer Holiday and Philip Bailey. And you only have to hear genuine gospel to realize that secular and sacred music share much in terms of technique and performance, and that pop owes a huge debt to the black church."[97] *Mama, I Want to Sing* encourages spectators to celebrate the rich tradition that is Black music—in all its forms. Higginsen remembers: "We want to show Black theatre, Black music, Black culture, Black history . . . and its contribution to the American musical landscape and we tell that story through *Mama, I Want to Sing* and that's why it's lasted forty years. . . It's even more important *now* to celebrate the ancestors, the music, the spirit, and the culture."[98] Higginsen and Wydro continue to share this vision by adapting the musical into other mediums.

After the success of *Mama, I Want to Sing*, Higginsen and Wydro continued to reimagine their original source material, creating musical sequels, a book adaption, and a film adaption based off of the musical. In 1990, Higginsen and Wydro introduced the musical's sequel, *Mama, I Want To Sing: Part II*, which captures Doris Winter's marriage and birth of her first child. Higginsen followed this musical sequel with a 1992 young adult novel with the same title. With the support of writer Tonya Bolden, the novel not only expands upon major plot points of the musical but also Doris's interiority. Told from the third-person perspective, readers get a glimpse into Doris's feelings of anger, guilt, and eventually numbness after her father's passing.[99] The novel also highlights Doris's developmental transition from a child to a teenage girl, including her confusion brought on by physical changes.[100] A highlight of the novel happens within the safety of Doris's bedroom. Her imaginative play allows her to experience the thrill of performance and transform herself from a "church girl" into a sexy diva. Higginsen and Holden write:

> Evenings when Geraldine was at church, Doris turned on her radio, pulled out her treasure chest, and transformed herself into a star. Her lips became flamingo red; her cheekbones, a swatch of deep rose. She'd fling a long scarf around her neck, tie a sash around her waist. She strolled, sauntered, and switched around her room in her three-inch heels. She'd strike poses in her doorway, trying hard to look as sultry as Dorothy Dandridge or Hazel Scott. She purred like Eartha Kitt. Sometimes she stood before the mirror and did a little bump and grind. Then she'd stand straight and tall—right foot pointed out, hands on her hips, chin up, cheek sucked in—batting her eyelashes away.[101]

Within the sanctity of her own room, Doris performs her burgeoning sexuality. The mirror and music help transform and she experiences pleasure from her sultry movements. The reader, of course, also experiences vicarious pleasure by witnessing her private, sexual acts. After publishing the novel, Higginsen and Wydro produced *Born to Sing: Mama III* in 1996. This third musical installment depicts Doris's international tour and her teenage daughter's desire to become a singer. Finally, in 2012 Higginsen and Wydro turned to film, adapting *Mama, I Want to Sing* into a musical drama released straight to DVD. Charles Randolph-Wright directed the film adaptation, which loosely follows the story of Doris Troy. The film stars real-life R&B singer Ciara, who takes on the role of Amara Winter, who dreams of becoming an R&B singer. As with the musical, Amara's mother Lilian Winter (Lynn Whitfield) takes over as pastor after her husband's death and advises her daughter against following her dream until Sister Carrie (Patti LaBelle) intervenes.[102]

Higginsen and Wydro's expert marketing of their secular "lost faith-regained plot" would usher in a new wave of gospel musicals in the

1980s–1990s. The theatre historian Samuel A. Hay writes that these new plays often feature "young female characters who . . . stopped believing" and "the Sacred/Gospel musical, then, existed solely because producers sought to capitalize on the strong appeal of both gospel music and theater."[103] Rashida Z. Shaw McMahon also credits the successful efforts of Higginsen, Wydro, and Shelly Garrett for popularizing what would become known as Urban Theatre, the Black Circuit, or the Contemporary Chitlin Circuit. McMahon writes:

> Early circuit playwrights such as Vy Higgensen [sic] and Ken Wydro, creators of the popular musical *Mama I Want to Sing* (1983), and Shelly Garrett, author *Beauty Shop* (1989), set a number of important precedents for the more recent wave [of performances], achieving commercial success, wide recognition, and loyalty among African American audiences, extended runs, and consistent tour bookings. They likewise laid the groundwork for the independent, community-based nature of these productions, in which playwrights continue to serve as their own directors and producers. Financial support, then as it does now, came largely from the pockets of the playwrights themselves and from family, friends, and interested community members.[104]

Higginsen, Wydro, and Garrett's financial models and aesthetics—which include "highly interactive theatre environments in which audiences were seen singing, dancing, and engaging in dialogue with performers, from their seats"—created the foundation for playwrights such as Tyler Perry, David Talbert, Je'Caryous Johnson, and Gary Guidry to become household names.[105] Angela Barrow-Dunlap, however, is among the very few Black women playwrights to successfully break into the male-dominated Contemporary Chitlin Circuit theatre.

Church Girl

Barrow-Dunlap's *Church Girl* (2010) introduces audiences to Emily Franklin, the daughter of the Redeeming Love Church pastor, Lamar Franklin. Similar to Doris Winter, Emily is at a crossroads in her life, performing in the church choir but dreaming of becoming a professional singer. When a church scandal erupts and her father is sent to prison, her mother Maya leads the congregation and raises Emily to value the church and education. Emily initially obeys, attending church choir and college to become a nurse. However, Emily when she meets a club owner named Jacob, she becomes seduced by his promises of fame and attempts to have one foot in "the church" and the other on "the streets" as an exotic dancer. Eventually, Pastor Maya, Emily's grandmother, and other churchwomen gather, storm Jacob's club, and use gospel music and the power of Christ to save Emily from Jacob's control. Pastor Maya then delivers a soul-stirring sermon to remind Emily of her divinity, which allows her to rediscover her faith and love of Jesus. The musical concludes with Emily finding redemption in the bosom of the church, an ending that suggests a need to cultivate religion within the hearts of the rising generation of Blackgirls.

Barrow-Dunlap's concerns about a decline in intergenerational faith are not unfounded. The 2021 Pew Research Center report attests to a decline in religious worship among young Black adults. A survey with more than 8,600 Black adults across the United States found that "young Black adults are less religious and less engaged in Black churches than older generations. Black millennials and members of Generation Z are less likely to rely on prayer, less likely to have grown up in Black churches, and less likely to say religion is an important part of their lives. Fewer attend church services, and those who *do* attend are less likely to go to predominantly Black congregation."[106] In terms of a numerical breakdown, "about one-in-five Black Americans (21%) are not affiliated with any religion and instead identify as atheist, agnostic, or 'nothing in particular,' and this phenomenon is increasing by generation: Roughly three-in-ten Black GenZers (28%) and Millennials (33%) in the survey are religiously unaffiliated, compared with just 11% of Baby Boomers and 5% of those in the Silent Generation."[107] Since Black women make up the majority of congregations within the Black Church, it's pragmatic for Barrow-Dunlap to consider the temptations, struggles, and faith journeys of Blackgirls. Barrow-Dunlap remembers: "For me, finding the balance between religion or church and enjoying life as a young person is a balance that we are constantly striving to achieve. . . . Young people have to understand that it is important to set boundaries and limitations for themselves and know those limitations. In the meantime, our parents, grandparents and pastors must help us define those limitations and help us understand that certain limitations in life are healthy and good."[108] Since Blackgirls are the future of the Black Church, it becomes paramount that parents, grandparents, and pastors set limits to ensure the spiritual and mental health of the next generation.

Before the debut of *Church Girl* in 2010, Barrow-Dunlap had already established her reputation as "a pioneer of Urban Theatre," having written and produced gospel plays for more than twenty-five years.[109] Indeed, *Church Girl* followed hits such as *If These Hips Could Talk*, *My Brother Marvin*, *Real Men Pray*, and *Why Good Girls Like Bad Boyz*, considered the "highest-grossing urban stage play of all time."[110] Barrow-Dunlap serves as president and founder of Faith Entertainment in Detroit, Michigan, an organization that allows her to produce her own musical works. "We literally had to invent this genre . . . There was no training or classes for this type of theatre. We had to invent and learn all at the same time," remembers Barrow-Dunlap.[111]After learning on her feet and establishing a following with audiences, Barrow-Dunlap produced and toured *Church Girl* across the United States and Canada from 2010–2011 before releasing a filmed recording on DVD in 2012. The recorded production was directed by Reuben Yabuku and featured an all-star cast of popular Black performers, including NAACP Image Award winner and *Tyler Perry's House of Payne* star Demetria McKinney (Emily Franklin), R&B singer and songwriter A'ngela Winbush (Maya Franklin), Emmy-winning actor Sean Blakemore (Jacob), Hollywood actress Robin Givens ("Cat" Jones), Grammy Award-winning gospel singer Karen Clark Sheard (Valerie), and Az Yet R&B group member Anthony "Tony" Grant (Lamar Franklin). Barrow-Dunlap hoped that this all-star cast could convey her vision and help spectators understand the message of the production.

Barrow-Dunlap wrote *Church Girl* for her ideal spectators: everyday Black women. She explains the "message" of *Church Girl* and the importance of Black women spectators in a 2010 press release. Barrow-Dunlap remembers:

> This is much more than just another production to me. . . . There is power and purpose in this piece, mainly because it was born out of the true story of someone very dear and close to me. But also because it will touch the hearts of so many hurting women. Women around the country are responding to the message of "Church Girl" because it resonates so powerfully within them . . . it's their story. Most every woman has at some point in her life given in to temptation, and as a result felt trapped. "Church Girl" simply says that you can choose to be free.[112]

The content of *Church Girl* not only entertains but also educates spectators about the importance of Blackgirl faith, agency, and mental health. In so doing, *Church Girl* functions as a "sermon" of sorts for everyday Black women spectators, who become a "congregation" during the performance. The poet and spoken word artist Dwain Wellington expresses similar sentiments about the musical's "message" and staging practices in his review of a Toronto production at the Sony Centre for the Performing Arts on September 3, 2011. "With scenes that often threatened to turn the audience into a congregation of worshipers, 'Church Girl' accomplishes the sometimes daunting task of pleasing theater goers [sic] at the very core. There are truths that you will recognize, truths you may want to shy away from. This story does not allow you to hide in the shadow of ignorance. More than quality entertainment, 'Church Girl' educates. The play is a social commentary of the possible mental state of our youth and the slippery slope done which they can slide," writes Wellington.[113] Thus, if the content of *Church Girl* acts as a sermon, telling the oft-ignored stories of Blackgirls who experience strife, the staging ensures that spectators bear witness to this "religious service." *Church Girl* celebrates the collective power of Black churchwomen by showcasing their ability to lead this service.

Figure 2.5 Gia Wyre (Mother), Wanda Nero-Butler (Regina), and Karen Clark Sheard (Valerie) stand, with Kourtney Lenton (Young Emily), Melanee Felton (Young Amber), and Damoli Harris (Young Kaleta) kneeling in *Church Girl* (2010). Film recording directed by Reuben Yabuku, still image courtesy of the author.

Church Girl presents Black churchwomen as god-like figures who wield gospel song to tend to the spiritual needs of Blackgirls. Barrow-Dunlap establishes the power and leadership of Black churchwomen within the very first moments of the musical. The filmed recording begins with a church service. Spectators are met with a striking image of three Blackgirls—a twelve-year-old Emily (Kourtney Lenton), Amber (Melanee Felton), and Kaleta (Damoli Harris)—facing the audience, on their knees in prayer (see Figure 2.5). Three choir members—Emily's grandmother named "Mother" (Gia Wyre), Emily's Aunt Regina (Wanda Nero-Butler), and a family member named Valerie (Karen Clark Sheard)—stand behind the girls, clothed in white robes with red stoles, and appear as if they represented the Holy Trinity. The three churchwomen bless and anoint the girls, singing a gospel prayer: "Holy / Most holy everlasting Father / Father we ask that you send your love on these young children / Lord, we ask that you cover / Let the angels walk beside them, Lord."[114] Afterward, the young girls harmonize a gospel rendition of the classic "Jesus Loves Me" alongside the church choir. The churchwomen's active protection of the Blackgirls—surrounding them with love, attention, and the truth of their divinity as children of God—stands in stark contrast to the Deacon Quartet, performed by Vincent Kelley, Jwyanza Gaines, Darrin Patterson, and Eric Deon Taylor. They sit on the front pew throughout the majority of the musical, passively looking on when temptation and trouble arise for the three girls. Afterward, Emily's voiceover discusses her love of singing and the important role the circle of women played in her childhood. "Mom always warned us that our gift could either be a blessing or a curse and I didn't understand it then. But looking back on it, I'm so glad my family prayed for me" Emily states. Gospel song provides a weapon for Black women, and if wielded correctly, offers protection for the rising generation of Blackgirls.

Church Girl also encourages spectators—through sermons, gospel music, testimony, and dance—to invite Jesus into their hearts. Emily's voiceover reveals that time has passed since the three girls formed a group called "Promise" and that she and Kelta continue to sing in the church choir. Unfortunately, Amber slowly stops attending church and choir practices. Emily, however, shares that everyone is welcome at Redeeming Love Church and encourages all to enter her mother's ministry. "Everyone is somebody and Jesus is the reason why," Emily states. At this point, Emily proudly boasts of her mother's efforts to restore the sanctity of the church. "Nobody preach like my mama," Emily states. In contrast to Mama, from *Mama I Want to Sing*,

Maya does not take a secondary role upon her pastor husband's departure. Instead, Maya uses her agency to do the unusual: she takes on the preacher's mantle to lead and guide the spiritual and temporal well-being of the Black community. Even today, while it is the norm for Black women to head church committees, it is a rarity for Black women to be senior pastors at predominately Black churches. A trailblazer in her own right, Pastor Maya, dressed in red robes, red stilettos, and a diamond-incrusted cross, delivers a soul-stirring sermon using the rhythms of the Black preacher, eliciting call-and-response from the congregation. In discussing the Second Coming, Pastor Maya repeats the phrase, "Be ready," as found in the Gospel of Matthew (24: 44), and the congregation responds, "Amen!" Afterward, the church choir and soloists perform a spirited number, "Since Jesus Came Into Your Life," as four adolescent Blackgirls dance. Barefoot and dressed in modest dresses, the four Blackgirls perform a "ring shout"—they form a circle, stomping their feet, leaping in the air, and clapping their hands while the soloists and choir perform their gospel number. Once the dance concludes, four women soloists look directly at the spectators and share their testimonies of Jesus in between belting a medley of classic gospel songs, including, "I'm a Soldier in the Army of the Lord." When combined, this opening church service performance leaves no doubt that spectators are the intended congregation. As such, *Church Girl* asks the spectators-congregation to bear witness to Emily's temptation, her fall from grace, and the redeeming love of Christ.

Church Girl warns spectators about the temptations of Satan and his desire to acquire the most vital force within the Black community: Blackgirls. Jacob (Sean Blakemore), a seedy night club owner, is the physical embodiment of Satan. He initially appears as a charming, well-spoken, and charitable businessman but the sinister-sounding music that accompanies his entrance suggests that perhaps appearances are deceiving. Amber, who has abandoned the church choir to work for Jacob, introduces Emily to him as a man who can jump-start their music career at his Sapphire Night Club. When Pastor Maya appears and interrupts these plans, Jacob flatters her, stating: "Well, I must say, there's nothing that compares to a strong Black woman." He then gives her ministry a check for $5,000 and quotes the Bible to demonstrate his churchgoing façade. Once Pastor Maya exits, he turns his attention toward Emily, insisting: "The world needs to hear your voice, Emily, and I can make that happen" and hands her his business card. His pious and charming demeanor belies his true desire: to lure innocent Blackgirls into a life of drugs and prostitution. For example, he convinces a poor and uneducated Amber that she is special and deserving of a glamorous lifestyle. He manipulates Amber into believing that stripping and prostitution will allow her to acquire the finer things in life, including dining at expensive restaurants and wearing designer shoes. He also convinces Cat to act as his "House Mother" by managing his club and sex workers. She, too, does so under the belief that Jacob loves her until she realizes that Emily has replaced her. Jacob's callous treatment causes Cat to threaten suicide. Finally, Jacob uses the promise of fame to break Emily from her close bond with her family and the church. Eventually, he uses drugs to dull her mind and manipulate her to not just sing at his club, but also strip and perform sex work against her will. In other words, audiences learn that Jacob, like Satan, understands the insecurities, desires, and strengths of Blackgirls. By striping Blackgirls of their self-worth and perhaps even their lives, Jacob takes away the future power of the Black community.

Church Girl also reveals what many Black queer feminist spectators already know: that preachers can be a wolf in sheep's clothing. Emily's flashback reveals the devastating impact that her father's choices have had on her family. *Church Girl* shows Young Emily sitting on a bench outside of Redeeming Love Church with her father (see Figure 2.6). As with the Reverend Winter in *Mama, I Want to Sing*, Pastor Lamar Franklin (Anthony "Tony" Grant) encourages Emily's love of singing. In one of the most endearing moments in the musical, Pastor Franklin teaches her how to sing a gospel rendition of the classic hymn, "Oh, How I Love Jesus." When they finish practicing, the pair walks hand-in-hand into the sanctuary and Pastor Franklin proudly watches Young Emily perform a solo with the church choir. Unfortunately, this heartwarming scene comes to an abrupt end with the entrance of Reporter (Bryant Woods), who confronts Pastor Franklin about owing back child support. When Pastor Franklin denies the accusation, he is confronted by a visibly pregnant parishioner who questions when he will leave his wife and be with her, as well as a second parishioner who demands he pay her child support. As a married man of God, Pastor Franklin has not only broken his marital vows but also his sacred duty to protect his flock from harm. Instead, he exploits the most vulnerable among his congregation: single Black women. Within a few minutes of this discovery, Maya faints, the congregation demands answers, and a police officer arrests Pastor Franklin for acquiring $70,000 worth of unpaid child support. This event, which led to Pastor Franklin's absence in Emily's life, had a profound effect on her, making her vulnerable to the machinations of any man who offers her affection.

Figure 2.6 Kourtney Lenton (Young Emily) and Anthony "Tony" Grant (Lamar) in *Church Girl* (2010). Film recording directed by Reuben Yabuku, still image courtesy of the author.

Lamar, the former Pastor Franklin, also provides an example of the positive change that can occur through repentance. When he asks why Emily she is at the Sapphire Night Club, she explains how difficult it was for her to "worship a father" only to realize that he didn't love her. Lamar admits that he was "selfish, arrogant, and self-centered," that he should have protected her but failed, and would love her forgiveness. Emily, however, remains unmoved until he breaks into a gospel ballad entitled, "Little Girl." Against the backdrop of an organ and drums, Lamar sings a soulful plea for Emily to abandon the Sapphire Night Club, come home with him, and finish singing their favorite song together. She responds by pretending as if she'll forgive him, pauses and says "Go to hell," and walks away. In addition to praying to God (through gospel song) for forgiveness, Lamar has to literally stand between Emily and a bullet for her to forgive him. While Lamar finds forgiveness for his past predatory behavior, spectators never learn the extent of the harm that he has inflicted upon his parishioners and unacknowledged/unsupported children. *What of their fate? How can Blackgirls survive the devastation wrought by selfish, arrogant, and self-centered Black clergymen?*

Emily's journey not only reveals the dangers of "the streets" but also the importance of Black families, friendship, and testimony in the lives of Blackgirls. Flashbacks of Young Emily sitting beside her father show how important this relationship is to her. He tells her that he wants her to know that she is "beautiful" and that her mother did her hair "very, very nice" before complimenting her singing. In this moment, her father not only reinforces respectability politics (i.e., she receives praise for her grooming), but also socializes her to believe in her beauty and talent. As he teaches her how to sing, he provides advice about navigating life's challenges. "Now, you did that kind of easy but let me tell you: in life, everything's not that easy. But I'll tell you what: if you trust in the Lord with all your heart—'lean not to your own understanding but in all your ways acknowledge Jesus,' I guarantee you—He will direct your path." Without her father's guidance, Emily struggles to cope when life becomes difficult. Rather than tell Pastor Maya she's working at the Sapphire Night Club to jump-start her professional career as a singer, she lies and says she had to work a double shift at the hospital. When Pastor Maya reminds her of her house rules (i.e., Emily must attend choir practice and nursing school at Howard University), Emily runs away from home and into "the streets." Emily's estrangement from her parents causes her to seek refuge with Jacob at the Sapphire Night Club. Emily's church friend Kaleta visits her at the club and tries to get her to leave with her but Emily refuses and accuses her of being jealous. Kaleta, who represents Blackgirls who stay on the straight and narrow path, tries to convince Emily of gospel truths, stating: "That's not love, it's lust… it's manipulation! Emily, a man who loves you is going to respect you, honor you, and protect you… He's not going to defile you or compromise your integrity. You can do better than Jacob. You deserve better, Emily. You are so much more than this. Emily, you belong to God. Amber belongs to God. I belong to God." Before Kaleta leaves, she reminds Emily of Pastor Maya's sermon, based on Romans 6:23. "She taught me that we have choices and that 'the wages of sin is death, but the gift of God is eternal life.' I choose life. Choose life, Emily," Kaleta states. These gospel truths may be spoken to Emily, but the message is just as important for Black women spectators to hear. When Pastor Maya finally convinces Emily to return to the fold, she cannot separate herself from Jacob's power and attempts to live in both worlds. Jacob, after all, provides her with drugs and affection, constantly reminding her: "I'm here for you. I didn't leave you like your father left you. All you see, all I do is for you, baby" (see Figure 2.7). Emily meets other Blackgirls who have been hardened by living in Jacob's den of sin, including Mystical, a menacing gun-toting stripper who tries to beat up

Figure 2.7 Sean Blakemore (Jacob) and Demetria McKinney (Emily) in *Church Girl* (2010). Film recording directed by Reuben Yabuku, still image courtesy of the author.

Amber for stealing her clients. Emily's road to a sure death at the hands of drugs or gun violence only comes to a halt when the churchwomen intervene.

Church Girl concludes the same way the musical began: depicting Black churchwomen as the most powerful force on earth; fully capable of bringing Satan to his knees. Before their arrival, Jacob has complete control of Emily—mind, body, and spirit. For example, when she grabs a fallen gun during Jacob and Amber's fight, he only gestures with his finger and she hands him the gun, with full knowledge that he will likely kill Amber for trying to steal his stash of drugs. Emily and Amber plead for mercy, but just like Satan, Jacob requires total submission. He orders Amber to "bow down" and rants at Emily: "After all I've done for you! You try and bite the hand that feeds you. I created you from nothing to something. Did you really think that you and this common street thug could pull this on me?" Enraged by their friendship and resistance, Jacob grabs Emily by the hair and threatens to kill her. Luckily, Pastor Maya, Mother, Regina, Valerie, and an unnamed churchwoman enter singing and cast out the demon in Jacob in Jesus's name. As he falls down, the churchwomen circle him, point their fingers, and sing, "You're lie!" The churchwomen continue to sing/pray while Jacob lies crumbled on the ground, trying unsuccessfully to rise, assault them, or use his gun (see Figure 2.8). As Jacob writhes in pain, Mother belts: "We claim victory in the name of the Father, in the name of the Son, in the name of the Holy Ghost!" Unfortunately, Jacob does manage to rise, throw Emily on the ground, and aim his gun at Emily. Pastor Franklin miraculously appears and pleads with Jacob: "You and I will handle this man to man." An undeterred Jacob responds: "If you'd handled it like a man she wouldn't be here in the first place." Lamar, in turn, admits his failures, positions himself in front of Emily, and advises her to take back her will: "You got to tell the devil 'no. Tell him 'no.'" However, Jacob doesn't take Emily's "no" for an answer, insisting that she bow before him. Knowing that he will not release Emily, the churchwomen return to their singing and, in the name of Jesus, permanently incapacitate Jacob as the sound of police sirens play. While this interaction shows Lamar risking his life for Emily, Jacob's admonishment also acknowledges his failures. Ultimately, it is the churchwomen who use gospel song to cast out Jacob/Satan's "lies" and save Emily.

Figure 2.8 Gia Wyre (Mother), Angela Winbush (Pastor Maya), Wanda Nero-Butler (Regina), Demetria McKinney (Emily), Teisha Jaretta Lott-Brown (Amber), Zeeky Minnis (Kaleta), and Karen Clark Sheard (Valerie) surround Sean Blakemore (Jacob) in *Church Girl* (2010). Film recording directed by Reuben Yabuku, still image courtesy of the author.

As heroes of the tale, the churchwomen offer Emily and the spectators a message of religious "truth." Pastor Maya begins this message by embracing Emily, telling her she loves her, apologizes, and praises Jesus for her safe return. At no point do the churchwomen condemn Emily for "sinning." Rather, they rejoice and welcome her home, with Pastor Maya telling Emily, "Thank God Jesus spared us! Go ahead, baby. Be who you are in Christ. Mom's proud of you." Aunt Regina then expresses womanist "truth" to Emily, helping her (and the audience) understand that Jesus loves her and that His love is redeeming and inclusive. "Oh, how God loves you! Do you see what He did for you? While you were yet in your sin, He kept you. Who wouldn't serve a God like that? God's love is redeeming, it's inclusive, and the best thing about the love of God is. You don't have to do anything to earn it. It just is. He loves you, baby. Talk to Him. Talk to Him. Just as you are," Regina states. Emily struggles at first, but eventually sings a song/prayer about her blessed Savior, entitled "I Surrender." The musical ends with Kaleta, Amber, and the churchwomen joining Emily in song. This didactic ending acts as a sermon, reminding Barrow-Dunlap's ideal spectators, or everyday Black women, that they too are loved unconditionally, just as they are. This message of love, acceptance, and community would prove particularly powerful for Black queer feminist spectators who all too often do not have the privilege of hearing this message.

Collectively, *Prodigal Sister*; *Your Arms Too Short to Box With God; Mama, I Want to Sing*; and *Church Girl* demonstrate the faith, agency, and power of Blackgirls. Gospel music, in turn, becomes a vehicle for self-expression and the articulation of gospel truths, including the beauty and divine heritage of Blackgirls. These truths, which articulate a womanist sensibilities, can counteract the effects of religious violence. In addition to centering the desires, struggles, and faith journeys of Blackgirls, Black women artists have also used musical theatre to celebrate their wit and imagination, a topic which is explored in more detail in the following chapter.

3
Blackgirl Wit and Imagination

I'm nine years old. I cannot alter what I have seen. I am marked. An unintentional spectator of rape. I spend the next thirty years trying to forget by imagining alternative realities: I walk in the bedroom, and my uncle is actually wrestling with my twelve-year-old sister. I don't turn the doorknob to enter my sister's bedroom. I walk through the door with a knife, toss my uncle off my sister, and stab him straight through the heart.

Of course, none of these scenarios take place. They are not wrestling. I do turn the doorknob. I do not have a knife. My imagination, though strong, cannot compensate for my eighty-pound body and tiny hands. I cannot overpower my uncle, and he threatens to kill me if I tell anyone. There is only *before* and *after*.

I gaze. I lie. I tell.
I am no longer a child.

My uncle is convicted of statutory rape and serves a few months in jail. Afterward, he continues to live his life, leaving my family in shambles. I help raise their daughter, who is my biological niece and cousin.

Their silence shatters my world. Their silence lets me know that my sister is not the first in my family to survive rape and incest. Their silence teaches me an important lesson: Blackgirls are not safe, even inside their own homes.

A few years later, I learn that my home truth resonates with a greater historical truth: Blackgirls have *always* been vulnerable to the many forms of violence. Charlene A. Carruthers writes that although this violence occurs structurally and interpersonally, both levels impede living life with dignity.[1] "Poverty is violence. Lack of autonomy over reproductive decisions is violence. Stripping away access to cultural practices and traditions that allow us to live with our human dignity is violence. Allowing rape to happen generation after generation is violence," writes Carruthers.[2] Blackgirls are particularly vulnerable to these forms of violence because they lack the protection of hegemonic masculinity. By "hegemonic masculinity," I refer to hierarchies

Black Queer Girlhood on the Musical Theatre Stage. La Donna L. Forsgren, Oxford University Press.
 DOI: 10.1093/9780197661444.003.0004

that use ideologies of gender, class, sexuality, age, and race in opposition to one another to empower those closest to dominant social norms (i.e., wealthy white heterosexual men), and subordinate those furthest away from social norms (i.e., Black and Indigenous men).[3] While society may place Black people in subordinate positions, we have always had the ability to counter these narratives by using the Black imagination. Carruthers writes that "we've never accepted that the bottom rung is where we will remain. And that's where the black imagination lives. It lives in our ability to create alternatives, whether those are alternative economies, alternative family structures, or something else entirely."[4] Thus, even while Blackgirls remain on the bottom rung of the social ladder, they *can* and *do* use their imagination and wit to resist their subordination, reaffirm their humanity, and create new liberatory possibilities.

Black women writers have long understood Blackgirl wit and imagination allow Blackgirls to survive the many forms of violence in their lives. Early writers such as Harriet Jacobs exposed the horrors of chattel slavery through the plight of Blackgirls. *Incidents in the Life of a Slave Girl* (1861) provides some clues about the precarious position of fifteen- or sixteen-year-old Blackgirls, describing their situation as "prematurely knowing" violence. Jacobs writes:

> Soon she will learn to tremble when she hears the master's footfall. She will be compelled to realize she is no longer a child. If God bestowed beauty upon her, it will prove her greatest curse. That which commands admiration in the white woman only hastens the degradation of the female slave.... I cannot tell how much I suffered in the presence of these wrongs, nor how I am still pained by retrospect. My master met me at every turn, reminding me that I belonged to him, and swearing by heaven and earth that he would compel me to submit to him.[5]

Her account reveals that Blackgirls survived hostile conditions by creating strategies of resistance from an early age. For example, Jacobs remembers outmaneuvering her white slave owner by sleeping on the floor of her mistress' bedroom, avoiding interactions, and turning to her grandmother for protection. Jacobs's ability to forge a sense of self despite suffering psychological trauma and degradation provides one of the few glimpses into the interiority of nineteenth-century Blackgirls. Her account of "prematurely knowing" degradation and sexual violence to the world helped stir readers to actively protest the brutality of slavery.

Early Black women writers used Blackgirls as a symbol of their Black abolitionist agendas. In her groundbreaking study, *Black Girlhood in the Nineteenth Century* (2016), the Black girlhood studies scholar Nazera Sadiq Wright notes that while both men and women writers used the image of Blackgirls to further their political agendas, Black women writers departed from the flat, idealized representations. "Black women writers tended to focus on the interiority of the girls. They wrote about their inner thoughts, their plans, their dreams and aspirations. They emphasized the determination and grit black girls exhibited as they formed successful strategies for fighting and rejecting oppression. They outlined trajectories that led to adulthoods that did not necessarily include wifehood and motherhood," writes Wright.[6] Contemporary Black women musical theatre artists continue the tradition of using Blackgirls as a symbol of Black America and, in so doing, reveal how anti-Blackness and gendered violence are anything but a "new" phenomenon.

Following the tradition of their literary foremothers, musical theatre artists Kirsten Childs and Aisha Rahman used their creative talent to illuminate the interior lives of Blackgirls, often privileging their transition from what Wright describes as "youthful childhood" to "prematurely knowing" violence. In Childs's *The Bubbly Black Girl Sheds Her Chameleon Skin* (2000), California native Viveca (also known as Bubbly) discovers the violence reaped upon Blackgirls as she reads a 1963 newspaper account of white supremacist terrorists bombing the 16th St. Baptist Church in Birmingham, Alabama. This real-life event left dozens injured and four Blackgirls—all between eleven and fourteen years—dead. These highly publicized murders awaken Viveca to the brutality of racism. Childs continues exploring Black girlhood with her more recent musical, *Bella: An American Tall Tale* (2017), which delves into the interior psyche of a nineteenth-century Blackgirl storyteller and fugitive named Bella. Forced to leave her Tupelo, Mississippi home with the threat of incarceration or death looming, fifteen-year-old Bella boards a train heading out West to evade arrest for a crime she did not commit.[7] Any distinction between fact and fiction becomes blurred as Bella's tales of adventure and romance come to life. As Bella's stories—filled with song, action, and humor—become more real than her present reality, audiences discover her innermost desire for love, family, and safety. Rahman's biographical blues musical *The Tale of Madame Zora* (1986) also engages with Black girlhood through the life of anthropologist, novelist, and playwright Zora Neale Hurston (1891–1960).[8] Using the framework of the "annual lie Swapping Festival," community members compete to tell the best account of events in Hurston's life. As narrators perform their folk tales and relive Hurston's resistance to violence, they create multiple visions of Hurston's interiority, leaving her legacy as rich and complex as her writings. Collectively, these contemporary musicals act as a bridge between the historical struggles of nineteenth- and early twentieth-century Blackgirls and the violence Blackgirls encounter today.

Black queer feminist spectators witnessing the works of Childs and Rahman can understand the irony that the historical violence reaped upon Black people—especially Blackgirls—has never gone away. While the US legislature eradicated chattel slavery and many of the twenty-first-century Jim Crow laws, Blackgirls, including queer, straight, cis, trans, or otherwise, have yet to experience the freedom of moving about the world unencumbered by violence and death. The Sexual Assault Support Center Inc. reports that Blackgirls and women remain particularly vulnerable to sexual assault and homicide with the following statistics:

- 4 in 10 black women have been subjected to intimate partner violence in their lifetimes.
- Black women comprise 8% of the U.S. population, but account for 20% of the intimate partner homicide victims.
- African American girls and women 12 years old and older experienced higher rates of rape and sexual assault than white, Asian, and Latina girls and women from 2005–2010.
- 40–60% of black women report being subjected to coercive sexual contact by age 18.[9]

These statistics are truly alarming and only become further compounded for queer and trans Blackgirls.

While the murders of transwomen of color have more recently skyrocketed to an epidemic, the sad truth is that queer Blackgirls have always been targets of heteropatriarchal violence. When I consider this terrible reality, the names of three Blackgirls always come to mind: Marsha P. Johnson (1945–1992), Sakia Gunn (1987–2003), and Shelley Hilliard (1992–2011). The body of Johnson, a pioneering LGBTQ activist and drag queen, was found floating along the Hudson River following the 1992 Pride Parade. Gunn, a fifteen-year-old lesbian, refused the advances of a group of Black men while waiting at a bus stop with friends in Newark, New Jersey. When she told them she was gay, Richard McCullough stabbed her in the chest, and she died of her injuries. Hilliard, a nineteen-year-old trans Blackgirl, was last seen alive on October 23, 2011. A few weeks later, her charred torso was discovered on Detroit's east side, near the I-94. While these egregiously violent deaths are not uncommon, we will never know the exact number of Black queer and trans girls who have been assaulted or killed in the United States. Yet, we know that this violence continues. In 2019, of the twenty-six transgender or gender-nonconforming people killed, most identified as Black transwomen. By June 1, 2020, the number of transgender or gender-nonconforming people had already reached fourteen.[10] As we mourn the white-authored murders of Trayvon Martin, George Floyd, Breonna Taylor, and so many others, we must also remember the names of Riah Milton, Dominique "Rem'mie" Fells, Iyanna Dior, and many other queer, trans, and gender-nonconforming Black folx who have been violently beaten, raped, or murdered because of their identity. If we truly desire our society to value Black life, Black queer feminists and their allies must increase efforts to reaffirm the sanctity of *all* Black life. Those keenly aware of these harms can certainly read performances of *Bella*, *Bubbly Black Girl*, and *Madame Zora* within this sociopolitical context.

Black queer feminist spectators understand that anti-Blackness and acts of violence not only destroy Black communities but also the Black imagination.[11] By the "Black imagination," I mean the ability of Black folx to be able to form new ideas, images, or concepts of external objects not currently present in our society. The ability to imagine new and better possibilities has always been an integral component of the Black freedom struggle. In other words, visions of an equitable and just society could not exist without the Black imagination. *Bella*, *Bubbly Black Girl*, and *Madame Zora* all pay tribute to the importance of the Black imagination. As Blackgirl protagonists encounter all forms of violence in their daily life, they employ their wit and imagination—through storytelling, song, and dance—to empower themselves and, perhaps by extension, the spectators who witness and take pleasure in their triumphs.

Celebrating the interiority of Blackgirls and the *process* by which they overcome their seemingly more powerful adversaries becomes a source of pleasure for spectators. In *Bubbly Black Girl*, Viveca realizes that Addie Mae Collins, Cynthia Wesley, Carole Robertson, and Carol Denise McNair were victims of murder because they were Black. Armed with the knowledge that society does not value Blackgirls, Viveca turns inward to protect herself from these realities. In the comfort of her bedroom, she uses her imagination to conjure Black historical figures and fairy tale characters to assist her. When these attempts fail, she creates a new (and safer) identity as a stereotypical white girl. Similar to Viveca, Childs's Western heroine Bella also needs psychic relief from her experiential knowledge of sexual assault. She creates a new identity and imagines a new world of possibility by envisioning herself as a Black folk hero. Bella's fantastic tale allows her to use her intellect and creativity to outmaneuver her assailant, a wealthy white southern plantation owner named Bonny Johnny Rakehell. Just as Childs crafts Bella's intellect and imagination as instruments of survival during the Reconstruction era (1861–1865), Rahman fashions similar tools for her larger-than-life depiction of folklorist Zora Neale Hurston. Borrowing from Black folklore tradition, Rahman allows narrators to use storytelling and embodiment to capture multiple visions of Hurston. They invite spectators to envision Hurston as "Zora," a spirited child of nine, a teenager forced to trade sexual favors for educational opportunities, a controversial figure of the Harlem Renaissance (1918–1930s), a social pariah following sexual misconduct accusations, and finally, an infirmed maid. As resistant readers, Black queer feminist spectators might consider these musicals symbolic of their struggle to navigate a society that does not recognize Black queer humanity, their daily acts of resistance, and their efforts to create a world filled with Black queer love and empowerment.

Bella: An American Tall Tale

As a gifted storyteller in her own right, Childs crafted *Bella* to expose historical mythologies that render Black and brown people's bodies—especially girls—invisible in the Old West. Newspapers, Western dime novels, literature, plays, television, and film romanticized the West as a wild frontier populated by cowboys, ranchers, sheriffs, and miners. These frontier heroes—all rugged white heterosexual men—used their brawn to conquer their enemies and claim the bounties of the Wild West, including gold, cattle, land, and women. Frontiersman such as Daniel Boone, Davy Crockett, William F. "Buffalo Bill" Cody, and Christopher "Kit" Carson became the stuff of legend. At the same time, the stories of Black, Indigenous, and People of Color (BIPOC) who migrated West often remain forgotten in the public imagination. Childs remembers knowing very little about how Black people contributed to and were impacted by Western expansion (1829–1870). In keeping with most Americans, Childs did not learn about the Exoduster

Movement in public school, nor did she see Black people represented in Western films. Childs remembers: "Clearly, there were Black people in the South and then other Black people in the West. How did they get there? I got really excited when I started to learn more and more about Black, Asian, Latino, and Native American people in the West. It was an eye-opening way of learning about American history, and it spawned flights of fancy that were so much fun."[12] Armed with her newfound historical documentation of BIPOC in the Old West, Childs crafted *Bella* as a means to restore Black and brown bodies on the historical stage.

Childs admittedly filled historical "gaps" with her creative imagination to fashion this new tall tale for contemporary audiences. By blending "fact" and "fiction," historical and contemporary popular culture, Childs engages with much larger historiographical questions. She invites performers to join her in this quest in her "Author's Notes." Childs writes that "this American tall tale is a big-assed lie created to point out outrageous American home truths. So please, my dear actors, put your booty in it."[13] Childs understands that these "big-assed lies," or white-authored visions of the past, not only ignore anti-Black and gendered violence but also justify and explain Black subjugation. These "big-assed lies" become the "facts" needed to create "history," which is nothing more than "outrageous American home truths." When asked how *Bella* relates to larger historical truths, Childs explained: "If George Washington saying, 'I cannot tell a lie. I chopped down the cherry tree' is a big-assed lie, then why can't I tell an even bigger-assed lie that has an essential truth in it?"[14] For far too long, white-authored narratives have been regarded as "Truth," regardless of evidence that would suggest otherwise. In contrast, Black women rarely have been afforded the privilege of documenting the reality of their lives.

Childs reimagines a Blackgirl-centered history, one in which they are the heroes of their own big-assed tales. The 2017 Playwrights Horizons production begins with Bella (Ashley D. Kelley) performing the opening song, "Big Booty Tupelo Gal." Decked out in a rich, floor-length red dress, Bella sings: "History is the tall tale/ that you learn/ from the book of the scholar/ but there's another history/ you can learn." With this number, Bella reveals the musical's conceit: history is naught but a construction, tailored to suit the needs of those who write it. In a direct address to the audience, Bella (as narrator) looks audiences in the eyes and asserts her right to claim her place as a legend of the Old West. She tells the audience that "this is the legend of the Big Booty Gal. She was a Wild West figure with a Wild West figure, and

Figure 3.1 Ashley D. Kelley (Bella) in *Bella: An American Tall Tale* (2017). Playwrights Horizons production trailer. Still image courtesy of the author. https://www.youtube.com/watch?v = wVTfT_7QqUs

her story starts around 1877, on a journey that was a true locomotion of hot steam and cool dreams." As performed by Kelley, a beautiful dark-skinned actress, Bella accentuates her narration with a flirtatious glance and slight bend of the hips, striking a sensual pose that invites spectators to appreciate her plus-sized figure (see Figure 3.1). As the audience laughs at her pun, she gives them a knowing look, followed by a gaze that asserts her control over her body and narrative. Indeed, Bella's enormous behind—a symbol of power and beauty—provides a means of subverting Western beauty aesthetics and reclaiming Blackgirl agency.

Childs based Bella's characterization on her experience witnessing the reactions of men watching a beautiful Black woman walk down a street. "I saw this woman who had this Hottentot behind, and she was with her boyfriend or her husband and every man that passed by her turned around and looked at her behind. They were all ethnicities. They were all stratums of the economy. There were rich, poor, homeless, Black, white, Asian, Hispanic, young, old, you name it. She was like, 'Yes, I know I look good,'" remembers Childs.[15] Her experiential knowledge affirmed that Blackgirls *are* beautiful and sexually desired by all races. The contradiction between Childs's reality and what she was taught to believe about Blackgirls made her angry. Childs remembers returning home and thinking: "I have to bear witness to this. Well, she is larger-than-life: it is a tall tale." This experience led her to deconstruct what she terms "outrageous American home truths," or American mythologies that render Blackgirls invisible.

Childs crafts Bella as a larger-than-life American frontierswoman who undergoes a series of adventures in her quest for freedom. Deeply rooted in American history, Bella encounters the actual dangers of navigating Mississippi society as a Blackgirl during the Reconstruction era (1865–1877). As such, her adventure begins *after* she narrowly escapes the machinations of a slave owner, Bonny Johnny. Childs pairs this history with the fantastic qualities of tall tales, endowing Bella with a great source of strength: a "large, voluptuous behind."[16] In contrast to the nineteenth-century Black folk hero John Henry, who dies in a strength competition against a steam-powered rock-drilling machine, Bella *survives* her trials. Furthermore, she saves others by using her wit and derriere. For example, in one of the most humorous moments of the musical, Bella rescues a porter named Daniel from the threat of white train robbers by holding him on her lap while bouncing on her buttocks down a mountainside. Bella's ability to outmaneuver her enemies (and how she does so) invites Black queer feminist spectators to take delight in their own beautiful Black bodies and imagine creative ways to defeat their seemingly more powerful foes.

The art of storytelling allows Bella to imagine the Old West as a world populated by talented and courageous BIPOC adventurers. Bella creates these tales based on her lived experiences navigating the world as a Blackgirl. For example, the love-struck cowboy Diego Moreno resembles a picture of a Mexican man from her travel book, *The Passenger's Companion: A Compendious Account of Picturesque Places and Objects of Interest for the Well-Seasoned Traveler*. Bella constructs other fantastic characters based on the personalities of the Black women in her life. Similar to the iconic musical *The Wonderful Wizard of Oz*, the production modes provide a visual layering of worlds through double casting. For example, Mama encourages Black respectability politics in the real world, advising Bella to avoid contact with men on the train and keep her appearance orderly while traveling. However, Bella's stories allow her to resist Black respectability politics. Within her world, she fashions Mama into the character Miss Cabbagestalk, a prim mail-order bride. Actress Kenita R. Miller performs both characters and delights audiences when she abandons propriety and dances with

Diego. Similarly, Bella's strong-willed Aunt Dinah morphs into a determined Exoduster named Ida Lou Simpson (Miranda Anderson). With an infant in her arms, Ida treks West to help build a strong Black community, a dream she once shared with her husband before white vigilantes lynched him. Grandma, the family historian, transforms into the Spirit of the Booty (NaTasha Yvette Williams), who resembles their legendary ancestor, Itty Bitty Gal.[17] Collectively, these characters help reclaim the historical presence of BIPOC in the Old West and Blackgirl interiority.

The modes of production, specifically the projection designs, helped spectators visualize Bella's dreams, hopes, and fears. The Playwrights Horizons production, directed by Robert O'Hara, used color to distinguish Bella's interiority from her actual life circumstances. Saturated colors represented the richness of Bella's imagination, while beige and muted colors designated life in nineteenth-century Mississippi. The Tony Award-winning video and projection designer Jeff Sugg remembers that "the dreamscape needed to be something that correlated to her: the power, the glory, the lifting up that it gave to her. It took her from this unempowered place to an empowered place. I felt we had to make a world for her that showed that—bright, open, and full. [I placed] dense greens and blues and reds on top of [the set] as a way to make those moments pop."[18] In addition to color, Sugg created a "cartoon aesthetic" projection and video designs to capture Bella's fantastic imagination. Sugg's cartoon aesthetic combines artistic and technological inspirations, including early American golden age cartoons, zoetropes, Polynesian shadow puppetry, and late nineteenth- to early twentieth-century optical technology. For example, Sugg depicted Bella's comical escape down the mountainside using Polynesian shadow puppetry. He framed her descent by using a Road Runner and Wile E. Coyote-inspired matte-painted backdrop. Sugg then connected these styles using handmade animations and a zoetrope to give an overall appearance of stop animation. Using familiar designs or, in this case, popular child's cartoons invited spectators to take pleasure in Bella's child-like imagination. The use of seemingly "strange" or older technology created a moment of surprise or even delight in spectators who witnessed the beauty of Bella's creative imagination.

However, Bella's exceptional imagination cannot eradicate the realities of life as a nineteenth-century Blackgirl. The threat of rape launches Bella into a liminal space between girlhood and womanhood. She must traverse dangerous roads independently, without protection from her mother, aunt, and grandmother. Aware of her flights of fancy, Mama warns her of these realities before she boards the train West. "Please remember that life is real—it's real, and it's hard. So try not to let your imagination run away with you all the time," Mama advises. She understands the systems that allow wealthy white men like Bonny Jonny to remain unaccountable for their actions. As a walking stereotype of the worst nineteenth-century white Southerner, Bonny Johnny lacks respect for Bella as a human being. He makes his stance clear in his upbeat ballad, "Bonny Johnny Rakehell." Set to the tune of a lively nineteenth-century-sounding Irish ballad, Bonny Johnny reminds audiences that he is as powerful as Jesus and above earthly laws. Later, when Bella's psyche returns her to the memory of her walk near a swamp along the Natchez Trace road, spectators witness Bonny Johnny's act on his assertion of power and dominance. He blocks Bella's passage and as she tries to push him away, he grabs her wrist and presses her against his body. The stage becomes cloaked in blue as a verbal battle ensues:

JOHNNY: You ain't nothin' to me, but I know who you are. You belong to the Patterson plantation.

BELLA: I don't belong to nobody. My daddy left the plantation to fight a war to make it so.

JOHNNY: Your daddy left the plantation in a pine box after he tried to stop Old Man Patterson from beddin' your big booty mama.

The abrupt shift in lighting—from a basic warm wash to a heavy, rich blue—suggests that this conversation likely occurred in her imagination. Rather than remember her (probable) sexual assault and her father's murder, Bella uses her imagination to create an alternative account, one in which she asserts her agency, her mother is never raped, and her father dies as a Civil War hero, rather than a victim of lynching.

Despite her mother's efforts to discourage her from imagining a better life for herself, Bella continues to read and dream of a world of new possibilities for Blackgirls. However, literacy was, in fact, a rarity for the Black population of the time. The National Center for Education Statistics reports that "in 1870, 20% of the entire adult population was illiterate, and 80% of the black population was illiterate. By 1900 the situation has improved somewhat but still 44% of blacks remained illiterate."[19] History has shown that denying Black people access to education ensured their subjugation well beyond the institution of slavery. At fifteen years old, Bella would have been born enslaved, her formative years would have been shaped by the US Civil

War (1861–1865) and Reconstruction era, and her literacy would have been a rarity at the time. She, therefore, represents a rising generation of Black women and girls who aspired for upward mobility. The social justice scholar Monique W. Morris discusses the significance of literacy in black women's lives in her book, *Pushout: The Criminalization of Black Girls in Schools* (2016). Morris writes that "to read challenged the oppressive, controlling logic of slavery and the presupposed inferiority of Black people. For many enslaved Black women, learning to read represented a reclamation of human dignity. . . . Many Black women's commitment to education was so strong that she risked incarceration or other penalties just to attain it."[20] Blackgirls accepted the risk because they believed that education would grant some semblance of social mobility in a society that did not recognize their humanity.

Bella's colorful world of erotic social dance allows her to experience vicarious sexual pleasure and escape (albeit, briefly) the oppressive forces in her life. Dance has always provided a productive means for Blackgirls to express their subjectivity, meaning their thoughts, emotions, and experiences about themselves and the world around them. Dance has also served as a site of resistance, empowering Blackgirls to critique dangerous ideologies and

Figure 3.2 Ashley D. Kelley (Bella), Yurel Echezarreta (Diego), and Kenita R. Miller (Miss Cabbagestalk) in *Bella: An American Tall Tale* (2017). Playwrights Horizons production trailer. Still image courtesy of the author. https://www.youtube.com/watch?v=wVTfT_7QqUs

practices that harm them and their community.[21] While Bella shares a love letter from her Buffalo Soldier, Aloysius, she hesitates to embrace her sexuality. Instead, she allows her deepest sexual fantasies to unfold by imagining a sensual dance with the amorous Mexican cowboy, Diego (Yurel Echezarreta). Mirroring Aloysius's passionate love letter, Diego sings an ode to her beauty in the romantic, salsa-infused ballad, "¡Quién Fuera Luna!-Pt 1." However, when Diego's complicated "fancy footwork" and well-placed pelvic thrusts prove too provocative, a timid Bella allows Miss Cabbagestalk to intercede on her behalf (see Figure 3.2). Miss Cabbagestalk abandons all notions of Black respectability politics of the Victorian era by performing a complicated cakewalk from her childhood. Originating from the "prize walks" by enslaved Blacks in the mid-nineteenth century, cakewalks developed into a popular form of dance exhibited at the 1876 World's Fair in Philadelphia and on minstrel stages across the nation. Performing the cakewalk allows Miss Cabbagestalk to reclaim her agency by reliving her first-prize-winning performance in "Miss Tidwell's Colored Orphans Dancin' Fool Contest." While opportunities were minimal for poor Blackgirls—especially orphans—of the era, Miss Cabbagestalk's moment of wild abandon creates space for her to reconsider the implications of matrimony to her unattractive fiancé. Miss Cabbagestalk performs a "pas de deux of Afro-Mexican ecstasy," or sexually charged salsa dance with Diego. In the Horizons Playwrights production, Miss Cabbagestalk (Kenita R. Miller) runs her hand from Diego's chest to her vagina, raising her leg to his hip during their dance number. At this moment, Miss Cabbagestalk refuses to accept the drudgery of marriage to an unknown man and father of six children, leans into a sexual awakening with Diego, and exits the stage arm-in-arm.

Camille A. Brown's anachronistic choreography presents Black queer feminist spectators with a much-needed image of Blackgirls as active agents, fully capable of pursuing sexual pleasure on their terms. As a choreographer, Brown centers her work on "reclaiming the cultural narratives of African American identity."[22] She comes from a long line of Black choreographers who challenge white cultural hegemony and use dance as a liberatory force on the musical stage. In the Horizons Playwrights production, Brown used her expertise to reclaim the experiences of Blackgirls through Black and queer popular dance references.[23] For example, her choreography included having Miss Cabbagestalk twerk during her erotic dance with Diego. Twerking refers to the Bounce style of social dance, which encompassed the Black LGBTQ culture of New Orleans during the 1980s.[24] Performed by

Black cis and transgender folk, twerking includes "stylized and rhythmically-timed gestures" such as "dropping, popping, locking, and bouncing with the fleshy part of one's ass to articulate through kinetic orality different aspects of a rap song."[25] Today, twerking has become an important form of Blackgirl expression in a highly digitized world that often marginalizes their voices. The ethnomusicologist Kyra D. Gaunt writes that "twerking is a form of vlogging for adolescent black girls whose bodies speak more powerfully than their voices."[26] Therefore, the act of twerking allows Miss Cabbagestalk to abandon society's dictates and give voice to her sexuality and power. Bella continues to imagine dance as a source of empowerment in her own life. For example, when the train robbers enter her car and shoot Nathaniel, Bella does not flee. Instead, she jumps out of her hiding place and into the line of fire, singing the uptempo song, "A-Bouncin' Back from Adversity." As she sings the lyrics, "But I'm from a line of women / who know how to turn a lemon into lemonade," she rotates her right wrist in homage to Beyoncé's 2008 Blackgirl anthem "Single Ladies (Put a Ring on It)."[27] In borrowing movement from Beyoncé's iconic dance video and uttering a lyrical reference to her 2016 visual album *Lemonade*, Bella embraces Blackgirl power and becomes her own hero. The powerful thrust of her buttocks incapacitates the train robbers, allowing her to rescue Nathaniel and escape down the mountainside. Brown's use of popular Blackgirl and queer dance references enables her to achieve her goal of creating "bold work [that] taps into both ancestral stories and contemporary culture to capture a range of deeply personal experiences."[28]

In addition to empowering Blackgirls, the Playwrights Horizons production of *Bella* also used dance as a means of reclaiming Black, Asian, and Latinx queer existence within historical narratives. While the script does not include overtly queer references, O'Hara's direction and Brown's choreography infuse subtle and overtly queer elements into the production modes. O'Hara, an openly Black queer artist, discussed the importance of queer representation in a 2014 interview with Playwrights Horizons artistic director, Tim Sanford. O'Hara remembers:

> For the most part when you say the word gay, one thinks of a white upwardly mobile man. Look at the TV, movies and magazines, most of the images of homosexuality surround white men: "Modern Family," "Will & Grace" and of the various sitcoms through the years that even introduced homosexuality limited it to white men. . . . We've been taught to believe that

> the window out of which we are gazing has to always be that of a white male gaze. It is not. I don't live my life like that although most of society and especially American theater would have us believe that the white straight male gaze was the default. It is not.[29]

Simply put, Black queer representation and subjectivity matter. O'Hara fostered greater visibility of queer relationships through movement. Childs remembers that "He infused certain things within the actual stage production that embraced queer characters in the piece. In 'Gal Over Yonder,' the square dance men are dancing with men."[30] Jeff Sugg also recalls O'Hara's incorporating both subtle and overt celebrations of Black queer identity. "Even on that train, there were probably queer and unspoken queer relationships of people in adjoining cars. Then that Tommie Haw number: that's a big striptease. [O'Hara] had that overt jovial version be the thing that people will specifically remember and be able to smile and joke about but also had all of these smaller signs throughout the piece," remembers Sugg.[31] Indeed, O'Hara's decisions to have men and women admire Bella's figure, conjure the image of the queer cowboy, and incorporate same-sex social dance celebrate the Black queer gaze, allowing Black queer feminist spectators to see their identity manifested onstage.

While Bella's colorful world of song, dance, and Black queer possibilities helps her escape the threat of Bonny Johnny, her imagination cannot help her entirely avoid the realities of white-authored violence. For example, when she meets Ida Lou Simpson aboard the train, she tells Bella about her late husband Matthew's vision of land and opportunity beyond the South. According to Ida Lou, Matthew spoke of his dream "until the day they took his land and his breath away, the day they strung him up, and invited their friends and neighbors and children out on a bright noonday picnic to watch. My Matthew was guilty of three crimes. The crime of bein' uppity. The crime of believing in the United States Constitution. And the crime of thinkin' that, for the south, the war would ever be over." Bella's construction of Ida conjures the spirit of Ida B. Wells-Barnett (1862–1931), a sociologist, suffragist, and journalist who began documenting the cruelties of lynching in the 1890s. Similar to her namesake, the fictitious Ida testifies to the barbaric practice, noting how Matthew's assertion of his rights as a citizen led to his "crime." Ida notes the contrast between a "bright noonday," the frivolity of whites (including children) gathering for a picnic, and the source of entertainment: her husband's lynched body. The irony is that despite their newly acquired citizenship, Blacks will not receive justice. Instead, Matthew was murdered in broad daylight with witnesses present. His white murderers will never be held accountable for their crimes. Kansas's "Promised land" offers Ida hope and an opportunity to escape the Ku Klux Klan. While Bella considers the dream of a new life in Kansas, by the end of the song, "Kansas Boun,'" she discovers life is just as difficult for Black pioneers, as the "town" is nothing more than makeshift dugouts on a hillside.

Bella's awareness of the intricacies of lynching—enough to incorporate the fine details into her dreamscape—speaks volumes about the dangers of nineteenth-century Black girlhood. Ida's recollections are, in fact, a product of Bella's imagination. Their imagined conversation of lynching supports the realities of white vigilante justice. Scholar Patricia A. Young writes that "lynching prayed mainly on African-Americans and was used primarily to mock, to degrade, and to control blacks throughout the southern and border states from Reconstruction to the mid-twentieth century."[32] While Black men, women, and children were lynched, Black men were more often the target of such "justice." Young notes that "going to the negative image of the black male during reconstruction, the African American man was the specified prey of the lynch mob. Stereotyped as 'the Brute Negro,' the black man was perceived by whites to be an insolent beast who constantly raped white women and who threatened to undermine white society."[33] In reality, Black women who worked near white men experienced rape and the threat of rape. These white men were not held accountable for their actions. Bella highlights this contradiction, showing that white men have the law on their side, allowing serial rapist Bonny Johnny to criminalize his victim. With a $5,000 bounty on her head, Bella must leave everything she knows and everyone she loves to avoid capture. Even still, Bonny Johnny continues to haunt her dreams. Ida B. Wells-Barnett, the NAACP, and countless other activists worked tirelessly to eradicate white terrorism throughout the nineteenth and twentieth centuries. Despite the long campaign to secure an anti-lynching legislature—nearly two hundred anti-lynching bills were introduced in the first half of the twentieth century alone—their efforts failed due to opposition by conservative Southern Democrats.[34] It was not until 2022, with the passage of the Emmett Till Antilynching Act, that lynching would become a federal hate crime offense punishable by fine, a prison term of up to thirty years, or both. In other words, it took decades upon decades for the federal government to offer Black people basic human protections against white vigilantes.

Bella's tale also reveals the long history of white men exploiting cis Black female bodies for monetary gain. More specifically, the attention garnered from Bella's large behind resonates with Sarah (Saartjie) Baartman (*c.* 1775–1815), whose experiences in life and death are often cited today as one of the most egregious cases of Blackgirl exploitation and commodification. In 1810, Baartman was captured from her village in (what is now) the Eastern Cape of South Africa and exhibited as a freak show attraction at fashionable Parisian parties and on English and French stages. Her perceived *steatopygia*, or large amounts of tissue on the buttocks and thighs, captivated European audiences, scientists, and businessmen who poked and prodded her body. Shortly following her death in 1815, Henri de Blainville and Georges Cuvier, known today as the "father of modern anatomy," made a cast of her body, dissected her remains, and preserved her brain and genitals and skeleton at the Musée de l'Homme in Paris. Cuvier then used his findings and interpretive images of her nude body to prove that the so-called Hottentot body more closely aligned with apes than homo sapiens.[35] His "discoveries" were later published in his brother Frédéric Cuvier's monograph *Histoire Naturelle des mammifères* (1817), one of many nineteenth-century European writings to mark the cis Black female body as primitive, sexualized, and devoid of beauty. Bella's participation in a "freak" show hearkens back to this terrible history. After being separated from Nathaniel after their escape down a mountainside, Bella meets circus master CP Conyers, a P.T. Barnum-esque showman, and his disfigured brother, Gabriel. Jobless and homeless, Bella agrees to perform in their "freak" show for one hundred dollars a week (see Figure 3.3). While she does achieve fame—her derrière, after all, inspires the creation of the bustle—she soon realizes that spectators do not view her as an artist; she is nothing more than an object of curiosity.

While historical records cannot verify whether or not Baartman willingly participated in her commodification, Black queer feminist spectators know beyond a shadow of a doubt that Bella uses her agency to resist white-authored primitivist fantasies. Indeed, white audiences of the nineteenth century flocked to performances that reinforced the wrong-headed belief that Blacks held a simple and unsophisticated culture. Conyers exploits the popularity of exotic Black savagery by creating a "jungle scene" performance that features Bella as Princess Unga Bunga. He insists Bella wear an unattractive, knee-length cheetah print cloth costume and large white bone in her small afro. He justifies the costume by reminding Bella that her performance will garner spectators, who will consume her image. Conyers

Figure 3.3 Ashley D. Kelley (Bella) and Yurel Echezarreta (CP Conyers) in *Bella: An American Tall Tale* (2017). Playwrights Horizons production trailer. Still image courtesy of the author. https://www.youtube.com/watch?v=wVTfT_7QqUs

states: "Nothing says Africa like a half-naked woman with a big booty. The crowds are gonna eat you up, gal." Bella responds by appearing to acquiesce to his wishes, but in reality, she and Gabriel stage a coup during the "jungle scene." As soon as Conyers mentions the inferiority of Blacks and orders the villagers to prepare a meal, Bella changes the script. She rips off the offensive jungle costume to reveal "a fabulous Josephine Baker outfit," transforming herself from an object of curiosity to a subject fully capable of speaking truth to power as she orders the villagers to cook Conyers in the unsanctioned song, "White People Tonight." Rather than sing unintelligible lyrics, a now glamorous Bella leads the villagers in a spirited song about preparing and consuming white people. Similar to Josephine Baker (1906–1975), Bella's use of feminine wit, humor, and wile makes her an instant sensation that allows her to send money home to support her family. Yet, her international acclaim cannot withstand the blight of systemic racism when she returns to US soil.

Although Black queer feminist spectators might experience pleasure witnessing Bella claim her agency and symbolically kill white-authored mythologies, they might also find her inability to achieve acceptance in her homeland quite tragic. Perhaps the latter hits too close to home, as many Black queer folks continue to face ostracism from their own families. Indeed, another important historical "truth" is that many Black communities have also turned their backs on so-called "sexually deviant" Black folks. Consequently, Black LGBTQ+ members and other outliers have had to use their wit and imagination to create new alternative family structures for support. However, as *Madame Zora* demonstrates, not every Blackgirl can successfully do so.

The Tale of *Madame Zora*

Similar to Childs's *Bella*, Rahman's *Madame Zora* uses the art of storytelling to critique the concept of "truth" and the process of writing history. Before he begins his narration, Doctor Mo invites spectators to consider the importance of historiography. Doctor Mo states that "in every tale there are two truths. That's why we call our tales 'lies.' Our truth is on the top of the tale. Out there in front of everyone's eyes: the naked truth. What folks may even call the historical truth. But turn a tale bottoms up and what you got is the second truth. Profound. Mysterious. Each side is an exaggeration in deformity of the other inside. Another truth. Still the truth, yet not the same."[36] Doctor Mo, who expresses many of the theorizations of the Black Arts Movement (1965–1976), understands that two truths coexist: one tailored by dominant white society and a second "naked truth" that expresses Black experiences in America. The latter truth, embedded within Black folklore, only appears "mysterious" because biased scholars never thoroughly examined the richness of Black history and culture. Instead, the truth of Black existence has been either distorted beyond recognition or consigned to the margins of history. For these reasons, Spirit of Zora encourages spectators to assess the "truths" within the musical. She sings: "So I'm asking you darling/When I live in your thoughts/ As my tale is told/Make up your own mind 'bout me." In so doing, Spirit of Zora positions spectators as critical agents, fully capable of drawing their own conclusions.

Rahman often described herself as the most "well-known obscure playwright" because many of her works have been anthologized and often appeared on college stages and in small theatres, but never on Broadway.[37] Her works were, after all, inspired by the Black Arts Movement, which eschewed the staleness of Broadway stages. "My theatre sensibilities were forged in the crucible of the sixties, downtown in the Off and Off-Off

Broadway avant-garde theatre and uptown in the Black Arts Revolutionary Theater Movement. It was always my opinion that both groups could learn from one another; Downtown playwrights needed to anchor their experimental forms in less abstract experiences and Uptown playwrights could tell their tales of racial oppression and revolution in less traditional, more experimental forms," remembers Rahman.[38] Her love of experimental works and concern for racial and gender oppression led to her crafting her second play with music, *Madame Zora*. Thadious M. Davis writes that "for the second time, Aishah Rahman took a famous black woman and eschewed the usual nostalgic, one-dimensional portraits that ignore the complex realities of black female life in America. Rahman again used music as an organic part of the characterizations but this time, however, it was the blues music of the southern rural African-Americans."[39] Rahman's depiction of Hurston, coupled with her deep appreciation for blues music, helped *Madam Zora* "become another one of her underground classics performed in alternative venues nationwide."[40]

As a playwright of the Black Arts Movement, Rahman believed the Black aesthetic—including Black folklore and music—could distill the truth of Black existence to everyday Black audiences. The Black Arts Movement theorist Larry Neal discusses the importance of the Black aesthetic in his seminal essay, "The Black Arts Movement" (1968). Neal writes that "the motive behind the Black aesthetic is the destruction of the white thing, the destruction of white ideas, and white ways of looking at the world. The new aesthetic is mostly predicated on an Ethics which asks the question: whose vision of the world is more meaningful, ours or the white oppressors'? What is truth? Or more precisely, whose truth shall we express, that of the oppressed or the oppressors?"[41] Rahman invites everyday Black audiences to engage with these fundamental questions through an accessible medium—a biographical blues musical. Rahman writes that "I was committed to the truth telling of black lives (especially women's) in the face of silence and I knew we African Americans were a jazz people who lived improvisatory lives in multi-realities so why couldn't The Music be adapted as dramatic structure? Form following content. [. . .] And through the years in all my plays and prose my goal remains to reveal Afro-American stories framed in African-American cultural forms."[42] *Madame Zora* realizes this artistic mission, using Black folklore as both form and content to reclaim Black history and culture as a sight worthy of intellectual inquiry. Zora Neale Hurston spent her career collecting hidden truths found within Black folklore, and so it is only fitting that *Madame Zora* uses Hurston's life as an entry point into these broader critical discussions.

Director Glenda Dickerson told Hurston's story through a Black feminist vision of Black folklore. Dickerson wanted the Ensemble Studio Theatre's premiere production of *Madame Zora* to celebrate what Hurston called the "drylongso" or "ordinary, plain, everyday people of color."[43] Inspired by Hurston's critical and creative writings, Dickerson's artistic sensibilities included a desire to reclaim the beauty of Black storytelling, Black womanhood, and everyday Black life. Dickerson expresses these concerns in her article, "The Cult of True Womanhood: Toward a Womanist Attitude in African-American Theatre" (1988). Dickerson writes:

> The image of the African-American woman has been sullied on the world stage. The trick for her now is to reclaim that image through self-definition, using Nommo, the magic of the word; uncategorically rejecting the stereotypes which are not "my shame" (as Harriet Tubman said). They are the shame of the perpetrators. In my work I try to replace stereotypes such as mammies, coons, bucks, tragic mulattoes with the archetypes embodied and preserved in the myths, tales, folklore that document the Black experience in America; the stories that "Grandma say."[44]

Dickerson's direction of *Madame Zora*, a musical deeply embedded within Black women's history and culture, allowed her to realize this artistic vision. Her incorporation of a Black folkloric aesthetic provided visual means of inviting spectators to document the Black experience in America. Dickerson framed Rahman's blues musical with the backdrop of a general store, the site of everyday conversations celebrated in Hurston's folkloric research. Hurston recorded her girlhood fascination with eavesdropping on adult conversations on the general store's porch in her hometown in her memoir, *Dust Tracks on a Road* (1942). Hurston writes that "for me, the store porch was the most interesting place that I could think of. [. . .] There would be, for instance, sly references to the physical condition of women, irregular love affairs, brags on male potency by the parties of the first part, and the like [. . .] But what I really loved to hear was the menfolks holding a 'lying' session. That is, straining against each other in telling folk tales. God, Devil, Brer Rabbit, Brer Fox, Sis Cat, Brer Bear, Lion, Tiger, Buzzard, and all the wood folk walked and talked like natural men."[45] Dickerson's general store allows spectators to also "eavesdrop," if you will, in on the stories told at the

Lie Swapping Barbeque Festival. Her simple set encouraged spectators to focus on Rahman's language, the beauty of blues and gospel music, and the art of Black storytelling traditions.

Dickerson's use of a Black folkloric aesthetic was celebrated by Black theatre critics and misunderstood by white theatre critics of the time. The *Madame Zora* cast included Stephanie Berry (Happy Sweet), Keith David (Doctor Mo), Willie Barnes (Black Herman), Jean-Paul Bourelly (Town's People and Musicians), and Deborah Malone (Town's People and Musicians), who perform multiple roles. Musician Olu Dara, choreographer Dianne McIntyre, and designers Charles H. McClennahan, Marshall Williams, and Sydney Inis brought Rahman's story to life. The Audience Development Committee, Inc. (AUDELCO), which recognizes Black theatre and dance excellence, praised Dickerson's production and honored Rahman with the 1986 Outstanding Musical Creator Award for her efforts. The *New York Times* critic Mel Gussow also lauded the onstage talent—specifically Berry's "lithe physicality" and Malone's singing abilities—but dismissed much of the culturally specific elements of the production.[46] For example, he refers to the simple set as a "cracker-barrel," Rahman's book as "inconclusive," and Rahman/Dara's score as "perfunctory."[47] Gussow then writes that the production "only rarely captures the uniqueness of this sizable literary and historical figure. . . . Both the play and Glenda Dickerson's production would benefit from additional work."[48] Rather than engaging with Black women intellectuals and their innovative use of Black folklore on the musical stage, Gussow compares the musical to Western theatrical modes. Consequently, Gussow can only attest to what the musical *does not do* and misses the transgressive nature of the piece altogether.

Madame Zora uses the art of Black storytelling to recover the forgotten legacy of Hurston's pioneering scholarship. Hurston provided one of the earliest definitions of Black folklore in her essay "Characteristics of Negro Expression" (1934). Hurston writes that "Negro folklore is not a thing of the past. It is still in the making. Its great variety shows the adaptability of the black man: nothing is too old or too new, domestic or foreign, high or low, for his use. God and the Devil are paired, and are treated no more reverently than Rockefeller and Ford. . . . Ole Massa is sometimes a smart man and often a fool."[49] Hurston understood Black folklore as a continuation of West African culture brought to the Americas during enslavement. Later in this essay, she situates the Black cultural hero Jack as the "blood brother" of the West African trickster-hero Rabbit.[50] She also recognized that Black folklore, often hidden from the purview of white listeners, functioned as a transgressive site, continuously adapted to meet the needs and concerns of Black people. As such, Black folktales centered the experiences of Black cultural heroes who use their wit to defeat their seemingly more powerful foe (i.e., Ole Massa) and, in so doing, overturn violent hierarchies of power and authority. While most white and some Black intellectuals degenerated the significance of Black folklore, Hurston understood its beauty and value.

Madame Zora situates Hurston as the most prolific Blackgirl writer of the Harlem Renaissance, whose work quickly fell into obscurity by the time of her death in 1960. Interest in Hurston's legacy revived with the publication of Alice Walker's *Ms.* magazine article, "In Search of Zora Neale Hurston" (1975).[51] A decade later, Rahman continued these recuperative efforts with *Madame Zora*, which uses Black folklore to restore Hurston's rightful place as the "mother" of Black folklore studies. In the musical, narrators Doctor Mo, Black Herman, Cora Mae, and Spirit of Zora "swap lies" about Hurston's ethnographic research, artistry, and political thought during their annual Lie Swapping Festival in Eatonville, Florida. As they embody their differing accounts, speculation about Hurston's life emerges. Cora Mae establishes this premise as she ponders: "Some folks said she was an early Black nationalist speaking against integration while others thought she was only a pawn for the southern racist." The narrators respond by presenting moments from Hurston's controversial life. They begin with Hurston's pursuit of education, her early encounter with sexual abuse, and critical acclaim during the Harlem Renaissance. Next, narrators depict charges of sexual deviancy and her fall from grace. The narrators provide several plausible accounts rather than a concrete explanation of what happened during the "lost" or undocumented ten years of Hurston's life.[52] They conclude their tale with Hurston's death in a county welfare home. In sharing Hurston's triumphs, challenges, and ambivalence, the narrators create space for Hurston to rise as a three-dimensional Blackgirl.

Hurston conceptualized "drama" as the everyday movements of Blackgirls, a concept which Rahman enfolded into her musical dramatization of Hurston's life (see Figure 3.4). In her essay, "Characteristics of Negro Expression" (1934), Hurston remarks that "every phase of Negro life is highly dramatized. No matter how joyful or how sad the case there is sufficient poise for drama. Everything is acted out. Unconsciously for the most part of course."[53] Hurston then provides examples of "little plays" within daily life. Hurston writes: "A Negro girl strolls past the corner lounger. Her whole body

Figure 3.4 "Portrait of Zora Neal Hurston, smoking." Schomburg Center for Research in Black Culture, Photographs and Prints Division, The New York Public Library. New York Public Library Digital Collections. https://digitalcollections.nypl.org/items/8e0981a2-4b28-a10a-e040-e00a18063089

panging and posing. A slight shoulder movement that calls attention to her bust, that is all of a dare. A hippy undulation below the waist that is a sheaf of promises tied with conscious power. She is acting out 'I'm a darned sweet woman and you know it.'"[54] *Madame Zora* captures this everyday movement of Blackgirls—their attitude, sexual agency, and conscious power.

Madame Zora presents Hurston's cultivation of a "womanist" attitude during girlhood as essential for her folklorist work. By "womanist," I refer to Walker's definition in her book *In Search of Our Mothers' Gardens: Womanist Prose* (1983). Walker writes:

> **Womanist 1.** From *womanish.* (Opp. Of "girlish," i.e., frivolous, irresponsible, not serious.) A black feminist or feminist of color. From the black folk

> expression of mothers to female children, "You acting womanish," i.e., like a woman. Usually referring to outrageous, audacious, courageous or willful behavior. Wanting to know more and in greater depth than is considered "good" for one . . . Interchangeable with another black folk expression: "You trying to be grown."[55]

While Hurston's actual lifespan and Rahman's musical dramatization predate Walker's term, the narrators nonetheless depict Hurston as the embodiment of womanist thought. For example, Black Herman begins his tale by describing Hurston as a "rambunctious" Blackgirl. "Too hot spirited for a gal. Womanish. Always listening to grown folks talk," Black Herman states. Spirit of Zora confirms Black Herman's narrative, providing a specific example of how Hurston's audacious behavior challenged her father's pursuit of toxic masculinity. "I was my Mama's child and I knew she wasn't happy. Though my tongue did not, my eyes accused him of the thing I heard from the neighbors," says Spirit of Zora. While Spirit of Zora cannot vocalize her innermost feelings about her father's infidelity—he is, after all, a respected Baptist preacher—she does use her agency to align herself with Black women's culture and challenge Black male authority through her gaze. Her father, portrayed by Black Herman, responds to her outrageous behavior by reinforcing male dominance. He declares: "I'm the man!" These early experiences of overhearing "grown folk talk" instilled womanist sensibilities and an abiding interest in Black folklore.

As Spirit of Zora and Happy Sweet share the story of Hurston's "prematurely knowing," they also reveal the truth about Blackgirls' vulnerability to exploitation and sexual abuse. The women present Hurston as a nine-year-old girl with a strong desire to obtain an education. Her father sends her to boarding school but does not provide the necessary funds to secure her enrollment. Lacking both protection and funding from her father, a young Zora finds herself destitute. Spirit of Zora uses song to express Zora's innermost thoughts: "No time for childhood dreams/ It's all over now/ Why did I have to see my destiny/ No time left for fantasy." Resigned to a life of domestic servitude, Zora puts away her "childish toys" and "childish joys" and secures employment as a maid at the boarding school. However, her spirit is not crushed for long because, much like Childs's Bella, she continues to imagine a life beyond the limitations society places on Blackgirls. Zora dreams of obtaining an education—her only hope for social mobility—even while the realities of being a poor Blackgirl during the turn of the twentieth century resurface.

Happy Sweet performs Zora's encounter with a male boarder—perhaps a teacher—while making a bed. Happy Sweet states: "Yes, sir, I'm trying to earn money for school. Because I'm going to be a writer someday, sir. No sir I am not joking. Oh yes sir I could use a nickel tip. Oh! Don't do that sir. I'll talk if you wanna but that's all. Cut it out. Stop it! Don't!" This story reveals several dark truths embedded within American history: Blackgirls have long been perceived as ignorant and sexually available to any man. As such, the nameless man finds her intellect, dreams, and aspirations of greatness humorous at best. However, Happy Sweet/Zora uses Black folk expressions to assert her agency and dismiss unwanted sexual advances. She responds: "Yes I do need the money. . . but you know you couldn't even steal a feel from a midget mosquito for a nickel so why offer it to me." In so doing, Happy Sweet portrays Zora's wit and humor as a much-needed shield of protection.

Happy Sweet's narration represents the dangers that countless Blackgirls encountered while working as domestic laborers. Indeed, scholars such as Hazel V. Carby, Darlene Clark Hine, and others have revealed the heretofore forgotten history of Blackgirls experiencing verbal abuse, sexual harassment, and rape while working in close proximity to their employers. Carby's pioneering work, *Reconstructing Womanhood: The Emergence of the Afro-American Woman Novelist* (1987), brought critical attention to early Black women writers and their focus on Black women's sexual vulnerability. Hine builds on Carby's reclamation efforts, delving deeper into how their work as domestic laborers fostered their vulnerability, finding that during and following chattel slavery, Black women navigated their hostile working conditions by developing a culture of dissemblance. As stated in Chapter 1, Black women could retain a sense of self and find relief from white oppressive forces by giving the appearance of openness to employers while keeping their innermost lives private. Happy Sweet gestures towards this tool of survival by maintaining a deferential appearance, referring to the nameless boarder as "sir." However, it is not until she lets her guard down and expresses her innermost thoughts and desires that the nameless boarder assaults her. In other words, showing genuine emotions in the workplace has always been risky business for Black women and girls. *Madame Zora* issues a call for Black communities to respect and protect *all* Blackgirls from abuse and sexual exploitation.

Rahman's concern for the safety of Blackgirls stems from her own experiences of navigating an abusive home life and the streets of Harlem as a foster child. She details her experiences transitioning from youthful childhood to prematurely knowing in *Chewed Water: A Memoir* (2001). Rahman writes that "girlhood to me means 103 West 120th street, apartment #123, my address in Harlem; Mrs. Farel, my foster mother; and that day in March 1956 when, in New York City's Family Court, I relinquished my three-month-old son for adoption."[56] Unfortunately, neither her religious zealot foster mother nor the Harlem neighborhood offered much protection. Rahman remembers Mrs. Feral telling her that she was inherently sinful and would follow her mother's footsteps by becoming sexually active before marriage. To avoid this unwanted outcome, Rahman remembers Mrs. Feral using physical punishment for any perceived misstep. For example, she received a beating after Mrs. Feral discovered her "dirty" DC and Marvel comic books stash.[57] Rahman writes: "On the floor, on my knees, I scuttle in every direction. I shield my face from the rope with my hands and OOUAWAHHH! blood leaks from my fingertips. . . . Every inch of flesh stings. Open cuts dot my legs, arms, and face. And then the storm is over."[58] Rahman's horrific description places her in a subservient, nonhuman position. In addition to suffering abuse at home, Rahman remembers predators using money as a means to lure her and other Blackgirls into the sex trade. She writes: "Jumping Double Dutch in the street in front of my house, I came to understand what society thought of black females, children included, as cars with New Jersey license plates cruised up and down and the drivers beckoned us, waving dollar bills in the air."[59] Despite these challenges, Rahman "chewed water"—meaning, she achieved the unthinkable after defying societal expectations—by graduating from Howard University, just like her idol, Hurston.

The storytellers depict the limits society places on Blackgirls, portraying Hurston as a Blackgirl who refuses to follow traditional heteronormative gender roles. While Hurston married Herbert Sheen (m. 1927; div. 1931), Albert Price (m. 1939; div. 1943), and James Howell Pitts (m. 1944; div. 1944) during her lifetime, the narrators depict only one marriage. Doctor Mo/Reporter asks Happy Sweet/Zora about her experiences with marriage, so she and Black Herman/Husband perform their early courtship. Happy Sweet/Zora and Black Herman/Husband express their undying love for each other in the bedroom. Immediately following this scene, Cora Mae/Zora and Black Herman/Husband depict life three weeks after marriage. Black Herman/Husband conveys that he finds Cora Mae/Zora's writings "cute" until she insists she won't accompany him back to Chicago but instead will return to her research with Langston Hughes in the South. The couple has the following exchange:

BLACK HERMAN/HUSBAND: I don't want you in another man riding around in the backwoods alone.... You are *my* wife now. Your research days are over.
CORA MAE/ZORA: If I was a tongue I'd refuse to speak those words that just came outta your mouth. If I was ears I wouldn't hear what you just said. If I was arms I'd be packing all my bags and if I was feet I'd be making tracks away from here.

The contrast between the two scenes is telling. Before marriage, Black Herman/Husband and Cora Mae/Zora take comfort in each other's arms as equal partners. However, the balance of power shifts upon marriage, wherein Black Herman/Husband positions Cora Mae/Zora as his property. He embodies the sexist ideology that Blackgirls must relinquish her identity and cease having a career upon marriage. Instead, he expects her to accompany him to medical school so he can pursue his dream. Cora Mae/Zora responds to his male bravado with Black folk expressions. Her cutting remark—the use of her tongue, ears, arms, and feet—allows her to reclaim agency over her own body. Her self-determination will enable her to resist society's limits for Blackgirls and wives and continue her career.

The storytellers engage with the controversial aspect of Hurston's life: allegations of sexual deviancy. On September 13, 1948, New York City police officers arrested Hurston on one count of assault, one count of "placing a child in such a situation as likely to impair morals," and three counts of sodomy.[60] The next month, the juvenile court case was leaked, sensationalized, and printed in two Black newspapers: the *New York Age* and *Afro-American. Madame Zora* uses "Community Voices" to depict Hurston's downfall. They say: "Extra Extra Extra / Read all about it! / Zora accused of unspeakable / Unmentionable, Unpardonable / Illicit, immoral abominations / With a ten-year-old!" Spirit of Zora also denies the accusation, but the court of public opinion condemns her. As a result, she becomes a social pariah, publishers show little interest in her work, and she dies penniless and forgotten. Although the real-life Hurston was proven innocent, the false accusation of sodomy linked her with a homosexual act, effectively destroying her reputation.

The history of criminalizing homosexuality continues to resonate with Black queer feminist spectators. Just twenty years before Hurston's arrest, conservatives waged a campaign against queer folks, many of which found solace in Harlem nightlife. The theatre historian James F. Wilson writes that "the greater conspicuousness of lesbians and gay men on the stages and streets throughout New York aroused increased cultural anxiety about their supposed assaults on traditional morality."[61] Conservatives counter-attacked queer visibility through stigmatization and enforcement of sodomy and indecency laws. Wilson writes that this counter-attack "propelled lesbians and gay men to develop underground social networks and institutions."[62] In other words, the unjust legislature effectively consigned queer folk to prisons or what we now call "the closet." Unfortunately, many Black artists—including many blues women and possibly Hurston's collaborator, Langston Hughes—were forced to remain in the closet to avoid public shaming and imprisonment.

Madame Zora further illuminates Black queer history and visibility through Doctor Mo and Black Herman's embodiment of the historical figure Langston Hughes and Hurston's real-life white patron, Mrs. Rufus Osgood Mason. Indeed, the world of storytelling allows performers to embody different personas, making constructions of race, gender, and sexuality more visible and less fixed. The fluidity of identities becomes especially pronounced when actor Keith David (Doctor Mo) transforms himself into the legendary Langston Hughes, and actor Willie Barnes (Black Herman) embodies Mrs. Rufus Osgood Mason, known simply as "Godmother." During their exchange, Black Herman/Godmother agrees to continue her patronage as long as Doctor Mo/Langston remains an "exotic primitive savage." Black Herman/Godmother states: "In your art I want to feel the heat of the jungle / In your poems I want to hear the beat of the drums. / A beat to match the drums throbbing inside of me / A sound to match the hot blobs dancing wildly in my head / My bare breasts are painted red / My face is painted yellow / Yeeeeeeeow! I am in the jungle!" Doctor Mo/Langston rejects her primitivist understanding of Black identity, insisting: "I am not an exotic primitive savage. After all, this is 1929 and I wasn't born in the jungle but in St. Louis, Missouri!" On one level, this exchange uses excess to lampoon Black stereotypes and expose the long history of white fetishization of Black bodies. While there are no extant recordings of the Ensemble Studio Theatre production, Gussow's review suggests that Barnes portrayed Godmother as a caricature rather than a three-dimensional human being. Barnes' decision to interpret these characters as "broad on both counts" aligns with the humor and representational aspects of the Black storytelling tradition.[63] On a deeper level, Barnes's performance of excessive white womanhood heightens awareness of his own masculine body. Therefore, Black queer feminist spectators might read his words of sexual desire for another

Black man—representing the historical Langston Hughes—as an acknowledgment of Black queer desire and visibility throughout history. *Bubbly Black Girl* similarly suggests a need to excavate the (often) untold history of Black queer artistry.

The Bubbly Black Girl Sheds Her Chameleon Skin

As with *Madame Zora* and *Bella*, *Bubbly Black Girl* uses narration to express the innermost thoughts and experiences of Blackgirls. In the Playwrights Horizons production, LaChanze (Viveca) opens the musical by directly addressing the audience. She introduces herself as "Bubbly" and invites spectators to bear witness to her imaginative world. She enters the small stage sporting an All-American look: red t-shirt, blue skirt, white sneakers, and two afro puffs. Behind her, a simple white set provides a neutral backdrop to help illuminate her interiority. For example, when Viveca first appears as "an energetic little girl," lighting reflects her positive outlook on life.[64] As Viveca sings about natural elements that bring her joy (i.e., breezes, palm trees, etc.), the set is bathed in a calm blue. Later, when Viveca matures and experiences the barriers that limit Blackgirl artists, lighting designer Michael Lincoln casts the stage in shadows and an ominous red, reflecting her frustration, disappointment, and anger. The production modes, coupled with representations of Viveca's everyday activities—walking home from school with a crush, reading a newspaper, playing with a doll, and daydreaming—create a sense of intimacy, allowing spectators to see the world from a Blackgirl's perspective.

Childs exposes society's misconception of Black girlhood by juxtaposing Viveca's subjectivity with her neighbors' pathological understandings of Blackgirls. Childs first presents Viveca as a determined young girl who claims the right to navigate the streets of 1960s Los Angeles unencumbered by violence. Viveca exudes energy and has a large smile plastered on her face as she walks home from school, singing "Welcome to my L.A." with her friends. As a child of the 1960s, Viveca embodies the youth culture and "California Sound" of the day. Her world revolves around her love of the sea, a schoolyard crush, and a fascination with fast cars. However, when she returns to her neighborhood, spectators witness a strong contrast between Viveca's behavior and society's perception of Blackgirls. While Viveca views herself as a typical Blackgirl, spectators discover that her neighbors consider her an *exception* to the rule. For example, Neighbor 3 states that Viveca is "very bright," Neighbor 4 remarks that she "has both parents in the home," and Neighbor 5 interjects, "and not a welfare check in sight!"[65] Viveca's intelligence, middle-class background, and two-parent home astonish her neighbors who have internalized racist beliefs about Blackgirls. They assume that all Blackgirls are ignorant, raised by a single parent (most likely, a mother), and their families are financially dependent on government-supported welfare programs. Immediately afterward, the neighbors, Daddy, and Mommy boast in unison: "She's one of the good ones!" In this world, being "one of the good ones" means not having sexual relations. Thus, even while adults—including her well-meaning parents—praise her behavior, it is at the expense of other Blackgirls. The stereotype of Blackgirl promiscuity remains intact, and Viveca has the added pressure of maintaining the illusion of Blackgirl exceptionalism.

Viveca escapes the stigma of Black girlhood by turning inward, using her imagination to craft a new identity drawn from the Western fairy tale tradition. She begins this process from the safety of her bedroom, comparing her "Negro baby doll" to her white Chitty Chatty doll. She ultimately finds that if she looked more like Chitty Chatty, the world would love and protect her too. Viveca responds to this painful truth by using her imagination. Mirroring the 16th Street Baptist Church explosion, Viveca "kills" her Negro baby doll. After making the sound of a bomb exploding and tossing her Black doll to the floor, she reveals her new identity to Chitty Chatty. Viveca explains: "I've decided I'm gonna be white! Just like you, Chitty Chatty. Uh-huh. And one day a prince is gonna come and rescue me from this evil, awful spell that a wicked witch has cast upon me. My prince shall kiss me, and my kinky, kinky hair shall straighten and grow down, down, down to my behind. My eyes shall turn as blue as a robin's egg, my skin as white as the virgin snow." After her declaration, a white fairy tale prince sporting a fur-lined red cape with matching tights arrives in her bedroom. In the Playwrights Horizons production, Prince (Jerry Dixon) drops to his knee and declares: "How glad I am that you were so clever as to hide inside the little white girl chamber of your mind while you waited so, so patiently for me! But wait no longer, Viveca, for I am here and ready to carry you off in my brawny, brawny arms." While Black queer feminist spectators may find this fairy tale absurd and may correlate the notion that a Blackgirl can just "decide" to be white with the wrongheaded belief that one can "choose" to be gay. Furthermore, they might also find Viveca's desire to find acceptance and love quite painful. The reality is that these canonical fairy tales socialize Blackgirls to equate "love" or "happily ever after" with heterosexual unions and "beauty" with having white skin, blue eyes, and long straight blond hair. Thus, these limiting beliefs discourage Blackgirls from acknowledging queer desire and Black beauty.

Despite Viveca's best efforts to assimilate and imagine all of her problems away, her feelings of isolation and fear of white-authored violence surface as nightmares. In the Playwrights Horizons production, Viveca's anxieties come to life before the audience's eyes. A cross is positioned at the top of her bed as five nightriders surround her bed cloaked in white sheets. Harriet Tubman (Cheryl Alexander) enters leading four runaway slaves, points a pistol directly at Viveca, and declares: "Be free or die, you Oreo, you Oreo, you O-reo-reo!" In her daily life, Viveca's peers also identified her as an "Oreo," suggesting that she may be a Black person on the outside but has actually internalized white identity politics. "Oreo" carries a tremendous stigma because the term implies self-hatred and a lack of racial solidarity within the Black community. As such, an "Oreo" is perceived as a threat to the Black liberation struggle. Consequently, Viveca experiences feelings of pain and isolation as expressed in the ensemble's jazz-infused song, "Sticks and Stones." The lyrics include hate speech hurled against Black queer folk—including "fag," "dyke," and "nigger." Viveca's precarious positionality—her outsider/within stance—resonates with the struggles of many Black queer folks. Black queer feminist spectators understand that all too often, queerness is perceived as a "white thing." The assumption is that Black queer folk have internalized white identity politics and therefore lack a commitment to the Black community. In other words, their very identity makes them suspect and a threat to the Black freedom struggle. This erroneous thinking only alienates the most vulnerable within the Black community and undermines the Black freedom struggle.

Ultimately, Viveca's imagination and assimilation efforts cannot fully protect her from the realities of state-sanctioned violence against Black people. After Viveca attends a party on her graduation night, her schoolgirl crush Gregory walks her home. Romance is clearly in the air. The set is bathed in a night sky as Gregory (Darius de Haas) discloses his feelings for Viveca in the R&B-funk song "Beautiful Bright Blue Sky." After the song, Viveca and Gregory lean in to kiss but are interrupted by the sound of a car breaking and car doors slamming shut. Four police officers approach the couple, with one officer standing center stage while three others surround Gregory. As Viveca tries to explain their innocence, Policeman brushes past her and checks Gregory for weapons. Policeman quickly places Gregory in handcuffs while the other officers stand with face shields, batons, and guns drawn. This standoff culminates in the song, "Legacy," in which Policeman orders Gregory to hold his hands up, yield his concealed weapon, and remain silent while Gregory and Viveca proclaim innocence. Afterward, Policeman's partner receives additional information—presumably from dispatch—and he states, "Wait a minute—wrong one." Gregory's unprovoked arrest confuses Viveca, who has been taught the middle-class ideology of racial uplift. She even pleads with the officers, stating, "Gregory's not like that—he comes from a good family—we both come from good families." However, she discovers that "positive" representation of Black people (i.e., a "good family") does not diminish anti-Black violence. Combining racial profiling with weaponized white supremacy, the officers identify Gregory's Black male body as a threat that must be immediately immobilized and silenced. When they do discover they have erred, the officers reassert their masculinity with the threat of retribution, warning Gregory, "Be careful, son." Viveca's encounter with white-authored gun violence only motivates her to continue to smile, pretend as if the episode did not happen, and pursue her dream of becoming a dancer.

Similar to the other Blackgirl protagonists, dance provides a means for Viveca to express her awakening sexuality. While Gregory asserts his manhood by insisting he must "protect" her by walking her home, Viveca barely glances his way. Instead, she begins a sensual dance a la Gwen Verdon's 1958 performance of "What Lola Wants." Viveca explains: "I'm dancing around in my underwear, like Lola, in that movie *Damn Yankees*." Unfortunately, Viveca's bold declaration of sexual desire upsets Gregory, who adheres to Black middle-class respectability politics. Gregory upbraids Viveca, stating, "Oooh, you better stop that! It's not nice for little girls to swear and dance around in their underwear! And if you keep on doin' it, I'm not gonna marry you when we grow up." Viveca responds by turning inward, expressing her innermost thoughts to the audience: "Marry me! Oh no . . . then he'll start bossing me around, and I'll never become—(Starry-eyed, as dancing music rises.) the greatest dancing star in the world (The music is now discordant.) And I'll be miserable for the rest of my life—no way, Jose! That'll never, ever happen to me." Even as a young girl, Viveca understands that marriage and prescribed gender roles will lead to her loss of agency and happiness. After all, only through dance can she fully express her creativity, strength, and sexual desire. Viveca refuses to relinquish her dream in exchange for hearth and home and instead enters the world of professional dance.

The New York dance scene of the early 1980s provides a space for Viveca to find acceptance and camaraderie with the Black queer community. When she arrives, she enrolls in many classes, including modern dance, where she meets Keith (Duane Boutté), a Black queer dancer. The two immediately become friends after expressing her attraction to a white male dancer who resembles Prince Charming. Keith sets her straight (pun intended) in the following exchange:

VIVECA: He's really cute.
KEITH: He's really gay.
VIVECA: How do you know?
KEITH: 'Cause I'm really gay, too.
VIVECA: Shoot!
KEITH: Sorry, mush nose. All the good ones are gay.

Their humorous rapid-fire exchange reveals Viveca's naïveté about the world and a Black queer presence in the arts. Keith unabashedly asserts his queer identity and teases her with the trope that "all the good men are gay." In contrast to Viveca's previous exchanges with peers, Keith does not ostracize her for not being "Black enough." Instead, he befriends her, tells her about upcoming auditions, and offers advice to help her nail her next audition. Unfortunately, Keith only appears in this scene and one other brief moment to congratulate her on receiving her first Broadway role. While Keith may only appear as a dramatic foil for Viveca, he represents the queer dancers Childs knew and lost during the AIDS crisis of the early 1980s. Childs explains: "What made me go to creating musicals is that I was a musical theater performer in the time of the AIDS crisis. I would say almost 95% of my very good friends died at a very early age. They were in their twenties or thirties, and every day, there was somebody to [mourn]. I had to check out. It was just too hard to perform. You would be on stage, and you would feel like you were with ghosts, and it was just too difficult."[66] Black queer feminist spectators might understand Keith's disappearance as an homage to the tremendous loss in the arts and a bleak period of queer history more broadly. Viveca and Keith's camaraderie suggests a strong need for allyship within the Black community.

While Viveca does not identify as queer, she remains in a "closet" of sorts, hiding her innermost thoughts and feelings for fear of rejection or violence. With Keith's help, Viveca achieves her dream of landing a Broadway audition but quickly discovers that Director Bob finds her not "Black" enough. This moment becomes Viveca's breaking point. Although her father socialized her to smile in the face of adversity, maintaining the image of Black feminine strength comes at a cost. She has spent her life unable to voice her true feelings to her family, friends, or community. As a result, her psyche has become fractured, and she has been forced to withdraw inward, creating new worlds and possibilities through her imagination. As such, only spectators glimpse the depth of her genuine emotions—from the joy of discovering dance to the excitement of romance to fear that white vigilantes or police officers will kill her or her loved ones. Now pushed to her limits to perform stereotypical blackness during her audition, Viveca makes the difficult decision to be her authentic self. She removes her wig, stops self-censoring her words, and claims the right to take up space, an essential first step towards self-definition. Her fears, as well as her decision to forgo a fractured life and come out of the "closet," might resonate with and inspire Black queer feminist spectators to do the same, despite the risks.

In conclusion, Black women intellectuals have long understood that storytelling is key to our survival as a people. Toni Cade Bambara testified of this profound truth in her essay "Salvation is the Issue" (1984). Bambara writes that "stories are important. They keep us alive. In the ships, in the camps, in the quarters, fields, prisons, on the road, on the run, underground, under siege, in the throes, on the verge—the storyteller snatches us back from the edge to hear the next chapter. In which we are the subjects. We, the hero of the tales.[67] Unfortunately, it is still a rarity for Blackgirls to appear as heroes of their own tales within US popular entertainment. If Blackgirl protagonists surface as subjects, they frequently appear as flat, one-dimensional victims of (often Black) male brutality, delinquents, or otherwise pathological. Regardless of their falsehood, these stereotypes persist and have detrimental consequences to Blackgirl psyches. Black women musical theatre artists undermine such mythologies by crafting new images of Blackgirl heroes. While Black queer feminist spectators can admire the courage, achievements, and noble qualities of Bella, Viveca, and Zora, what truly sets them apart as heroes are their ability to imagine and articulate their interiority—their hopes, dreams, and fears—despite the hostile forces within society that would render them voiceless and powerless. In essence, storytelling functions on multiple levels within the scripts and production modes of *Bella*, *Madam Zora*, and *Bubbly Black Girl*. Yet, all forms of storytelling create space for Blackgirls to imagine themselves heroes of their own tales, fully capable of conquering forces that would harm them. The following chapter continues this line of inquiry, exploring how Black women musical theatre artists use the fairy tale tradition to create new images of Blackgirl strength.

4

Blackgirl Fairy Tales

It's the spring term of my sophomore year of college. I'm finally eighteen, but I feel like Peter Pan. I want to stay a kid forever, so I enroll in a Theatre for Young audiences course at Western Oregon University. The professor tells us that together, we will write, produce, and perform our own adaptation of a fairy tale. We'll then tour the production to public schools in the surrounding towns at the end of the term.

I'm super excited, so I toss out ideas: *Cinderella, The Little Mermaid, Alice's Adventures in Wonderland.* Nothing sticks. A classmate suggests *Snow White.* There are enough roles for all ten of us: Snow White, Huntsman, Witch, and the seven dwarfs. Everyone agrees. I have to stop this. I speak up. I tell them that I never really liked that story.

Why not?

All eyes are on me. I am hyper-aware of the lack of melanin in the room. If I share my truth, I'll probably get laughed at. If I don't share, then well, I look like a jerk. Like I'm making random excuses so they'll pick my idea. My throat feels so tight, my face is so hot, but I decide to share. I tell them I've always been bothered by that fairy. *Snow White* taught me that white skin is beautiful. That story always made me feel bad. Like I was ugly and could never be beautiful.

Silence.

Now we have to adapt Snow White, *but only if you play Snow White.*

I hesitate because I don't want to make this about me.

This isn't just about you. We gotta shake this story up. Let's make a feminist tale that teaches children that Black is beautiful and that girls can save themselves.

We go to work, and a few weeks later, we present out musical adaptation to elementary school kids (see Figure 4.1). Most of the kids smile, cheer, and sing along when we perform. However, there are always a few kids whose brows furrow when I enter the stage.

A Black Snow White?!

Black Queer Girlhood on the Musical Theatre Stage. La Donna L. Forsgren, Oxford University Press.
 DOI: 10.1093/9780197661444.003.0005

Figure 4.1 Author (Snow White) in rehearsal for *Snow White*, a 2000 devised musical production at Western Oregon University, directed by Dr. Adelaide Palagi. Still image courtesy of the author.

Black women have long understood the importance of fairy tales in Blackgirls' lives. By fairy tale, I refer to the subgenre of folklore that entails "dark stories of violence, hardship, and strife" and contain "magic and wish fulfillment," and offer "the promise of victory over villainy."[1] Fairy tales are more than made-up stories meant to entertain children. As one of the oldest forms of communication, storytelling has helped transmit values, beliefs, and cultural mores of pre-literate societies. However, fairy tales take on special meaning for Blackgirls, who, from an early age, must navigate violence in their everyday lives. This violence takes many forms, including denying Blackgirls access to an essential human habitat (i.e., clean air, shelter, water, and food); policing their speech, bodies, and behavior; and socializing them to believe in their own inferiority. These and other forms of violence negatively impact the physical, psychological, and economic well-being of Blackgirls. Black women musical theatre artists have also recognized that canonical European fairy tales such as *Snow White, Sleeping Beauty*, and *Cinderella*—which valorize alabaster skin, red lips, and other markers of white feminine beauty—could harm Blackgirls' psyche. Yet, if radicalized, these same fairy tales had the potential to create new images of Blackgirl joy, resilience, and victory over their seemingly more powerful adversaries.

Black Arts Movement (1965–1976) writers Aduke Aremu (Gwendolyn Holmes), Jackie Taylor, and Rosa Guy fostered the Black aesthetic through a radical re-evaluation of the Western fairy tale canon. As Black radical thinkers, Aremu, Taylor, and Guy understood that many classic European fairy tales originated within the African folk tale tradition. As revolutionary artists, they crafted works that rejected white visions of the world and, in so doing, reclaimed African diasporic traditions while also celebrating Blackgirl subjectivity. Indeed, Aremu's children's musical *The Liberation of Mother Goose* (1972), Taylor's popular musical *The Other Cinderella* (1976), and Rosa Guy's 1985 novel *My Love, My Love or The Peasant Girl* (later adapted into the 1990 musical, *Once on This Island*) allow audiences to appreciate the richness of Black culture through the perspectives of Blackgirl protagonists.

Aremu, Taylor, and Guy's critique of Western fairy tales parallel conversations within feminist fairy tale studies during the 1970s. Sparked by Alison Lurie's "Fairy Tale Liberation" (1970), feminists launched critical debates about the role of fairy tales, positioning the promise of "happily ever after" within the larger cultural and political struggle for gender equality.[2] However, these early feminist critiques focused on depicting fairy tale heroines and limited the scope of their analysis to European and Anglo-American texts and writers.[3] For example, Donald Haase's collection *Fairy Tales and Feminism: New Approaches* (2004) offers one of the first studies to explore the reception of fairy tales, including those beyond the borders of German, French, and English-speaking countries. Hasse writes that "it is time for scholars to assess the impact of feminism and feminist criticism itself on the way contemporary readers experience fairy tales [and] expand the focus of feminist fairy-tale research beyond the Western European and Anglo-American tradition, and even within those traditions to investigate the fairytale intertexts in the work of minority writers and performers."[4] Unfortunately, fairy tales created by Black women and the socio-political meaning spectators garner from their works have yet to receive sustained study by feminist fairy tale scholars.

Literary and Black studies scholars credit Black Arts Movement women writers for fostering greater diversity within the fairy tale tradition. In her edited collection, *Fairy Tales with Black Consciousness: Essays on Adaptations of Familiar Stories* (2013), the children's literature scholar Laretta Henderson credits the Black Arts Movement for furthering the representation of Black children's subjectivity in the twentieth century. Henderson writes that "African-American retellings of European fairy tales resist an all-White world of fairytales thereby serving as a mirror for the African American child and a window for others. The rationale for these stories may have rested in evolution of postmodern literature, the Black Arts Movement and the increase in the publication of multicultural children's literature in the mid-20th century."[5] Black women writers, in particular, used their talent to create new images, allowing Blackgirls—queer, trans, or otherwise—to see themselves projected on the stage. Musical theatre scholarship has yet to appreciate or acknowledge these contributions.

Aremu, Taylor, and Guy's adaptations not only restore images of feminine strength within the early folk tale tradition but also critique systems that oppress Black people (especially Blackgirls) and offer alternative visions of a more just and equitable society. Adaptation has always been an essential element of the oral folk tale tradition. Jack Zipes writes that "folktales were to be shared and exchanged, used and modified according to the needs of the tellers and listeners."[6] For example, cultural researchers and authors Jacob and Wilhelm Grimm famously modified their collection of oral tales to suit their own German middle-class values and cultures. Their "editorial interventions" have been well-documented by fairy tale scholars Ruth B. Bottigheimer, Donald Haase, and many others.[7] Haase writes that the Brothers Grimm's deliberate act "weakened once-strong female characters, demonized female power, imposed a male perspective on stories voicing women's discontent, and rendered heroines powerless by depriving them of speech, all in accord with the social values of their time."[8] As an outgrowth of oral storytelling, literary fairy tales similarly reflect the needs, concerns, and cultural practices of both author and reader. Musical fairy tales work in a similar fashion; allowing artists to adapt canonical works to meet their needs and share their specialized knowledge with spectators. In return, Black queer feminist spectators have the ability to use and/or modify the artists' vision to address their needs and concerns.

Aremu, Taylor, and Guy's works challenge the Western fairy tale canon as depicted by the Brothers Grimm, Hans Christian Andersen, Charles Perrault, and Walt Disney. Zipes writes that "collecting folktales was a social and political act of some kind—and it still is. Not only did educated middle-class collectors give voice to the lower classes, but they also spoke out in defense of their native languages and in the interests of national and regional movements that sought more autonomy for groups with particular interests."[9]

Indeed, Aremu, Taylor, and Guy's works celebrate Black women writers' tradition of amplifying the experiential knowledge, history of resistance, and the interior life of Blackgirls. More specifically, Aremu's "The Liberation of Mother Goose" empowers Blackgirls to center themselves in classic fairy tales. In so doing, she dramatizes the everyday action of Blackgirls who "engage with literary texts through counter fairy tales (CFT) as a resistive literary strategy to reclaim Black girls' narrative and be reflective of their own experiences."[10] This is important because "Black students are rarely afforded opportunities to see themselves with the texts that they are reading, or if a Black character is referenced, it is often through slave narrative of racial subjectification."[11] Taylor's *The Other Cinderella* actualizes scholars Jemimah L. Young, Marquita D. Foster, and Dorothy Hines's call for the "(re)centering of Black girls' voices in ways that challenge the idea that 'even Cinderella is white' . . . while also given the opportunities for counternarratives and resistance to injustice."[12] Taylor's musical does just that, encouraging the next generation of Blackgirls to empower themselves. Finally, Guy's novel *My Love, My Love*, adapted into musical hit *Once on This Island*, provides an important glimpse into the desires and trials of poor Blackgirls coming of age in the aftermath of slavery in the Caribbean islands. Collectively, these musicals attest to the power of fairy tales and the beauty of Blackgirls.

The Liberation of Mother Goose

From its musical debut at New York public schools in 1972, Aremu's *The Liberation of Mother Goose* quickly became a staple of the Harlem Children's Theatre Company's (HCTC; 1971–1990) repertoire. Aremu, along with artist Omodele Folayan, co-founded the HCTC just one year prior and at the time, held the distinction of being the only Black children's theatre repertory company in the United States.[13] At its inception, the HCTC provided a space for nearly one hundred Black and Puerto Rican children—from ages 4 to 18 years old—to hone their craft in the basement of Harlem's P.S. 57. Students received free music, dance, voice, drama, art, and technical theatre training, which gave birth to Aremu's first musical, *Land of the Egyptians*. Aduke's next musical, *Mother Goose*—a reimagined mashup of Charles Perrault's *The Tales of Mother Goose* (1696), Lewis Carroll's *Alice's Adventures in Wonderland* (1865) and *Through the Looking Glass, and What Alice Found There* (1871), and classic English nursery rhymes—became their most popular touring production and included a cast of sixty to eighty-five children.[14] The HCTC's successful tour led to a May 22, 1973 television debut of *Mother Goose* on Black Journal (WNET/13), the first nationally televised news program focused on Black American issues. Their televised performance brought the company greater exposure, and within a few short years, the company garnered rave reviews and received a second Off-Broadway run at Joseph Papp's Public Theater during the 1975–1976 New York Shakespeare Festival season.

The juxtaposition of the Off-Broadway success of *Mother Goose* and Aremu's inability to move the production to the next level of commercial theatre speaks volumes about the barriers that prevent Black women writers from breaking into Broadway. In a *New York Amsterdam News* interview following the Public Theatre production, Aremu publicly declared, "I want 'The Liberation of Mother Goose' on Broadway!"[15] Working under the belief that Papp would help make her dream a reality, she collaborated with Jimmy Justice, a well-known English pop singer and Broadway composer, to prepare *Mother Goose* for a Broadway debut. Aremu remembers charging her new musical director with the task of transforming *Mother Goose* from a "jazz music" sound into a "commercial-sounding" Broadway musical which would include rock and modern music.[16] She then secured Lilias White to choreograph a combination of jazz, rock, ballet, modern, Caribbean, and breakdance numbers. Finally, Aremu stepped down as long-time director of *Mother Goose* and hired Gilbert Moses, the original (and recently fired) Broadway director of *The Wiz*, to direct the musical. In other words, Aremu spent all of her time, energy, and resources lining all of her ducks in a row.

Unfortunately, Aremu's dream of a Broadway production of *Mother Goose* never came to fruition. When asked to discuss the circumstances of this failed venture, Aremu remembers:

> Oh God, Joseph Papp and I had a long conversation. He took that Elizabeth piece [*Runaways* (1978)]. I was so over it. He was mentoring this white hippie writer. She became very famous for a long time. Elizabeth Swados; whoever she was. She had a lot of plays running at the same time. She went to Broadway. Yes, she did. That's how it works in Black theatre. He took her to Broadway.[17]

Similarities abound with *Mother Goose* and *Runaways*. Both musicals were produced by Papp at the Public Theatre, included a large cast of multiethnic children performers, and had the potential to meet commercial success if transferred onto Broadway. However, the most glaring difference is that the white woman artist had the continued support of a famous Jewish producer; the Black woman artist did not. In addition, one production provided an accounting of the struggles of inner-city youth as presented by a white woman; the other captured the interiority of a Blackgirl as envisioned by a Black woman artist. Finally, one production garnered five Tony Award nominations, including Best Musical, Best Book of a Musical, Best Original Score, Best Direction of a Musical, and Best Choreography; the other production never even had the opportunity. Without Papp's support, Aremu turned to her mentor, Black television and theatrical producer Ellis Haizlip, for guidance. While her dream of a transfer to Broadway never came to fruition, the HCTC went on to tour *Mother Goose* at New York's Lincoln Center, Town Hall, the Apollo Theater, the Brooklyn Academy of Music, and the John F. Kennedy Center for the Performing Arts in Washington, D.C. before embarking on an international tour across Europe, Africa, and the Caribbean.[18]

Mother Goose provides a glimpse into the imaginative world of Alice Washington, a fifteen-year-old Harlem resident. As she walks home from school, she uses her creative power as a coping mechanism to escape the harsh realities of urban living. Rather than engage "busy, uninterested, and somewhat cruel" vendors and everyday people, Alice turns inward and talks to herself. She reflects on her inability to stay awake during her history test or comprehend "all those wars, dead people, madness and cruelness" within history.[19] Convinced that Mother will punish her for failing her test, she daydreams about better possibilities and creates a whole new world of "wild, luscious colors" populated with "the most exciting people you ever could imagine." When she arrives home from school, Mother insists that she abandon her imaginative play and enter the realm of womanhood. Mother states, "You are to stop this silly daydreaming, locking yourself in your room until all hours of the morning reading those fairy tales and talking to yourself. You are too old now for such nonsense." When Mother openly expresses love and physical affection for Alice, she also questions her daughter's sanity. Alice's self-isolation and obsession with fairy tales—on the eve of her sixteenth birthday—convinces Mother to have her evaluated by a "doctor." However, Mother fails to understand the value of fairy tales in her daughter's life. Fairy tales are so much more than an escape for Alice. In their article "Fairy Tales, Myth, and Fantasy" (2016) the fairy tales scholars Christina Phillips Mattson and Maria Tatar write:

> Fairytales in fantasy literature have often been positioned as escapist. But they are less a way out than a way in, and escape into perils and possibilities. Moving in the optative mode, they tell us how things might be, should be, could be, or ought to be. The stories give us a great "what ifs?" and they introduce [youth] to hypotheticals, giving them worlds that may not be real yet also characters who shape their identities in much the same way as people do in real life.[20]

The mere mention of her age and looming psychiatric treatment causes Alice to flee to the safety of her bedroom where she can dream about the "what ifs" and create stories that are more meaningful to her than historic figures and events. Staring off into the stars, she takes a mental flight down a rabbit hole in pursuit of her longed-for birthday present: a rabbit. Alice's creation of Wonderland and her journey through the "Forest of Discontent" and "Land of Wisdom" provide the cognitive space needed to explore her innermost desires.

Alice's search for her rabbit symbolizes the innermost desires of Blackgirls, including their ongoing need to validate their existence. In her "Character Analysis" of the unpublished playscript, Aremu writes: "Who is her rabbit? Is her rabbit a he? Is Alice searching for beauty, freedom, love, companionship, or does her rabbit represent a teenage girl's sexual fantasy[?]." Indeed, these themes appear throughout the musical but are particularly pronounced in Alice's "I want" song. Confused, sad, and lonely, Alice delivers a heart-wrenching solo titled "Searching" while in the "Forest of Discontent" at the conclusion of Act I. Alice repeatedly sings that she needs "communication," "truth," "reality," and a "friendship of love and peace." Her wish is granted at the beginning of Act II with the arrival of Little Red Riding Hood, a mystical Blackgirl. Little Red listens to Alice, offers her friendship, and grounds her in truth and reality by teaching her about Black history and culture. Perhaps most importantly, when Preacher fails to offer Alice any tangible help during his revival meeting, Little Red uses her Voodoo powers to guide Alice along her path to the powerful Mother Goose, who she believes will help Alice find her rabbit. Ultimately, Aremu finds that, "Who or what her rabbit represents is not as important as *how* she decides to fulfill her fantasy."[21] Indeed, the *how* of Alice's journey deserves further critical attention.

The HCTC's staging of *Mother Goose* invites spectators into the bright, colorful interior life of Blackgirls. HCTC administrator Dawn Alli directed the

1978 John F. Kennedy Center production of *Mother Goose* and remembers their unique staging practices as follows:

> At that time, we were innovative. We had people come from the audience. We had people come down from the sky and from backstage, left stage. . . . We wanted to paint the floor. We wanted to do lots of lighting. Hanging material from the back. All of those things because we didn't bring big sets. We were moving little things around the stage: blocks, trees, [and set pieces] that were moveable.
>
> [E]very character had a color scheme. When the character came out . . . fabric would come down and the color scheme would come out.[22]

By employing the "extended audience concept" and eliminating the traditional division between actor and audience, spectators functioned as co-travelers along Alice's journey. Furthermore, the use of simple set pieces and fabric to indicate place encouraged spectators to join Alice by similarly using their imaginations to fill in the gaps (see Figure 4.2).

Figure 4.2 Actresses perform as "Alice in Wonderland" and "Little Red Riding Hood" in Billie Holiday Theatre's 2014 production of Aduke Aremu's *The Liberation of Mother Goose*, directed by Abdel Salaam. Photo by W. Calvin Anderson, courtesy of W. Calvin Anderson.

Alice's colorful world and imaginative travel is not without purpose and meaning for spectators. Her vision of Wonderland incorporates characters drawn from an amalgamation of Harlem archetypes and classic European nursery rhymes and stories. Her creation includes lively music, song, dance, Voodoo rituals, and Black church practices. Perhaps most importantly, Alice's creation still manages to attend to the problems facing Black communities. Indeed, the theatre critic Patricia Ann Spence describes the 1975 production of *Mother Goose* at Douglas Turner Ward's Negro Ensemble Company as not only "consciousness-raising" but also a "scintillating and power-packed musical satire for children [that] exposes the illusions inherent in familiar nursery tales and re-adapts them to meaningful everyday Black experiences."[23] Alice's retelling of nursery rhymes—which prove humorous, ironic, and exaggerated in nature—provides a means for her to expose and critique problems within urban living. The subversive nature of Alice's world is in keeping with traditional Mother Goose nursery rhymes and picture books. Julia L. Mickenberg writes that the Mother Goose tradition includes "content that is, arguably, inappropriate for children" and "a history of being rewritten for satiric, and/or political effect through a process that Berthold Brecht . . . and Walter Benjamin called '*umfunktionierung*' or 'refunctioning.'"[24] Rather than begin the tale with the typical line, "once upon a time," the musical begins with an older cast member shouting, "the time is now!"[25] Issuing an SOS of sorts, the performers call Black spectators to attention—to learn from the satirical tale and take immediate action to better their own communities.

Alice's imaginative play helps her make sense of how historical atrocities continue to harm Black communities. Following the example of her history teacher, who she believes "changes the stories every day for her own amusement," Alice takes action to adapt beloved Western fairy tales for her own pleasure. She combines her knowledge of Harlem with her love of fairy tales and active imagination to create a Wonderland replete with well-known fairy tale characters and everyday archetypes which she places in the "Forest of Discontent." Alice imagines the criminal underclass through characters such as Alcoholic and Junkie, two homeless men who only care about getting their next "fix." Alice reimagines Carroll's larger-than-life flowers as beautiful prostitutes clad in "bright, carnival costumes" who perform modern dance. Alice revises Old Woman from the nursery rhyme "There was an Old Woman Who Lived in a Shoe" into a poverty-stricken, ex-convict who bemoans her poor housing situation. Old Woman tells Alcoholic, Junkie, and Solomon Grundy (reimagined from the nursery rhyme as "the derelict, and the dropouts of society"): "This is supposed to be the richest place in the world to live with such high standards of living, yet my house is so raggedy that no one wants to live near me." Old Woman also challenges contradictions within history, questioning why she is placed in jail for theft (regardless of her guilt or innocence) while "they," meaning colonialists, "stole all the gold from Africa" without negative consequences. After acknowledging this violent past and the continued policing and criminalization of Black people, Alice turns to a religious archetype named Preacher (a reimagined Mad Hatter) for guidance. However, when Alice attends his revival meeting, Preacher is too busy singing about his love for Jesus in the spirited jazz-rock number, "I Get High on Life," to offer Alice any tangible help locating her rabbit. Through these interactions, Alice critiques the historic exploitation of Africa's riches, its devastating impact throughout the Black diaspora, and the continued assault on Black communities through systematic social, political, and economic disenfranchisement. Indeed, the "Forest of Discontent"—with its issues of poverty, homelessness, alcohol and drug addiction, prostitution, and unjust judicial system—runs parallel to the realities of life in Harlem.

Fairy tales allow Alice to explore her somewhat fractured relationship with her mother through her interactions with mothers and othermothers in Wonderland. Her fraught relationship with her mother manifests itself within the dream world of Wonderland as a matrilineal society ruled by powerful and knowledgeable Blackgirls. Mother Goose and her daughter Mary, Mary Quite Contrary, along with Mother Hubbard and Witch, share their knowledge of Black history and culture to re-educate and empower Alice to continue her search for her rabbit. These Blackgirls appear to understand Alice's stubbornness, fear, and miseducation and help transform her from a tearful, lonely child into a strong, knowledgeable, and liberated Blackgirl capable of writing her own history.

Mary, Mary Quite Contrary represents a part of Alice's psyche that wants to resist Eurocentric standards of beauty and embrace Black culture and identity. Spectators learn in the opening song, "Just a Plain Little Girl," that society has taught Alice that she lacks beauty. As the crowd of street vendors and passersby sing about Alice, they refer to her as "plain" and devoid of "strawberry curls." However, Mary, Mary Quite Contrary encourages Alice to disavow these opinions and instead, embrace the Black is Beautiful cultural movement. She declares:

> I looked in the same mirror as Snow White and my mirror saw Mary, Mary Quite Contrary, how does my garden grow? My garden grows black and

> comely. Yes, I'm contrary, I don't believe nothing they tell me against myself. My name is Mary, Mary Quite Contrary and the land of Dreams of Truth taught me to love my contrary positive comely black self. My mirror told me to take my fine black self and comb my fine black Afro and put on my fine red, black and green and green, red, and black, and red, green and black super mind, and tipped on down the street right beside Snow White with my head up high because I am Black and Comely!

Alice transforms "Mary, Mary Quite Contrary" from a British nursery rhyme that alludes to perhaps the Biblical Virgin Mary; Mary, Queen of Scots (1542–1587); and Mary I of England ("Bloody Mary"; 1516–1558) into a Blackgirl's tale of emotional abuse and resilience. In an ultimate act of defiance, Mary, Mary Quite Contrary upsets the idol of white feminine beauty, Snow White. Rather than allow the magic mirror to judge her beauty and sense of self-worth, Mary, Mary Quite Contrary asserts her control of her narrative. She makes the choice to actively ignore those who seek to control her mind and instead, chooses to love her blackness and proclaim her beauty. This allows Mary, Mary Quite Contrary to walk beside Snow White with confidence and pride in her freshly combed afro and Afrocentric garb. Mary, Mary Quite Contrary then sings her solo, "I Am Black and Comely," a song which celebrates the diversity of skin colors, ending with the line: "Do recognize the beauty in you."[26] By sharing her experiential knowledge through monologue and song, Mary, Mary Quite Contrary teaches Alice that she too has the power to control her own mind and love herself completely.

Mother Hubbard stresses the importance of education and Mother Goose reinforces the importance of self-determination as a pathway to the "truth" of her condition. Mother Hubbard steps out of "Old Mother Hubbard," a British nursery rhyme about a charitable woman who tends to a dog, and enters Wonderland as "Mother earth" or the "grandmother of the world." Having lived for centuries trying to liberate her "hard-headed children," Mother Hubbard cares for a lost and lonely Alice. She orders everyone to sit down while she teaches them through her song, "Each One Teach One."[27] The title of this song derives from the African American proverb originated during enslavement, a time when it was understood that if an enslaved person learned to read, they had a responsibility to pass down this knowledge to another enslaved person and so on. Mother Hubbard sings, "A girl has to learn to be a woman / Each one teach one" and warns "The strong survive, the weak will fold." In other words, for Alice to become a woman, she must surround herself with strong role models to disseminate information that will help her survive. Unfortunately, at the beginning of the musical, Alice lacks this knowledge. "She's the new urban Black kid who don't know nothing about nothing. . . . She doesn't know culture. She doesn't know anything so these characters are bringing her into her own. It's like a rite of passage," remembers Aremu.[28] Mother Goose, another mother figure, directs this rite of passage. Described as "the educated, down-to-earth mother . . .with a deliberate Southern accent," Mother Goose "makes a point of stressing her upbringing, knowledge of foreign languages, and in-control attitude." As the matriarch of Wonderland, Mother Goose welcomes Alice and orders Witch, a "sexy foreign lady" to give her "sight." Witch informs Alice that "black is beautiful" and gives Alice a "little bitty drop" of her "powerful dew drops to clear [her] head." This potion allows Alice to eliminate the false narratives she has been told about herself and her culture, and begin embracing her identity and truth.

Alice would never reach the "Land of Wisdom" and become liberated without the love, friendship, and healing powers of another Blackgirl, Little Red. As stated earlier, Little Red appears immediately following Alice's ballad, "Searching." Alice bears her soul, singing: "I'm just a lonely little girl / Without a face / In the massive race toward reality / I'm just a lonely little girl / Searching for the truth." Alice repeatedly sings that she needs, "communication," "friendship," "love," and "peace of mind." Upon the song's conclusion, Little Red appears looking for her grandmother (later revealed as Mother Hubbard). Aremu remembers the symbolic meaning behind Little Red and her search. "Little Red's costume has kente on it and all these different rags but she's really a collection of a civilization that woke up in another world and they're trying to put together their culture. Little Red was trying to put together her culture," remembers Aremu.[29] This frayed connection with the past does not stop Little Red from using her knowledge of the swamp culture, Voodoo, and other world secrets taught to her by her grandmother to help them move forward on their search. Little Red begins by pouring a libation, goes into a trance, and conjures two "Swamp Creatures or Voodoo Spirits" known as Grumpsons who use African dance to force the wall to crumble. While Alice does not fully understand the importance of Little Red in her life, spectators might view her as the "rabbit" Alice has been searching for. Indeed, Little Red listens to Alice's concerns, offers friendship, comforts her when scared, and heals her mind when she becomes confused or upset by making her chamomile tea from the herbs around her waist. As a keeper of culture, Little Red's use of conjuration and trance allows her to break down walls that would otherwise trap them in the Forest of Discontent. Little Red's efforts allow them to move forward in their journey, meet mother figures, and discover "truths" about themselves in the "Land of Wisdom."

While Aremu's script does not explicitly imply a lesbian relationship between Alice and Little Red, resistant readers can view their relationship as an intimate friendship blossoming alongside Alice's sexual awakening. In fact, sexual undertones permeate many fairy tale stories, including Aremu's source material, "Little Red Riding Hood." Indeed, the earliest version of the "Little Red Riding Hood" story—found within Perrault's collection, *The Tales of Mother Goose* (1696)—is replete with sexual innuendo. In Perrault's version, Little Red meets Gaffer Wolf ("gaffer" meaning an older male), who races her to Grandmother's house in the next village.[30] Wolf takes the shorter route, pretends to be Little Red to gain entry, and eats Grandmother. Later, Little Red arrives at Grandmother's house, undresses, and hops into bed with Wolf. When Little Red finds "Grandmother's" arms, legs, ears, eyes, and teeth to be "great," Wolf, of course, makes excuses for these oddities. The story ends with Perrault writing: "this wicked Wolf fell upon Little Red Riding-hood, and ate her all up."[31] Despite its lack of a "happily ever after," fairy tales scholar Sandra L. Beckett writes that the Little Red Riding Hood tale is "considered by many to be the most popular fairy tale of all time."[32] Scholars have noted the sexual undertones within this early variant, arguing that Perrault "penned the first literary version of the tale to warn girls and women against predatory males."[33] Indeed, from Little Red's disrobing, to laying in bed with an older predatory male, to the Biblical use of the term "fell upon" to connote sex—Little Red Riding Hood has been used a cautionary tale for centuries. Furthermore, the fairy Tales scholar Jack Zipes notes the lack of consent within the tale, arguing that "it is because rape and violence are at the core of the history of *Little Red Riding Hood* that it is most widespread and notorious fairy tale in the Western world, if not in the entire world."[34] In *Mother Goose*, Little Red is not a passive victim of child abuse or rape. Instead, Little Red she emerges as a powerful Voodoo practitioner, leader of swamp creatures, and helpmate to Alice. Wolf never makes an appearance and Little Red lavishes affection and care onto Alice as they journey to her very much alive grandmother, Mother Hubbard. Rather than offer a cautionary tale about the dangers of sex, Aremu allows Alice to use fairy tales as a lens to openly explore her sexuality within the safety of seemingly innocuous children's rhymes, riddles, and songs.

Aremu intended the sexual nature of Alice's Wonderland to be read on multiple levels, depending on the knowledge of spectators. Aremu remembers:

> You had the children's spectacle part, which is the singing, the dancing, and all of that. But then there's a dialogue running through that has what we call *double entendre*. . . . When they say, 'Little Bo Peep has lost her sheep,' 'Little Jack Horner sat on the corner, put in her thumb and out come . . . ' All of it had all kinds of implications that were adult-themed. The rabbits were really deep. They could be prostitutes.[35]

Indeed, as the rabbits recite English nursery rhymes such as "Rub a Dub Dub," "Peter, Peter Pumpkin Eater," "Little Jack Horner," and "To Bed, To Bed," their double meanings emerge. Perhaps the most obvious example occurs when Male Rabbit and Female Rabbit exchange the English riddle, "Two Legs Sat Upon Three Legs" and recite the English song, "Pussy Cat Male Jumped Over a Coal." While some might read the answer to the riddle of one leg (a leg of mutton), two legs (a human), three legs (a stool), and four legs (a dog), the riddle might also suggest a variation of sexual acts. For example, "three legs" might also represent a man and his penis. "Pussy Cat Male Jumped Over a Coal" also alludes to the act of sexual intercourse with the lines "Pussy cat male jumped over a coal/And in her best petticoat burnt a great hole." Of course, the use of the terms "pussy" and "great hole" might hold multiple meanings for audiences "in the know." Theatre critic Patricia Ann Spencer notes that while Aremu offered spectators a "sophisticated" musical, based on "the response of the audience, children seem to know what it's all about."[36] Thus, fairy tales offer Alice—and spectators who share her vision—much more than escapism; they provide an opportunity for Blackgirls to explore their own curiosity about human anatomy, sex work, and sexual desires.

In contrast to many of her male comrades who correlate the acquisition of manhood with Black liberation, Aremu presents Blackgirls and their search for identity as emblematic of Black empowerment. While Aremu privileges Black girlhood most overtly through the protagonist, Alice—spectators literally see her vision of the world presented onstage—she also provides a more subtle critique of male-centered nationalist discourse through the characterization and interaction between Little Red Riding Hood and Humpty Dumpty. After Alice befriends the fairy tale characters Little Red, Old Woman, Solomon Grundy, as well as derelicts Alcoholic and Junkie, they come upon a wall (projected on a screen) that blocks their path. Next, the stage directions indicate that "Humpty Dumpty enters with his slaves in front of him." When Little Red removes the wall, Humpty Dumpty, who "represents the colonial powers of the past" tells his story through his solo, "I Am a Man." The title of the song has particular meaning within the Black nationalist struggle, as the phrase became the slogan for Black workers during the sanitation strike which began on February 12, 1968, just a few years prior to the musical debut. In his song, Humpty Dumpty laments the loss of his manhood, which he inextricably links to his lost African kingdom, wealth, and pride. Little Red counters his story with one of her own experiences through the song, "I Am the Orphan Child." Little Red sings: "I have no name. / Not even fame like / You did / I am an orphan child." As a Blackgirl, Little Red never held the power of a kingdom, nor was her story included in historical records. Instead, Little Red has faced two hundred years of abandonment, using her only resource (i.e., knowledge of Voodoo) to help her search for her grandmother. Although a fictional tale, the reality is that Blackgirls rarely make the cut of history. Their stories of activism (i.e., breaking down walls for the betterment of the entire community) and resilience continue to go untold, undervalued within history and Black nationalist discourse. Alice offers Humpty Dumpty friendship and advises him to "have faith, willpower and have a little love" and invites him along their journey out of the "Forest of Discontent" and into the "Land of Wisdom." Through Alice and Little Red's example of tenacity and grit, Humpty Dumpty gains a desire to take action (i.e., "try to do something") and better his community in the Forest of Discontent.[37] In other words, *Mother Goose* showcases Blackgirl magic at its finest.

The Other Cinderella

Long before Taylor ever conceived of her African-inspired musical fairy tale variant, the Cinderella tale was deeply embedded within racial politics of the West, and used as a weapon to further antiblackness. While contemporary scholars acknowledge that the Cinderella tale has been told thousands of times across many different cultures for hundreds of years, early anthropologists and folklorists focused solely on European tales and completely dismissed African variants.[38]Fairy tale studies scholar Deborah L. Thompson writes that leading nineteenth-century folklorists Joseph

Jacobs and Andrew Lang "presented arguments as to whether savages (the term both used to refer to Africans) or Red Indians (also their term) could produce such a tale as Cinderella and her glass slipper. Jacobs thought no because at the heart of the story were marriage rituals established during feudal or medieval times. Lang, on the other hand, thought Cinderella could not have evolved from a 'naked, shoeless race.'"[39] These wrong-headed and racist beliefs led early compilers to elevate three European tales as the foremost Cinderella variants: Giambattista Basile's "The Cat Cinderella" (1634–1636), Perrault's "Cinderella, or the Little Glass Slipper" (1696) and Jacob and Wilhelm Grimm's "Cinderella" (1812).[40] Cinderella variants from Africa were largely dismissed until 1893, with the publication of Marian Roalfe Cox's *Cinderella: Three Hundred and Forty-five Variants of Cinderella*.[41] Taylor envisioned *The Other Cinderella* as an Afrocentric response to the whitewashing of the Cinderella fairy tale.

While anthropologists and folklorists have since shifted away from Eurocentric visions of the Cinderella tale—even acknowledging that the oldest recorded Cinderella variant, *Yeh Shen*, originated from ninth-century China—Taylor understood that the titular character remains fixed as a symbol of white feminine beauty within popular imagination. Yet, Taylor dared to imagine Cinderella as something more than a submissive, beautiful, young, and (often blond) white girl toiling away at her cruel stepmother's behest as depicted in Walt Disney's 1950 animated film and Richard Rodgers and Oscar Hammerstein's 1957 televised production starring Julie Andrews. Indeed, one can not underestimate the influence Disney has had on the fairy tale tradition. Jack Zipes writes that "although fairytales had been adapted for film as early as the 1890s, Disney was the first to use technicolor to embrace the Broadway and Hollywood musical as a formula for fairytales and to print books, records, toys, and other artifacts to accompany his films. . . . Disney corporate artists have made a profitable business out of the fairytale." Indeed, the Disney corporation has literally commercialized the classical fairy tale as its own trademark.[42]

Taylor's decision to write, direct, produce, and (eventually) star in her own African-inspired Cinderella musical variant stood in direct opposition to the corporatization of fairy tales. Taylor remembers writing *The Other Cinderella* as an "experiment" while teaching children at a "difficult school" in inner-city Chicago. "I said, 'Well we can't do *Cinderella*.' The children had just seen the Rodgers and Hammerstein version of *Cinderella*. I said, 'We can do *The Other Cinderella*. Let's make it relevant to who we are.' That's how *The*

Other Cinderella was born."[43] While Rodgers and Hammerstein's televised production may have sparked Taylor's interest in writing her own adaptation, she envisioned *The Other Cinderella* as an outgrowth of the African storytelling tradition. Taylor writes:

> The story of Cinderella originated as an African folk tale. . . . The universal message of *The Other Cinderella* comes from Fairygodmama and I hope her words will be forever entrenched in your heart: 'You'll have a lifetime of hopes and dreams, of successes and failures in planning life's schemes, there will always be heartaches that you must go through—but you'll live through them all because of the Spirit in you.[44]

In other words, *The Other Cinderella* celebrates the "Spirit"—or resilience—of Blackgirls.

After the success of this first iteration, which was performed *by* children *for* children, Taylor transformed the script into a production performed by adults for Chicagoland spectators of all ages.

Taylor directed and produced the first professional production of *The Other Cinderella* at Black Ensemble Theatre, a Chicago-based theatre company that she founded in 1976. As an actress in her own right, Taylor later starred in the titular role to help increase interest in the musical. Her local celebrity—she appeared in the popular Hollywood film, *Cooley High* (1975)—boosted ticket sales. "Word-of-mouth is the best form of advertisement in the world. They kept coming. I could have kept running it but I was sick of it. People loved the message: 'find the greatness in yourself because it is there. No matter your circumstances. No matter what, it's there. Find it and use it,'" remembers Taylor.[45] Her message takes on even greater depth when compared to Disney's messaging. Zipes writes that "what counts most in the Disney fairy tale is the repetition of the same message: happiness will always come to those who work hard and are kind and brave."[46] While Disney emphasizes the importance of capitalist labor, personal attributes, and "happiness" as the end goal, Taylor acknowledges the importance of "circumstances"—how poverty, racism, heterosexism, etc. *can* and *do* harm Black people, especially Blackgirls. In other words, she amplifies the struggles of those who have been "Othered" by society. She doesn't deny the importance of happiness within their lives, but rather celebrates agency and self-discovery and valorizes resiliency as an important end goal. Ultimately, Taylor wants spectators to gain the knowledge of who they are and gain the confidence to do great things with their lives. *The Other Cinderella*, with its forty-year production history, remains a mainstay of the Black Ensemble Theatre and continues to transfer this message throughout Chicagoland.

The Other Cinderella takes place in the Kingdom of Other, ruled by Black royalty: King Harry (Dwight Neal), Queen Mildred (Chantee Joy), and their son, Prince Charles (Blake Hawthorne). Spectators quickly learn that speculation about Prince's sexuality abounds throughout the kingdom. Indeed, Prince's friendship with an openly gay young man, known simply as "the Duke's son," has caused quite a stir, and King vows to put an end to these rumors, as well as instill a sense of responsibility into his son, by decreeing a royal ball. King sends invitations to women throughout the land and orders Prince to select a wife. Having established the musical's premise, Taylor then introduces audiences to Cinderella, a twenty-one-year-old orphaned Blackgirl who suffers abuse from Stepmama and her stepsisters, Geneva and Margarite. While Cinderella expresses a desire to leave her toxic home environment, she does not take action because she believes that she can't secure a job without her high school diploma. However, Fairygodmama (Robin DaSilva), who practices Voodoo, sees her worth and encourages her to attend the ball, providing her with a dress, transportation, and dancing lessons. As with the classic fairy tale, Cinderella and Prince fall in love at the ball and her abrupt departure leaves behind a silver high heel. After a search throughout the kingdom for the owner of the glass shoe, Prince arrives at Cinderella's home. However, unlike other Cinderella tales, when Geneva tries on the shoe, it fits her foot. Fairygodmama returns, threatens harm to Cinderella's family if they continue interfering, and uses her Voodoo to confine the family to the couch. At last, Cinderella tries on the perfectly fitted shoe, and the couple agrees to marry. Taylor then fuses these major plot points together with musical numbers and interludes drawn from gospel, funk, rhythm and blues (including doo-wop), rock and roll, calypso, rap, and popular music.

As this plot summary suggests, *The Other Cinderella* includes many of the motifs audiences would expect from a Cinderella variant. Thompson defines a "motif" as "a repeated element common among folktales, such as magic mirror, incantations, and formulaic beginnings—'once upon a time'—and endings—'and they lived happily ever after.'"[47] Thompson writes that within the Cinderella tale, twenty-two common motifs emerge (see Figure 4.3).[48] Perhaps what makes Taylor's musical most unique is her ability to incorporate what Thompson has identified as the persecuted/abused heroine, cruel stepmother/stepsisters, supernatural helper, selecting the appropriate object, incantation/chant, significance of three, magical/helpful animals, and taboo

"Important Motifs Across All Cinderella Tale Types" (Excerpt) compiled by Deborah L. Thompson	Use of Cinderella Motifs in Jackie Taylor's *The Other Cinderella* compiled by the author
1. Persecuted/abused heroine/hero	Cinderella's stepfamily force her to work as an unpaid domestic worker.
2. Cruel stepmother/stepsisters	Stepmama and stepsisters, Geneva and Margarite, emotionally abuse Cinderella.
3. Kind/unkind siblings	Geneva and Margarite insult Cinderella.
4. Indifferent, absent, or deceased father	Cinderella's father is deceased.
5. Supernatural helper—i.e., fairy godmother, elderly woman, young boy	Fairygodmama aids Cinderella on her quest for love and freedom.
6. Special shoes—incredibly small and made of glass, silver, gold, or pink embroidery	Prince Charles uses Cinderella's lost glass shoe to determine the rightful owner (and his future bride).
7. Clothes produced by magic	Fairygodmama uses magic to produce a ballgown and glass shoes for Cinderella.
8. Hero/prince/suitor sees heroine at ball, in the forest, at the market, and is enamored	Prince Charles instantly falls in love with Cinderella at the royal ball.
9. Good deeds rewarded and evil doers punished	Cinderella becomes engaged to Prince Charles and will reside with the royal family. Stepmama, Geneva, and Margarite must spend their days washing the palace walls.
10. Older person helps hero/heroine on quest	Fairygodmama teaches Cinderella how to dance and develop confidence in herself.
11. Person who complies with request of an older person is rewarded	Cinderella follows Fairygodmama's advice and becomes engaged to Prince Charles.
12. Selecting the appropriate object: eggs, gourds, etc.	Dorothy must distinguish three varieties of collard greens to become a citizen of the Kingdom of Other.
13. Provisions received from a tree	None
14. Incantation/chant/refrain	Fairygodmama chants and uses incantation to conjure magical apparel, a chauffeur, and a vehicle to take Cinderella to the royal ball.
15. Opening and closing lines	The show begins with the musical number, "The Kingdom of Other," in which the characters are introduced. The musical concludes with a reprise of the "Kingdom of Other," in which Cinderella confides that she now lives "happily."
16. Significance of three	Newcomers must pass three tests to become citizens of the Kingdom of Other.
17. Magical/helpful animals	Humans have animal names such as "Groundhog."
18. Tasks	Cinderella must clean the house while her stepfamily attends the royal ball.
19. Transformations	Cinderella transforms from an unpaid domestic worker into a royal princess.
20. Tests of recognition	Prince Charles recognizes Cinderella as the woman he fell in love with at the royal ball only after she tries on the glass shoe and it fits.
21. Taboos	Prince Charles remains committed to his friendship with the Duke's queer son, despite criticism from the realm. Prince Charles and Cinderella fall in love, despite their difference in socioeconomic status. The king's attendant and queen's lady-in-waiting refuse to allow colorism to hinder their love for each other.
22. Ordinary objects with magical powers	None.

Figure 4.3 Cinderella Motifs Table, courtesy of the author.

motifs into a tale that is meaningful to Black queer feminist spectators.[49] Taylor does so by blending these familiar motifs with her own experiential knowledge of Black cultural practices and identity politics.

The Other Cinderella and Taylor's artistic mission is shaped by her experiences of navigating the effects of systemic racism within the city of Chicago as a Blackgirl. In fact, each iteration of the Cinderella tale has, in fact, been "shaped by large-scale cultural, political and historical influences such as invasions, colonization, and migration."[50] Taylor remembers that "the Kingdom is a reflection of my reality of the people who I know. You can only write about what you know. The brothas from the hood were a very strong part of my community. So, of course, they would be in the Kingdom of Other."[51] These brothas from the hood appear as supporting characters—Page (Stewart Romeo), Groundhog (Vincent Jordan), Peanut Butter (Michael Adkins), and Pee Wee (Blake Reasoner)—who embody the magical/helpful animal motif. Using the "extended audience concept," the actors emerge from the audience and welcome everyone to the Kingdom of Other. At the November 15, 2019 production, performed in a 299-seat theatre for a predominantly Black audience, their "welcome" included improvised banter and flirtations with women in the audience, call-and-response, seemingly spontaneous moments of hip-hop dance, and singing a few bars from popular R&B and hip-hop songs while accompanied by a four-piece live band (i.e., drums, keyboard, bass, and guitar).[52] Eliminating the "fourth wall" and the use of familiar music promoted a spirit of celebration and community before the production even began. These sentiments are in keeping with Taylor's own artistic mission, which is to eradicate the pain and suffering caused by antiblackness and all forms of racism. "We are highly segregated in Chicago. Chicago is a very racist city. The systems that are here are at the core based on a highly racist attitude of white superiority and . . . we need to stop this nonsense," remembers Taylor.[53] Inspired by their real-life counterparts (she based these lively characters off of actual Black men in her life), Taylor humanizes everyday Black men, showcasing their humor, wit, and talent. While Taylor opens her show spotlighting her vision of Black masculinity, the majority of the musical focuses on the trials and resiliency of Blackgirls.

The Other Cinderella utilizes the familiar "persecuted/abused heroine" Cinderella motif as a vehicle to show the unique experiences of Black girlhood, including their navigation of racial trauma. In the 2019 production, spectators first meet twenty-one-year-old Cinderella (Jayla Williams-Craig) performing menial cleaning tasks. When Cinderella questions her family's treatment of her, Stepmama (Rhonda Preston) attempts to gaslight her back into submission. "Oh, no now, Cinderella. Don't go makin' no villain outta me. I made you drop outta school for your own good. You were just too stupid to learn. I wouldn't have the other children makin' fun of you. I did it for your own good. Wasn't no sense in wastin' a good education," Stepmama states.[54] Her belief that Cinderella lacks intelligence and must be disciplined for her perceived behavioral issues (i.e., "backtalk") replicates stereotypes within the larger society. For example, in their 2011 study on racial trauma and Black youth, Maryam M. Jernigan and Jessica Henderson found that Black children and youth are more often on the receiving end of school system policies that use stereotypes to identify them "as recipients of disciplinary actions, and lack thereof with regard to academic opportunities when compared to White students."[55] These educational practices and policies simply reinforce society's perception that "Black youths are intellectually inferior and prone to behavioral issues."[56] While Stepmama is an unreliable source to know whether or not Cinderella experienced this trauma at school, spectators do know she experiences the similar treatment at home. Stepmama weaponizes stereotypes to manipulate Cinderella into doubting her intelligence and abilities which ultimately allows Stepmama to control her. Spectators learn that after removing her from public schools, Stepmama forces her to work as a domestic servant in her own home and refuses to let her attend the royal ball, thus stifling Cinderella's autonomy and sense of community. In addition to gaslighting, Stepmama draws unflattering comparisons between Cinderella and her "two babies" to provoke an emotional response from Cinderella. Thus baited, Cinderella insults twenty-eight-year-old Geneva and twenty-nine-year-old Margarite, noting that they still live at home and "haven't worked a day in [their] lives." Upset by her loss of control, Stepmama stands her ground by reminding Cinderella of her precarious situation. "My babies could stay with me forever if they want to! And so can you Cinderella; if you stay in your place," states Stepmama. With the threat of homelessness looming, Cinderella must mask her emotions and suppress her aspirations to survive.

Stepmama's treatment of Cinderella mirrors the very real contempt society has for Blackgirls. Unfortunately, there were no other parents or adults present in the home to counteract Stepmama's emotional assault on Cinderella. In her "I want" song, a doo-wop number titled, "The Spirit Inside of Me," Cinderella reveals that she never met her mother and cannot remember her father. As a result, Stepmama was been charged with the task of socializing Cinderella from an early age. By socializing, I mean "a process in which parents and families communicate to their children an understanding of values, roles, and statuses that allow their children to acquire beliefs about the social structure of the larger society."[57] For Black, Indigenous, and People of Color (BIPOC), socialization becomes essential as they must learn, from an early age "to have a positive individual and group identity within the context of a society that discriminates against people of color."[58] In their study on racial trauma, Jernigan and Daniel found that a parent's ability to socialize their children "is essential to their ability to survive and thrive in racially oppressive environments. For Black children, many of the lessons about racism and strategies for how to resist oppression begin in the home environment."[59] Blackgirls like Cinderella, who have not been taught positive individual and group identity become more vulnerable to racial oppression and discrimination. As a result of Stepmama's use of verbal abuse and isolation, Cinderella is left feeling unloved and struggles to form a sense of self and community.

Despite her family's cruelty, Cinderella finds moments to stand up for herself and speak her mind. Spectators catch a glimpse of this spirited side of Cinderella during one of her first conversations in the musical. After Cinderella essentially calls her stepsister lazy, Margarite justifies her unemployment by stating, "I'm just waiting on a position that suits my talents." Cinderella rejoins, "You got a looooong wait, baby." Cinderella's quick and witty comeback garnered laughter from the audience before Margarite went in for the kill:

MARGARITE: You getting smart again, Cinderella?!
CINDERELLA: I was born smart.
MARGARITE: You were *born* in the projects.
CINDERELLA: So what? Ain't nothin' wrong with bein' born in the projects. Lots of people was born there.
MARGARITE: And your mama went off and left you. If it wasn't for our mother marrying your father, you wouldn't have nothing.

Far removed from the traditional docile, voiceless, and dispirited heroine, Taylor's Cinderella confronts her foe head-on in what appears to be a pattern of resistance (i.e., "getting smart again"). Cinderella asserts her intelligence and refuses to let the financial circumstances of her birth make her feel inferior. It is not until Margarite reminds her of her status as an orphan and repeats a narrative of abandonment that Cinderella becomes somewhat dispirited. Luckily, Fairygodmama works as her parent-by-proxy, resocializing

Figure 4.4 Jayla Williams-Craig (Cinderella) and Robin DaSilva (Fairygodmama) in the 2019 production of *The Other Cinderella*, Black Ensemble Theatre trailer, directed by Jackie Taylor. Still image courtesy of the author. https://www.youtube.com/watch?v = sDd-sf0d0Yk

her to believe in herself and reclaim the spirit inside of her through the use of magic, song, and sound advice (see Figure 4.4).

Fairygodmama (Robin DaSilva) provides Caribbean-infused supernatural guidance to Cinderella at lowest emotional moment in the musical. After Cinderella laments her inability to control her own destiny in the classic rhythm and blues number "Souvenirs," the sound of a harpsichord breaks the silence and Fairygodmama makes her magical appearance. She enters from the audience to the stage and repeatedly talks directly to the audience throughout her lively performance. Sporting a gold turban, large teardrop earrings, and fitted red floral print costume designed by Taylor, Fairygodmama performs the uptempo number, "You Make The Wish" to the beat of a steel drum. "We all have work to do. To do. Oh Oh," Fairygodmama sings along to calypso music, ending with the refrain, "You make de wish/I make de wish come true." In a Caribbean accent, she tells Cinderella that she has arrived to help her but she must "believe" in her. In contrast to Stepmama who tries to manipulate and control Cinderella, Fairygodmama seeks to empower her. "Can't nobody help you til you learn how to help yourself," Fairygodmama advises. She further admonishes Cinderella to not allow others to treat her poorly and the two have the following exchange:

FAIRYGODMAMA: You're twenty-one. Don't you think it's about time you started taking care of yourself?"

CINDERELLA: I can't. I don't even know how . . .

FAIRYGODMAMA: Can't, can't can't . . . Who says you can't? There's nothing you cannot do.

Parents and greater society often socialize Blackgirls by telling them what they cannot do—whether to help or harm them. Blackgirls also need encouragement, opportunities, and autonomy so that they can maintain a sense of self and *thrive* while also navigating a world that does not recognize their humanity. For this reason, Fairygodmama removes every possible barrier that stops Cinderella from taking action to better her life. She uses Voodoo to conjure an invitation to the ball, transportation (an unseen red Bugatti driven by actor Michael B. Jordan), styles her unkempt hair into braids, and transforms her drab servant's uniform into a beautiful silver and white knee-length dress (see Figure 4.5). However, the most powerful transformation does not occur by magic. Rather, the true magic happens when Fairygodmama sings: "You are somebody / Spirit" and "never say goodbye to the greatness of yourself." At last, Cinderella internalizes Fairygodmama's message and recognizes her worth as she sings the beautiful ballad, "The Spirit Inside of Me."

"The Spirit Inside of Me" not only showcases actress Williams-Craig's rich, soulful voice but also allows Cinderella to model Blackgirl resilience. The R&B song includes the lines: "I'll have a lifetime of hopes and dreams / Successes and failures in planning life's schemes / There will always be heartaches that I must go through / But I'll live through them all because of the spirit from you." The literal manifestation of her struggles appears as a large scar on actress Williams-Craig's leg. While Taylor could have asked Williams-Craig to cover the actual scar with makeup, but she made the decision to give audiences the opportunity to make this connection. "Everybody wouldn't get it. I knew that. But some people would see it and respond to it and understand it," Taylor remembers.[60] As the song suggests, Blackgirls will experience "a lifetime of hopes and dreams" but also encounter struggles that may leave them scared but they will survive because of their spirit. However, spirit alone does not initiate Cinderella's path toward personal autonomy. Rather, Cinderella needed Fairygodmama to encourage her, to provide her with vital resources, and to create an opportunity for her to gain control of her life. However, *all* Blackgirls need encouragement, resources, and opportunities, and fairygodmamas are in short supply.

Figure 4.5 Jayla Williams-Craig (Cinderella) and Blake Hawthorne (Prince Charles) in the 2019 production of *The Other Cinderella*, Black Ensemble Theatre trailer, directed by Jackie Taylor. Still image courtesy of the author. https://www.youtube.com/watch?v=sDd-sf0d0Yk

In addition to privileging the interior lives of Blackgirls, *The Other Cinderella* addresses homosexuality within Black communities, demonstrating how heterosexism harms (already vulnerable) Black LGBTQ youth. In one of the most powerful conversations in the musical, King Harry discusses his disdain for his son's friendship with the duke's queer son and his concern for his son's reputation. Queen Mildred counters King Harry's homophobic rhetoric in the following conversation:

QUEEN: [The duke's son has] done more with his position than any of his predecessors.
KING: I don't like the young man, Mildred.
QUEEN: Well, like him or not he deserves your respect. He's earned it.
KING: How?
QUEEN: By being alive, Harry. Simply by being alive.

Their disagreement indicates that, even within this wealthy, harmonious kingdom ruled by seemingly just Black sovereigns, heterosexism continues to divide Black communities. Within the fictional Kingdom of Other, Black LGBTQ subjects may acquire lands, titles, and wealth; yet basic respect remains out of their reach. In contrast to King Harry, who denigrates and openly loathes his queer subjects, Queen Mildred demonstrates a keen understanding of the struggles of Black LGBTQ youth and explains that the act of merely *existing* should command respect from the Black community, including its leaders. While the duke's son never actually appears onstage, his given name is never revealed, and the word "suicide" is never uttered, his precarious situation may linger in the minds of spectators who understand the mental health challenges facing Black LGBTQ youth.

Taylor wrote about the mental health challenges of Black queer folx more than forty years ago, yet the topic remains just as relevant today as suicide rates continue to rise exponentially. Taylor remembers writing the Black queer subplot in the original production and insists that her attention to intersectionality was not ahead of her time. "I think whatever it may be—sexism, homophobia, or whatever it may be—human beings tend to want to destroy what they don't understand or what is different from them and that has just never been my belief. We should embrace our differences. We are different on all kinds of levels and I never was of the ilk that if you were gay you were less than. That is stupid to me," remembers Taylor.[61] Unfortunately, Blackgirls—queer, trans, or otherwise—remain particularly vulnerable to experiences of racism, homophobia, sexism, and other social ills which do have a devasting effect on their mental health. In their 2022 article "An Intersectional-Contextual Approach to Racial Trauma Exposure Risk and Coping Among Black Youth" Chardée A. Galán et al. found that "Black youth experience racial discrimination at significantly higher rates than any other ethnic-racial minority group in the United States . . . . averaging five discrimination experiences per day."[62] Repeated discriminatory experiences can cause a host of psychological harm, including racial trauma. Perhaps unsurprisingly, mental health studies have found that "Black youth have the fastest rising suicide rate among their peers of other races and ethnicities. . . . In a 13-year period between 2007 and 2020, the suicide rate among Black youth ages 10–17 increased by 144%. Black boys ages 0–19 have more than twice the suicide rate as compared to Black girls of their age group."[63] According to the Johns Hopkins Center for Gun Violence Solutions 2023 report entitled, "Still Ringing the Alarm: An Enduring Call to Action for Black Youth Suicide Prevention," Black queer youth are particularly vulnerable and at high risk for mental health crises:

> In 2019, the year for which most recent data is available, 51% of Black LGB youth reported feeling sad or hopeless during the past year and 35.1%

> reported seriously considering attempting suicide. Additionally, the percentage of Black LGB youth making a suicide plan in the past year doubled between 2015 and 2019, from 18% to 36%, and 27.2% of this group reported a suicide attempt. . . . These data are consistent with a 2002 survey by The Trevor Project finding that about 50% of Black LGBTQ youth had considered suicide in the past year and about 20% had attempted suicide in the past year.[64]

Black queer youth contend with daily race-based discrimination but also suffer from feelings of rejection; many lack safe spaces and encounter physical threats and violence. Queer Blackgirls have yet another added layer of concern for their safety and well-being as they navigate racism, homophobia, sexism, and other ills.

Placing the mental well-being of Black queer youth within the subplot of a deceptively simple fairy tale musical allowed Taylor to make an important intervention that could, in fact, save lives. The "Still Ringing the Alarm" report issues a call for community, state, and national interventions, including the need to "create safe and supportive spaces for Black youth," "make mental health services more accessible," and "engage the Black church in suicide prevention initiatives."[65] The intervention section concludes with a powerful statement on the use of cultural expression as a protective measure for Black youth. "Racial identity and racial centrality are associated with positive impacts on psychological well-being and self-esteem. Culture as an intervention can help one cultivate a strong sense of cultural identity and/or reconnect with cultural traditions, and beliefs that were repressed due to historical trauma."[66] Taylor understood that there is an ongoing need to provide representation of the complex, multidimensional lives of Black women, men, and children—queer, trans, or otherwise. *The Other Cinderella*, with its celebration of Black culture, helps fill this void. In fact, Williams-Craig considers the musical a celebration of Blackness, with Cinderella functioning as a model of strength and perseverance for everyday Blackgirls in the Chicagoland area. Williams-Craig remembers:

> The whole show is Black. We have Black royalty, Black jobs, and Black cultural references or Black "Easter eggs" within the show that only Black people would understand or relate to. I think that's the point that Jackie [Taylor] went for. She's like: "I wanted a story of the Black Cinderella. Her circumstances and her lifestyle and what she would be going through." She

> knew her audiences would be Black and understand and relate. I want to cry because the little girls that would come up to me after the performance made me feel so good about what I did. They rarely see that so the production was very special to me. For me to show them that we can do this, too. We have our own story and we can *always* have our own story. We just have to have those opportunities. If the door is closed, how can we get in?

While queer folx and Blackgirls encounter ostracism within this imagined world, they ultimately find the acceptance, love, and community they so desperately seek.

In addition to critiquing homophobia within Black communities, *The Other Cinderella* also challenges spectators to reject the harmful nature of colorism and classism. In another subplot, which Taylor integrated into the script in the late 1980s, King Harry's Attendant (Lemond Hayes) falls in love with Queen Mildred's Lady-in-Waiting (Micah Materre) but fears their love will not survive public scrutiny due to his dark complexion. However, the fair-skinned Lady-in-Waiting asks a series of questions that allow him (and the audience) to question the absurdity of colorism. Among other questions, Lady-in-Waiting asks: "don't you think it's time that our people get past this whole color thing?" Similar to her thoughts on homophobia, Taylor finds colorism abhorrent. "[Colorism] is a big issue within the African American community and we got to stop doing that to each other. It is just stupid. We're still self-degrading each other and it is ridiculous," remembers Taylor.[67] Issues of classism are also treated as a blight within Black communities. Taylor, who was raised in the Cabrini Green housing project believes: "It's classism that we have to stop."[68] In addition to Cinderella unashamedly acknowledging the projects as her original home, the brothers from the hood speak fondly of their neighborhood and assert their right to exist. For example, during the opening number, "The Kingdom of Other," when the entire cast introduces their characters, Groundhog sings, "we all from the hood but we all have souls." Later, when Groundhog, Peanut Butter, and Pee Wee perform a hip-hop dance and sing their uptempo number "Respect the Brothers from the Hood," they declare: "Brothers from the hood / Are misunderstood" (see Figure 4.6). In resisting stereotypes of Black men as aggressive or lazy, the brothers from the hood reveal their innermost desire to gain economic opportunities. Unfortunately, the game of chance provides the only viable economic opportunity. Spectators see this unfair system when Page wins the King's Lotto which grants him with a position in the palace. Page excels at

Figure 4.6 Vincent Jordan (Groundhog), Stewart Romeo (Page), Michael Adkins (Peanut Butter,) and Blake Reasoner (Pee Wee) in the 2019 production of *The Other Cinderella*, directed by Jackie Taylor, Black Ensemble Theatre trailer. Still image courtesy of the author. https://www.youtube.com/watch?v = sDd-sf0d0Yk

this new position and quickly becomes a trusted confidant to Prince Charles. Page's upward social mobility demonstrates the power of opportunity and lack thereof for everyday brothers in the hood. In other words, winning lotto tickets are just as scarce as the appearance of fairygodmamas. Social mobility should not come by chance or magic; but by expansive economic opportunities.

Decades after its premiere, *The Other Cinderella* continues to appeal to the cultural sensibilities of Black audiences, allies "in the know," and those who desire to know more about Black cultural expression and experiences in America. As such, the production takes a tongue-in-cheek approach to white allyship, depicting it as a three-part test to become a citizen of the Kingdom of Other. In the 2019 production, Dorothy (Colleen Perry), a white girl, desires citizenship in the Kingdom of Other. When she arrives at the ball, she sports flowing brown hair, a long floral gown, and introduces herself as "Dorothy from Kansas." The all-Black cast immediately respond by singing a few bars from "Somewhere Over the Rainbow," for they recognize the white traveler is none other than Dorothy from *The Wizard of Oz*. Despite the incredulity of his subjects, King Harry declares, "This is the Kingdom of Other where everyone is welcome!" and invites Dorothy to take a three-part citizenship test:

1. The Royal Watermelon Test: Dorothy tastes the Kingdom's watermelon and correctly declares: "That's the sweetest and juiciest watermelon I've ever tasted!"
2. The Royal Greens Test: as Dorothy begins to correctly distinguish three varieties of collard greens, she stops eating and states, "Well, how am I supposed to eat these greens without the cornbread?" The cast expresses shock at her nuanced answer and Dorothy identifies the dishes as collard, mustard, and turnip greens.
3. "Get down and boogey" Test: Dorothy enthusiastically gyrates across the stage to the sound of 1970s funk music, ending with her twerking as the cast chants, "Go Dorothy!"

When Queen Mildred interrupts and challenges Dorothy to sing the blues, she complies and belts out the show-stopping number, "The White Girl Blues." After her performance, she becomes a full citizen, and is embraced by the all-Black Kingdom of Other. Their acceptance of Dorothy only calls attention to the fact that more than a hundred and fifty years after the abolition of slavery, Black people have yet to gain full citizenship in the United States. As of date, the dream of a multiethnic democracy remains but a fairy tale.

While humorous and in keeping with the traditional "selecting the appropriate object" Cinderella motif, Dorothy's tests also take on the serious task of debunking racial stereotypes. Popular imagery of the past depicted Black people with exaggerated coal-black skin, wide eyes, and thick red lips. This animalistic imagery often depicted Black people happily chomping down on watermelon. Dorothy's love of watermelon and collard greens disrupts this historical trauma, showing that people of all races enjoy eating watermelon and appreciate Black southern cuisine (i.e., collard greens). Dorothy's ability to sing the blues and dance similarly counters the stereotypes that white people lack rhythm and cannot dance or learn how to perform vocal belting. Taylor remembers that she incorporated food tests because she "thought they were funny" and was "based on our cultures."[69] Furthermore, Taylor insists that "watermelon is something that *everybody* loves, not just Black people. Even though we were scrutinized—the images that they had of us were very, very degrading—we got to get past it. It is just a fruit! . . . We don't know where Dorothy grew up, but wherever she grew up, it was similar to what we do! So, she was a kindred soul."[70] As a kindred soul, Dorothy feels connected to the "Others." As a white traveler, she does not attempt to usurp the throne or conquer the rich kingdom as colonists have done throughout actual world history. Rather, she shows a deep appreciation for their culture and remains humble, curious, and happy to take on the difficult task of demonstrating her commitment to their way of life. The Other citizens reward Dorothy's behavior by embracing her into the fold. Thus, Dorothy's embodiment of humility, a genuine love of Black culture, and a desire to build community serve as a model for interracial coalition-building.

Despite the popularity of *The Other Cinderella* and having successfully produced more than a hundred musicals for Chicago audiences, Taylor has no desire to ever transfer *The Other Cinderella* to a Broadway theatre in New York. "Broadway has nothing on Chicago except it costs *way* more money to produce a show on Broadway and it has to have a certain formula. It has to be 'safe' and I am not a safe person. Even though Broadway definitely is far more diverse than it has ever been, it still ain't there," remembers Taylor.[71] Writing, directing, and producing high-quality musicals in Chicago provides greater opportunity for Taylor to pursue her mission, which is to eradicate racism. However, she did once dream of a career on Broadway. When she initially produced *The Jackie Wilson Story* at the Apollo Theatre in New York, she even discussed a venture with Broadway producers. However, these conversations quickly halted, in part, because she was unwilling to sacrifice her artistic mission and vision. Taylor remembers:

> I've talked to Broadway producers. I'm not their flavor. They want to change my shit. I ain't changing nothing because it's like it is for a purpose. I'm not going after your purpose. I'm going after mine which is being true to my mission to eradicate racism. Period. . . . I have had in the past Broadway producers who found my work of some interest but, again, wanting to control it and wanting to change it. This is my work. These are my words. This is my music. There is not enough money to have me change my beliefs.[72]

Taylor believes that producing her musicals in Chicago not only surrounds her with more cultural diversity but also the ability to do more for her community. "If I had $10 million, I wouldn't be putting it on Broadway. If I had $10 million, I would increase all of my actors' salaries, I would put it in my organization," remembers Taylor.[73]

In contrast to Taylor, Rosa Guy allowed white Broadway producers and writers to take her work—in this case, her novel *My Love, My Love, or, the Peasant Girl* (1985)—and transform it into a Broadway musical, *Once on This Island*. On the one hand, this deal resulted in eight Tony Award nominations and recognition of Guy's outstanding narrative. On the other, the transformation also sanitized Guy's work, altering or simply omitting key features that gave the narrative Black cultural nuance and artistic beauty.

Once on This Island

Once on This Island presents the story of Ti Moune, an orphaned "peasant" Blackgirl who falls head over heels in love with a wealthy, light-skinned grand homme named Daniel. After barely surviving a car crash, Ti Moune finds the injured Daniel and against her adopted parents' wishes, devotes all of her time and energy to healing him. The two seemingly fall in love and begin a physical relationship only to have Daniel's father return to collect him and bring him back to their grand hotel. Saddened by his abrupt departure, Ti Moune follows him into the city with the hopes that the two can rekindle their love, and become man and wife. Ultimately, Daniel rejects Ti Moune and marries Andrea, a girl from his own social class. As this story unfolds, their taboo relationship becomes a source of sport or entertainment for the powerful gods Erzulie (Goddess of Love), Asaka (Mother of the Earth), Agwe (God of Water), and Papa Ge (Demon of Death), who wreak havoc upon the lives of the villagers. By the conclusion of the one-act musical, Ti Moune has proven her unwavering love and is rewarded after her death. In the 1990 premiere production at Playwrights Horizons in New York, a storyteller relates that the gods take Ti Moune, bless her, and transform her into a tree. The all-Black ensemble cast of storytellers spread their arms to create a human tree and lift Ti Moune (LaChanze) high into the air. While doing so, a woman storyteller states, "And one day, as Daniel's young son sat in the shade of the tree, he noticed a beautiful young peasant girl high in the branches, looking out at the world. And the spirit of Ti Moune touched their hearts, and set them free to love."[74] Afterward, the ensemble cast begins to dance, concluding the musical on a hopeful note. However, this sanitized ending is a far cry from Ti Moune's tragic ending in the original source material. *Once on This Island* was adapted from Rosa Guy's novel, *My Love, My Love, or, the Peasant Girl* (1985), and is a retelling of the Danish author Hans Christian Andersen's fairy tale, "The Little Mermaid" (1837).

Andersen's "The Little Mermaid," with its emphasis on love, beauty, and subjectivity, embodies the Romantic spirit of nineteenth-century Europe. Indeed, the artistic and philosophical movement known as Romanticism dominated Europe from the late eighteenth century into the first half of the nineteenth century. The historian Ken Mondschein writes that "while, as a movement, Romantics had no credo or manifesto, and their beliefs ranged from the revolutionary sentiment of the French novelist Victor Hugo to the reactionary politics of the German composer, Wilhelm Richard Wagner, all shared certain commonalities."[75] These commonalities include the celebration of "nature and wild beauty" with a "focus on emotion (particularly romantic love), personal subjective experience, and authenticity of feeling."[76] Andersen captures these sentiments by painting a magical portrait of Little Mermaid and her life under the beautiful sea. As one of six sea princesses, Little Mermaid is described as the youngest and the "most beautiful of them all" with "skin as soft and tender as a rose petal."[77] As "an unusual child, quiet and wistful," Little Mermaid spends her days playing in the palace and tending to red flowers in her idyllic garden.[78] Her grandmother, the dowager queen, tells her stories of people, animals, ships, and cities above the sea, which rouse her curiosity. Upon her fifteenth birthday, she receives permission to see these wonders firsthand and eventually rescues a prince, who has fallen from a ship during a sea storm. Little Mermaid continues to ruminate about him and the possibility of gaining an immortal soul to be with him for eternity until she finally decides to take action. After her concert, she secretly visits a sea witch in the hopes that she can help her "win" the prince.[79] Andersen's portrayal of Little Mermaid—her desire to see the wonders of the earth and her single-minded pursuit of love, despite the impossibility of such a match—aligns with the cultural sentiments of the day.

Andersen's tale not only constructs an idealized vision of the world but also a Romantic Christianity that fuses love and sacrifice as essential attributes of moral goodness. Upon entering her lair, Sea Witch offers Little Mermaid a "draught" to turn her fins into legs. Unfortunately, this painful transformation will forever cause Little Mermaid's feet to feel as if she "were treading upon knife blades so sharp that blood must flow."[80] In addition to this suffering, Sea Witch warns: "if you do not win the love of the prince so completely that for your sake, he forgets his father and mother, cleaves to you with his whole heart, and lets the priest join your hands in marriage, then you will win no immortal soul. If he marries someone else, your heart will break on the very next morning, and you will become foam of the sea."[81] As with Disney's 1989 animated film *The Little Mermaid*, Andersen's mermaid must "pay" for her "draught" with her voice. Andersen's Sea Witch, however, includes her own blood in the potion and does permanent harm by cutting out Little Mermaid's tongue. Afterward, Little Mermaid awakens with "the loveliest pair of white legs any maid could hope to have."[82]The prince finds her, clothes her in fine apparel (even palace slaves dress in finery), takes her riding and hiking, and gives her "a velvet pillow to sleep on outside his door."[83] Andersen writes that "Day after day, she became more dear to the prince, who loved her as one would love a good little child, but he never thought of making her his queen."[84] Instead, the prince marries a neighboring "beautiful princess" of his parents' choosing and who he mistakenly believes saved his life.[85] Unbeknownst to Little Mermaid, her sisters trade their hair to Sea Witch for a magical blade to save her. Unfortunately, in order for the magic to work, Little Mermaid must plunge the sharp blade into the prince's heart. Little Mermaid enters the prince's tent and sees him asleep with his new bride, but ultimately loves him too much to kill him. Instead, she tosses the knife blade and hurls herself into the sea where she dissolves into the foam. Mondschein writes that Little Mermaid's death is "not as a punishment for hubris or curiosity, but seemingly as a direct result of her sacrifice, love, and compassion."[86] In so doing, Andersen depicts "a very emotional religion of love and forgiveness, not one of sin and retribution—a Romantic Christianity, steeped in the Lutheran tradition of a forgiving, loving God."[87] Indeed, Little Mermaid's willingness to sacrifice her very life for love qualifies her to become one of the "daughters of the air," meaning a transparent and "spiritlike" singer who performs good works for three hundred years to achieve an immortal soul.[88] In other words, Little Mermaid's very goodness in life and in death saves her eternal soul.

Guy's adaptation transforms Anderson's Romantic Christian vision of love, forgiveness, and sacrifice into a tale deeply embedded within African spirituality and the history of colonization. *My Love, My Love* tells the story of a sixteen-year-old orphaned girl Désirée Dieu-Donné, whose name means "god-given desire."[89]As a young girl, she miraculously escapes the bands of death by hiding in a mango tree during a terrible storm on the island. Afterward, an elderly couple named Mama Euralie and Tonton Julian rescue her, give her the nickname Ti Moune, and embrace her as their daughter. Désirée blossoms under their care but daydreams about "unknown pleasures" not found in her village and "racing away in a car" as she has seen the wealthy, light-skinned grands hommes do.[90] One day, she discovers an incoherent Creole named Daniel Beauxhomme who is injured during a car crash. Against Mama Euralie's wishes, Désirée nurses him back to health and an intimate relationship develops between the two. "She bared her breasts and held his head to the soft warmth of her bosom," writes Guy.[91] Mama Euralie questions this misalliance, stating, "She gives up honor to this man, born of a world as different from hers as land is from the sea. And haven't seen these days what happened when land meets sea? What disorder? What disaster? Is it not better, then, that we be sucked down into these rising waters, to nourish another generation, than to suffer such shame!"[92] Eventually, Daniel's father collects him and brings him back home and Désirée makes the decision to leave her village and reunite with them. However, before she leaves, Mama Euralie pulls Désirée along to a ritual being performed by the villagers in a clearing to help guide Désirée on her journey. They chant along to the beat of the drum, conjuring Agwe "god of waters, of floods, of the sea"; Asaka, "goddess of living things / Goddess of the trees, of the earth, of growing things"; Erzulie, the goddess of love; and the "evil demon," Papa Ge.[93] Agwe wants to "force" the couple to fall in love but Erzulie insists the gods "help" them fall in love.[94] Thus, the gods play a major role in the lives of the people. As such, they are capable of both destruction and protection, fostering feelings of wickedness and love on the island. Guy presents the gods as also having a competitive streak, with Erzulie intent on proving her power by assisting the most unlikely of love matches: that of a poor, dark-skinned "peasant" girl and a wealthy, light-skinned Creole hotelier. In so doing, Guy demonstrates that a union between a Caribbean girl and Creole boy is just as fantastically impossible as marriage between a human and a mermaid.

As a fish out of water—in this case, a dark-skinned Blackgirl from the "peasant" class—Désirée does not and cannot belong in Daniel's opulent world populated by fair-skinned Creoles. As a descendent of French colonists, Daniel and his family reap the rewards of enslavement, owning land and living in what Désirée describes as a "palace." After Désirée arrives at Daniel's home, the two reconnect and share a bed together, and Daniel orders Madame Mathilde to provide Désirée with a fine wardrobe so she can appear "a grand demoiselle whom even my father will be unable to resist."[95] Madame Mathilde also befriends Désirée, describing her as "the best in us—our humanity," and tries to convince Désirée to leave the hotel before it's too late.[96] Madame Mathilde warns: "We peasants hate them because they reject our blackness. They hate us because we remind them of theirs. My child, that is the curse of the Antilles, created by the enslavement of our fathers."[97] Désirée does not heed her words and finds herself at a reception with the bride of Daniel's father's choice: Andrea Galimar. Guy describes this encounter as follows:

> Andrea Galimar was easily the most perfect woman at the reception. Tall, white-skinned, with hair the texture of cornsilk, she moved from group to group in a long, golden gown, greeting each group to turn. And as she did, she spoke different tongues; German to the young millionaire, Italian with the count, French with the Island guests, English with the African. Hearing her, Désirée, who had been forced into a numb, smiling silence when confronted with the same guests, felt a chill growing, growing inside.[98]

Andrea's perceived beauty and interactions with guests only heighten the differences between the two classes. Andrea appears confident, educated, and accepted in Daniel's social world while Désirée must maintain the outward appearance of calm in the face of silence and contempt. Désirée experiences further humiliation when Daniel introduces her to Andrea, and she responds, "Daniel, how lovely. Never have I seen such a beautiful black girl. Can we keep her?"[99] Andrea perceives Désirée's beauty as a potential threat and establishes her superiority by dehumanizing and reminding Désirée of her "peasant" status. As the wedding approaches, Papa Ge appears and tries to convince Désirée to seek revenge by stabbing Daniel to death. "He has betrayed you—betrayed us all. Only then will the gods be assuaged," Papa Ge urges.[100] As with Andersen's tale, Désirée cannot harm her beloved and drops the knife. Rather than hurl herself into the sea like Little Mermaid, Désirée stops caring for herself and is mistaken for a peasant and removed from Daniel's property. As she watches the newlyweds depart for their honeymoon, she is trampled to death by partygoers near the gate entrance. In other words, Guy does not give Désirée a "happily ever after," nor provide an eternal reward for her moral goodness. Instead, readers can only grieve at her tragic loss, for she represented "the best in us—our humanity."[101]

Guy envisioned Désirée and Daniel's ill-fated love as an allegory of the devastating impact of slavery in the Caribbean. In her 1983 unpublished book proposal, Guy writes:

> The tenderness of Hans Christian Anderson's fairy tales has been haunting me for years—none more than the LITTLE MERMAID. For years I have

> wanted to write an allegory. But to what setting? . . . What about South America? Central America? The Caribbean? Haiti! Probably under another name. That island where the most beautiful waters of the world flow, where lyricism can be retained, in the lyrical pattern of the proverbial language and where, European culture, left over from the bloodiest period in the hemisphere's history, has grown old, decadent, insulated against change by its watery boundaries in the passage of time, makes it the ideal setting for this tale of love and despair?[102]

As a native Trinidadian, Guy was fully aware of the legacy of colonialization, including the creation and policing of racial hierarchies, economic disparities between European, African, and mixed-race people, and the social inequalities that disproportionately affected people of African descent. She also had a firm understanding of the long tradition of Black activism across the African diaspora, including the Black nationalist thought of Jamaican political activist Marcus Garvey (1887–1940) and his Universal Improvement Association and African Communities League (UNIA-ACL). As such, the call for Black Power went beyond the shores of North America. Throughout the 1960s and 1970s, Caribbean nations—including Trinidad and Tobago—grew inspiration from protests in the United States and actively resisted colonial rule. Brinsley Samaroo writes that "The February (or Black Power) Revolution in Trinidad and Tobago can be defined as the efflorescence of a movement in which thousands of citizens revolted against the status quo and demanded substantive changes in governance."[103] Guy's decision to set the story on an unnamed island reminiscent of Haiti—which won independence from French colonial rule in 1804—allowed her to consider the long-term impact of so-called liberation. The abject poverty in *My Love* demonstrates that it is not enough to wage battle for an independent Black nation; Black people must also gain economic power and educational opportunities, and abandon any colonial practices that divide and dehumanize Black people.

While Guy did not situate herself within the Black Arts or feminist movements of the time, her writing nonetheless reflects the ethos of the Black Arts Movement. Imamu Baraka (formerly Leroi Jones) reflects back on this era of Black cultural flowering in his 1981 essay, "Black Literature and the Afro-American Nation: The Urban Voice." Baraka describes the movement as follows:

> Just as the Harlem Renaissance literature had reflected the lives and struggles of the people, so the young Afro-American writers who were

> part of the Black Arts Movement of the 1960s consciously wanted to create a contemporary Black art that was: (1) *Black* (an art that utilized the forms and content of Black life); (2) *revolutionary* (an art that would transform America, that would help Black people transform it); (3) *mass-oriented* (a literature that would reach and educate the masses of Black people); and (4) *oral* (a literature that would be spoken and public, not an academic literature conceived and received and read in deadly silence).[104]

Guy's novels engage with Baraka's notions of Black art, with particular attention to the intersections of identity, in order to educate Black people and transform their communities for the better. However, rather than foster a more masculinist approach to the Black aesthetic, Guy captures these concerns from the perspective of Blackgirls. Her interest in these ideas predate the institutional development of the Black Arts Movement of the sixties and the rise of the Black feminist movement of the seventies.[105] "Long before feminism came in I was by myself. And long before the Black is a Beautiful thing came in, I was a part of my cousin's household where everyone was talking about the Garvey movement. So that I find that, yes, I'm black and a woman, and I write from my perspective of being black and a woman, but not from somebody else's idea of it," remembers Guy.[106] Furthermore, Guy did not situate her work as the embodiment of the Black Arts ethos. Jerrie Norris, who interviewed Guy following the success of *My Love, My Love,* perhaps best summarizes this critical tension in her 1988 book, *Presenting Rosa Guy*. "Although not a proponent of the black arts movement, Guy was influenced by the tone it set in the literary community and the interest it provoked in the country at large," writes Norris.[107] The Black Arts and feminist movements, coupled with her own experiential knowledge of Black girlhood, directly influenced Guy's writing.

Guy's writings reflect a Black Arts Movement and feminist influence, while also attending to her experiential knowledge of poverty, the Caribbean, and life as an orphaned Blackgirl. Margalit Fox writes that "Ms. Guy's own childhood was like something from a fairy tale, though not the kind suffused with light. . . Hearing the personal narratives of the children she met [in foster homes] made her realize that her vocation lay in storytelling."[108] Indeed, losing both of her parents, coupled with moving from the Caribbean to Harlem, had a major impact on Guy's life and led to her passion for writing. Norris further explains:

> The outsider's viewpoint informs everything she writes; her life has so shaped her consciousness. Growing up black, female, West Indian, and orphaned, and consequently many times removed from the mainstream of majority culture, she empathizes with the outsider. She has a special affinity for the "new" girl, the kid who talks, dresses, or thinks differently, the inner-city kid negotiating outside home turf, and all those who most struggle to shape a life in the face of overwhelming odds.[109]

Her novels, which included the themes of "race, class, poverty, sexuality and simmering tensions between American blacks and Afro-Caribbean immigrants newly arrived in the United States," often centered on the lives of Blackgirls.[110] Her gripping young adult trilogy, *The Friends* (1973), *Ruby* (1976), and *Edith Jackson* (1978), for example, capture the joys and challenges of Black girlhood. The first installment focuses on the formation of an uneasy friendship between Phyllisia Cathy, a well-educated West Indian immigrant, and Edith Jackson, a poor Blackgirl from Harlem. *Ruby* centers on Phyllisia's sister, Ruby, and her lesbian relationship with a sophisticated Blackgirl named Daphne Duprey. *Edith Jackson* circles back to Edith, who is now in foster care and must choose between continuing her pregnancy or having an abortion. As these plots suggest, Guy was not afraid to explore social taboos within the framework of young adult fiction. These and other novels were well received by critics of the time, garnering *The New York Times* Outstanding Book of the Year Award, the Coretta Scott King Award, and the American Library Association's Best Book for Young Adults Award.

Despite her gift for storytelling and knowledge of the theatre, Guy chose not to adapt *My Love, My Love* for the stage. Guy initially wanted to become an actress and honed her craft at Abram Hill and Frederick O'Neal's American Negro Theatre (1940–1951) in Harlem before co-founding the Harlem Writer's Guild (1950–) with novelist John Oliver Killens. Although surrounded by like-minded artists, Guy quickly discovered the lack of opportunities afforded Black performers during the 1950s. "At that point the prejudice in the U.S. made it very difficult. You hardly could get a play on or anything. So I decided to write a play. And I did a one-act play which was called 'Venetian Blinds' and showed off-off-Broadway," remembers Guy.[111] Writing her own play assured Guy a part in the production, which debuted at the Topical Theatre in New York in 1954. Unfortunately, Guy recalls, "it was a one-shot deal and after this play I started writing short stories."[112] Guy wrote on a much-needed trip to Haiti following the murder of her husband (whom she had been separated from). While we do not know for certain why Guy would later forgo adapting *My Love, My Love,* her early experiences of ostracism within the commercial world of Broadway theatre likely influenced this decision. After her "one-shot deal," Guy continued to write throughout the sixties, garnering a reputation as a superb young adult novelist at a time when other Black artists were also demanding greater representation and opportunities in the arts.

The process for securing the rights to adapt *My Love, My Love* included Lynn Ahrens and Stephen Flaherty presenting a "treatment" of songs for Guy's approval. The white writing duo began searching for a new project following their 1988 hit musical farce, *Lucky Stiff.* American playwright Bill Rosenfield writes that Ahrens and Flaherty wanted a project that would allow them "to create a musical that would be keyed into human emotions and have a deeply melodic score, rather than a fast-paced clever musical comedy."[113] This search led Ahrens to purchase a copy of Guy's *My Love, My Love.* "Here was the story she'd been seeking. It was at once beautiful, simple, compelling and *musical.* The rights were secured with one stipulation Ahrens and Flaherty had to do a presentation of four songs from the show for Ms. Guy to obtain her approval for the project," writes Rosenfield.[114] Guy reportedly approved the project and Ahrens and Flaherty adapted the novel into a musical, which included nineteen original songs with a book and lyrics by Ahrens and music by Flaherty. The majority of the music attempts to capture the "feel" of the island through a calypso-reggae sound but, unfortunately, fail to deliver. The scholar of education Julia Eklund Koza writes that "Stylistically, the music has only a remote (if any) relationship to indigenous Haitian music. Indeed, it is most closely related to the popular American styles typically found in recently composed American musical theater."[115] The *Chicago Tribune* theatre critic Michael Kilian, for example, notes the "Caribbean flavor" of the music and dance but also concedes that "the music has more in common with the contemporary stage music of Stephen Sondheim or Andrew Lloyd Webber."[116] In terms of engaging issues of race and class, Ahrens's book and lyrics provide only a passing acknowledgment of how institutional white racism harms Black people. Koza rightly argues that "the race/class politics are represented largely as problems among blacks rather than as the result of white presence on the island."[117] Indeed, the island's race and class hierarchy—which allows the light-skinned descendants of colonists to hold land, power, and wealth, and forces dark-skinned people to till the soil and struggle to survive—becomes a source of intraracial strife. While Ahrens

Figure 4.7 swope_1199987. Swope, Martha. Scene from Playwright's Horizon production of "Once on This Island." (New York) 1990. Photo by Martha Swope. ©Billy Rose Theatre Division, The New York Public Library for the Performing Arts.

and Flaherty did use their creative license to make significant changes to the narrative—such as using the protagonist's nickname "Ti Moune," rather than the name Désirée, and altering the ending, among others—their treatment did help reach an even broader audience than Guy's novel was able to. In so doing, their collaboration offered a rare opportunity for Broadway audiences to glimpse into the interior life of a Blackgirl.

Once on This Island allows spectators to experience (albeit briefly) the sense of community, gendered norms, and the joys and trials with life on French Antilles islands, but from the perspective of Blackgirls. In keeping with the novel's use of third-person perspective, the musical adaptation uses a small group of peasants to tell Ti Moune's story (see Figure 4.7). However, they do so through the use of narration, song, and dance and for the purpose of distracting and soothing a young Blackgirl who is frightened by the violence of a tropical storm. This change gives spectators the opportunity to recognize that the so-called "peasants" of the French Antilles have a rich oral tradition, a strong sense of community, and protect every member of their society—including Blackgirls. As the ensemble dance in a circle to the upbeat song, "We Dance," spectators continue to learn about the defined gender roles of their society. While the men sing about laboring to plant, weed, and chop sugar cane, the women rejoin: "And bear the child / and bear the load / and bear the pain."[118] While men perform manual labor, women take on domestic responsibilities and child care, bearing this burden for the sake of the community. At the conclusion of the song, the once-frightened Blackgirl joins in the community celebration, taking on the role of Little Ti Moune as the narrators sing, "One Small Girl." Despite her poverty, Little Ti Moune appears happy, loved, and energetic about life. She darts across the stage in an animated game of hide and seek while her adopted parents Mama and Tonton chase after her and envelop her in their arms. Little Ti Moune, however, flourishes under this care, as Mama and Tonton repeat the line "and growing" four times. Little Ti Moune exits and Ti Moune (LaChanze) appears as "a beautiful, full-grown version."[119] This heart-warming moment captures the importance of familial bonds, which can be forged on the love of a "chosen family," rather than simple biology; a sentiment that would be particularly important for Black queer feminist spectators. All Blackgirls—queer, trans, or otherwise—need and deserve nurturing homes, community support, and protection. Unfortunately, this is not always the case.

LaChanze's rendition of the Calypso-inspired song, "Waiting for Life," provides audiences with a glimpse into Ti Moune's interior life. As a child, Mama socializes Ti Moune to believe in her worth and the power of the gods. "Saved by the gods for something special!" Mama emphasizes.[120] This feeling of specialness and notion of spiritual protection stays with Ti Moune as she grows into a teenager. Discontent living an ordinary life working beside her parents in the fields, Ti Moune sings/prays to the gods to help her begin an adventure of a lifetime. "Waiting for Life" functions as her "I want" song, allowing her to vocalize a fantastic life beyond the fields. Throughout this song/prayer, Ti Moune fantasizes about what it would be like to take control of her life and meet the handsome stranger she sees racing a car down the beach. As she kneels in prayer, she sings to the rhythm of the steel drum: "Oh Gods, Oh Gods / Let me fly / Send me to places where / no one before me has been / You spared my life / show me why." Knowing that her life has a purpose beyond anything her community can imagine, LaChanze/Ti Moune concludes her prayer with the passionate refrain: "Waiting for / life to / begin!" This powerful song/prayer acts as a bridge between the human and divine, inviting the gods into Ti Moune's world. As she sleeps, the gods surround her and respond with their own song, "And the Gods Heard

Figure 4.8 swope_1199993. Martha Swope. Scene from Playwright's Horizon production of "Once on This Island." (New York) 1990. Photo by Martha Swope. ©Billy Rose Theatre Division, The New York Public Library for the Performing Arts.

Her Prayer." During this musical number, three of the gods mock Ti Moune's heartfelt prayer and suggest ways to humble her. Asaka recommends finding a mango tree and dropping a mango on her head to make her see reason, Agwe suggests sending a wave to knock her down, and Pape Ge proposes scaring her to death. Erzulie, however, persuades the other gods to give Ti Moune her heart's desire, allowing her to meet Daniel and pursue her ill-fated love in the city (see Figure 4.8).

As with the novel, the musical adaptation uses Ti Moune and Daniel's ill-fated love as an allegory for the "afterlife of slavery" in the Caribbean. Saidiya Hartman defines the afterlife of slavery as "skewed life chances, limited access to healthcare and education, premature death, incarceration, and impoverishment."[121] The song "The Sad Tale of the Beauxhommes" perhaps best captures the legacy of enslavement in the former French colony, Saint-Domingue (today Haiti). Staged as a comic pantomime in the Playwrights Horizons 1990 production, the performance reveals how colonial thought and culture have divided Black people, created wealth disparities, and established violent social hierarchies based on the color of their skin. An ensemble member dons a mask and narrates Daniel's family history, revealing that he is a descendant of Armand Beauxhomme, a French colonist who lived during the reign of Napoleon Bonaparte (r. 1804–1814). As the storyteller sings about Armand acquiring a fortune, building a mansion, and marrying a pale blonde lady (i.e., Madame Armand), cast members put on masks and act out the story. Madame Armand appears onstage and sings: "But Armand took his pleasure / with the women who served him / Black peasant girls from / the village beyond." A second storyteller tells the audience that the Black "peasant" girl bore him "A beautiful child. The pale color of coffee mixed with cream." Afterward, Daniel (Jerry Dixon) puts on his mask and becomes Armand. He gives the Black "peasant" girl a coin and mimes fighting for the French in the Civil War and sailing away to France in defeat. The first storyteller reveals: "But Armand left behind a terrible, terrible curse. Your black blood will keep you forever on this island . . .While your hearts yearn forever for France!" The circus-like music and use of exaggerated movement present a seemingly lighthearted pantomime which stands in direct contrast to the tragic tone of the remainder of the show. Indeed, the humorous delivery of devastating content (i.e., slavery, rape, and the Haitian Revolution) provides a satiric "history lesson" which may not be read by all spectators.

Black queer feminist spectators "in the know" might read the "The Sad Tale of the Beauxhommes" as a satirical performance of the history of slavery, rape, and war in Haiti. Chattel slavery began in Saint-Domingue upon the arrival of Christopher Columbus in 1492 and became the primary source for the island's economy as more Portuguese, Spanish, and French colonists followed suit. Saint-Domingue officially came under French rule in 1625 and remained so until the Haitian Revolution of 1791–1803. While performers of the pantomime do not utter the words "Haitian Revolution," the narrators nonetheless portray one of the bloodiest battles in history. Inspired by the ideals of the French Revolution—namely liberty, equality, and fraternity—the enslaved population of Saint-Domingue began to demand their freedom. Led by iconic figures such as Toussaint Louverture, Jean-Jacques Dessalines, and Henri Christophe, revolutionaries eventually gained their independence from slavery and colonial rule, forming the first Black republic in the Americas. However, winning the war did not liberate formerly enslaved Haitians. Whereas Guy's novel takes great pains to describe the aftermath of slavery, the musical falls short. In her comparison of the novel and musical, the scholar of education Julia Eklund Koza writes that "Unlike readers of the novel, however, theater goers are not schooled in the reality that hunger drives peasants to eat the seeds that should have been reserved for planting. The musical does not describe the distended bellies of poor undernourished children, nor does it tell how peasant food crops wither in times of drought while wealthy landowners selfishly irrigate only their rich soil."[122] While the actors' pantomime merely scratches the surface of this history, the performance does showcase the plight of Blackgirls under colonial rule. This unnamed Blackgirl ancestor is either forced or coerced into having sex with Armand, giving birth to a mixed-race class that would eventually rule over dark-skinned Africans like herself. This new mixed-race class would inherit wealth built upon enslaved Africans and secure their power by affirming their proximity to whiteness, controlling land and other vital resources, and degrading dark-skinned Africans. In so doing, the uptempo pantomime presents a rather grim understanding of the world in which Ti Moune must navigate.

With all of its merits, Ahrens and Flaherty's inclusion of a "happy ending" undermines the allegorical nature of Guy's original tragic ending. In the Playwrights Horizons production, Mama Euralie enters the stage and begins to sing the ballad, "A Part of Us" as Ti Moune lies on the ground. Little Ti Moune, Tonton, and storytellers enter the stage and join Mama Euralie in song. Storyteller/Asaka says "And the gods began to cry—tears of compassion for the orphan Ti Moune. Who proved that love could withstand the storm, and cross the earth and survive even in the face of death."[123] Erzulie lifts Ti Moune and hands her to Agwe, who then gently passes her to Papa Ge and Asaka. After Ti Moune's death the performers return to their original role of storytellers comforting Little Girl. Storyteller/Asaka relates that the gods take Ti Moune, bless her, and transform her into a tree. The storytellers then create a "tree" and lift Ti Moune high into the air. Finally, Storyteller/Erzulie recalls: "And one day, as Daniel's young son sat in the shade of the tree, he noticed a beautiful young peasant girl high in the branches, looking out at the world... And the spirit of Ti Moune touched their hearts, and set them free to love."[124] After Ti Moune's death breaks the island's curse, the storytellers turn outward and sing and dance to the upbeat number, "Why We Tell The Story." Several storytellers relate that they tell Ti Moune's story because of "life," "love," "grief," "hope," and "faith."[125] The storytellers then sing in unison: "It will help you feel the anger and the sorrow."[126] Storyteller/Ti Moune completes the lyric with a solo, singing: "and forgive . . . "[127] By the end of the song the Little Girl happily sings along with the storytellers. The musical concludes with a return to calm. The torrential downpour has ceased, stars and a night sky are projected on the backdrop of the set, and the storytellers return to their previous position by the campfire. Ahrens and Flaherty's ending provides a neat, uplifting, and circular narrative that emphasizes the moral value of forgiveness. By forgiving, Storyteller/Ti Moune asserts her value—she did not deserve to be wronged and Daniel should not have wronged her. But by forgiving, she retains her dignity and status within her moral community. In so doing, the race/class divide becomes insular, disconnected from institutional white racism and the much larger allegory of the afterlife of slavery.

Guy originally did not want to alter Désirée's brutal death scene in *My Love, My Love*, but was persuaded to do so by Ahrens and Flaherty. In the original novel, a groundskeeper named Lucifus mistakes Désirée for a peasant and removes her from the hotel, injuring her shoulder in the process. Despite her pain, she remains standing at the hotel gates for two weeks, not eating or sleeping—only staring at the wedding preparations at Hotel Beauxhomme.[128] Immediately following Daniel and Andrea's wedding, a drunken crowd of partygoers chase after their limousine and trample Désirée until "only the corpse of the girl remained."[129] Guy concludes the story with one final moment of injustice performed by Lucifus. "Picking up the corpse by an arm and a leg, he dumped it at the side of the road to await the garbage collectors," writes Guy.[130] This ending provides a powerful visual representation of the treatment of Blackgirls in post-colonial Haiti. Although slavery has ended, the life chances for Blackgirls remain skewed because they lack the privilege of whiteness or proximity to whiteness. Désirée's impoverishment, lack of access to healthcare and education, and premature death represent the ongoing plight of Blackgirls in Haiti. Without community protection, Blackgirls do not stand a chance of battling these forces. Unfortunately, this important message was replaced by a much more cheery ending. While we do not know the exact reason Guy acquiesced to the alteration, journalist Judith Weinraub's *The Washington Post* article, "The Writer's Happily Ever After: Rosa Guy and the Musical With a Fairy Tale Ending" (1992), provides some detail. Weinraub writes that: "There are some forces that Guy finds hard to resist, however, such as when Flaherty and Ahrens, the writers of 'Once on This Island,' wanted a somewhat more uplifting ending than Guy (or Hans Christian Andersen) had provided. It took them a while to talk her into it, but eventually they won her over. 'I'm glad they did,' she says. 'Everyone leaves the theater happy.'"[131] Theatre critics applauded the cheeriness of the production, with the *Village Voice*'s Michael Feingold writing that

Once on This Island "is, for the most part, such a cheery, skillfully made little entertainment that I can't imagine anyone taking violent exception to it."[132] Obviously because including the destruction of the Black cis female body would not allow the production to maintain its charm, seemingly noncontroversial politics, and appeal to young audiences.[133]

While Guy may have wanted Désirée's story to serve as an allegory of the afterlife of slavery, Black queer feminist spectators can also read the Playwrights Horizon's production of Ti Moune's as an allegory of Black queer life. Ti Moune's experiences of ostracism—being shunned by the wealthy light-skinned grand hommes—might resonate with spectators who also experience rejection and hatred from their dominant heteronormative society. Ti Moune's decision to embrace a "chosen family" after losing her blood-related kin redefines the meaning of family. Spectators learn that should they too "lose" family—whether through death, separation, or ostracism—they can form familial bonds and experience love through *chosen kinship*. Ti Moune's ability to express her desires and boldly enter into a socially taboo sexual relationship with Daniel might also empower spectators to reclaim their own sexuality. Finally, Ti Moune's premature death might resonate with Black queer feminist spectators who continue to experience the "loss" of loved ones due to high rates of suicide, hate crimes, incarceration, limited healthcare, food insecurity, racialized violence, and other problems within Black and Black queer communities. While not written into the libretto, Black queer feminist spectators can and do have the capacity to make these connections and in so doing, make themselves visible.

In conclusion, the need for greater visibility is an ongoing project for both Black women artists and their spectators. As the experiences of Aremu, Taylor, and Guy demonstrate, navigating the business of theatre is fraught with obstacles—even for the most talented of artists. Black women artists, in particular, are more vulnerable to discriminatory practices due to their position as Black and as female (queer, trans, or otherwise). Yet, Black women musical theatre artists continue to persevere and craft fairy tale musicals that speak to the concerns of Black America. The following chapter, "Blackgirl Fantasy," continues this discussion, exploring Black women artists' contributions to one of the most beloved all-Black musical fantasies of all time: *The Wiz*.

5
Blackgirl Fantasy

My six sisters and I are sitting on the hardwood floor, gathered around the television set watching *The Wiz* for the thousandth time. Actually, that may not be true. I actually don't remember our very first time watching *The Wiz*. It's the 1980s and *The Wiz* is as much a part of my life as the countless hours I spend removing my Jheri curl activator from the sofa, practicing the moonwalk, or listening to my mom and older sister's annual Thanksgiving argument about how much salt should go into the collard greens. What I do know is that we enjoy watching *The Wiz*. We love watching our hero Dorothy (Diana Ross) travel from her aunt's Harlem apartment to the magical land of Oz. We celebrate the fact that Dorothy ultimately vanquishes her seemingly more powerful foe Evillene, the Wicked Witch of the West (Mabel King). As young Blackgirls, we identify with Dorothy's plight. While we are not battling powerful witches, we are constantly resisting our mom's attempts to socialize us into "respectable" young women. As such, we were fascinated by Evillene, the most oppressive force in Dorothy's life. The gargantuan size of Evillene's body, the hideousness of her face, and the force of her supernatural powers both excite and repulse us. We eagerly anticipate her first appearance in the film, bursting through the doors of her sweatshop belting, "Don't Nobody Bring Me No Bad News." We revel in drawing comparisons between Evillene and our mom, hoping that one day we, too, can defeat her.

The Wiz took on greater meaning as I traversed the waters of Black girlhood. When I was about seven years old, I learned that the 1978 film was adapted from a 1975 all-Black cast Broadway musical. At about ten years old, I discovered—what to me felt like a rip-off of *The Wiz*—Judy Garland's rendition of Dorothy in *The Wizard of Oz* (1939). When my mom revealed that both films were derived from Frank L. Baum's beloved children's novel *The Wonderful Wizard of Oz* (1900), I was incredulous that Dorothy could be anything other than a Blackgirl. Yet, I also felt a sense of pride that some artist had thought to create a hero for me and other Blackgirls to emulate. However, it was not until I reached late adolescence, when I began to

Black Queer Girlhood on the Musical Theatre Stage. La Donna L. Forsgren, Oxford University Press.
 DOI: 10.1093/9780197661444.003.0006

resist heteronormative ways of viewing the world, that I fully appreciated Dorothy's plight. At the beginning of *The Wiz*, Aunt Em presents Dorothy with a potential suitor named Gil in the hope that she will marry him and bear children of her own. Before Aunt Em's matchmaking plans come to fruition, Dorothy creates an alternative fantasy world (i.e., Oz) to escape these familial pressures. Even without the advantages of graduate school training, I interpreted Dorothy's behavior as *transgressive*. I found Dorothy's refusal to conform to heteronormativity refreshing and delighted in her ability to construct alternative visions of Black girlhood with queer possibilities.

With the advantage of hindsight, I now conceptualize my experiences watching *The Wiz* as that of a "resistant reader."[1] By suggesting that Black queer feminist spectators might interpret Dorothy's fantasy as a Black lesbian narrative, I continue the tradition of challenging notions of an *ideal* spectator, typically defaulted as white and cis male. Unfortunately, Black women—whether queer, trans, or otherwise—rarely meet the criteria as an ideal spectator of popular entertainment. Yet, Black queer feminist spectators have *always* existed, and their representation—on and off our stages and film and television screens—continues to matter. I therefore offer multiple points of entry into understanding how Black queer feminist spectators might engage with four major productions of *The Wiz*.

Standing at the crossroads of larger critical debates, *The Wiz* is uniquely situated to engage with issues of Black queer feminist spectatorship, racial authenticity, and politically engaged popular entertainment. For more than forty years, *The Wiz* has enjoyed prestigious awards, commercial success, and a cult following among marginalized subcultures. Indeed, many Black queer folx—whether from the privacy of their own home or the glamorous world of *The Wiz*–themed public vogue balls—have embraced the film as exemplary of the Black queer experience.[2] For Black queer bloggers such as Kenyon Farrow, *The Wiz* and its "Black gay anthem . . . 'Home'" resonates with those who came of age during the "Classic Era (meaning you're over 30, or at least have Classic Black Gay Sensibilities, or CBGS)."[3] Farrow writes:

> One reason that the Black gays of the classic era love this song, in my opinion, is that it speaks to the pain of feeling cast out of the larger Black community—we have no "home" in a sense. The song is about a stateless person—someone who has dreams of a physical place, but the lesson that they learn is that home has to be made in the family and community we create.[4]

Yet, scholars of both African American theatre and media studies have, for the most part, shied away from exploring how potential Black queer audiences might respond to the political relevance and Black queer representations in the various productions of *The Wiz*. This is in part due to the privileging of the heteronormative gaze in reception studies, the unease of positioning an artistically miscegenated work within the canon of African American theatre, and the longstanding binary opposition between popular entertainment and politically engaged theatre.

The few studies that do explore *The Wiz* focus almost entirely on the 1978 film adaptation and often privilege Black cis male subjectivity. The philosopher Tommy J. Curry, for example, analyzes *The Wiz*'s unsuccessful political campaign as a metaphor for Black political marginalization and the Lion's pursuit of courage as a how-to guide for acquiring Black masculinity.[5] The media studies scholar Ryan Bunch goes a step further by interpreting Dorothy's journey through Oz as a metaphor for building strong Black communities and briefly acknowledges queer undertones in the Black liberation song "Everybody Rejoice (Brand New Day)."[6] In contrast, the musical theatre scholar Stacy Wolf celebrates the original Broadway production's social significance, noting that *The Wiz* depicts a woman as "the leader or initiator of [a] community."[7] In so doing, she addresses the importance of spectatorship, writing that "*The Wiz* motivated the formation and enactment of a community of black theatergoers and critics who defied the hegemony of white critics . . . and negated the presumption that a white perspective is objective or universal."[8] The media studies scholar Rhonda Williams takes Wolf's woman-centered and spectatorship-focused approach a step further by championing Black women's spectatorship and the Black feminist possibilities of Dorothy's journey. Unfortunately, Williams frames her study within a heteronormative lens.[9] While important to our understanding of the film's political and social relevance, these readings cannot fully account for intersectionality within the Black experience, nor envision Black queer feminist spectatorship.

A Black queer feminist reading of major productions of *The Wiz* provides important insights into the curious silence of Black queer feminist spectatorship, as well as creates the ontological space for Black queer spectators perhaps to identify with and celebrate Black queer feminist subjectivity. The performance studies scholar Laura Alexandra Harris locates Black queer feminist criticism "at the intersections of pop culture, intellectual culture, and cultures of race, class, and sexuality."[10] Black queer feminist praxis illuminates the gaps and silences within queer and feminist histories and theories by reclaiming and writing Black queer feminist subjectivity into history.[11] This chapter, therefore, situates *The Wiz* as a Black lesbian fantasy constructed out of the innermost desires of Dorothy, a Blackgirl navigating betwixt and between adolescence and womanhood, who must come to terms with her own burgeoning sexuality. Dorothy consistently—in all major theatre, film, and television adaptations—creates an Oz brimming with Black queer cultural references and visions of Black queer womanhood.

Dorothy's fantasy not only renders the Black queer body visible within popular culture, but also demonstrates how the cis Black female body has been used as a site to reinforce and *transgress* heteronormativity, sexism, and racism. The original producer Ken Harper conceptualized *The Wiz* as a transgressive and entertaining production: "*The Wiz* says this. 'Alright America, you have this story, it can be told but it is so universal that it can be told with Blacks as well as whites and we're showing it and telling it in a humorous, entertaining and delightful way.' "[12] By staking a claim to Blackness as universal, Harper resists the supposed universality of whiteness and renders Dorothy's Black female body a transgressive site of possibilities. In the original 1975 Broadway production, 1978 film adaptation, 2015 *The Wiz Live!* televised event, and 2024 Broadway revival, Dorothy must kill Evillene in order to return home. Whether portrayed by actress Mabel King as a dangerous dyke or more recently by Mary J. Blige as camp personified, Evillene disrupts patriarchy, wreaking havoc upon the Black community. Though Evillene ultimately dies in all four versions, her dangerous pursuit of power and pleasure transgresses the boundaries of benign Black womanhood. The more recent televised adaptation further complicates gender norms through actress Queen Latifah's drag king performance as The Wiz. This contemporary wizard lives their life as a powerful male ruler, yet remains in constant fear that others will discover that they are, in fact, a powerless woman. Evillene and The Wiz's rejection of normativity are but two of many subversive elements within the musical.

By staking a claim to the queerness of this canonical text, I hark back to the film critic Alexander Doty and the queer theatre scholarship of Jill Dolan and Stacy Wolf, whose pioneering efforts helped decenter heterocentrism and sexism within audience reception theories of popular culture. Dolan's *The Feminist Spectator as Critic* (1988) encourages resistant readership; Wolf's *A Problem Like Maria: Gender and Sexuality in the American Musical* (2002) reveals the implications of signifying "lesbian" on the American musical stage; and Doty's *Flaming Classics: Queering the Film Canon* (2000) situates Judy Garland and *The Wizard of Oz* as significant to the LGBTQ community. Although Doty does not offer criticism of *The Wiz*, I am drawn to his analysis because of his celebration of queer subjectivity. For example, Doty draws parallels between his own coming out journey and Dorothy's trek through Oz, noting the campiness of the cult classic and taking pleasure in reading the Cowardly Lion as a "drag queen who just didn't give a fuck."[13] Doty situates the film as "lesbian narrative" constructed from Dorothy's own queer adolescent fantasies, which culminate in her rendition of "Over the Rainbow," a "Queer National Anthem."[14] By reclaiming this canonical film, Doty disrupts the supposed universality of heterosexism within audience reception studies of popular culture.

While the present analysis owes a debt to Doty's work, my study also departs by simultaneously engaging with race, class, gender, and sexuality within audience reception theories. This reading not only reclaims Black queer feminist subjectivity and Black queer imagery and culture, but also celebrates the *pleasure* Black queer feminist spectators might experience from the critical moments wherein heterocentrism, sexism, and white cultural hegemony are (intentionally or not) subverted. This pleasure—whether derived from the black lesbian narrative, the use of subversive song, a pulsing disco beat, stylized vogue movements, the black tradition of signifyin', or a camp sensibility—helps to explain why *The Wiz* has achieved both mainstream success and a cult following among Black queer spectators.

The Wiz Arrives on Broadway

The Wiz premiered during the Black Arts Movement (1965–76), a time of Black cultural flowering and civil unrest. Rebellions swept the nation, as Black Americans and their allies protested police brutality, the assassination of Black leaders, and the failure of the Civil Rights Act (1964) in instituting civil liberties. High rates of unemployment, substance use disorders, prostitution, inadequate housing, and underfunded public school systems continued to threaten the fabric of many Black communities. Black artists responded to these social ills, as well as to their invisibility on Broadway stages, by turning inward, creating new works for Black audiences.[15] While the plays of this era vary in tone and style, they often depict a didactic conversion process whereby Black audiences could witness a Black protagonist's journey from a "Negro" (i.e., passive, individualistic, and politically uninformed) to a "Black" (i.e., politically active for the betterment of the community). We see this most clearly in works such as Amiri Baraka's *Madheart* (1971) and Martie Evans-Charles's *Where We At?* (1971). Both one-act plays feature "Negro" characters who are figuratively and literally "lost," meaning that they are ignorant of their cultural heritage, have internalized racist beliefs about Blacks, or are unmoved by the suffering of the Black community. These lost souls must rely on a Black revolutionary guide to help them return to the Black community and realize their potential as strong Black leaders.[16] Plays such as *Madheart* and *Where We At?* exemplify how prescribing and policing the boundaries of blackness were a constant source of artistic and political tension in the 1970s (as today). Unfortunately, these often narrowly defined conceptions of Blackness largely excluded the most vulnerable within an already marginalized community: Black queer women.

The Wiz, with its all-Black cast and mostly Black creative team, sits uncomfortably within the ethos of the Black Arts era. Hearkening back to W. E. B. Du Bois's 1926 call for a new Black theatre that would meet the needs of Black America, revolutionary artists of the sixties and seventies attempted to create black theatre that was *by*, *for*, *about*, and *near* the Black masses.[17] Harper's decision not to produce the musical at a historically Black theatre could potentially have alienated Black audiences, many of whom did not live near the Majestic Theatre, a Broadway house located in midtown Manhattan. Yet, the 1975 production included the talents of Stephanie Mills (Dorothy), Tiger Haynes (Tinman), Hinton Battle (Scarecrow), Ted Ross (Lion), the openly Black queer actor André De Shields (The Wiz), Mabel King (Evillene), and Dee Dee Bridgewater (Glinda). Behind the scenes, Black artists Charlie Smalls (music/lyrics), George Faison (choreography), Tom H. John (set design), Tharon Musser (lighting), Geoffrey Holder (costumes; codirector), and Gilbert Moses (codirector) worked with white book writer William F. Brown to realize Harper's vision. Harper's decision to hire Brown, rather than use the talents of a Black playwright, also stood in direct conflict with the Black Arts ethos of creating Black art for the Black masses. The question of audience continued to plague Harper, as "many potential backers doubted that theatregoers would accept the 'Blackening' of a work so dear to White America."[18] The implications were that (1) whites had staked a claim to Frank L. Baum's beloved children's classic, (2) the Broadway production would privilege white spectators, and (3) a Black-centered narrative of Oz would alienate white audiences.

Situating *The Wiz* within the Black theatre canon engages with larger critical debates about what constitutes Black theatre. *Does Black theatre only include works written by Blacks and performed for Black audiences?*[19] If so, *The Wiz* does not qualify. Yet, *The Wiz* created greater visibility of Black talent and widely appealed to Black audiences. Despite Broadway's exclusionary practices, the expense of a $30 Broadway ticket (about $175 with current inflation), and the theatre's geographic distance from de facto segregated Black communities, the production was supported by Black audiences during weekend matinees.[20] The theatre critic Judith Cummings credits this high attendance to "word of mouth within the black community," who believed the show "offer[ed] them something to identify with."[21] Queen Latifah admits to being inspired to pursue a career in entertainment after witnessing Mills (Dorothy) sing "Home" as a child: "It's one of the first plays I'd ever seen. . . . To see people who looked like me and had my color skin, my body type. People who looked like my aunts and my uncles and people I knew—black people. I had never seen anything like it."[22] Perhaps she, too, connected with Dorothy's Black queer fantasy of acceptance from the Black community?

In addition to affirming the skill of Black artists, the Broadway production also entertained Black audiences through the use of culturally specific humor, slang, dance, and music (i.e., a mixture of gospel, rock, soul, pop, and protest songs). Black audiences, according to the Black theatre critic Bryant Rollins, experienced *pleasure* through the production's subversion of cultural white hegemony: "Blacks responded in a special way at certain dramatic points in the show, and to some of its songs and dances. . . . Black theatergoers, especially, seem to appreciate the irony of hearing explicit protest songs right on the Great White Way."[23] Though the show's book was written by a white writer, the production modes—orchestrated by a team of talented Black artists and performers—demonstrated the possibility of popular culture rising to the level of political importance. Yet, one must not forget that the production—to channel Du Bois—was not exclusively created *by* Black artists, *for* Black audiences, or *near* Black communities. *The Wiz* also needed to appeal primarily to white audiences, who made up the majority of spectators who attended Wednesday matinees: Harper needed to ensure the financial marketability of his venture, and this meant carefully packaging his "Black vision" for racially mixed audiences.[24]

To secure a return for his investors, it was essential that Harper market a codified blackness that would appeal to white consumers. After years of careful maneuvering, Harper finally persuaded Twentieth Century–Fox to invest $1.2 million in the Broadway production.[25] Unfortunately, racial biases remained embedded in the quest for profit. The song lyrics walk a fine line between catering to the sensibilities of white and Black audiences by, for example, using symbols and metaphors that reference slavery, emancipation, the Great Migration (1916–70), the dangers of urban living, domestic servitude, the Black church, and law enforcement's untenable relationship to the Black community.[26] Yet, within the safety of a child's fantasy and from within the modes of production, these references could go unnoticed to audiences unfamiliar with these historical and cultural references. The use of vibrant, futuristic sets and costumes helped disconnect the day-to-day struggles of the average Black American from this fantastic world. An all-Black cast further obscured the impact of institutional white racism, instead highlighting intracultural conflict. Thus, while the book itself alludes to Black political struggle, the modes of production also establish *The Wiz* as a consumable product for a broad (meaning white) audience. Playing to sold-out houses and grossing $18.5 million in ticket sales, *The Wiz* culminated in seven Tony Awards, including Best Musical.[27]

The Wiz's critical and financial success demonstrated the viability of Black theatre and subverted (albeit, briefly) the racial barriers of the Great White Way. For this to happen, Harper had to convince the white businessmen of Twentieth Century–Fox that white audiences would attend an all-Black Broadway musical. There were, of course, a number of precursors to the all-Black Broadway musical, including Bob Cole and Billy Johnson's *A Trip to Coontown* (1898) and Noble Sissle and Eubie Blake's *Shuffle Along* (1921), which "legitimized the black musical [and] proved to producers and theatre managers that [white] audiences would pay to see black talent on Broadway."[28] Yet, by the 1970s, Harper's insistence on producing an all-Black musical was considered controversial, in part because of his race. Black producers encountered "charges of racism" for supporting all-Black musicals, whereas white producers remained virtually unchallenged for continuing the practice of all-white casts.[29] *New York Times* critic Mel Gussow exemplifies this double standard in his article "Casting by Race Can Be Touchy" (1975). "The crucial question is whether a play should be cast entirely with black performers or with a mixed company. The former can seem racist if there is no artistic validity for the switch in color. Then its only justification is to give minority actors employment. The mixed company makes far more sense" writes Gussow.[30] While well-intended, arguing for an interracial cast simply ignores the underlying issue of systemic racism within the arts and society as a whole.[31]

The fact remains that Broadway directors, producers, designers, playwrights, and audiences remain predominately white and cis male. The problem is so pervasive that in 2011, when the works of three Black women playwrights—Katori Hall, Lydia R. Diamond, and Suzan-Lori Parks—were produced on Broadway, their presence became a newsworthy headline. Kenny Leon, director of *The Wiz Live!*, reflects: "I can't remember the last time there were three women playwrights on Broadway during the same season, let alone three African-American women."[32] Furthermore, actors of color deserve more than the occasional nontraditional casting opportunity. Gary Anderson, the artistic director of Plowshares Theatre Company (Detroit), reports:

> For every exceptional situation where an artist of color has found work—such as *Hamilton*—there remains an 8-to-1 advantage white actors have over the random actor of color. Administrators of color who are put into associate or deputy positions below senior management are tasked with masking the reality that American Theatre has become no more progressive on race and inclusion than their fathers and grandfathers. . . . [T]here seems to be a growing awareness among many sociologists that "colorblindness" of any kind—including color blind casting—does more to entrench racial disadvantage rather than rectify it.[33]

Black, Indigenous, and People of Color (BIPOC) need employment opportunities at *every* level of theatre production. *The Wiz* showcased the talent of Black artists and also brought public scrutiny to these topical issues.

Although I have briefly discussed *The Wiz* in terms of its cultivation of Black talent, popularity with Black audiences, and consumption by white spectators, it is also important to consider the play's popularity among subcultures that operate within marginalized cultures. Black lesbians—whether playwrights, characters onstage, or spectators—are often rendered invisible within discussions of the Broadway canon and in audience reception theories of popular culture. The remainder of this section, therefore, provides a more nuanced reading of spectatorship, privileging the less visible intersections of Black identity. I offer my own resistant readership of *The Wiz* and consider how Black queer feminist spectators might derive pleasure from Dorothy's Black queer adolescent fantasy, paying particular attention to the critical tension between the book and song lyrics, modes of production, and Black queer feminist spectatorship. In so doing, I hope to continue the practice of queering the canon.

If Oz is a product of Dorothy's Black queer adolescent fantasy, just what is she attempting to escape? The Broadway book describes Dorothy as "a girl of thirteen or fourteen" who is "as bright and alive as can be."[34] Conflict arises as she uses her agency to daydream of a different life, rather than perform domestic tasks such as helping Aunt Em with laundry. Daydreaming allows her to escape, albeit briefly, the drudgeries of life on a "ramshackle little farm house in Kansas" (9). The book states that "somehow, it would seem she's built a life of her own on this dreary farm, and would probably rather remain a child as long as possible instead of accepting the responsibilities of adulthood" (9). As heterosexual kinfolk with clearly delineated gender roles, her family assumes that she will follow in Aunt Em's footsteps and tend to the home. Dorothy copes with the pressure to conform to gendered and sexual norms by creating an interior life and disavowing the physical growth Aunt Em refers to in her song, "The Feeling We Once Had," by literally turning away from her (11). Dorothy is not alone in this journey, as many Black queer youth tend to live in heterosexual families, are isolated from their peers, and "do not even recognize this [queer] part of their identity until adolescence."[35] Feelings of isolation, coupled with the burden of conforming, become manifest in a "Tornado Ballet," taking Dorothy to a new world of Black queer possibilities.

Dorothy's journey through Oz serves as a metaphor for her path to Black queer womanhood. *Will she continue to repress her desires, or will she find the strength to embrace her queer identity and gain acceptance from the Black community?* Unable to cope with this internal battle in everyday life, she imagines multiple visions of what Black womanhood might look like for her. Black queer feminist spectators are left to wonder which path Dorothy will follow. Will Dorothy emulate the Black churchwomen and wait for a Black man to "save" her from her own queer desires? Or, will Dorothy suppress her feelings and become Glinda, a surrogate mother figure to the Black community? Even still, will she choose a more dangerous path and abandon the Black community altogether in pursuit of her own power, like the Wicked Witch of the West? Finally, will Dorothy decide to discard her inhibitions and embrace an isolated life of queer BIPOC dance culture behind the gates of Emerald City?

The churchwomen of Oz represent the important role the Black church has played in shaping Black queer experiences in the United States. The sociologist Patricia Hill Collins writes that during the turn of the twentieth century, "the majority of LGBT Black people . . . remain[ed] deeply closeted" in rural areas of the South.[36] Already marginalized within society because of their race, many Black queer folx, fearing further abuse, felt pressed to pass as heterosexual.[37] As previously mentioned in Chapter 2, as the twentieth century dawned, Black religious and political leaders promoted a politics of respectability as a weapon to combat institutional racism. Black homosexuality was viewed by churchgoing folks not only as morally repugnant but also as a threat to the Black family structure and the Black political struggle.[38] At the heart of this homophobic rhetoric rests a concern about the supposed weakened state of Black queer men and their inability to fulfill their role as providers, protectors, and leaders of the Black community. (With the Black church's view that women should head neither the family nor the liberation movement, Black lesbians do not factor into such discussions.) Black homosexuality is therefore seen by many churchgoing Blacks as an enemy to Black liberation, perhaps even reflecting "a sinister plot by White racists as a form of population genocide (neither gay Black men nor Black lesbians have children under this scenario)."[39] Pressured by the Black church to adhere to the politics of respectability—which supports dominant ideologies of gender and sexuality—Black queer folx often self-censor by remaining in the closet to support and protect the Black community.

The churchwomen of Oz adopt a similar politics of respectability by situating Evillene as the embodiment of pure evil. Similar to the Black women's club movement at the turn of the twentieth century, the Black women of Oz organize a religious society to aid their community. The Wiz explains that the churchwomen promote benefits and insist that he perform another miracle when he is mistakenly identified as a pastor of sorts. The churchwomen turn to the Wiz for leadership and protection against Evillene, whom he describes as "the most evil . . . the most wicked . . . the most powerful of all the witches in Oz" (53). It is important to note that the Wiz has never actually met Evillene and that his description presumably comes from the churchwomen's previous encounters with her. Now, what makes Evillene evil, wicked, and powerful? She is physically unattractive (by Western standards of beauty), flourishes without the companionship of a Black man, and aligns herself with feminism and capitalism. In other words, she embodies the attributes of what I term the *dangerous dyke*. While she perceives herself as beautiful and powerful, the Black community finds her queer body repulsive and her power dangerous. However, what conservative Black Christians may deem repulsive or "dangerous," Black queer spectators may find *thrilling*.

As a so-called "dangerous dyke," Evillene represents a heterosexist view of Black queer womanhood. Described in the book as lacking "a kind bone in her imposing body or a good thought in her rotten mind," Evillene surrounds

Figure 5.1 swope_1131074. Swope, Martha. Actress Ella Mitchell in a publicity shot from the replacement cast of the Broadway musical "The Wiz." (New York) 1977. Photo by Martha Swope. ©Billy Rose Theatre Division, The New York Public Library for the Performing Arts.

herself with "slave-like" Winkies who labor in her factory (55). Performed by actress Mabel King in both the original Broadway and film version of the musical, the character situates herself as the epitome of Black beauty (see Figure 5.1). However, her appearance is meant to read as a conglomeration of controlling images of Black womanhood. Onstage, Evillene appears as a large, animalistic, domineering Black matriarch. She sports small, sharklike teeth; grotesque red, black, and silver makeup; an oversized black wig that resembles a fruit tree; an excessive amount of jewelry; and a long black dress with large movable eyes at her chest. As master of her own castle, Evillene rests on a throne made of carcasses and intimidates any man who undermines her authority. For example, when the leader of the Winged Monkeys questions her decision, she threatens to put a spell on his "coconuts," and he quickly defers to her judgment (60). She also displays her contempt for Black male agency by ordering (the once-powerful) Lord High Underling to speak to her only while on his knees. Obeying, he immediately "drops to his knees, groveling" (57). She then makes him kiss her foul-smelling boot and declares: "It's so good to be a liberated woman" (57). While Lord High Underling's response to her body odor is likely meant to elicit laughter from audiences, her statement, coupled with her appearance and masculine behavior also provides a warning against the dangers of feminism. Evillene, after all, appears to associate Black women's liberation with the emasculation of Black men.

Black queer feminist spectators, however, can use their agency to challenge interpretations of Evillene as a heterosexist nightmare and instead read her as an *exciting* image of Black queer feminist strength whose only "fatal flaw" is her inability to work *with* the Black community of Oz. Evillene's plight parallels the actual concerns that many Black lesbians encounter in everyday life. In her study of motherhood and gay identities, the sociologist Mignon R. Moore found that Black lesbians "live in black communities, not 'gay ghettos,' and that social location shapes their identities, family formation, and other understandings in ways that differ from some white LGBT people."[40] Indeed, finding a way to express one's sexual agency and remain within the Black community is an ever-present tension within Black lesbian identity formation. Evillene's betrayal of her own community perhaps serves as an example of what to avoid. In contrast to the other witches and churchwomen of Oz, Evillene achieves power and financial independence to the detriment of others. Her source of power lies with her mind and body as she uses her business savvy and knowledge of Voodoo to maintain order. For example, when the groveling Messenger tries to escape her wrath, she performs a Voodoo chant using the movable eyes at her chest to force him to crawl back to her (59). Dorothy and the other witches of Oz are likewise strong and decidedly queer, but unlike Evillene they use their power to protect and uplift the Black community. Evillene, however, uses her strength solely for her own empowerment, leaving her ostracized from the Black community.

In contrast to Evillene, the churchwomen turn to a cis male spokesman for protection. Though the Wiz describes the churchwomen as assertive and capable of leading, they ultimately turn to a pastor of sorts for direction. The Wiz, who desperately craves social mobility, explains to Dorothy that, before landing in Oz, he sold used cars, worked as "a pitchman in a carnival," and "even peddled bleaching creams from door to door" in Omaha (73). He insists that God called him to "spread the Good Word" (i.e., host a revival meeting) so that he could acquire "the simple things in life . . . power . . . prestige . . . and money" (73). Before he could make his grand entrance inside a hot-air balloon, a "violent wind" tossed him in the middle of a ladies' social in Oz (73). "They thought a miracle had delivered me to them," says the Wiz. "And before you could say 'wizard' . . . they promoted me all over town, and sold tickets for a benefit, at which they said I was going to perform *another* miracle. . . . Naturally, I did!" (74). Unfortunately, the churchwomen put their faith in an individualistic man who sees spirituality as nothing more than a used car: a commodity to be sold. Furthermore, his open admission to manipulating Black women's faith and beauty for personal gain suggests a severe moral deficiency and cements him as an enemy to the Black liberation struggle.

Ultimately, it is not the Wiz's "miracles" but Dorothy's strength that liberates the churchwomen. Their inability to understand their strength as Black women allowed them to be controlled by the Wiz. Black queer feminist spectators might read the churchwomen's reliance on the flawed teachings of a male pastor as a very real problem within actual Black communities. The Black church has historically provided Black women with "a place of refuge, of solace and hope" from the horrors of enslavement to the battle for civil rights, with Black women making up 70–90% of today's Black congregations.[41] Yet, the Black church has also been slow to admit women formally into high-ranking positions. Black women continue to find themselves consigned to the margins while Black men assume leadership positions.[42] Meanwhile, these same ministers continue to view homosexuality as "a 'white disease'" and reaffirm heterosexist ideologies that render Black queer women at best invisible or at worst: an enemy to the Black community.[43] Manipulated by the smooth-talking Wiz, Dorothy makes the decision to kill Evillene in exchange for his aid in returning home.

However, by killing Evillene, Dorothy runs the risk of silencing her innermost desires. Evillene, after all, is created from Dorothy's own queer subconscious and embodies her own feminine strength. Dorothy perhaps best exemplifies this attribute through her interactions with Lion. When she first meets Lion, he takes pleasure in scaring her friends as he boasts about his masculine strength in the song "Mean Ole Lion." Dorothy, however, sees through his male bravado. While Tinman and Scarecrow cower in fear, she becomes her own hero by delivering a roundhouse punch to Lion, followed by a sound spanking for upsetting her friends. Black queer feminist spectators can perhaps derive pleasure from watching Dorothy disrupt gender norms through her skillful defense of her terrified friends.

Unfortunately, Black queer feminist spectators may find that the book later undoes this subversive scene by reinforcing the belief that strong Black mothers hinder Black communities. In a moment of contriteness Lion reveals why he behaves like a hypermasculine hero from a Blaxploitation film: "Daddy left home when I was born, and Momma was such a strong lady. It was either 'do this' or 'don't do that' . . . 'you call them paws clean?' . . . 'Lick behind your ears, child, or you don't get no dessert'" (34). The juxtaposition of his affected machismo and actual ineptness is meant to illicit laughter. Yet, using a strong-tongued single mother as a scapegoat for Black men's personal failings is no laughing matter. By blaming his broken home on his mother's strength, Lion reinforces both superwoman and Black matriarchy mythology.[44] Early Black feminists such as Michele Wallace worked tirelessly to disrupt these mythologies, as well as the correlation of Black liberation with the acquisition of manhood.[45] Unfortunately, using single Black mothers as scapegoats for the ills of the Black community is nothing new. From *The Negro Family: The Case for National Action* (1965), to welfare reform debates of the 1990s, to today's myth of the "missing Black father," single Black mothers continue to encounter stigmatization within US politics and greater society.[46] *The Wiz* reinforces these dangerous mythologies by making it clear that, in order to liberate herself, friends, and the Winkies, Dorothy must kill Evillene. This she does by tossing a bucket of water on her; but when exorcizing Evillene from the Black community does not immediately allow Dorothy to return home, she turns to Glinda, the Good Witch of the South, for advice.

Glinda embodies attributes of the blueswoman figure and, as such, represents a more viable vision of Black queer womanhood for Dorothy to emulate. Glinda, described in the book as "the prettiest of all the Witches," appears at Dorothy's most desperate moment (86). Dorothy has won the Wiz's favor by killing Evillene only to experience abandonment by his abrupt departure in a hot-air balloon. He does, however, counsel Dorothy and the citizens of Oz to "stop . . . holding on to the things that make us feel safe! [. . .] And embrace what we fear" (81): sound advice for those who fear their sexuality might lead to ostracism from their community; yet, difficult to execute for those who lack confidence in themselves. As a seasoned performer in the land of Oz, Glinda uses the power of her voice to help restore Dorothy's confidence. Much like the classic blueswomen of the 1920s who advised women listeners through themes of "abandonment . . . homosexuality . . . returning home [and] traveling,"[47] Glinda offers guidance through song. This is perhaps best exemplified through her musical number, "A Rested Body Is a Rested Mind." Glinda sings, "Oh, the journey that you had to make / I've watched you bear the load / But you can always stay at my place / When you come off the road" (86). With these words, Glinda conjures the spirit of Gertrude "Ma" Rainey, the "Mother of the Blues," who also privileged Black women's subjectivity and openly discussed her women lovers in her songs. The Black feminist activist Angela Y. Davis writes that Rainey's songs about Black women's travels to and from home "are frequently associated with the exercise of autonomy in their sexual lives."[48] These poor Black women "travel because they have lovers in other cities, or because they wish to find new lovers."[49] Glinda's song likewise validates Dorothy's freedom to explore her sexuality and maintain acceptance from the Black community.

In contrast to Evillene, Glinda has negotiated a space for her Black queer womanhood within the Black community. While technically a witch, Glinda uses her crystal ball to bear witness to the plight of her community. She serves as a cultural healer, using performance to unify and strengthen Oz from divisive forces. It is not the community-minded Glinda, after all, whom the churchwomen join forces to defeat. Glinda shares her wisdom with Dorothy in her reprise of The Wiz's song "Believe in Yourself." Glinda sings, "believe in yourself, right from the start / Believe in the magic that's inside your heart / Believe what you see / Not what life told you to" (88). Glinda understands that Dorothy's life experiences have taught her to doubt her strength and question her heart's desires. Blackgirls are often socialized from an early age to believe that they are somehow inferior, or that having queer desires makes them undeserving of protection from the Black community. Glinda, however, validates the "magic" of Black queer womanhood and invites Dorothy to reach a new understanding of her worth and role within the Black community. Dorothy now has the choice either to follow Glinda's footsteps by taking on the difficult task of unifying the Black community, or to devote her energies to pursuing unbridled pleasure on the dance floor behind the gates of the Emerald City.

For Black queer feminist spectators, Emerald City might symbolize the hidden world of Black queer nightlife in New York City. The book describes Emerald City as gloriously "futuristic," replete with "Beautiful People, [who are] very much aware of it, and as such, are haughty and proud" (44). The gate protects the "exquisitely and exotically dressed" citizens from society's censor, allowing them to form their own community based upon their love of dance. To gain entrance into this exclusive world, Dorothy and her friends must first win the approval of the Royal Gatekeeper. Unfortunately, the Royal Gatekeeper perceives them as "trash" and allows them to enter the "Big Green Apple" only under threat of bodily harm (i.e., Tinman swings an axe at him; 43–4). The Royal Gatekeeper immediately regrets his decision, for once the friends enter Emerald City he declares: "Well, there goes the neighborhood" (44). While this exchange satirizes racist housing covenants that denied Blacks entry into select white neighborhoods, this moment also mirrors the racist and sexist practices that occurred within the disco nightlife of New York City.[50] Originally a subversive social dance, disco allowed queer dancers in the early 1970s to circumvent New York State law, which forbade male–male dancing.[51] The cultural historian Tim Lawrence reminds us, however, that by the late seventies, disco spaces were co-opted by party organizers who formed groups based on restrictive concepts of identity. "*De facto* white-only male gay venues" secured the "self-anointed 'A-list' crowd," leaving lesbians and minorities mostly excluded from elite New York dance culture.[52] Black queer feminist spectators familiar with queer New York nightlife might experience a moment of joy when witnessing Dorothy and her friends resist these exclusionary practices and secure their right to enter Emerald City.

At the conclusion of her journey, Dorothy must make an important decision that will determine her future. Will she repress, embrace, or negotiate her queer identity? The iconic song "Home" provides clues to Dorothy's choice. Toward the end of the song Dorothy pleads with God: "Please, don't make it hard / To know if we should believe the things we see / Tell us, should we try to stay / Or should we run away / Or is it better just to let things be?" (90). Dorothy understands that no matter which path she takes, she will encounter difficulty. Blackgirls of this time (and arguably still today) encountered a barrage of images that did not reflect their reality. Representations of Blackgirls as hypersexual jezebels, angry bitches, or emasculating matriarchs were pervasive within US popular culture. Yet, positive images of Black queer womanhood were rare. Gross misrepresentations and invisibility within society are equally damaging. Dorothy's song invites spectators also to question what "we" see and to choose either to "stay" who they are, run away from their troubles, or continue to submit passively to society's pressures. Dorothy ultimately decides to embrace her queer fantasy as "real," or as a part of her identity, and returns home with a newfound love for herself and community (90).

The Wiz Moves to Film

Despite a profitable and critically acclaimed run on Broadway, a series of artistic compromises were made to ensure the production's successful transition into film. To begin, the 1978 film adaptation was produced during the height of the Blaxploitation era of filmmaking. By this point, major Hollywood production companies had taken notice of the financial success of small, independent Black film companies and marketed Black-themed films to their newly identified "Black audience."[53] Berry Gordy's Motown Productions, the film and television branch of the Motown Records label, readily seized the opportunity to profit from this trend by producing a Black-themed film that had already proved popular with Black and white audiences. Motown Productions acquired the rights to produce the film but replaced most of the original Black creative team with commercially successful white filmmakers. Executive producers Ken Harper and Gordy headed this new creative team comprised of Jewish Hollywood producer Rob Cohen (who'd worked with Gordy and Diana Ross before), Jewish director Sidney Lumet, white/Jewish screenwriter Joel Schumacher (of the multiracial comedy-with-music *Car Wash* [1976]), and Black composer-arranger Quincy Jones.

The new production team's major visual and aural changes included a revised book and additional songs that catered to the strengths of their all-star cast, including Motown royalty. These changes allowed living legend Lena

Horne to dazzle spectators with her diva-like persona as Glinda; Motown veteran and superstar Michael Jackson (Scarecrow) to shine in the added song, "You Can't Win"; comedian Richard Pryor to perform as a non-singing Wiz; and entertainer Julius "Nipsey" Russell (Tinman) to provide additional lighthearted humor to the story. The music-driven film also provided the perfect platform to transition Motown darling and gay icon Diana Ross into serious acting. Prior to *The Wiz*, Ross had only made brief cameos on television, performed *An Evening with Diana Ross* (1976) on Broadway, and starred in *Lady Sings the Blues* (1972) and Gordy's film *Mahogany* (1975). Universal Pictures, however, was willing to support the film (to the tune of $1 million) if Ross starred as Dorothy in the film.[54] Gordy eventually conceded, and Schumacher changed the screenplay accordingly. Now a thirty-three-year-old Ross would perform as a timid twenty-four-year-old schoolteacher who refuses to travel beyond the bounds of her Harlem neighborhood. In a surprising move, the megastar (known for her glamorous wigs and diva persona), abandoned her affected look to play the role. Ross appears "natural" in the film, sporting a short afro, light makeup, a conservative lavender top, and a white knee-length pleated skirt. Only two original cast members reprised their roles in the film: Mabel King (Evillene) and Ted Ross (Lion).

In keeping with their parent company, Motown Productions omitted the more overtly political messages within the original Broadway production to appeal to the broadest possible audience. The performance studies scholar Wendy S. Watters contends that "Motown was not committed to delivering a political message [but instead] celebrated traditional themes in popular music of the time such as: romantic love, dancing, and parties."[55] Through his careful engineering of his recording artists' voices, song lyrics, fashion choices, and dance moves, Gordy was able to introduce "a new performance of blackness into mass media."[56] The 1978 screenplay follows a similar pattern by excluding any overt reference to Black feminism, enhancing the elaborate dance sequences within the world of Oz, and situating the central conflict in terms of Dorothy's inability to secure romantic love. These alterations invited spectators—Black, white, queer, or otherwise—to consume this new vision of Blackness.

Years after the release of the film, members of the original creative team have expressed their displeasure with the changes made in the film adaptation. For example, in a 1993 interview book writer William F. Brown and choreographer George Faison described the film as "awful" and "dreadful," respectively.[57] Brown, in particular, expressed displeasure with Hollywood producers restoring Scarecrow's "You Can't Win" song to the narrative. "The movie had a song that was dropped from the [Broadway] show. It went, 'You can't win / You get even,' and that was considered a black message song. But it's all changed. Black people *can* win," stated Brown.[58] Since Motown eschewed (for the most part) political messages within its songs, one is left to speculate that this song was more likely added to highlight the talents of Michael Jackson than to deliver a "Black message song" to audiences.

Despite their attempts to appeal to popular tastes, Universal Pictures and Motown Productions did not receive a complete return on their nearly $30 million investment. Many critics panned the screenplay and Ross's acting abilities. Yet, the production also received critical acclaim, garnering four Academy Award nominations for costume design (Tony Walton), cinematography (Oswald Morris), production design (Tony Walton and Philip Rosenberg), and music (Quincy Jones).[59] The adaptation has also enjoyed a strong following among marginalized subcultures. This is perhaps, in part, due to the resistant readership of Black queer feminist spectators. Thus, despite the limitations of the screenplay, Black queer feminist spectators have the capacity to "read" Black queer cultural references—whether through Ross's portrayal of Dorothy, the use of disco within Emerald City, or Lena Horne's camp performance as Glinda.

Ross's Dorothy reflects a Black queer feminist sensibility through her eschewal of a heterosexual union. Well beyond her adolescence, Dorothy faces the more immediate pressure of conforming to her community's dictates of Black womanhood or risking a fate worse than death: spinsterhood. These pressures are perhaps best exemplified in the opening sequence of the film when Aunt Em summons Dorothy from the kitchen to meet a potential suitor named Gil, a well-dressed son of her friend. After introductions are made, Dorothy takes Gil's coat and quickly retreats to the safety of the kitchen, leaving him standing with a look of dejection on his face. Clearly, this meeting was no choice encounter, but a carefully arranged meeting concocted by Aunt Em. Despite Dorothy's evasive actions, Aunt Em continues her matchmaking, explaining: "Don't worry Gil, she's just a little shy."[60] It becomes clear in the next scene that by refusing Gil's amorous attentions, Dorothy may also surrender her chances of motherhood. As the entire family surrounds the newest arrivals—a young woman, man, and infant—Dorothy stands by herself several feet away, staring longingly at the mother and baby. Dorothy's innermost desire is motherhood and not a relationship with a man. Yet, is

Figure 5.2 Diana Ross (Dorothy) and Michael Jackson (Scarecrow) in Motown Productions' *The Wiz* (1978). Still image courtesy of the author.

it possible for her to have one without the other? Dorothy's trip through Oz provides the answer she so desperately seeks.

A Black queer feminist interpretation of this moment could suggest that Dorothy's ability to embrace both motherhood and a Black queer identity allows her to empower the Black community of Oz. She mothers Lion, Scarecrow, and Tinman throughout the film: protecting them from Evillene's wrath, the hallucinogenic charm of the Poppies, and The Wiz's bullying. She encourages them during their weakest moments, helping them obtain their dreams of courage, a brain, and a heart, respectively. She also works collectively with Black men. For example, she and Scarecrow help Tinman escape a mammy figure who has literally crushed him (see Figure 5.2). Liberating Tinman from the weight of stereotypes and encouraging him to free his mind from self-loathing allows him to "ease on down the road" to empowerment. Her newfound strength culminates in the soulful song "Home," which has been regarded in heteronormative spaces as "an anthem of self-determination."[61] As Ross stares directly into the camera, she testifies to viewers, singing: "And I learned that we must look / Inside our hearts to find / A world full of love / Like yours, like mine / Like home." Using the collective "we," Ross invites audiences to join her in building strong black communities filled with love. In so doing, Ross/Dorothy becomes a "Black feminist model . . . for the appropriate and necessary behavior that all of the

Black, female moviegoers should emulate with the Black men in their lives," writes scholar Rhonda Williams.[62] Yet, Dorothy also provides an image of Black queer motherhood and models how to have productive (nonsexual) relationships with Black men. Through her efforts to establish community, Dorothy becomes a leader in her own right, perhaps encouraging Black queer feminist spectators to do the same.

Black queer feminist spectators might also derive pleasure by identifying the film adaptation's use of Black queer culture references, namely the celebration of disco. From the cotton fields to drag balls of the Harlem Renaissance, social dance has provided Black folx the opportunity to commune with one another and take part in "expressive release" from day-to-day concerns.[63] The emergence of disco following the Stonewall Rebellion (1969) provided yet another space to express Black queer possibilities. Merging elements of soul, funk, gospel, and R&B music into a "queer aesthetic," disco music allowed dancers to experience "an affective and social experience of the body that exceeded normative conceptions of straight and gay sexuality."[64] The Emerald City citizens embrace these queer possibilities, creating a vibrant disco nightlife that privileges a glamorous Black LGBTQ community. The citizens wear couture clothing and strike poses to a disco beat in a *Vogue*-like photo shoot while a human-sized camera records their efforts. However, in contrast to disco music of the time, the dancers are not guided by the voice of Black female divas such as Gloria Gaynor or Donna Summer. Rather, The Wiz serves as M.C. and encourages the dancers to focus on beauty and fashion. It is Dorothy, after all, who creates this Black queer disco fantasy from *her* imagination. As such, it is Dorothy (and by extension, the viewer) who discovers pleasure and belonging within the gates of Emerald City.

While the screenplay does not allow Dorothy to create a Black female diva figure within her Black queer disco fantasy sequence, the spectator can still derive pleasure from witnessing Lena Horne's camp performance as the *mother of all divas*. By camp, I refer to filmmaker and activist Susan Sontag's conceptualization that "the essence of Camp [is a] love of the unnatural: of artifice and exaggeration."[65] This sensibility, which is most often associated with gay male subculture, is not something that is universally shared or appreciated. Camp is a subjective, often solitary, experience whereby spectators take pleasure in androgyny, outrageous spectacle, and "convert[ing] the serious into the frivolous."[66] While seemingly unintentional, Horne's performance embodies many elements of camp. She first appears as a godlike Black femme mother sporting an extravagant diamond-encrusted ball gown, bedazzled headpiece, and diamond earrings. The night sky, artificial snowflakes, and a dozen Black babies suspended in midair surround her as she makes a grand entrance. She demonstrates her supernatural power by using her breath to create a "snow tornado" to carry Dorothy into Oz. In her second and final scene, Horne again appears suspended in midair against the artificial snow-covered heavens. She advises Dorothy to remember that, "Home is knowing . . . knowing your mind, knowing your heart, knowing your courage" before delivering an affected gospel-like rendition of "Believe." Horne's earnest performance as Glinda appears unnatural, replete with exaggerated facial expressions, one-dimensional characterizations, and awkward arm movements during the spirited gospel number "Believe." While encouraging self-knowledge, celebrating Black motherhood, and empowering Black queer women is no laughing matter, the modes of production produce an extravagant spectacle ripe for camp enthusiasts.

Acknowledging the camp sensibilities of Black queer feminist spectators furthers the efforts of feminist film critics to decentralize camp spectatorship from white urban gay male subjectivity. As media studies scholar Pamela Robertson persuasively argues, camp is both performed by and experienced by lesbians and heterosexual women who use their agency to "appropriate aspects of gay male culture" and "knowingly produce themselves as camp."[67] Black queer feminists *can* and *do* experience the pleasure of camp performance as both spectators and subjects of camp.

The Wiz Live! On Television

Similar to the original Broadway production, *The Wiz Live!* was produced during an era of social injustice and civil unrest. While Black Americans and their allies have protested racially motivated crimes against Black folx throughout history, the dawn of social media has helped make these concerns more immediate, visible, and potent. Social networking has provided a platform for activists to share news and strategize ways to address the alarming rates of unarmed Blacks being killed by police.[68] Yet, even as the Black Lives Matter and Say Her Name movements gained national attention, counternarratives formed to disrupt the momentum. Active and retired law enforcement officers formed Blue Lives Matter to dispute accounts of systemic wrongdoing on the part of police officers, and white supremacists formed White Lives Matter supposedly to prevent white genocide.[69] While *The Wiz Live!* does not directly address police brutality, white supremacists situated the production within social justice narratives as an example of liberalism gone awry.

Although the vast majority of the Twitter community praised NBC's decision to produce an all-Black musical, more hostile Twitter users condemned the casting practice as "reverse" discrimination or racism. For example, @KoneyDetroit wrote: "@nbc why are there no whites starring in #TheWiz? this is racist! can u imagine if it were the other way? #whitelivesmatter."[70] While racially insensitive and wrongheaded, @KoneyDetroit's comment presents a fascinating paradox. By acknowledging racism, the tweet disrupts the mythology of a supposedly post-racial society. Yet, their willful ignorance of the political and aesthetic context from which *The Wiz Live!* emerged allows institutional white racism to remain intact. Unfortunately, these more inflammatory tweets were then circulated by media outlets, including *The View*, which aired a "Hot Topic" segment on the production's casting practices. While erroneous, these sensationalized tweets remain important because they helped bring national attention to issues of racism within the theatre and television industries.

The Wiz Live! represents a moment of Black cultural trafficking within the white-dominated television industry. Executive producers Craig Zadan and Neil Meron (both white and openly gay) decided to mount a live televised adaptation of *The Wiz* in the hopes of improving lackluster ratings for their previous project, *Peter Pan Live!* (2014). "What we learned is we wanted to do something that was cooler and hipper and contemporary. And something that had a lot of stars," remembers Zadan.[71] Greenlit as a live televised event, *The Wiz Live!* was conceived of and controlled by white executives who marketed the musical to both white and historically marginalized audiences. Appealing to the broadest possible audience meant omitting or whitewashing the more overt symbols and metaphors of Black history and culture found within the original book; infusing hip-hop into the land of Oz; and casting popular Black entertainers Queen Latifah, Mary J. Blige, Ne-Yo (Tinman), Uzo Aduba (Glinda), Amber Riley (Addaperle), and Common (The Bouncer)—in addition to original *The Wiz* Dorothy, Stephanie Mills, as Aunt Em. Zadan and Meron also hired the Tony Award-winning Black director Kenny Leon, critically acclaimed Black hip-hop choreographer Fatima Robinson, and openly gay Tony Award-winning actor Harvey

Fierstein to realize their vision. While Fierstein initially refused to adapt the book—he was concerned that his Jewish heritage might undermine the cultural legacy of the production for audiences—he readily agreed once he learned that the original book writer was white.[72] Fierstein's camp aesthetics, coupled with Zadan and Meron's hip-hop vision, proved successful, with the resulting production garnering 11.5 million television viewers and 6.4 million Twitter views.[73]

Fierstein's adaptation emphasizes the Black queer cultural references found within the musical's original book, and the production modes more overtly produce a camp aesthetics. In fact, one might argue that the televised musical is itself a distinct form of camp—intentionally marketed to both mainstream and marginalized audiences. Openly gay writer Rob Smith provides an astute observation of why he and other camp enthusiasts experienced pleasure while watching *The Wiz Live!* Smith credits gay dancers voguing in the Emerald City, "baby gay icon" Amber Riley's rendition of "He's The Wiz," Blige's exaggerated bitchiness, and Queen Latifah's drag king performance as being "just subversive enough to fly over the heads of most in middle America."[74] This does not mean that viewers unfamiliar with queer cultural references did not enjoy the production's camp aesthetics, nor that all viewers in-the-know experienced pleasure while watching the overtly camp production. After all, "camp is a reading/viewing practice which, by definition, is not available to all readers; for there to be a genuinely camp spectator, there must be another hypothetical spectator who views the object 'normally,'" writes Pamela Robertson.[75] As such, spectators experienced pleasure knowing that others "missed" the Black queer cultural references embedded in *The Wiz Live!*

While the TV event's book cannot account for racism in the United States, the modes of production unapologetically celebrate Black queer identity and recover queer Black and Latinx voguing traditions. Despite popular memory, voguing existed prior to Madonna's popularization of the dance in her 1990 video "Vogue." *The Wiz Live!* critiques this historical erasure by transporting Dorothy and friends into the inner sanctuary of a Black queer ballroom community. Initially undisturbed by their arrival, the queer citizens chant, "Fierce, slay, serve, beat, twirl" as they Vogue Fem to house music.[76] Once the citizens notice Dorothy and her friends, they immediately perceive them as house rivals and begin throwing "shade" or insulting them by performing intricate handwork. When Dorothy asks to see The Wiz, the queer citizens laugh at her and continue to strut around the stage. Tinman recognizes this slight and asks, "Why the shade? She asked a perfectly *normal* question."[77] Normality does not, however, sit well with the queer citizens. They respond to Tinman's challenge by holding an old way vogue battle, performing precise floorwork, spins and dips, hands, duckwalks, and catwalks until they win the battle by pinning the motionless intruders into a tight circle. Having won the battle, the queer citizens return to their neutral positions on the dance floor and ignore Dorothy's pleas for assistance until she proves her mettle by voguing with them. Taking her rightful place on the ballroom dance floor allows Dorothy (and spectators) to challenge the concept of *normal*, embrace Black queer feminist identity, and stake a claim to the heretofore culturally appropriated dance form.

The Wiz Live! questions the normality of gender binaries through Queen Latifah's drag king performance. Audiences first encounter The Wiz as a tower of strength wearing emerald green pants and a floor-length suit coat (see Figure 5.3). An oversized lapel and additional pieces of sequined fabric create the illusion of bulk at the shoulders, as well as obscure any semblance of breasts. In contrast to many drag king performers, Queen Latifah does not sport facial hair to signal gender illusion. Rather, she relies on exaggerated makeup and movements to create the appearance of masculine features and behavior. A gender-neutral silver and green pompadour provides greater height to the looming figure. The Wiz commands respect from all their

Figure 5.3 Queen Latifah (The Wiz) in NBC's *The Wiz Live!* (2015). Still image courtesy of the author.

subjects, including the newly arrived Dorothy, who addresses The Wiz as "sir." Unfortunately, this deferential treatment quickly vanishes once The Wiz's original sex assignment is revealed. The following conversation ensues:

DOROTHY: You mean The Wiz is . . .
LION: A fraud.
TINMAN: And a woman!
DOROTHY: And what's wrong with being a woman?!
TINMAN: Nothin'.
DOROTHY: That's right, nothin' wrong with being a woman. I don't know where y'all fools learned y'all manners.

The consequences of The Wiz's decision to embrace gender ambiguity can be read by Black queer feminist spectators as a metaphor for the very real battles the Black LGBTQ community encounter. The Wiz—performed by an actress who has consistently refused to make a public statement about her reported relationships with women—lives in constant fear that their social position will be taken away should others discover that they are, in fact, a "fraud" or sex-assigned female. Unfortunately, US society is not that far removed from the prejudices of Oz. One need look no further than the US Supreme Court's decision to uphold the Trump administration's policy of barring transgender soldiers from serving in the military.[78] To prevent this social death, The Wiz lives a solitary lifestyle, completely disconnected from friends or family. Thus, even the fantastical land of Oz cannot escape the pressures of gender constructs.

Once their sex assignment is discovered, The Wiz must choose between their desire for personal autonomy and position within their community. While liberal-minded Dorothy can accept The Wiz as a strong woman leader—doing otherwise would be rude—she cannot accept their deception (i.e., gender fluidity). Dorothy now refers to them as "Ms. Wiz" and pressures them to come out to the world. The Wiz reluctantly complies, revealing that they began their career as an assistant for a magician named Alfred. After constant strife with their employer, The Wiz took off in a hot-air balloon, never suspecting that a storm would take them to Oz. Once surrounded by the people of Oz, The Wiz was left with no alternative but to don Alfred's hat and perform. While the new book implies that The Wiz was *forced* to perform—Scarecrow, after all, likens their secret lifestyle unto a "fancy prison"—Black queer feminist spectators can delight in the fact that the

Figure 5.4 Queen Latifah (The Wiz) and dance ensemble in NBC's *The Wiz Live!* (2015). Still image courtesy of the author.

actress Queen Latifah *gets* to perform as a drag king. Eventually Dorothy convinces The Wiz to return to the "real world" so as to experience family, friendship, and "warm hugs." To achieve this community, The Wiz must first abandon their source of power: a queer identity. They do so by concealing their innermost desires behind a neutral, shapeless, floor-length dress (see Figure 5.4). The Wiz's new, socially acceptable facade not only renders them powerless, but also stabilizes gender binaries.

Mary J. Blige's camp performance provides a more pleasurable alternative to The Wiz's disappointing narrative arc. At first glance, Blige (Evillene) appears to embody some of the characteristics of Mabel King's performance as the dangerous dyke. To begin, Blige delivers nearly every line as a shout and wields a knife on an unsuspecting Dorothy (Williams). Exposition reveals her merciless nature and business savvy. According to Lord High Underling, Evillene declared "a corporate takeover," which forced him (and presumably others) to relinquish his factory and become her lowly worker. Her callous disregard for others is further exemplified by her grand arrival in a large cart pulled by two exhausted Winkies.

Stripped of the prosthetic nose, acne, fat suit, intentionally terrible wig, and garish costume of earlier Evillenes, Blige invites viewers to imagine a more humane and physically *desirable* vision of Black queer womanhood. As an attractive Black femme, Blige wears a corseted top that accentuates her small waist, tight leggings that emphasize her slim figure, and high-heeled boots that elongate her 5′ 9′′ frame. Sporting red lipstick, large false eyelashes, and artfully placed makeup that emphasizes her cheekbones, Blige appears as a far cry from King's Evillene. Blige's costume does, however, maintain the semblance of authority and cruelty through a bejeweled tie and numerous decorative whips placed at her shoulders and hips. However, in contrast to previous depictions, the new book allows Evillene to appear quite logical. For example, when Dorothy calls her "plain old everyday passable mean," Evillene delivers the rejoinder, "Well if I'm mean, what does that make you?" She then accuses Dorothy of committing such vile acts as killing her sister, stealing her sister's shoes, and gathering a "crew" to kill her. Similar to the sympathetic Elphaba from *Wicked* (2003), Evillene challenges audiences to consider her suffering caused by Dorothy's actions. Her attractiveness and ability to situate herself as a victim encourages Black queer spectators to desire her and relate to her pursuit of power.

The disconnect between Blige's sincere desire to channel human behavior and her exaggerated performance of evil could become camp for some viewers. Blige remembers that when she first accepted the role, she felt like "a fish out of water" because of the play's cultural significance.[79] "I played in something that meant so much to our culture for so many years and to be a part of that [now] when you [were once] a little girl at home watching this? It's like 'wow,'" remembers Blige.[80] To add to this pressure, *The Wiz Live!* marked her first performance on a Broadway stage. Blige understood that spectators would compare her performance to King's, which meant that she needed to conceptualize her own unique interpretation of Evillene. "I made the role my own by channeling what I already knew, which is everybody has an Evillene. Everyone has a bad side. Everyone has a good side. Also studying Mabel [King] in her role. But mostly just looking at life, how it can actually bring the Evillene out in you," remembers Blige.[81] Her glorification of character over authenticity resulted in a heightened bitchiness best exemplified in her harsh remarks to her noncompliant henchman. In her performance, Blige uses exaggerated arm movements to emphasize her points as she bellows, "You some kind of Eddie Murphy or something? Well, don't try me 'cause I am evil with all y'all today!" Blige's sincere attempt to deliver such drivel within the spectacular world of Oz creates a sense of artifice and frivolity in which Black queer feminist spectators may take delight.

Blige, however, is not merely an *object* of camp, but a cultural producer in her own right, fully capable of signifyin' to her subculture. While Blige has yet to describe her performance as camp, her 2016 interview with Zach Laws suggests an awareness of the humor her performance elicited. "I watched it several times and I thought it was hilarious. It was funny to watch me just be so *mean*," remembers Blige.[82] Central to her delight, it would seem, was her ability to convey meanness to others. This meanness takes the form of a confrontational attitude and aggressive behavior. For example, she all but snarls as she plots her revenge, bellowing, "So, Dorothy thinks she can walk her skinny ass up in here and destroy me?! Well, it ain't my first time running a nursery. I know how to handle a brat like that. Unleash my winged warriors!" Taken at face value, Blige's performance may appear to reinforce the Black bitch stereotype, a controlling image that "is designed to defeminize and demonize" working-class Black women, according to Patricia Hill Collins.[83] Blige's outrageous performance of bitchery, however, creates an *excess* that effectively destabilizes this mythology. Her seemingly aggressive barbs also create a space for the Black cultural expression of signifyin'.[84] Blige and Williams exchange a series of insults back and forth throughout the production (see Figure 5.5). Their seemingly cruel words more accurately represent "snaps," or the linguistic acrobatics needed to play the dozens. Spectators familiar with this African American game would find additional pleasure in witnessing Blige's display of mental acuity. Blige's performance—which can be understood as both queer and Black cultural expression—functions as an important site of reclamation.

Figure 5.5 Mary J. Blige (Evillene) and Shanice Williams (Dorothy) in NBC's *The Wiz Live!* (2015). Still image of courtesy of the author.

Although *The Wiz Live!* is set in the contemporary United States and features an all-Black principal cast, the televised production remains silent on important issues impacting Black America today. The executive decision not to use the production as a platform to confront US society's racial problem does a disservice to the legacy of *The Wiz*. The original Broadway book and production did not shy away from symbols and metaphors of police violence and Black political struggle. *The Wiz*'s critical and financial success on Broadway demonstrated that it is possible to produce politically engaged popular entertainment. Rather than integrate the growing numbers of unarmed Black people killed by police and white vigilantes into its narrative, *The Wiz Live!* book takes jabs at dated references for cheap laughs. Nevertheless, *The Wiz Live!* also presents new images of Black queer feminist strength and unapologetically celebrates Black queer culture. In this sense, *The Wiz Live!* accomplishes what many Black liberation movements of the past have failed to do: it demonstrates why Black queer visibility matters. Artists now, more than ever, have a responsibility to create meaningful art that boldly attends to the intersections of Black identity.

The Wiz Returns to Broadway

The 2024 revival of *The Wiz* marked another moment of greater Black visibility on Broadway stages and behind the scenes of commercial theatre. *The Wiz* included Black producers and creatives Brian Anthony Moreland, Kandi Burruss, Todd Tucker, Common, MC Lyte, Deborah Cox, and Lascelles Stephens, as well as white producers Kristin Caskey and Mike Isaacson. Black creative team members included the Academy Award-winning production designer Hannah Beachler (scenic design), the two-time Academy Award nominee and Emmy Award-winning costume designer Sharen Davis, and award-winning choreographer JaQuel Knight (Beyonce's "Single Ladies" and *Black is King*). Non-Black creatives included Ryan O'Gara (lighting), Jon Weston (sound), and Daniel Brodie (video and projection). The openly Black queer comedian Amber Ruffin provided additional material for the production, including updating the book to include Black queer references and contemporary Black cultural expression. Schele Williams, a prominent Black producer and Broadway director, provided direction for the production, which opened for a limited run at the Marquis Theatre from April 17, 2024, to August 18, 2024. As with *The Wiz Live!*, the revival included a mixture of newcomers to the entertainment industry, Broadway veterans, celebrities, and well-known R&B singers to draw in audiences. The all-Black cast included Nichelle Lewis (Dorothy), Deborah Cox (Glinda), Melody A. Betts (Aunt Em/Evillene), Kyle Ramar Freeman (Lion), Philip Johnson Richardson (Tinman), Avery Wilson (Scarecrow), and Wayne Brady (The Wiz). Despite the musical's inability to secure any Tony Award nominations, *The Wiz* did receive moderately positive reviews from theatre critics and garnered commercial success, grossing $29,699,923 after playing eighteen previews and only 142 performances.[85]

In contrast to previous iterations, *The Wiz* revival was greatly shaped by a Black queer feminist creative, Amber Ruffin. Prior to working on *The Wiz*, Ruffin had already established herself as a comedian, television writer, and theatre artist. Ruffin became known in the entertainment industry after a failed audition for *Saturday Night Live*. This experience led to Seth Meyers offering her a writing position at *The Late Show With Seth Meyers*, which led to her writing for the Comedy Central show *Detroiters* and HBO's series *A Black Lady Sketch Show*. Ruffin also served as a regular narrator for the Comedy Central show *Drunk History* before landing her own late-night talk show, *The Amber Ruffin Show*, on NBC's streaming service Peacock in 2020. The next year, she joined the Tony Award-winning Latino playwright Matthew Lopez in co-writing the book for a musical adaption of *Some Like It Hot*. Their combined efforts secured a Tony Award for Best Book of a Musical. These prior writing credits and achievements led to her joining *The Wiz* production team and revising the musical for contemporary Black audiences. Working under Williams's direction, she recrafted Lion, Tinman, and Scarecrow to become Dorothy's peers, rather than "uncles." Making Dorothy's friends more youthful also led to more novel and surprising characterization changes to well-known characters. For example, Lion now behaves as a spoiled, petulant child reared by loving Black women. He appears much younger than Dorothy, sporting a red double-breasted vest and purple kente print skirt at his waist. Rather than belittle the women of his pride, he welcomes their unconditional love for him. However, as a member of Gen Alpha, Lion is also "built different" and stomps his feet when Dorothy doesn't follow suit and let him have his way. Dorothy sees right through his "fierce" act and wallops him soundly when he misbehaves. Ruffin also gives Scarecrow a new backstory, presenting him as a former scientist who questioned the changing weather patterns caused by Evillene's magic. Evillene punishes him for questioning her by turning him into a brainless scarecrow. Tinman also receives a new backstory. He tells Dorothy that Evillene transformed him to tin and cursed him to live an isolated life as a rusty lumberjack for making fun of her "rusty" performance of the Fugees' "Killing Me Softly With His Song" (1996) during karaoke night at the club. Finally, Ruffin envisions our hero Dorothy as a sad teenager who must grieve the loss of her mother and build a new home with her Aunt Em while also battling bullies at school. By envisioning a younger cast, Ruffin could tap into the more immediate concerns of today's Black youth.

Williams reconceptualized *The Wiz* to address the needs of contemporary Blackgirls, including their need to embrace their difference and find belonging. Williams's foundational work on *The Wiz* began from her personal experience as a young Blackgirl watching Mills perform the role of Dorothy. The original touring production was Williams's first opportunity to witness (what she believed to be) authentic Black representation on a theatre stage. "Stephanie Mills' voice did not sound like it had come out of a conservatory. She sounded like she came out of Church. . . . What Geoffrey Holder did in his direction and his costumes. . . it's like: that's *us*. George Faison's choreography showed the world that Black bodies can do all kinds of things. It was the first time I saw contemporary dance on Black bodies. A real elevation of what I had seen . . . I didn't know we could do that. So *The Wiz* taught me so much about my Blackness at a young age [of six or seven] when I saw it in Dayton, Ohio. . . . It was the first time I saw *me* onstage and that was exciting," remembers Williams.[86] Later, during her senior year of high school, Williams landed the iconic role of Dorothy and this experience "changed everything."[87] Williams remembers, "It synthesized all the things that I loved. I got to dance, I got to sing, I got to act (which was fairly new for me). When you're on stage, you get to really embody the music in a whole other way, and so all the hats that I had worn in my life got to all come together, and I felt for the first time that I wasn't segmented."[88] Now, as a mother of two young Blackgirls, Williams wanted to make Dorothy's journey meaningful to their lives and the theme of belonging emerged. Williams remembers:

> What I saw was a girl who was seeking belonging, who felt like she didn't fit in where she was and she gets put on an adventure where she has to go beyond her comfort zone and she finds her tribe. Every person she finds is a little quirky and they're all seeking their own sense of belonging and they have challenges. . . . They have to face their fears, and they have to overcome [them], and then they meet someone who says, "I can fix everything for you." But what they realize is that they have to solve their own problems. They have to be brave. They have to learn how to rely on each other. At the

> end of the story, [Dorothy] learns that she must believe in herself, and she is exactly where she needs to be, and she has exactly what she needs to have, and she has great purpose. When I saw that in the story, I was like, "Oh, that's a gift to my daughters." This is a Black girl who has to figure it out and I'm excited to tell that story to [them].[89]

Furthermore, Williams felt that changing the ages of the Scarecrow, Lion, and Tinman from "uncles" to peers allowed Dorothy to "navigate the world with her friends."[90] Their individual quirks and unique challenges become the glue that binds them together, creating space for a deep appreciation for *difference* (see Figure 5.6). It was Williams's hope that Dorothy's ability to build community might inspire the Black youth today who view themselves as "different" to do the same. "I feel like young people today really do have to find their tribe—especially when they're a little different in some way. They have to find people who accept their differences and love them and celebrate them and grow with them," remembers Williams. While Williams does not elaborate on these "differences," Ruffin's revised script and the production modes certainly present Black queer identity as a prime example.

Figure 5.6 Nichelle Lewis (Dorothy), Kyle Ramar Freeman (Lion), Philip Johnson Richardson (Tinman), and Avery Wilson (Scarecrow) in *The Wiz* (2024), directed by Schele Williams. Photo by Jeremy Daniel, courtesy of Jeremy Daniel.

Queerness abounds in Ruffin's characterizations and in Wilson and Freeman's embodiment of Lion and Scarecrow, respectively. As openly Black queer men, both Wilson and Freeman have become fan favorites among the Black queer community. Wilson, a celebrated R&B singer, rose to stardom after appearing on season three of the popular television show *The Voice* in 2012. His fandom continued to grow in 2015 with the release of his single "If I Have To," which became a hit on the R&B charts. Already admired for his talent, Wilson only further cemented his popularity among Black queer communities when he came out as bisexual in 2020. Freeman had also established a following among Black queer communities before ever stepping into the land of Oz. Freeman rose to prominence in 2023 after performing as "Usher," the Black gay lead, in a West End production of Michael R. Jackson's Tony Award- and Pulitzer Prize-winning musical, *A Strange Loop*. As notable Black queer men, Wilson and Freeman were given the creative freedom to incorporate their "difference" into their embodiment of the Tinman and Lion characters. Wilson reflects on this artistic freedom during his 2024 interview with Ricky Cornish. "I am a bisexual man, but I feel like my character, naturally, . . . is going to have a little bit of that in it. And I just think it's a beautiful thing to see joy, Black joy, and queer Black joy. To be able to have no boundaries in that way is beautiful," remembers Wilson.[91] Black creatives did not try to mask his embodiment of a bisexual Scarecrow. "I think it's clear . . . maybe not to little ones that are figuring their lives out and things like that but to adults that see it. . . I don't think it's anything is being hidden. I think it's very clear and I love that," remembers Wilson.[92] Ruffin's additional material supports Wilson's characterizations. For example, the crows—portrayed by cis-male and female ensemble members—consider him their dear queer friend. Rather than stigmatize Scarecrow's effeminate speech and mannerisms, the crows refer to him as "sister" as a term of endearment as they comfort, advise, and care for him during his banishment. Not alone in his efforts to incorporate his authentic self into his characterization, Wilson remembers Freeman also crafting a decidedly queer Lion. "He's one of the girls and we love that," remembers Wilson. Drawing on the multiple meanings of "pride" as the consciousness of one's own dignity, a lion kingdom's non-biological family structure, and the celebration of gay liberation protests, Lion (Freeman) gains the self-confidence, additional fictive kinships, and courage to "be a lion" and accept every facet of his identity. Lion comes to this realization as he joins Dorothy (Nichelle Lewis) in the gospel-fused duet, "Be A Lion." As Dorothy encourages him to be his authentic self,

Lion abandons his macho demeanor and declares, "I'm standing strong and tall / I'm the bravest of them all / If on courage / I must call [. . .] I'm a lion / In my own way / I'm a lion."[93] However, when performed by the openly gay Freeman, the song takes on additional meaning, acting as a Black queer anthem, reminding Black queer spectators that they, too, can be accepted by the Black community just as they are.

The Wiz revival intentionally embraces a breadth of Black music—from 1970s funk to Black gospel music to contemporary R&B vocalizations—to simultaneously tap into the nostalgia of older spectators and create new meaning for younger audiences. "I really wanted this to be a celebration of Black excellence. I wanted the show to look timeless, to feel timeless. I wanted every generation who comes to see it to see themselves inside of it and to see the incredible impact that Blackness has had on culture. So you're going to hear different musical styles, you're going to see fashion that kind of gleans from all of these different periods of time. I'm really excited to show that broad, vast impact that Blackness has had on culture," remembers Williams.[94] Perhaps the strongest example of blending 1970s funk and soul with current musical genres occurs with the performance of "Slide Some Oil To Me." Following Joseph Joubert's new musical arrangement, Richardson (Tinman) begins his performance of "Slide Some Oil To Me" with a slightly more uptempo beat that also stays true to the original soulful source material. However, at the conclusion of his song, the 1970s soul music abruptly stops. Silence and darkness suddenly engulf the stage before a new drumbeat drops. Neon-colored shapes are projected onto a scrim, transforming the stage into a nightclub. After the music drops, the familiar sounds of "Slide Some Oil To Me" return but with a fresh hip-hop beat. A spotlight shines on Tinman as he begins to breakdance and repeat the chorus a final time. This moment of Black excellence exemplifies the seemingly effortless blending of old and new into a cohesive whole.

In addition to fusing past and present-day Black vocal stylings, the production modes blend the 1970s call for Black power with today's concern for Black lives. To begin, the Emerald City and the Poppies' costumes hearken back to the Black Power era. At first glance, Brodie's projection design appears as an innocuous garden-like vision of the Emerald City. However, upon a closer look, spectators discover that Emerald City is not an ordinary lush garden but, instead, a garden riddled with cultural references to Black Power and Black hair. The spiraled "gate" leading into the Emerald City takes the form of braided hair, the "shrubs" that cover the landscape are actually an array of gigantic afro puffs, and the spire on top of the golden building leading into the Emerald City sports an oversized Black Power fist. Beachler's scenic design, which includes The Wiz's throne room (featuring a throne attached to an oversized crown made out of afro/fist picks) only adds to the visualization of the Black Power theme. By using the iconography of the Black Power movement, reaching the Emerald City becomes more than just an audience with The Wiz; the journey represents a much grander concept of achieving solidarity, community, and self-determination. Unfortunately, once Dorothy and friends make it past Gatekeeper 1 (Kolby Kindle) and Gatekeeper 2 (Cristina Raé), their quest meets another derailment. The Poppies consist of eight beautiful Black women of all complexions, shapes, and sizes dressed in green skin-tight body suits with hot pink flowers in their large afros.[95] As they perform provocative dance moves—slowly moving their hips, extending their arms, and sashaying to 1970s funk music—they chant in unison, imploring the newcomers to "Wake up. Lounge. Sleep. Repeat." Afterward, the Poppies encircle their guests, luring their guests into massage-type chairs. Rather than use drugs to distract the group from their goal, these Poppies use the temptation of mindless entertainment and consumerism. When Lion expresses feeling scared, a Poppie soothes him, stating: "Don't be scared, be lazy." As the Poppies massage Dorothy's scalp, place product in her hair, and read to her, her determination wavers and she becomes distracted from her goal. However, when the Poppies encourage her to "relax and take off your shoes," she wakes up from her stupor and tries to convince her friends to do the same by using reverse psychology. "Who cares if we lay around on our manes until they're all matted up," Dorothy tells Lion. "Too bad sitting around and doing nothing will make us dumber and dumber," says Dorothy to Scarecrow. "Let's just give up. Who cares if people call us 'heartless,'" Dorothy tells Tinman. Dorothy then admonishes all of her friends: "Do better. This behavior is *toxic*. We gonna see The Wiz." Dorothy's challenges causes her friends to wake up out of their trance and take collective action to continue on their journey to the Emerald City, ultimately leading Dorothy back home to Kansas. Of course, their waking up symbolizes the need for the entire Black community to abandon their individualistic ideologies, pursuit of superficial comforts, and complacency, and instead become "woke" to the systems of oppression that harm the most vulnerable among them. Dorothy's final admonition to "Do better" and pursue their goal further symbolizes the need for the Black community to strengthen their efforts and take collective action to realize Black liberation.

While Williams was able to realize her directorial vision and dream of bringing a talented Black cast and creative team to Broadway, the reality is that this achievement remains a rare occurrence on the Great White Way. Williams, who remembers her early painful experiences working as a Black actress in commercial theatre, understands just how extraordinary the experience was to not fight for the one spot allotted for a Black creative. "When I started auditioning thirty-two years ago, I was one of *three* in the room and knew all three of us weren't going to get that job. Only one of us would be that representative in that show," remembers Williams.[96] Rather than limit Black talent to one "token" role, *The Wiz* revival created space to truly *recognize* and *celebrate* the incredible talent of innumerable Black theatre makers. This process began in the audition room. Williams remembers:

> I've been in this business for thirty-two years; I never had that. I never walked into a room and saw a creative team telling a story about my culture that looked like me, and that was not lost on anyone in that room. You could see the hope, the awesomeness of what we were about to do. . . . People would come in and look in a room where everyone looked like them and they knew that they weren't going for one slot, maybe two. They knew they authentically had opportunities to fully be themselves in that space and it would be *respected*, it was *cherished*, it was *wanted*, fully *wanted*. You know, if I ever felt that way, I might still have been performing.[97]

It is truly heartbreaking to ponder the amount of lost talent and stories that have never been told due to anti-Blackness in the theatre industry. While some may read this production as a signpost of positive change, I certainly do not.

One diverse, equitable, and inclusive Broadway musical production cannot repair the harm caused by centuries of institutional white racism, nor does this *one* musical signal large-scale change. In addition, why does it take the re-mounting of a historically all-Black musical for Black theatre makers to feel respected, cherished, and wanted? How can we create spaces wherein the work of Black creatives *always* matter? The following chapter, "Blackgirls Navigate Show Business," continues this conversation, using Aisha Rahman's *Lady Day: A Musical Tragedy* (1972), Katori Hall's *Tina: The Tina Turner Musical* (2018), and the *King Kong* (2019) musical as a lens to explore the perils and possibilities that await Blackgirl artists working in the theatre, film, and music industries.

6
Blackgirls Navigate Show Business

I am ten years old and considered quite learned in my family. I read every single day. During the summer. For fun. *National Geographic* magazine, *Sweet Valley High*, or even the back of a cereal box; doesn't matter. The magic of reading allows me to imagine that I am rich and popular like high schoolers Jessica and Elizabeth Wakefield. In my fantasy, I have a cupboard full of soft, fluffy bath towels and *tons* of friends. I *never* have to dry myself off with my dirty clothes or eat lunch alone ever again or pick roaches out of my food.

I hear the doorbell ring and see some white lady drop off a cardboard box full of books. A musty smell wafts up my nose as I dive into the box. I pick up a large hardcover book and discover a new type of storytelling. Plays. I read, and I read until I come across *The Boor*, a play written by someone whose name I can't pronounce. I laugh. A lot. This play is *hilarious*. I make the decision then and there that I am going to bribe my younger sisters into helping me stage *The Boor* and sell tickets to our neighbors. I figure three or four of my younger sisters can perform in the show and the baby can sell Kool-Aid, since no one can say "no" to her. I have three food stamps. I can pay my sisters and, hopefully, make a lot of money from the ticket sales.

This show has to be really good. Like, my sisters have to memorize all their lines and wear costumes and everything. I demand practices every day leading up to the performance.

Stop being bossy. That's too many practices. I don't wanna pretend to be Sue Ellen Ewing from Dallas.

We argue. One by one, my sisters drop out of the show and return outside to play. My soul is crushed. . . for a spell.

It's 1998. I'm sixteen and audition for the theatre department's production of *The Bourgeois Gentleman*. I don't have much experience, but I am loud and eager. I land the role of the Fencing Master and learn stage combat. I am thrilled that I get to be a man and wallop an actor twice my size with

Black Queer Girlhood on the Musical Theatre Stage. La Donna L. Forsgren, Oxford University Press.
 DOI: 10.1093/9780197661444.003.0007

my rapier. The next few years fly by as I study my craft. I perform in nearly every available production but never land the lead. The department uses "color-blind" casting, which basically means all the plays are written by white playwrights for white actors and they pretend not to notice that I am the only Blackgirl theatre major. This means I get cast as the villain, the suicidal best friend, or the angry Blackgirl for comic relief. By my senior year, I am aware that I will never be cast as the ingénue and my girlhood dreams of entering show business are completely dashed.

When I enter graduate school and begin to study the critical writings of the Black Arts Movement theorist Barbara Ann Teer, I discover that the barriers that hinder my growth as an actress are not unique but a part of a much larger problem of systemic racism within society. Decades before my foray into educational theatre, Teer published a series of essays—many of which were published in the *New York Times*—that detail how discriminatory practices within show business mirror institutional white racism found within greater society. In her essay "Needed: A New Image" (1968), Teer writes:

> The problem of racial equality which confronts the Negro performer in Show Business is no different from that which he faces in any other field of endeavor. . . . He is at the end of the totem pole mainly because he is struggling to be a part of or integrated into Show Business. The name itself is self-explanatory. It is a trade, owned, operated, and formulated by white people for the purpose of making money. In order for the black performer to become successful and/or accepted in this business, it is mandatory that he adapt to the values of that white system physically, spiritually, and morally.[1]

Black performers of this era responded to their lack of representation, opportunities, and leadership within show business by bolding chanting slogans such as "Last to be hired, first to be fired," "Don't exclude us," "We exist," and "Employ us in roles that more realistically depict us as we really exist in America today" along their picket lines.[2] While these demonstrations may have garnered an increase in opportunities and role types for Black actors, these changes did not lead to long-term structural change within show business. "Look around you. The proof is in the pudding. The few directors, choreographers, television and movie actors we have are doing in fact the same thing as the white man and not even as effectively," writes Teer.[3] Rather than continue to fight a system that was never meant to honor the talent of Black performers, Teer opted to create her own cultural institution, the National Black Theatre of Harlem (1968–). As founder and CEO, Teer was able to realize her vision of a liberated theatre that would cultivate the talents of the rising generation of Black performers and designers. Unfortunately, show business continues to foster white cultural mores while simultaneously limiting, excluding, and harming the psyche of Blackgirls.

Audra McDonald, a six-time Tony Award-winning actress who broke racial barriers through her Broadway performance as Carrie Pipperidge, has documented her trials navigating anti-Blackness in show business. As with many actresses, McDonald began performing as a young Blackgirl. She remembers her mother recognizing her talent but also offering her important advice while participating in a teen pageant in Fresno, California at the age of twelve. "You're still an African American girl so you are going to work even harder," remembers McDonald.[4] Eventually, McDonald found her way into local theatre before landing a placement at The Julliard School in New York. Unfortunately, her experience earning her undergraduate degree at the prestigious conservatory harmed her emotional well-being. "I tried to off myself at Julliard. I don't know how serious of an attempt that was but it landed me in the mental hospital for a month. I look at that period of my life and I do remember quite a bit about it but what I remember the most is dreams I was having at the time. And all of them involved me just fighting in the ocean. Waves," remembers McDonald.[5] Somehow, she found the wherewithal to continue her pursuit of a career and made her Broadway debut at the age of nineteen as Ayah in *The Secret Garden*. By 1994, McDonald earned her first Tony Award for Best Actress in a Musical ("Carrie") in the Broadway revival of Richard Rodgers and Oscar Hammerstein's *Carousel*. In terms of being cast in nontraditional, or historically white roles, McDonald remembers not allowing external forces to limit her creative possibilities. "I just gravitated toward the roles that have felt right to me. Carrie was somebody who was a lot of fun and very funny, but maybe some of it has to do with voice. The voice is a bigger, heavier thing," remembers McDonald.[6] This performance proved eventful, challenging white Broadway producers to consider (albeit, briefly) the remarkable talents of Blackgirl performers for traditionally white roles.

While McDonald describes her experience performing in *Carousel* as "just magic," the same cannot be said for her experience performing in the 1999 film adaptation, *Annie*.[7] By the time *Annie* filmed, McDonald had garnered three Tony Awards and was greatly esteemed in the theatre industry. Yet, she was directly confronted with issues of racism while performing the role

Figure 6.1 Audra McDonald (Grace Farrell) and Victor Garber (Oliver Warbucks) in Chris Montan Productions, Storyline Entertainment, Columbia TriStar Television, and Walt Disney Television's *Annie* (1999), directed by Rob Marshall. Still image courtesy of the author.

of "Miss Grace Farrell," the personal secretary and love interest to "Daddy Warbucks" (see Figure 6.1) McDonald remembers:

> It was an exciting experience to get to play a role that I would never, ever be considered for normally. There were some battles that had to be fought with that production. We shot the finale where Daddy Warbucks presents a ring to Grace, and then we were informed that the powers-that-be wanted us to shoot an alternate ending where there was no proposal, just in case there were any issues because of the interracial thing. Craig [Zadan] and Neil [Meron] and Rob Marshall were so apologetic but their hands were tied. I was devastated and embarrassed. It was a terrible day for me to go in and shoot that scene.[8]

All too often, artists, critics, and scholars cite McDonald's commercial success within the white-dominated entertainment industry as an example of growing inclusivity. However, I read McDonald's success as a series of compromises that have had a negative impact on her mental health (i.e., suicidal, feelings of embarrassment). McDonald's experience serves as an example that even the talented Blackgirls who have "made it" will continue to experience the detrimental effects of anti-Black racism in the entertainment industry.

Despite ongoing issues of racism and sexism within the theatre industry, McDonald has managed to carve out a space for her craft by landing the coveted role of "Mama Rose" in 2024 musical revival of *Gypsy: A Musical Fable* (1959). The musical tells the story of Rose, an ambitious stage mother who pushes her daughters June and Louise toward stardom on the vaudeville stage, with Louise eventually transforming into the famous burlesque performer, Gypsy Rose Lee. Set against the backdrop of show business in the 1920s–1930s, Arthur Laurents' book, Jule Styne's music, and Stephen Sondheim's lyrics explore themes of ambition, identity, and the cost of success. The more recent revival not only breaks ground by its inclusion of Black creatives in senior leadership roles—the two-time Tony Award winner George C. Wolfe provides direction, alongside the choreography of four-time Tony Award nominated choreographer Camille A. Brown—but also breaks ground by casting three Blackgirls in the lead roles. The production manages to showcase the talents of McDonald, Joy Woods (Louise), and Jordan Tyson (June) but does not change any of the original material. McDonald addresses this creative choice during her 2025 interview on *The Late Show with Stephen Colbert*. "We have not changed a single, solitary line of dialogue, we have not changed one lyric, we have not changed anything about the show. It just hits differently. There are different layers. There are certain lines that Rose has in the show. One line is that she says, 'You know why I did it? Why I did it for you?' Speaking about why she did it for her kid. She said, 'Because I was born too soon and got started too late.' Now you can say that as any race and it means something. Think about that coming out of a Black woman's mouth in the 1920s and it just hits in a different way," McDonald remembers.[9] For McDonald, taking on this challenging role—often considered the "King Lear" of parts for women in musical theatre—and not changing one iota of the script, functions as a form of resistance to the limitations put on Black actresses. One could argue that McDonald's critically acclaimed performance in a traditionally white role creates space (if but for a moment) to reimagine the possibilities for Black actresses on Broadway stages. However, just as many critics could counterargue that this one concession is *not* representative of the experiences of most Black actresses. In addition, why must "racial progress" typically be read as the integration of Black performers into white-authored scripts? *Why don't more Black women musical theatre artists have the opportunity to tell their own stories?*

Unfortunately, the diminishment of Blackgirl talent and creative genius does not start or end with McDonald's experiences. From Emmy, Grammy, Oscar, and Tony Award-winning actress Viola Davis, to Black Ensemble Company member Jayla Williams-Craig, to Broadway newcomer Christiani Pitts, many Blackgirls bear the emotional brunt of anti-Blackness in show business. For example, in her memoir, *Finding Me* (2022), Viola Davis remembers while auditioning early on in her career, being acutely aware that she was "dark-skinned, not a size two, not considered 'beautiful.'"[10] Her inability to meet white standards of beauty—which have become internalized within Black communities as well—coupled with stereotypes of Blackgirls meant that she was confined to limiting roles. "The roles, almost all where I fit the description, were drug-addicted mothers. My agent would send me in for the others. The roles for Black actresses that were described as 'pretty' or 'attractive.' I would put on my makeup, do my hair, and never, ever get those roles, even if the producers were Black. I took the jobs that were given to me," remembers Davis.[11] If this is the situation for one of the most talented actresses in show business, this surely does not set well for emerging Blackgirl talent. Williams-Craig, who starred in the 2019 Black Ensemble Theater production of *The Other Cinderella*, argues that "judgment and assumption" are two of the most pressing roadblocks for Black actresses working within mainstream commercial theatres.[12] Williams-Craig remembers:

> For one, it's hard enough as Black women. They only see me as this one type of character, but I want to show them. For example, the musical *Six* that's out [on Broadway] right now. Put me in as Catherine of Aragon (the Beyonce character) or as Anna of Cleves (the other Black character). But did you know that I can sing? I can do the "All You Wanna Do" song [that is performed by "Katherine Howard," a character modeled after pop stars Britney Spears and Ariana Grande]. I can be the pretty role. There are Black women out there that can *kill* that role. But they're never going to. They're not going to put you there because that's not what they assume. Prettiness is the tall, white girl with dark hair or with blue eyes and blonde hair. That's the only type of girls who have played that role.[13]

Despite these challenges, Williams-Craigs understands the value and beauty of Blackgirlhood and determination needed to pursue their craft. "Black girlhood is empowerment, confidence, strength, and togetherness. I think that we, as black girls, are an inspiration. Not only just for other races and other types of people, but for each other as well. *This world is very tough on us.* There's lots of pressure on us and we have to show the world that we're stronger than they already 'think' we are."[14]

In addition to advocating diversity, equity, and inclusion, Christiani Pitts, who starred in the Broadway musical *King Kong* (2018), recommends concrete action to remove the barriers that hinder Black theatre artists. Pitts calls for systematic change in representation that "goes beyond just what you see on stage."[15] "For a long time, it has been this idea that 'If we have representation with respect to the actors, we're doing something wonderful,' without considering the fact that there was not a single Black casting director or producer. These people exist. These people are going to college with degrees, but they are just not given that opportunity. They're just not," remembers Pitts.[16] Lack of diversity, equity, and inclusion, as well as the culture of sexual harassment within the entertainment industry, came to the forefront of social media as the United States simultaneously confronted its racist past.

As the call to value and protect Black lives from extrajudicial violence gained momentum following the 2014 murder of Eric Garner by the New York Police Department, Black artists and their allies began working collectively to make systemic changes within show business. For example, performers Adrienne Warren, Jackie Bell, Amber Iman, Cameron J. Ross, Britton Smith, Christian Dante White responded to Garner's murder by founding the Broadway Advocacy Coalition (2016–). The organization's mission is to provide a platform for anti-racist advocates to use the arts for social change. Broadway Advocacy Coalition's first of many events featured a three-day forum entitled "Broadway for Black Lives Matter Again" from June 10–12, 2016. Organizers intended for the event to provide space for the "Broadway community to heal, listen, and hold itself accountable to its history of white supremacy while moving towards becoming an anti-racist and equitable space."[17] "Broadway for Black Lives Matter Again" featured Broadway royalty, including McDonald, Tony Award-winning actor Brian Stokes Mitchell, and the most prolific female composer and six-time Tony Award nominee, Jeanine Tesori. By 2020, Warren expressed in a *Backstage* interview that while some positive changes had been made in the theatre industry, this progress directly correlated with the state of society as a whole and that much more effort is needed. "The systemic racism within our industry is in direct correlation to the systemic racism in our country. . . . I am excited about the willingness we're seeing right now to have tough conversations and the willingness to dive into investigating solutions for these issues. But I also don't expect these solutions to happen in my lifetime, because they go much deeper than we all even realize," remembers Warren.[18] However, even those who might claim ignorance of the depth of racial and gender disparity in the United States could not ignore these issues during the summer of 2020, as mass Black Lives Matter demonstrations spread throughout the country. Actresses Audra McDonald and LaChanze responded to these demonstrations by founding Black Theatre United on June 16, 2020, as theatres across the country sat "dark" during the COVID-19 lockdown. Producer and director Schele Williams remembers receiving a call from McDonald to join them, along with other Black artists, on Zoom to express their emotions during this turbulent moment in US history. "Because it was COVID, we were all isolated and brewing in all of this pain and frustration and anger. It was incredible to get on Zoom and just talk. The conversation very quickly went from 'how we were feeling' to 'what are we going to do about it.' That is a company of people that I always want to be in. People who can honestly express their feelings and emotions but also channel that into action and positive change. So, that is what Black Theatre United is," remembers Williams.[19] In addition to formal group efforts, countless Black women musical theatre artists have also used their individual voices to combat systemic racism within the theatre industry. This chapter—which explores the writing talents of Aishah Rahman, Katori Hall, and Christiani Pitts—provides just a small sample of how Black women musical theatre artists have used their talent to further diversity, equity, and inclusion within show business.

In their quest to create a more diverse, equitable, and inclusive entertainment industry, Black women artists have exposed the history of exploitation and sexual violence against Blackgirls within the show business. Long before Tarana Burke's formulation of the #MeToo movement (2006–), Rahman used the jazz musical as a platform to unearth predatory practices within the music industry. Her musical, *Lady Day: A Musical Tragedy* (1972), dramatizes the life and career of jazz woman Billie Holiday (b. Eleanora Fagan; 1915–1959), depicting her talent, grit, and survival in an industry and society that has yet to recognize the humanity of Blackgirls. However, the source material for Rahman's critique came from Holiday's own catalog of jazz music and her memoir, *Lady Sings the Blues* (1956), written with William Dufty. Hall's more recent musical, *Tina Turner: The Tina Turner Musical* (2019) continues to expose the music industry and society's treatment of Blackgirls. Hall uses the "jukebox" musical form to explore the life and music career of queer icon, Tina Turner (b. Anna Mae Bullock; 1939–2023) and in so doing, provides a platform for spectators to engage with "taboo" topics such as sexual abuse within the music industry, domestic violence, marital rape, and a host of other social ills. Similar to Rahman, much of Hall's source material came from the artists' own words—in this case, the memoir *I, Turner* (1986) written with MTV News correspondent Kurt Loder. Hall, in fact, credits Tina Turner's disclosure of sexual violence as a catalyst for more open and public conversations about gender oppression. "The #MeToo moment we are living in; a lot of women who are coming to terms with the intense oppression and sexism not only in the entertainment industry but in our world; the fact that so many women are standing up and saying this happened to me, too. I would say Tina was one of the first to start #MeToo, in that she was honest about the abuse she suffered and was willing to have people look at her life and how raw and vulnerable she was," remembers Hall.[20] While Turner did not formalize her critique into a social justice organization, her story helped break down the culture of silence regarding sexual violence. As a Black woman survivor who built a thriving career in the unlikely field of rock and roll, Turner's story touched the hearts of many survivors and continues to serve as a source of inspiration for many members of the LGBTQ community.

The rise of the #MeToo movement has created an even greater need for Black women musical theatre artists to create musical works that amplify the voices and stories of Blackgirl survivors. Burke, after all, founded the #MeToo movement as a direct response to the culture of silencing victims of sexual assault—especially Black women, Blackgirls, queer folx, and other vulnerable populations. Burke, a New York native, was inspired to found the movement after she began working at a camp for Black and brown youth in the early 2000s. She remembers listening to a young girl named Heaven following an all-girl bonding session and learning that she was suffering sexual abuse at the hands of her mother's boyfriend. Unfortunately, hearing the details of Heaven's story was too much of an emotional load for Burke to bear and she made the poor choice of silencing the young girl. Burke remembers:

> I was horrified by her words, and the emotions welling inside of me ran the gamut. . . . I listened until I literally could not take it anymore—which turned out to be less than five minutes. Then, right in the middle of Heaven sharing her pain with me, I cut off this little girl's story and directed her to another female counselor who I believed could "help her better." . . I will never forget the look on Heaven's face. . . . The shock of being rejected, the pain of opening a wound only to have it abruptly forced shut again—it was all on that precious little face. As much as I love children, as much as I cared about that child, I did not yet possess her courage. . . . As I stood there, I couldn't even bring myself to whisper the words circling my mind and soul: "me too."[21]

By 2006, Burke found the courage to break her silence about her own experience of sexual assault and began helping other survivors—especially "young people, queer, trans, the disabled, Black women and girls" find their voice and begin to heal.[22] A decade later, Burke began using the simple #metoo hashtag on social media to encourage survivors to share their stories and allow others to identify content on this important topic. Within a six-month period, the hashtag went viral, with Burke's message reaching survivors from around the world. The popularity of Burke's message broadened the stories being told, even catching the attention of celebrities such as actress Alyssa Milano, who used the moment to voice experiences of sexual abuse within the entertainment industry. For example, allegations of sexual misconduct were made against the Academy Award, Tony Award, Golden Globe Award, and BAFTA Award-winning actor Kevin Spacey. In addition to allegations, major figures in the entertainment industry were convicted of sexual abuse crimes and faced prison. Perhaps two of the most notable convictions were that of Tony Award and Academy Award-winning producer Harvey Weinstein, and Grammy Award-winning R&B singer, songwriter, and record producer Robert "R" Kelly. More recently, the Grammy Award-winning rapper and Bad Boy Records founder Sean "P. Diddy" Combs has also faced sexual assault allegations, lawsuits, and federal criminal case.[23] While accountability on the part of perpetrators is an important part of Burke's work, her greater mission is to dismantle the systems that foster sexual violence. "We're also galvanizing a broad base of survivors, and working to disrupt the systems that allow sexual violence to proliferate in our world. This includes . . . the implementation of strategies to sustain long-term, systemic change. So that one day, nobody ever has to say 'me too' again," writes Burke.[24] Black women theatre artists further these efforts by providing a platform to engage with the long history of the predatory behavior and sexual abuse of Blackgirls within show business and greater society.

The chapter offers a Black queer feminist reading of Rahman's *Lady Day: A Musical Tragedy*, Hall's *Tina: The Tina Turner Musical* (written with Frank Ketelaar and Kees Prins), and the 2018 Broadway musical, *King Kong*. All three musicals feature Blackgirl protagonists who experience the challenges of Black girlhood and the pitfalls of show business. Whether based on the lives of actual music superstars (i.e., Billie Holiday and Tina Turner) or adapted from a fictional character within popular film (i.e., Ann Darrow), each Blackgirl encounters a host of social ills ranging from issues of racism, exploitation, and addiction, to sexual harassment and sexual violence, while pursuing careers in entertainment. My analysis of these themes extends to a critique of the production modes, the critical interventions made by Black women creatives, and the reception of their work by Black queer feminist spectators. Thus, I simultaneously explore the *depiction* of show business within the world of the musical, the agency of Black women creatives working within the actual theatre industry, and what meaning might be garnered for Black queer feminist spectators who witness their artistry.

Lady Day: A Musical Tragedy

Lady Day: A Musical Tragedy (1972), a highly theatrical jazz musical, uses a three "beat" structure to tell the professional and personal life story of blues singer, Billie Holiday. In terms of structure, the musical employs metadrama using house lights to distinguish the play-within-a-play device. In the first beat, the house lights remain on as spectators meet Flim-Flam, a 1950s host of Amateur Night at an Apollo-like theatre. He speaks directly to spectators, addressing them as if they are actual audiences at his theatre. He introduces three musical acts, including the 1950s style all-male R&B group, the Vi-Tones; Mr. Bullfrog Hawkins, a Mississippi-born harmonica player; and Ma Horn, an older Black woman who calls out lucky numbers using her "sight." Afterward, he promises to make spectators laugh by going back in time to tell them a story about "the Lady."[25] With the help of the Vi-Tones, who act as a chorus/ensemble within the world of their musical, Flim-Flam transports spectators back to 1915, the year of Billie's birth. From there, spectators witness Holiday's relationship with her mother, early career as a nightclub performer, and friendship with saxophonist Lester Young, who gives her the nickname "Lady Day." Time has passed in the second beat, which opens at church with the funeral of Clarence Holiday, Billie's father. In her sorrow, Billie turns to her partner, Dan Sugarman, for guidance and he introduces her to the world of heroin. Holiday is eventually arrested and stands trial for drug charges and is imprisoned. In the final beat, the musical returns to the Apollo-like theatre. Flim-Flam tries his best to make spectators laugh—improvising jokes as he pulls objects out of his suitcase—as spectators see an ensemble imprison Billie, offering her drugs. Flim-Flam then tells the audience that it's 1943 and the metadrama continues. Billie gets sober and tries to obtain a cabaret card—a document now required to perform in nightclubs in New York—but is denied. Billie goes back and forth between sobriety and addiction before finally landing in a hospital, which has her arrested when she resumes heroin. Once she has given everything—her talent, love, and money—to the exploitative and abusive managers and lovers in her life, Billie dies penniless and alone at the age of forty-four. This "humorous" story Flim-Flam promises to deliver concludes with the entire company singing the musical number "Rest Enough," a tribute to Billie, who passes at the age of forty-four.

Rahman's interest in Billie Holiday's life and career stems from her own adoration of the living legend (see Figure 6.2). Rahman remembers first encountering Holiday as a young girl as she listened to her covers of popular love songs and Black anthems on the radio. "It seems to me I was born hearing Kate Smith and Billie Holiday on the radio. While Kate Smith's voice was allowed in my house, Billie's was not. But I still heard her beckoning from the juke boxes and record holes on 125th street and somehow I knew that the words she sang were only a minuscule part of the true message of her voice. Except for the song, 'Strange Fruit,' I ignored the lyrics and listened to what was beyond articulation, those complex, intricate modulations of sweetness and vulnerability, grief, passion, joie vivre, that Billie poured into every note," remembers Rahman.[26] Even as a young Blackgirl, Rahman demonstrated the power of resistant listening by perceiving the layered meaning behind even Holiday's (seemingly) innocuous love songs. As such, Rahman was able to understand Holiday's relationship woes as a broader love and concern for the Black community. Rahman also connected to Holiday's music on a personal level, applying Holiday's emotional experiences to her own struggles of surviving the New York foster care system. Holiday, who famously surmised her own challenges with the phrase "there's no damn business like show

Figure 6.2 Schomburg Center for Research in Black Culture, Photographs and Prints Division, The New York Public Library. 'Billie Holiday' New York Public Library Digital Collections. https://digitalcollections.nypl.org/items/bbecb27f-bec9-d9eb-e040-e00a18064061

business, you have to laugh to keep from throwing up," spoke to Rahman's own struggles in life.[27] Years later, Rahman finally had the opportunity to meet Holiday in person. "One blessed day, when I was 16 years old, I looked up and there she was. She had a fur coat and was walking two small poodles on a leash. She was in between two thin, ominous men with dark glasses.

I remember the map of her face, with all the rough roads and deep valleys carved deep in her beautiful golden brown skin, her full red lips slightly apart ready to smile or sneer, which one I couldn't tell."[28] The memory of this choice encounter stayed with Rahman for decades, with her eventually diving into the experiences or the "rough roads and deep valleys" that shaped Holiday.

Rahman's *Lady Day: A Musical Tragedy* uses the musical form to offer spectators a complex and multidimensional image of Holiday. As with Holiday's actual life, music allows Rahman's Billie to express the joys and challenges of being a Blackgirl in show business and in America more broadly. However, it is important to note that while scholars refer to *Lady Day* as a "jazz musical," Rahman eschewed the label of "musical" to describe her work. "I always like to describe *Lady Day: A Musical Tragedy* as a play with music. I never intended to write a musical. . . since I bore the form as it has been presented to me on Broadway. But in that play the characters insisted on singing. I did know that the music could not be a mere embellishment but an integral part of their consciousness," remembers Rahman.[29] Music allowed Rahman to give more depth to her characterization of Holiday, which was integral to her purpose in writing *Lady Day*. "In *Lady Day* I wanted to challenge the myths surrounding the legendary singer and make clear the confluence of gender and racial oppression that was Holiday's reality," writes Rahman.[30] Angela Y. Davis writes that during this era, "the most common portraits that Billie Holiday highlight drug addiction, alcoholism, feminine weakness, depression, lack of formal education, and other difficulties unrelated to her contributions as an artist. In other words, the image she has acquired in U.S. popular culture relies on biographical information about Holiday's personal life at the expense of acknowledging her role as a cultural producer, which is, after all, the reason for her enduring importance."[31] The 1972 Motown Productions film, *Lady Sings the Blues*, released the same month as Rahman's musical, provides a prime example of this problematic narrative approach. While based on *Lady Sings the Blues* (1956), an autobiography co-authored with William Dufty, the film largely depicts Holiday as a performer without agency (see Figure 6.3). Davis writes that "this image of Lady Day, who is played by Diana Ross, tends to imply that her music is no more than an unconscious and passive product of the contingencies of her life. If one accepts this construction of Holiday, 'Strange Fruit' appears to be an anomaly."[32] While Rahman's depiction does include Holiday's personal struggles with drug addiction and unfaithful partners, she does so from a place of empathy. Rahman allows spectators to see Holiday's addiction as a

Figure 6.3 Diana Ross (Billie Holiday) in Motown Productions' *Lady Sings the Blues* (1972) directed by Sidney Furie. Still image courtesy of the author.

medical ailment and her management/romantic partnerships with men as nothing short of abusive and exploitative. She also balances these moments by depicting Holiday as an artist in her own right, who used her gift of song to express concern for Black women and the collective well-being of the entire Black community. Unfortunately, despite Rahman's nuanced representation of Holiday, *Lady Day* presents a curious silence surrounding her bisexuality.

Lady Day was produced by the Chelsea Theater Center (1965–1984), a not-for-profit theatre company known for producing cutting-edge new plays, lesser-known European classics, and noncommercial plays by well-known playwrights. By the time *Lady Day* debuted, the Chelsea Theatre Center had moved from the Chelsea district of Manhattan to the Brooklyn Academy of Music, which operated from 1968–1978. The Chelsea Theater Center was led by three white men—founder and artistic producer Robert Kalfin and his producing partners Michael David and scenic designer Burl Hash—who oversaw what would become a strife-ridden production. To begin, the production costs ballooned to $143,209 (nearly $80,000 of which went toward salaries), more than double the cost of the Chelsea's next two shows combined.[33] Davi Napoleon's *Chelsea on the Edge: The Adventures of an American Theater* (1991), a definitive history of the Chelsea, notes that in addition to rising costs, the production also included internal strife among creative artists. "Kalfin recalls playwright Aishah Rahman and composer

Archie Shepp urged him to fire the director and stage the show himself. He declined, explaining 'it would have been war' if he replaced Paul Carter Harrison. . . . '*Lady Day* was like *Slave Ship*,' Kalfin said. 'It destroyed itself out of internal problems, blacks against whites and mostly women against men. . . . The director's attitudes toward women in the play were exactly like those the playwright was fighting against in her text.' "[34] While Kalfin did not offer any further details, his assistant Tim Wernet disclosed other points of contention, including instances of musicians and performers arriving to rehearsals stoned or drunk, Harrison's frustration that Bill Mintzer and Bob Taylor "didn't know how to design for blacks," and discord between Rahman and Harrison.[35] Despite financial woes, racial tension, and perceived gender discrimination, *Lady Day* debuted at the Brooklyn Academy of Music on October 17, 1972.

Lady Day received polarized responses from theatre critics of the time. The production included sixteen new songs by composer Archie Shepp—ranging from jazz and blues to gospel and 1950s R&B—along with renditions of Holiday's iconic social justice songs such as "Strange Fruit" and "God Bless The Child," as well as her interpretations of popular love songs of the era (i.e., "Lover Man," and "I'm Pulling Through"). The musical numbers served a variety of purposes, including providing exposition, expressing characters' inner thoughts, and serving as meta acts during the play-within-the-play moments. *Lady Day* featured a fifteen-piece band and a large all-Black cast, including performers Cecilia Norfleet (Billie), Rosetta LeNoire (Mother Horn/Mom), Maxwell Glanville (Mort Shazer), and Roger Robinson (Flim-Flam/Preacher/Miss Freddie Freedom).[36] The theatre critic Martin Gottfried described the production as "original, theatrical, intelligent and ultimately a powerhouse theatrical experience."[37]However, *The New York Times* critic Clive Barnes described the production as "something of the shape of a musical revue" and dismissed her script as "not entirely original," "unkempt," and in need of "cutting, trimming, and tidying."[38] More recently, the performance studies scholar Davi Napoleon has attempted to understand such strong responses to the piece. "Critics loved Robert U. Taylor's set—three circular stages, the center one on a revolve, and a sleazily decorated false proscenium. They enjoyed Randy Barcelos's symbolic costumes, including eerie masks for dream sequences. Although a few black and leftist papers appreciated the show for its pro-black or pro-feminist views, the praise of mainstream reviewers rarely went beyond design elements. Most complained about the unpolished book. Others faulted the director or performers also," writes Napolean.[39] In reality, criticism of an "unpolished book" often meant dissatisfaction with Rahman's depiction of Holiday. However, contemporary scholars such as Thadious M. Davis have celebrated Rahman's ability to complicate traditional depictions of Holiday. Davis, for example, writes that "*Lady Day* was not the usual sentimental and romantic portrait of Billie Holiday as a sentimental, weak, drug-sodden and 'naturally' talented singer. Instead Billie is shown against the background of a racist and sexist society, unscrupulous managers and husbands who exploited her emotional vulnerability and physical addiction."[40]Unfortunately, Rahman's more nuanced depiction of Holiday never went any further than the Chelsea Theatre.

The dream of taking the Chelsea Theatre's production of *Lady Day* to Broadway never came to fruition due to a lawsuit and subsequent settlement. As mentioned previously, the film *Lady Sings the Blues* was released within a month of Rahman's production. The film portrays Holiday's third husband, Louis McKay (m. March 28, 1957), who served as co-producer of the film, in a positive light. However, Rahman's *Lady Day* portrays him as exploitative and abusive. Napoleon writes that "economic and personal interests may have combined to prompt [McKay] to sue, alleging that the script distorted some facts and stole others. The suit named four parties—Shepp and Rahman (neither of whom could be found), Chelsea, and BAM. 'BAM had nothing to gain from a move to Broadway,' [Micheal] David pointed out, 'and we couldn't very well incorporate a $250,000 lawsuit into a pitch to backers.' The threat effectively stalled production until the suit could be settled. He dropped the suit when Chelsea signed an agreement promising never to remount the show."[41] McKay's suit effectively shut down any possibility of remounting the musical for Broadway audiences. Despite its abrupt end, *Lady Day* remains an important musical for countless reasons, including the fact the production provided a scathing critique of politicizing and criminalizing substance use disorders.

Lady Day premiered on October 17, 1972, a time when the phrase "War on Drugs" became popularized by the media following US President Richard Nixon's June 17, 1971 press conference. Rather than treat the growing rates of drug addiction as a public health concern, Nixon positioned "drug abuse" as a new threat. Nixon stated that "America's public enemy number one in the United States is drug abuse. In order to fight and defeat this enemy, it is necessary to wage a new, all-out offensive."[42] He would later ask Congress to approve $155 million in new funds to increase the budget (for drug abuse enforcement and treatment) to more than $350 million.[43] Nixon's speech not only brought the concern of drug addiction to a national audience but also positioned those who suffer from this health condition as the "enemy" that must be vanquished. In reality, the "War on Drugs" actually meant the "War on Black and Brown communities," as the criminalization of drugs worked in tandem with the mass incarceration of Black and brown people. Indeed, phrases such as "War on Drugs" and "law and order" are used as dog whistle politics to harm Black and brown communities. For example, the US Department of Justice reports that in 2018, the imprisonment rate for Black men in state or federal correctional facilities was 5.8 times that of white males, and the imprisonment rate for Black women was 1.8 times the rate of white women.[44] The New York Attorney General Letitia James acknowledges that "we've unfortunately seen the 'War on Drugs' be used as an excuse to declare war on people of color, on poor Americans and so many other marginalized groups."[45] Fifty years after Nixon's speech, the United States "still incarcerates more people than any other nation, with nearly half of the inmates in federal prison held on drug charges."[46] However, federal prisons are just one of several criminal legal systems, as the United States today holds a total of 1.9 million people in state prisons, federal prisons, local jails, juvenile correctional facilities, immigration detention facilities, Indian country jails, military prisons, civil commitment centers, state psychiatric hospitals, and prisons in US territories.[47] The cost of operating these criminal legal systems amount to at least $182 billion per year.[48] Imagine what positive change could happen if even a fraction of this budget were used to *medically treat* rather than *criminalize* substance use disorders. After all, Dr. Nora Volkow, head of the National Institute of Drug Abuse, believes that "the best outcomes come when you treat the substance use disorder [as a medical condition] as opposed to criminalizing that person or putting them in jail or prison."[49] US policies, however, lag behind this sound medical counsel.

Lady Day offers a scathing critique of the "War on Drugs" through Holiday's experiential knowledge of the criminalization of substance use disorder. Throughout about two-thirds of the musical, spectators witness the character Billie write songs and hone her craft as an entertainer. At the very end of the "Second Beat," she falls prey to her partner/manager Dan Sugarman, who pressures her to snort dope. Rahman uses a theatrical device to show how Billie becomes shackled by her medical disorder—long before her physical incarceration. At the beginning of "Beat Three" the stage directions note: "On the upper level pimps, dope peddlers, cops, etc. of previous scene imprison Billie with their bodies. She weaves in and out of them desperately, looking for an exit. Each one blocks her escape by stretching out hands which contain dope. At the end all hands are outstretched with dope, forming a prison. When she succumbs and takes the dope offered, they fall away. This is executed simultaneously with ['God Bless the Child']." This theatrical moment emphasizes the feelings of isolation, loneliness, and betrayal after being manipulated and discarded by the music industry. Flim-Flam and the chorus remind spectators that Holiday's legacy should not be confined to her medical challenges. Above all, Holiday was an artist. Flim-Flam and the chorus commend her for singing her "sad-ass songs" and composing original works such as "Don't Explain," "God Bless the Child," "Billie's Blues," "Now or Never," and "Somebody's On My Mind." Flim-Flam and the Chorus then make a historical connection between the rise of drug addiction in Black communities of the 1940s–1950s, Billie's incarceration for substance use, and the current "War on Drugs." Flim-Flam sings: "Then drugs were not a national problem / One that the President tried to ponder / Addicts were only them there niggers / In that ghetto over yonder." Flim-Flam sings that young wealthy whites were not perceived as "addicts"—only "nigger men" and "junkie nigger bitches" were given the label of "Dope Fiend Criminal Monster." Flim-Flam concludes that with the absence of programs and medication to treat Opioid Use Disorder (OUD), the public cried, "Jail the Nigger!" Holiday expressed similar disdain for incarcerating people with substance use disorders in her autobiography, *Lady Sings the Blues*. "People on drugs are sick people. So now we end up with a government chasing sick people like they were criminals, telling doctors they can't help them, prosecuting them because they had some stuff without paying the tax, and sending them to jail. [. . .] Imagine if the government chased sick people with diabetes, put a tax on insulin and drove it into the black market, told doctors they couldn't treat them, and then caught them, prosecuted them for not paying their taxes, and then sent them to jail. If we did that, everyone would know we were crazy. Yet we do practically the same thing every day in the week to sick people hooked on drugs," writes Holiday.[50] *Lady Day* taps into Holiday's intellectual thought, dramatizing her being caught within the larger web of dog whistle politics until she becomes a poster child for the criminalization of Black people.

Lady Day's depiction of Billie's drug use trial and subsequent incarceration highlights just how unjust the US criminal justice system is for Black people (especially Blackgirls), those who suffer from OUD, and other marginalized individuals. In another highly theatrical moment, spectators witness the Chorus transform into guards who bring a wooden stand and a large American flag onstage. The Chorus/Guards handcuff Billie to the flag and place a wreath of gardenias on her head as the Judge, a "grotesque figure," enters. The entire court proceeding—"Lady Day versus America"—is ridiculous. Billie and Judge have the following conversation:

JUDGE: You stand accused of use, abuse and misuse of drug codes sanctioned by these United States. Now what is your plea?
BILLIE: I'm sick.
JUDGE (*observing her lustfully*): Hmmm, not bad, not bad.... Why don't you sing that sexy song you're so famous for. You know, the one about the naked black bodies swinging in the trees?
BILLIE: I don't feel so good.
JUDGE: This is a court, we dispense justice, not medicine.

Judge's misreading of her famous rendition of "Strange Fruit" (1939) as a "sexy" song, rather than an anti-lynching protest song, only heightens the ridiculousness of this trial. In fact, this moment might make spectators wonder why the criminal justice system is targeting Billie for her health condition while allowing actual criminals to torture and kill Black people. In his quest for "justice," Judge ultimately finds Billie guilty, refuses to offer her mercy because she has "defied American society" and "offended Christian morality" with her music, and sentences her to a year and a day of incarceration. During this incarceration, Billie meets another Blackgirl named Cellmate, who has been sentenced to six months in prison for a reoccurring offense: prostitution. As the two begin to share their stories, Cellmate questions why Billie—a famous and presumably wealthy entertainer—is in prison alongside a street hustler. Billie responds with a painful truth: "Being born Black, well, that's tears enough to start with, but being a Black woman is a special kind of pain." Billie then discloses the story of her first incarceration at the age of ten.

Lady Day uses Billie's childhood memory of rape and incarceration to expose the long history of sexualizing and criminalizing Blackgirls' bodies and socializing them to believe in Superwoman mythology. Within her private conversation with Cellmate, Billie delivers a powerful monologue about the pain of being a Blackgirl. Billie states:

> Yeah, I know about life. It's being raped at ten by a forty-year old man and going to jail for it and nobody believing or wanting to hear about it. It's

> prostituting at fifteen and loving every minute of it because for the first time in your life you got a decent place to stay and a full stomach. It's helplessly watching Mom following tradition while her spirit was slowly corroding with loneliness as she did her Black-woman-sustaining-herself-no-man-around number. It's playing a maid in a Hollywood movie even after you are an international singing star, "Yes, mam, Miz Mary Lee." It's loving a no-good man because you think that's all you deserve and that's the only kind you can get. It's being a bitch dog lapping after some love from a guy you hope cares enough to beat you. It's writing ten songs and cutting hundreds of records and the most I've gotten from any one of them is $75. . . . I will kill the next person who tells me how big and black and strong I am.

This heartbreaking monologue captures the events detailed in Holiday's memoir. In *Lady Sings the Blues*, Holiday recounts being held down by a woman neighbor so her partner, "Mr. Dick" could rape her, only to have her mother storming in and a police officer storm in afterward. Rather than being treated as a victim of sexual assault and taken to a hospital to care for her injuries, Holiday was taken to a local precinct, charged with prostitution, and placed in a Catholic institution for her so-called crime. "They treated me like I killed somebody. They wouldn't let my mother take me home. Mr. Dick was in his forties, and I was only ten. Maybe the police sergeant took one look at my breasts and limbs and figured my age that. I don't know. Anyway, I guess they had me enticed this old goat into the whorehouse or something. All I know for sure is they threw me into a cell," remembers Holiday.[51] *Lady Day* not only recounts this and other horrific moments in Holiday's girlhood, but also similar abuse suffered as an adult in the entertainment industry. Despite having risen from a poor domestic worker in Harlem to an "international singing star," the Hollywood industry still confined her to the role of maid, men continued to abuse her and exploit her talent for their financial gain, and she remained in poverty. Furthermore, this childhood trauma continued to haunt Holiday throughout her later years. Holiday remembers that "for years I used to dream about it and wake up hollering and screaming. My God, it's terrible what something like this does to you. It takes years and years to get over it; it haunts you and haunts you."[52] Unfortunately, Holiday's experiences of sexual abuse and exploitation are all too common and should not be read as a narrative of "Blackgirl resiliency."

Rather, Billie's monologue invites Black queer feminist spectators to question the emotional toll that Superwoman mythology takes on Black women and girls. Psychologists have found that the value of "strength" is normalized for Black women and girls through a "racialized and gendered script for Black female identity" known as the Superwoman Schema. Five characteristics of the Superwoman schema include "obligation to manifest strength, obligation to suppress emotions, resistance to being vulnerable or dependent, determination to succeed despite limited resources, and obligation to help others."[53] Billie's refusal to accept praise—that she is "big and black and strong" for enduring such oppression—suggests that Blackgirls should not and cannot continue to bear the burden of society's ills on their shoulders. If anything, Black queer feminist spectators can read Billie's monologue as a testament that Blackgirls are deserving of love and protection from the Black community, justice from the criminal justice system, and more opportunities within the entertainment industry.

Lady Day encourages Black queer feminist spectators to consider the blues as an important space for Blackgirls to express their interior thoughts and feelings about the world around them. Rahman perhaps best expresses the layered meaning of the blues immediately following her conversation with her friend and colleague Lester, who dubs her "Lady Day." Billie expresses her thoughts on the title and the blues tradition as follows:

> Call me Lady if you want but just remember if you mean some glove wearing bitch who sticks out her pinky when she drinks a cup of tea and coughs to drown out the sound of her farts, that ain't me, honey. I'm the kind of broad that sings the blues, baby, like my moms here. Now the blues don't always mean you mad. The blues don't always mean you sad. It's weak man that can't cry and you got to be strong to *sing* the blues. The no money and no place to get none blues! My man don't love me treats me so damn blues. Funky blues! I'm gonna keep on gettin up blues! Sassy blues! Lowdown and dirty blues that wash away the pain and purify the soul! When I sing the blues I know that this Day will never break![54]

In this monologue, Billie defines the blues as an expression of the complex and multidimensional lives of Blackgirls. As such, the blues encompasses the "earthy" side of humanity, including feelings of joy, sorrow, love, anger, spirituality, sexuality, and everything in between. *Singing the blues*, however, provides a means for Billie to financially support herself and her mother (Rosetta LeNoire). In the "First Beat," spectators see that although Billie and her mother work full-time as domestic servants, they struggle to make their rent payments. With the threat of homelessness looming, Billie considers going back to sex work, but her mother pleads with her to find another means. Billie responds by hitting the streets for employment and is led to a club by the Chorus of Winos (formerly the Vi-Tones). When Billie asks Piano Player (formerly Flim-Flam) for a job, he offers to "manage" her, stating: "Don't you know you got a natural money-maker between yo legs. Fine as you be." Despite Piano Player's repeated sexual advances, Billie follows her mother's admonitions and declines his sexual advances. Instead, she auditions for the role of dancer and fails miserably. Undeterred by rejection, Billie performs the blues song, "Looking for Someone to Love." Similar to many blues songs, Billie sings about endlessly searching for love, concluding with the lyrics: "I hope he shows / Oh, how I love for someone for me to love." Rahman's decision to pair Billie's rendition of love songs beside her more socially conscious songs (i.e., "God Bless the Child" and "Strange Fruit") demonstrates that regardless of the genre, Holiday's powerful voice always evoked Blackgirl subjectivity; the desire to love, be loved, and be free. Indeed, Angela Y. Davis writes that "Billie Holiday could sing with prophetic conviction about the transformative power of love because it may have come to represent for her all that she was unable to achieve in her own life. In a more complex racial and cultural context, she was able to carry on a tradition established by the blues women and blues men who were her predecessors: the tradition of representing love and sexuality as both concrete daily experience and as coded yearning for social liberation."[55] *Lady Day* highlights how Holiday's musical gifts and expression of love and sexuality were celebrated by the Black community and often derided by critics of the time (see Figure 6.4). For example, when faced with criticism in the *New York Times*, Billie responds: "It's like I said, most words written are damn lies. I can't sing how people want me to. Most time I get up there I don't even know what I'm going to do till I'm singing it." Rather than changing her musical style to please her critics, Rahman dramatizes Holiday's conviction to stay true to her creative genius.

In addition to dramatizing Holiday's renditions of love songs, *Lady Day* also highlights her creative genius and more overt activism through Billie's performance of "Strange Fruit." In a highly theatrical moment in the musical, Flim-Flam narrates how the Black community responded to Holiday's music, stating: "And the people heard / Their secret hope/pain/love/fears / Hidden for years in their cocoons of silence / Finally gave birth to the world / In the Songs of the Lady Day." With this introduction, Billie performs the

Figure 6.4 Roger Robinson (Flim-Flam), Cecilia Norfleet (Billie Holiday), Don Jay (Vi-Tones/Wino), Eugene Riley (Vi-Tones/Wino), R.T. Vessels (Vi-Tones/Wino), and Joe Lee Wilson (Vi-Tones/Wino) in *Lady Day: A Musical Tragedy* (1972) directed by Paul Carter Harrison. Photo by Amnon Ben Nomis, courtesy of BAM Hamm Archives.

anti-lynching protest song, "Strange Fruit," written and composed by Abel Meeropol (pseudonym Lewis Allan). Holiday describes the meaning and the reception of the song in her memoir, *Lady Sings the Blues*. "The germ of the song was in a poem written by Lewis Allen. I first met him at Café Society. When he showed me that poem, I dug it right off. It seemed to spell out all the things that had killed Pop," remembers Holiday.[56] Her memoir relates that when her father, Clarence Halliday (whom she refers to here as "Pop"), fought overseas in the army, he suffered exposure to poisonous gas, which destroyed his lungs. According to Holiday, as his condition worsened and he fell ill with pneumonia, and segregated hospitals in the South refused to treat him, "Pop finally found a veterans' hospital [in Dallas, Texas], and because he had been in the Army, had ruined his lungs and had records to prove it, they finally let him in the Jim Crow ward down there. . . . By that time it was too late. He had a hemorrhage. All they could do was give him a bed to die in and notify his next of kin," writes Holiday.[57] This experience taught her that Jim Crow racism was just another form of lynching Black Americans and served as a catalyst for "Strange Fruit." Despite her convictions, Holiday initially worried about her audience's reception of the song. "I was scared people would hate it. The first time I sang it I thought it was a mistake and I had been right being scared. There wasn't even a patter of applause when I finished. Then a lone person began to clap nervously. Then suddenly everyone was clapping," writes Holiday.[58] It took further strength for her to convince Jewish producer Milton Gabler to let her record the single under his company, Commodore Records. "I had to crawl to get the song recorded, and recorded right. . . . People don't understand the kind of fight it takes to record what you want to record the way you want to record it. I've fought as long as ten years to get to record a song I loved or wanted to do," writes Holiday.[59] In *Lady Day*, Billie initially expresses her love for her father and grief at his passing with the original gospel song, "He's Gone." After his funeral, her sadness turns to righteous anger as she contemplates her father's service and injury for a country that denied him his most basic right as a citizen. Embodying the wealth of emotion in Holiday's "Strange Fruit," Billie (Cecilia Norfleet) sings of the sweet scent of magnolias, the harsh smell of burning flesh, and the sight of "Black bodies swinging in the Southern breeze / Strange fruit hanging from the poplar trees."[60] Unfortunately, this haunting ballad remains just as valid today as Black communities continue to experience extrajudicial murders, as well as health, educational, and economic disparities.[61]

With all of *Lady Day*'s strengths, Black queer feminist spectators will likely notice one major weakness: the production fails to capture Holiday's bisexuality. This glaring omission becomes more pronounced as Billie encounters cis-male lovers who abuse her emotionally and physically and exploit her talent for their financial gain (see Figure 6.5). Rahman is careful not to use the actual names of these men, instead using them as an amalgamation of the types of men Holiday encountered in her life. For example, spectators meet Dan Sugarman, a serial cheater who introduces her to harsh drugs and slaps her when she questions his whereabouts (see Figure 6.6). Spectators witness Dan take money directly out of Billie's purse and manipulate her into allowing him to manage her career. Although she expresses her dream of owning her own nightclub and publishing her own songs, he convinces her to sign a contract that positions her to perform at larger venues—concerts, radio, television, and film. Once she signs, Dan promises her that they'll be a team, stating: "With your voice and my brains we are going to be the greatest singer the world has ever known." He seals his coercive control on her by making her pledge the following oath to him: "From this moment I belong to Daddy / I will never question or doubt him again." In addition to depicting her toxic relationship with Dan, Rahman dramatizes how Holiday's lovers continued to exploit up to her early death (see Figure 6.7). In *Lady Day*, Billie speaks with her manager Levitt as her health declines, and she faces legal battles with the city of New York, who refuse to allow her to perform in nightclubs due to her status as a felon. Levitt enters her dressing room and catches her reading a law book to help her dispute her case with the Police Commissioner. "From what I can make out even in their own laws addicts have the right to work" Billie tells Levitt. "Bitch, have you lost your mind? You can't do it" Levitt rejoins. Rather than help Billie, he discourages her and supplies her with drugs so he can further control her. Rahman depicts Billie's final partner, known simply as "Unknown Lover," after her final relapse and subsequent arrest. As she lies in a hospital bed receiving treatment for her substance use disorder, Unknown Lover tells her he loves her, that he will punish those who have treated her poorly, and promises: "I always been trying to get to you." Unknown Lover gets into bed with a delirious Billie, "makes love" to her, and tries to abruptly depart until she offers him money to stay. "Take it… it's all I got," Billie pleads. There are no references to women lovers, only male lovers who use, abuse, and discard Billie.

Despite Rahman's curious silence in regard to Holiday's bisexuality, she does celebrate the history of gender impersonators on the Apollo Theatre

Figure 6.5 Rosetta Le Noire (Mother Horn), Cecilia Norfleet (Billie Holiday), and Clifford Jordan Jr. (Lester) in *Lady Day: A Musical Tragedy* (1972) directed by Paul Carter Harrison. Photo by Amnon Ben Nomis, courtesy of BAM Hamm Archives.

Figure 6.6 Al Kirk (Dan Sugarman) and Cecilia Norfleet (Billie Holiday) in *Lady Day: A Musical Tragedy* (1972) directed by Paul Carter Harrison. Photo by Amnon Ben Nomis, courtesy of BAM Hamm Archives.

Figure 6.7 Roger Robinson (Flim-Flam) and Cecilia Norfleet (Billie Holiday) in *Lady Day: A Musical Tragedy* (1972) directed by Paul Carter Harrison. Photo by Amnon Ben Nomis, courtesy of the New York Public Library.

stage through Flim-Flam's appearance as Miss Freddie. Flim-Flam first emerges from the audience wearing "bizarre women's clothes" and carrying a suitcase while a performer named Bullfrog plays the harmonica poorly. Unable to gain the interest of the audience, Flim-Flam stops his performance by stepping onstage, drawing his pistol, and firing at Bullfrog until he angrily exits." As host of Amateur Night, Flim-Flam validates the Black audience's role as arbiters of what constitutes good Black entertainment. As such, he likens Bullfrog's obnoxious performance to the pains of urban poverty, telling spectators: "Bullfrog just like roaches-a bitch to get rid of." Having established rapport with Black spectators, Flim-Flam uses witty wordplay to prepare them for his shape-shifting throughout the course of the evening. "We got melliferous, fanatferous show lined up for you folks tonight and I'm your man, Flim-Flam. I flams the flim and flims the flam. You got to catch me if you can. Now you see me, now you don't. You got to catch me if you can. Ah got flim flams for every sit-chi-action. I can Flim-Flam the whole damn nation." He flim-flams by taking on multiple roles: he makes unwanted sexual advances toward Billie as Piano Player, offers a soul-stirring sermon as Preacher, and finally, performs as a female impersonator from the Bis Box Revue, Miss Freddie Freedom.

Black queer feminist spectators in the know would understand that Rahman's use of the "Bis Box Revue" represents an actual female impersonator troupe known as Jewel Box Revue (1939–1975). The theatre historian Bud Coleman writes that after initially struggling to find a sustained audience in their home base of Florida, the Jewel Box Revue found financial success touring on the Chitlin' Circuit in the late 1950s–1960s and performing at preeminent Black theatres such as the Howard Theatre (Washington, D.C.), Regal Theatre (Chicago), and the Apollo Theater (New York). The interracial troupe, which toured the United States continuously for more than thirty years, began performing at the Apollo in 1959 and remained a mainstay at the 1700-seat theatre until the 1960s. Bobby Shiffman, manager of the Apollo Theater, remembers the Jewel Box Revue was "a most unusual show. It was something that was away from the normal fare of the Apollo. It was glamorous. It was good family entertainment. It was wholesome. There was nothing sleazy about it. It was a show that people came back to see time and time again."[62] The Jewel Box Revue advertised their show as "'Twenty-five men and a Girl,' featuring 'The World's Foremost Femme-Mimics.'"[63] From 1955–1969, the Black lesbian singer Stormé DeLaverié (1920–2014) was the "girl" of the show, performing as a male impersonator while emceeing the drag performances. Former company member Rick Colantino describes these performances as both glamorous and entertaining. "The show was opulent—feathers, sequins, rhinestones—it was just incredible," remembers Colantino.[64] Audiences continued to flock to the Apollo Theater to witness these mesmerizing performances well into the 1960s. However, by 1974 Shiffman ended the mutually profitable enterprise as Black nationalist groups began picketing Jewel Box Revue performances. "The shows came to an end because a nationalist group menaced the theatre in a most violent way, saying they would blow up the theatre if we put on the show. They said it glorified the homosexual, and that was a threat to black life and the black family," remembers Shiffman.[65] While most of the company members were queer—many identified as bisexual and homosexual, with some performers identifying as women—their queer and camp aesthetic was certainly less harmful to Black spectators than a potential bomb.[66] Nonetheless, as the Jewel Box Revue found fewer Chitlin Circuit venues to perform in, they performed their final show at the Bijou Theatre (New York) in 1975. Within the context of growing hostility towards the LGBTQ community, Rahman's decision to incorporate a Jewel Box Revue-type of drag performance into *Lady Day* certainly took courage.

Black queer feminist spectators can read Miss Freddie Freedom's performance of "Lover Man" as a celebration of Black queer iconography. Miss Freddie sings "Lover Man" following newspaper reports of Billie's relapse. Miss Freddie encourages Billie to continue fighting, reminds spectators that "She's showed them before. She'll do it again," and performs "Lover Man," a popular song written by Jimmy Davis, Roger "Ram" Ramirez, and James Sherman in 1941. Holiday recorded her bluesy rendition of the love song in 1945, and the song quickly climbed both R&B and pop charts. Rather than dismissing Holiday's renditions of white-authored popular love songs as lacking social consciousness, Angela Y. Davis positions them as an important aspect of her Black radicalism. "Billie Holiday's songs were subversive in that they offered special and privileged insights to black people about the dominant culture. She sang songs produced by its rapidly developing popular-culture industry. Unlike Gertrude Rainey and Bessie Smith, she did not concentrate on the musical creations of black culture. Rather, she boldly entered the domain of white love as it filtered through the commodified images and market strategies of Tin Pan Alley," writes Davis.[67] Indeed, by expressing her longing to "make love," hug, and kiss her man and hear him "whisper sweet / Little things in [her] ear," Holiday's "Lover Man" not only celebrates Black love but also Blackgirl sexual autonomy. However, when Miss Freddie (Roger Robinson) channels Holiday, performing the heartbreaking love song in a spectacular evening gown, "Lover Man" takes on additional meaning for Black queer feminist spectators. This drag performance—in which Robinson imitated the sultry vocal qualities and style of Holiday—can be read as both validation of queer sexual desire and reclamation of Holiday as a Black queer icon.[68]

As *Lady Day* can attest, Billie Holiday suffered greatly as she navigated the perilous terrain of a racist, sexist, and homophobic entertainment industry. Her premature death at the age of forty-four only confirms the physical and emotional toll that this navigation took on her. Yet, her tenacity, creative spirit, and love for the Black community provided the courage she needed to voice the most inexplicable horrors of the mid-twentieth century. From her overt social justice anthems to her more subversive love songs, Lady Day remains a Black queer icon for so many and a source of inspiration for Blackgirls who dare to enter show business. In other words, without Lady Day, there would be no Tina Turner.

Tina: The Tina Turner Musical

Tina: The Tina Turner Musical (2019) dramatizes the life and career of rock'n'roll legend and queer icon, Tina Turner. Based on the autobiography, *I, Tina: My Life Story* (1986) and the critically acclaimed biopic *What's Love Got to Do with It* (1993) starring Angela Bassett (Tina) and Laurence Fishburne (Ike), *Tina* offers Black queer feminist spectators a glimpse into the world of show business from the 1950s into the 1980s.[69] The musical opens in Rio de Janeiro, Brazil, in 1988, with Tina (Adrienne Warren) about to step out on stage to perform in one of the most famous concerts in rock history. As nearly two hundred thousand fans scream for her, she kneels on the floor in a red leather minidress and iconic lion's mane, and takes a moment to do a Buddhist chant to overcome her fear. The stage lights darken, fog surrounds the stage, and spectators are transported back in time and place to rural 1950s Nutbush, Tennessee. Spectators witness a Young Anna-Mae (Skye Dakota Turner) discover her gift of song in the church choir, only to have her mother Zelma (Dawnn Lewis) scold her for being "too loud." After Zelma leaves her abusive husband, Richard (David Jennings), spectators see a now sixteen-year-old Tina (Warren) being raised by her grandmother

Georgeanna (Myra Lucretia Taylor), who encourages her to cultivate her gift for song and join her mother and sister Alline (Mars Rucker) in St. Louis. From there, Tina meets Ike Turner (Daniel J. Watts), lead singer of the Kings of Rhythm. Ike pulls her onstage to sing with him and, afterward, offers her a spot on his tour around the Chitlin Circuit. The musical then hits major plot points from the 1993 film, namely Ike's formation of the Ike & Tina Turner Revue in 1960, Tina's rise to fame, tumultuous marriage with Ike, and financial ruin following her 1976 divorce. In contrast to the film, which concludes shortly after Tina meets her new manager Roger Davies, the musical continues Tina's story, devoting the entire second act to detailing her resurgence. After spectators witness Tina's creative talent recording her first solo album and fifth studio album, *Private Dancer* (1984), the musical closes by returning to the present. As Tina enters the Rio concert stage, spectators become concert attendees as she provides an energetic performance.

Tina Turner's mass appeal—from everyday Blackgirls, to drag queen performers, to King Charles III of England—helps explain why *Tina: The Tina Turner musical* was set up for success.[70] Tina Turner's decades-long musical career began alongside Ike Turner, with R&B hits such as her 1971 Grammy Award-winning rendition of "Proud Mary" and her semi-autobiographical R&B song "Nutbush City Limits" (1973). Her solo career in the field of rock, no less, included hits such as "What's Love Got to Do With It" (1984) and "The Best" (1989). In her lifetime, Tina Turner sold more than 200 million records and garnered eight Grammy Awards, three Grammy Hall of Fame Awards, a Grammy Lifetime Achievement Award, and seven Billboard Awards. She was inducted into the Rock and Roll Hall of Fame twice (with Ike Turner in 1991and as a solo artist in 2021), received a spot on the Hollywood Walk of Fame, is the first woman and first Black artist on the cover of *Rolling Stone* magazine, and the first female solo artist to fill stadiums.[71] In her book *Black Diamond Queens: African American Women and Rock and Roll* (2020), Maureen Mahon discusses how Turner navigated her race, gender, and genre boundaries to achieve these feats and become the "Queen of Rock." "She understood that to succeed in the field of rock she had to connect with a sound and scene that by the early 1980s had eschewed visible blackness, while continuing to rely on black musical sound. She capitalized on the authorizing participation of white men and symbolic distancing from blackness to facilitate her success, aligning herself with a white manager and . . . white supporters. . . . Sonically, though, Turner's repertoire maintained a connection to blackness index through blues-based roots, gospel-inspired vocals, and the polished energy of rhythm and blues venue," writes Mahon.[72] Self-fashioning a new image included efforts to broaden her fan base to find mainstream success. She notably turned down Stephen Spielberg's offer to play Shug Avery in the critically acclaimed film *The Color Purple* (1985) and instead performed as "Auntie Entity" alongside (then) superstar Mel Gibson in a post-apocalyptic dystopian action film, *Mad Max: Beyond Thunderdome* (1985). Her appearance in the *Mad Max* franchise only further cemented her status within popular culture. In terms of artistic legacy, her incredible vocal ability and energetic stage presence, combined with her ability to defy expectations for Blackgirl performers paved the way for women singers today (see Figure 6.8). As Hall rightly argues: "Without Tina Turner there wouldn't be a Beyoncé, there wouldn't be a Rihanna, there wouldn't be a Katy Perry. There wouldn't be this shining example for so many young female performers and singers to look up to in the way she was so authentically herself."[73]

In addition to her mainstream success, Black queer feminist spectators remember Tina Turner as a source of inspiration, political ally, and queer

Figure 6.8 Tina Turner (as herself) in Touchstone Pictures' *What's Love Got to Do With It* (1993) directed by Brian Gibson. Still image courtesy of the author.

icon. In his article, "Gay Iconography: Tina Turner Is Simply The Best," the journalist Bobby Hankinson writes: "Not only is she beloved for her powerful voice and high-energy performances, but the story of her overcoming an abusive relationship with Ike has cemented her status as a woman of immeasurable strength. . . . Beyond the inspirational story, Turner's catalog and style has inspired legions of gay fans young and old (and plenty of drag queens). She also has the distinction of performing at the opening ceremonies of the first ever Gay Games in San Francisco in 1982."[74] Indeed, Turner's decision to perform at the Gay Games—when other artists refused—was not a "popular" thing to do at the time.[75] Unfortunately, her early support of the LGBTQ community has been obscured within cultural memory. As the *PinkNews* journalist Marcus Wratten rightly argues, "while the likes of Madonna and Cyndi Lauper are routinely recognized for standing firmly in the LGBTQ+ community's corner during the '80s, when other celebrities turned their heads, Tina Turner was up there with them, making her support for the community known."[76] In addition to celebrating LGBTQ athletes on a global stage, Turner also advocated for people living with HIV and vocalized her support for same-sex marriage long before the Supreme Court (Obergefell v. Hodges) ruled in favor of marriage equality on June 26, 2015. "I think that men marrying men, and women marrying women, is a wonderful thing. I think that it's God's blessings on them, that's what I think," Turner famously stated in a 2000 interview with *The Advocate*.[77] Turner also collaborated with queer artists, performing duets with Elton John and David Bowie, and performing onstage with other gay icons, such as Cher and Beyoncé.

Even beyond Turner's actual expressions of support for the LGBTQ+, countless drag performers have been inspired by her music catalog and spirited performances. Turner's more "masculine" vocals perhaps lends itself to queer expression. She describes her early vocal training with Ike's Kings of Rhythm in her memoir *I, Tina: My Life Story*. "Now, when I say sing, I know that I don't have a 'pretty' voice. My voice is not the voice of a woman, so to speak. That's why when I choose my music, I think of men. I can relate to their delivery, I'm attracted to it. When I first started working with Ike, it was all men and just me, and I had to sort of keep up. So I had to take a lot of my training and my patterns of singing from the guys. It wasn't about girls and beauty and femininity," writes Turner.[78] Ike expressed similar sentiments in his memoire, *Takin' Back My Name: The Confessions of Ike Turner* (1999), with Nigel Cawthorne. "Tina she don't sing like a woman, she sings like a man," writes Ike.[79] Tina famously juxtaposed the masculine voice with high femme glamor, wearing heaps of sequins and short fringe dresses, and a long black wig while her limbs moved freely, sweat dripping from her chest and body. The journalist Joshua S. Mackey writes that "rousing performances of 'Proud Mary' have surfaced on various gay bars to lip syncs on *RuPaul's Drag Race*. Many drag artists, like Tina Burner, Vinegar Strokes, Peppermint, and even RuPaul herself, have gone on record to discuss her influence on their artistry."[80] Sadly, Hall's book does not address or even hint at Turner's cultural significance within LGBTQ communities.

Tina opened on Broadway at the Lunt-Fontanne Theatre on November 7, 2019 and met both packed houses until the production was forced to close due to the COVID-19 pandemic. Before arriving on Broadway, *Tina* premiered at the Aldwych Theatre in London on April 17, 2018 before transferring to Hamburg, Germany, in 2019. The Broadway production was directed by Phyllida Lloyd, known for her direction of both the 2001 Broadway production and 2008 film adaption of the jukebox musical sensation, *Mamma Mia!* The European company Stage Entertainment served as lead producer of *Tina*, with Tina Turner and her second husband, record executive Erwin Bach, serving as executive producers. Producers allotted *Tina* a $16.5 million budget, a figure considered pretty standard for most major musicals.[81] *Tina* proved a huge box office success, grossing nearly $72.5 million with 559,041 attendees at 479 performances and 27 previews.[82] The production also received critical success, winning one Tony Award for "Best Performance by a Leading Actress in a Musical" (Adrienne Warren) and another eleven nominations, including Best Musical, Best Book of a Musical" (Katori Hall, Frank Ketelaar, and Kees Prins), Best Performance by a Featured Actor in a Musical (Daniel J. Watts), Best Performance by a Featured Actress in a Musical (Myra Lucretia Taylor), Best Direction of a Musical (Phyllida Lloyd), Best Choreography (Anthony Van Laast), Best Orchestrations (Ethan Popp), Best Scenic Design of a Musical (Mark Thompson and Jeff Sugg), Best Costumes Design of a Musical (Mark Thompson), Best Lighting of a Musical (Bruno Poet), and Best Sound Design of a Musical (Nevin Steinberg). Since the Broadway production, *Tina* has been mounted in the Netherlands (2020), Spain (2021), and Australia (2023), as well as toured the United States (2022) and the United Kingdom (2025).

The popularity of *Tina* is part of a larger narrative about the rise of celebrity-driven jukebox musicals on Broadway. By "jukebox musical," I refer to musicals that use preexisting music for most, if not all, of its musical numbers. The musical theatre historian Millie Taylor writes that "the songs function differently in a jukebox musical than in an 'integrated' musical, in that rather than simply amplifying and expanding on their context, they leap from it and make connections with other parts of the audience."[83] "Jukebox musicals," also known as "catalogue musicals" or "back-catalogue shows," are not a new phenomenon. George Rodosthenous, for example, writes that "one could trace the jukebox musical's history from The Beggar's Opera (1728) to two of MGM's greatest successes—*An American in Paris* (1951) and *Singin' in the Rain* (1962)—as in all these famous works pre-existing songs were used to counterpoint a new narrative. Since the 1920s familiar songs have been reintroduced into other narratives to express love, anger, frustration, desire, and so on through the sung words."[84] More recent celebrity-driven jukebox musicals include *Beautiful: The Carole King Musical* (2013), *Head Over Heels* (2015; dramatizes The Go-Go's), *Ain't Too Proud to Beg: The Life and Times of The Temptations* (2017; book by Dominique Morisseau), *The Cher Show* (2018), *Summer: The Donna Summer Musical* (2017), *MJ: The Musical* (2022; dramatizes Michael Jackson; book by Lynn Nottage), and *Hell's Kitchen* (2023; semi-autobiographical dramatization of Alicia Keys). As this list can attest, most of these more recent jukebox musicals are about the life and times of aging or deceased musicians. *Why?* Why would aging musicians or a musicians estate want to resurrect the past? Hall remembers asking Turner this same question. "Why dive into the dark?" she remembers asking, to which Turner responded: "This is not about my stardom, this is about the journey that I took to get there."[85] For Hall, the jukebox musical offered the best way of capturing and preserving Turner's musical legacy. "*Tina* is meant to further preserve the legacy of this towering giant, a woman whose wail was cured in that Tennessee soil. Her story was meant to be told through song and dance because that is the essence of who she is—a vessel for the muses, a consummate show-woman, the queen of rock and roll," writes Hall.[86] As such, Hall's creative process began by listening to Turner's music. "From 'River Deep – Mountain High' to 'We Don't Need Another Hero,' the various hits in Tina's vast catalog lit my spirit ablaze just as they had done when I was a little girl belting along to records in my mother's kitchen. If anything, these songs resonated with me even more deeply, almost 30 years later. As a woman and a mother who has fought hard to achieve her dreams, I found a new kinship with Tina," writes Hall.[87] Building on this foundation of nostalgia, the hope was that spectators could also discover new facets of Turner's music and renew their connection to her story.

Despite Hall's enthusiasm for the jukebox musical, the subgenre is not without criticism from theatre artists and critics. Major opposition to the jukebox musical comes from accusations that jukebox musicals: are not "real musicals," have replaced the creation of new musicals on Broadway, lack essential elements of musical theatre (i.e., drama and characterization), are too predictable (many are biographical in nature, leaving little opportunity for surprise), and are simply entertaining and do not challenge spectators.[88] The composer-lyricist Michael John LaChiusa distinguishes between what he calls a "real musical" and a "faux musical," writing that "a real musical makes perfect symmetry out of the muck of diverse and eclectic sources, and transcends those sources. A real musical is organic in all its parts. It's equal parts intelligence and heart. It can never be realistic theatre, only realistic in its humanity."[89] Creators of "faux musicals," on the other hand, rely on formulae, becoming facsimiles that never transcend the original source material.[90] Writing in 2005, he predicted that the box office success of "faux musicals" such as the "dance play" *Contact* and "jukebox musical" *Mamma Mia!* would only exacerbate the trend of "*use[ing]* songs, rather than invent[ing] them."[91] Returning to his concern in 2014, LaChiusa writes that "the catalogue musical still seems to be thriving. I find the genre annoying. The familiar songs from the repertoires of famous pop and rock stars never seem to rise organically from the story at hand, and the music does little to advance action, much less explore character. But audiences and some critics apparently enjoy these concerts masquerading as musicals. They can go into the theater humming the tunes. What drama there is seems to come from the moment when the audience recognizes a familiar song."[92] The theatre critic Barbara Ellen expresses similar concerns, likening the jukebox musical to a "pop-theatre crossover" before questioning if they are simply the "repackaging of dusty back catalogues and fading reputations" and/or "just one big cynical tourist trap."[93] Regardless of the answer, Ellen foresees the jukebox musical a permanent mainstay on the Broadway stage. "What no one could deny is that these hybrids of pop nostalgia and theatrical sawdust are here to stay," writes Ellen.[94] However, the musical theatre historian, George Rodosthenous identifies both the positive and negative aspects of jukebox musical, surmising that they carry a double-edged sword. "Even though the jukebox musical has re-introduced the musical to a wider audience, it is also partly responsible for the stagnation of musical theatre as an art form," writes Rodosthenous.[95] Hall, however, believed that use of Turner's musical catalogue would actually strengthen her dramaturgy and the musical as a whole.

In many ways, *Tina* serves as an example of Hall's revitalization of the jukebox musical. Initially, even members of the creative team were less than enthusiastic about creating a jukebox musical. For example, the Tony-nominated projection designer Jeff Sugg remembers feeling hesitant to join the creative team not only because of the jukebox genre but also the lack of Black representation behind the scenes.

> For what's it worth, I carry stigma with jukebox musical. I think of that as like: blech. I wasn't necessarily involved in that part of it but I will say that when I first spoke to Phyllida and met her and talked about the piece, I was so grateful to hear that Katori was writing it. I don't know when she came into the process next to two other names that are attached to it who I believe are both Dutch guys. Having Katori at the center of this show that is, besides her—let's be very clear, is a bunch of white people. . . So, anyway, I felt great solace in having her there because I trust her and know how strong and succinct and insightful she is, remembers Sugg.[96]

As a Pulitzer-Prize-winning dramatist, she has always used her craft to further Black representation both on and off Broadway stages. "As a Black woman who has dedicated herself to telling stories about the Black experience, I know I'm coming from a culture that oftentimes is dehumanized no matter who and what you are or what your profession is –singer, stripper, or whatever. . . . To always be reaching for humanity is, for me, an act of social justice," Hall explains.[97] As a major Black voice within a white-dominated production team, Hall carried her social justice efforts into her work on *Tina*. Hall remembers:

> I believe in a "laying on of hands," this spiritual tradition where blessings are passed on through touch. So when I was asked to join the creative team and lay my hands on Tina's story for the stage, I was, of course, nervous as all get out; but I knew the honor and responsibility of shepherding that journey had to be mine –for all that she meant to this southern girl, my mother, and women around the world. I was raised on the music and legend of Tina by her biggest fan. In fact, my mama looooooved herself some Tina Turner so much that she named my eldest sister after her. In our household, Tina meant breaking all the rules, shattering expectations, and rising above the ashes and sometimes even the sun.[98]

Hall's own subject position gave her a firm knowledge of the South and what Turner's music and performances meant to Black women and girls. Building on this experiential knowledge, Hall returned to Turner's music catalog to capture the *feel* of the musical and its characters. Hall remembers: "I was astounded by the way the grit, power, and soulfulness of Tina's voice told her entire life's story. At the most pivotal moments in this piece—when Tina and the folks in her life were overcome by joy, heartbreak, pain, love, and hope—the melodies and lyrics of her records provided the perfect outlet for our characters to express their deepest truths. No original music could have come close to matching the authenticity and poignancy of Tina's catalog."[99] Rather than feel limited by Turner's catalog, Hall used her music as an entry point into the narrative, creating rich characters and dramaturgical complexity often absent in jukebox musicals.

Hall's use of Turner's catalog not only drives the action of the play but also provides a means for characters to express their innermost truths. Before writing *Tina*, Hall was already widely known for creating three-dimensional characters. The visionary Black Broadway producer Brian Anthony Moreland, for example, has praised the great emotional depth of her characters. "She writes human people that are your brothers and your cousins, your sisters, your uncles, your aunts, your grandparents, she writes people and she writes them in the rawest, most accessible way. . . . She literally crawls inside these people and reveals their innermost truths," remembers Moreland.[100] While Hall had no prior experience in musical theatre before writing *Tina*, she is no stranger to dramatizing the lives of important figures in US history. In fact, she became the first Black woman to win an Olivier Award for her drama *The Mountaintop* (2009), which offers a fictional account of the remaining hours of Martin Luther King Jr. before his assassination. "Because I did *Mountaintop*, that's probably why I felt I could do Tina. I did King. I can do Tina. . . . It was very helpful to have already had that under my belt," remembers Hall.[101] In addition to this experience, having grown up in Memphis—about an hour from Turner's hometown of Nutbush, Tennessee—Hall felt a special connection to Turner's story and the people who would (eventually) populate her musical. "I grew up in Tennessee. Tina grew up in Tennessee. I know that place. I know the culture. . . . I know the struggle of being a Black woman in the entertainment industry, especially if you are an unapologetic Black woman—how you have to bend the rules to the point of breaking because that's the way that you can keep yourself intact.

I know that personally," remembers Hall.[102] In addition to dramatizing the plight of Black Southern women entertainers, Hall also broke new ground by highlighting Turner's girlhood, which was largely overlooked in the biopic *What's Love Got to Do With It*. "Tennessee has a way of swallowing up little black girls' dreams. Some say it's why the soil is so fertile. Coming of age in this place bound by its racist past, I was led to believe that my feet belonged on the ground—that dreams were for the night, never to be seen by the day. But I looked to Tina Turner as a living, breathing, thriving example that some black girls were supposed to walk amongst the stars," writes Hall.[103] In addition to investigating how the Black Church and domestic violence influenced Turner's girlhood and sense of self, Hall also departs from the biopic film by extending the typical Tina Turner narrative beyond her divorce from Ike.

At the time of writing *Tina,* Brian Gibson's *What's Love Got to Do With It* provided the only major artistic examination of Turner's life and greatly shaped media perception of Turner as the "patron saint of battered women."[104] To begin, the film highlights Ike's coercive control of Tina's stage persona and its harmful effects. Early on in the film, Ike (Fishburne) takes Tina (Bassett) to a salon and tells her to bleach her hair blonde. Unfortunately, the bleach causes her hair to fall out and she masks the injury by wearing what would become her early iconic look: a long, straight black wig. From there, the two-hour-long film devotes ninety minutes to Tina and Ike's tumultuous marriage—which included physical, emotional, financial, and sexual abuse—and only spends the final thirty minutes detailing the start of Tina's solo career. At this point, spectators see a forty-three-year-old Tina perform a cabaret number in a hotel while patrons eat their meals. Manager Roger Davies sees the performance and sets up a showcase for her at the Ritz. The film concludes with Ike visiting her dressing room before the showcase and threatening her with a gun. Tina, now sporting her famous lion wig and black leather rock dress, refuses to reconcile and instead, performs "What's Love Got to Do With It" to adoring fans. The camera cuts away from her performance to show a (now) downtrodden Ike sulking in her dressing room, then Ike watching her perform, and finally, Ike walking away from Tina's showcase. When the performance concludes, the film uses placards to detail Ike's future prison sentence and Tina's future as a Grammy Award-winning solo artist. In other words, the film largely dramatized Tina's suffering and spent little time detailing her owning her creative genius during the later part of her career. As a result, Ike looms larger-than-life throughout the film and, at times, almost becomes the focus of the film. Highly critical of this narrative, the Black feminist scholar bell hooks asked: "Why is it that her success is less interesting than the period of her life when she's a victim?"[105] The popular music scholar Duncan Wheeler offers an answer to this query. "The film may have focused on Tina's victimhood as opposed to her victorious period, but producers and audiences were primarily interested in her years of suffering because of her renaissance. If she hadn't scored number one hits and won Grammy awards, Ike's reputation would likely have survived largely intact, as have those of other musical abusers from the period," writes Wheeler.[106] Yet, according to hooks, some Black audiences continued to support Ike, even questioning the veracity of Tina's account. "You know all these black people – particularly black men – have been saying to me, 'Ike couldn't have treated her that bad.' Why don't they say, 'Isn't it tragic that he did treat her so bad.' This just gets to show you how we, as black people in this country, remain sexist in our thinking of men and women," writes hooks.[107] Despite criticism of the film and its reception within popular culture, *What's Love Got to Do With It* remained the definitive artistic examination of Tina's life for decades.

While Hall's dramatization does detail instances of domestic violence, she also makes critical departures in previous narratives through her imaginative incorporation of Tina's music catalog, her character-driven story, and her focus on Tina's artistic agency and solo career. Wheeler analyzes how Hall used *I, Tina* and *What's Love Got to Do With It* as a foundation for her artistic vision:

> While replicating some of the key incidents from the film and autobiography (such as being told off for singing too loudly in church as a child and the reproduction of Ike's condominium replete with psychedelic aquarium), *Tina* expanded the temporal and thematic remit by taking her life-story up to the time of the record-breaking Brazilian concert, and employing songs to develop the narrative rather than in strict chronological order. Hence, for example, Turner addressed her performance to Ike of "Better Be Good to Me," a song from the 1984 comeback album *Private Dancer*, in marriage scenes set two decades previously. No attempt was made to shoehorn all her hits into the show (notable exclusions included "Steamy Windows," "Typical Male," and "Goldeneye"), avoiding tactics that could reduce gravitas.[108]

Indeed, Hall fills in narrative gaps from the film, devoting nearly all of the second act to depicting Turner's struggles to mount a solo career and using her catalog to express her interior life. Perhaps one of the best examples of Hall's artistic vision occurs after Tina (Warren) explains *why* she endures abuse from Ike. However, staying in an abusive marriage for the sake of her children comes to an end after her son is caught in the crosshairs of their physical altercation. This action occurs alongside Tina expressing her innermost feelings through song. Wheeler writes that "in this sequence, a montage of Tina performing her signature hit 'Proud Mary' and spousal abuse builds to a climax before the relative calm of a performance of the more contemplative 'I Don't Wanna Fight,' a song commissioned for the 1993 film biopic."[109] Rather than follow the chronological order in which Turner released her songs, Hall allows the songs to emerge organically and with intentionality. By "I Don't Wanna Fight," spectators witness an exhausted Tina, barely able to put one foot in front of another—a stark contrast to her public persona as a high-energy performer.

Hall not only provides spectators—many of whom are die-hard Tina Turner fans—with a glimpse into the inner workings of Tina's psyche but also her legendary public stadium performances (see Figure 6.9). However, Hall's

Figure 6.9 Angela Bassett (Tina Turner) in Touchstone Pictures' *What's Love Got to Do With It* (1993) directed by Brian Gibson. Still image courtesy of the author.

use of a metatheatrical concert at the conclusion of the musical runs the risk of reproducing what Rodosthenous describes as jukebox musical cliches. In his criticism of the jukebox musical, Rodosthenous asks three important dramaturgical questions about the incorporation of catalog music into a musical: "Why do these characters actually sing? Who do they sing to? And why do they use existing songs?"[110] He later answers these questions, writing that "jukebox musicals very often use pop songs and in so doing, they deny the audience songs which can in a subtle way portray character and communicate their thoughts. On some occasions, the amalgamation of narrative and existing music does not go beyond the cliched plot of the development of a band/tribute band and this does not allow for exciting new storylines or dramaturgical complexity. Due to the nature of the songs, easy narratological devices such as karaoke and concerts lead to predictable metatheatrical narratives."[111] Hall's use of song often furthers character development and her book finds moments to diverge from "fact" while still "staying true to the spirit of Turner's journey."[112] Furthermore, Hall's incorporation of what the theatre critic Natalie de la Garza describes as "an honest-to-goodness concert" does seemingly follow the standard fare with jukebox musicals.[113] However, rather than view this concert as a predictable flaw, the theatre critic Marilyn Stasio commends this artistic choice. "Unlike most biographical musicals, which tend to lose energy as their subjects grow older, wiser, and sadder, 'Tina' builds to a high," writes Stasio.[114] The concert, then, helps maintain the energy of the musical, keeping audiences entertained until the conclusion of the musical.

In addition to maintaining audience engagement, incorporating a concert also allowed Hall's narrative to come full circle. *Tina*, after all, begins with Tina in a meditative state, about to step onstage and perform. Most of the action of the musical occurs in her memories, in what the creative team referred to as "Etherland." Sugg describes Etherland as a "sort of liminal zone" that allows spectators to be transported into Tina's memory flashbacks as if watching a film.[115] "I think what was really important was for us—as frequently as possible—to make sure that we could tap back onto that moment and just acknowledge that we were in this elusive never fully rendered, never fully clear state. That is why there's not really any hard edges on the stage. Everything sort of disappears into blackness... there's always depth of field to it. That was something that I had actually never done or seen in a theater production before—to let all of the scenery be so domically presented insofar as the focus is on the downstage and everything else is not a focus with what is actually an artificial camera blur filter. I really treated all that stuff as if it was the background that was being shot way far away," remembers Sugg.[116] Having experienced the joys and sorrows of Turner's memories, the concert allows spectators to celebrate her legacy and perhaps tap into their own nostalgic memories associated with Turner's catalog.

While Hall certainly entertains spectators, she also challenges them to engage with difficult subject matter—including the relationship between the vestiges of chattel slavery and domestic violence in Black homes. Etherland begins with Tina's memory of her mother Zelma reprimanding her for singing too loudly at church, only to have her father, Floyd "Richard" Bullock (David Jennings), intervene on her behalf. Tina witnesses the following altercation:

RICHARD: Now that's enough there. *[slaps Zelma]* What the devil has gotten into you? You ain't gonna ride her just cause she gets happy more times than you in a week than you ever did in your whole life. . . . Just leave her.
ZELMA: Why you always put her first like she's some kind of angel?
RICHARD: Now, how am I gonna put a child before the woman I love?
ZELMA: Cause you do. You forced my hand. I was fine, I was just fine with Alline.[117]

First, Richard mistakes his subversive control over Zelma with feelings of "love." Zelma, who has been living with Richard's verbal and physical abuse for years, engages with Tina in a similar fashion, treating her with the same brutality that her husband has shown her. Richard, however, appears completely oblivious to the pain he causes and the domino effect that his words and actions have on the women in his life. Instead of communicating with Zelma about her unhappiness, he glowers at her and goes to take his anger out on the person she loves the most: Alline. When Zelma finds the courage to physically shield Alline from his clenched fists, Richard threatens: "Don't you think you're better than me. Woman, I ain't no field nigger. I'm the overseer. I oversee them fields. I oversee this house." Richard, who barely earns a living picking cotton in the same fields of his enslaved ancestors, endures dehumanizing treatment by his white employer. When he returns home, he feels a pressing need to reassert his masculine dominance by putting Zelma beneath his heel. Drawing on this history of generational trauma, Richard likens their marriage to slavery, wherein *she* is the Black fieldhand and *he* is the white overseer. As such, he imagines that his word is law and his cruel actions justified. Despite the ongoing abuse, some of Zelma's spirit remains and she makes the courageous decision to leave him. "You and Nutbush can go straight to hell 'cause I've done had enough of you beatin' on me. I am tired. I am sick and tired." With this exchange, Hall explains *why* Zelma cannot remain in her loveless, abusive marriage. Unfortunately, after surviving years of Richard's emotional manipulation, including forcing her to have a second child, she now conflates her hatred of him with her feelings for Anna-Mae. When Richard asks about her plans for Anna-Mae, Zelma responds: "You the one that made me have her. You wanted her so bad, you take care of her." As a helpless Anna-Mae looks on, she expresses her pain by singing/crying a repetitious, "Oh, mother!" Thus, *Tina* exposes the generational trauma caused by slavery continue to fracture Black familial relationships.

Tina dramatizes how domestic violence and abandonment irreparably harms Blackgirls' psyches, making them even more vulnerable to coercive control in their future relationships. Sadly, having never healed from the emotional trauma of her childhood, Tina does not recognize what a healthy relationship/marriage should look like. Instead of recognizing Ike's gradual escalation of violence and leaving him, she dismisses the "red flags" and pacifies him by deferring to his judgement. For example, after giving her the stage name "Tina" and forming the "Ike and Tina Turner Revue" (without asking her), Ike responds violently to her attempt to assert some creative control of a song during a recording session. Ike responds by yelling at her in front of the band. "Show me some respect. I'm the one who know what it's supposed to sound like!" screams Ike. "You're right!" Tina quickly responds. Ike then throws a cymbal at her, narrowly misses her head, and threatens the other band members. "Anybody got something else to say?" asks Ike. Afterward, Tina justifies Ike's actions to a band member by stating, "He's just passionate, that's all. Ike was just giving me some advice." When questioned how this attack could be "advice," Tina playfully responds, "Well, I bet I won't do that again." As their revue becomes more popular, Ike holds her financially hostage, refusing to pay her for her work on the tour. When Tina asks how they can afford to hire road manager Rhonda Graam but not pay her a salary, Ike slaps her and asks: "I made you a star and this how you repay me?" He then turns to beat Tina and only stops when she tells him she's expecting their first child together. Hall then provides a montage of Ike's escalation of violence over the course of a decade or more while Tina performs "I Want to Take You Higher." In quick succession, spectators witness Ike cheat on Tina while berating her for wanting to care for their baby rather than record or go out with him. Next, the Ikettes leave the band because of Ike's abusive behavior and try to convince Tina to do the same. When Tina refuses to leave Ike, one of the women teaches her a Buddhist chant to give her strength to endure his abuse. In the third sequence, Rhonda asks Tina why she stays with Ike, and she explains that she stays for her children. Finally, spectators witness Tina intentionally overdose on medication as Ike threatens to kill her. After being admitted into a hospital, Zelma visits Tina and advises her: "If you gonna survive this, then you need to teach Ike a lesson. You need to beat his ass just like I did your daddy's ass. . . love got nothing to do with this." The use of a montage allowed Hall to condense years of domestic violence into a brief chapter within Tina's life. However, some critics felt that the swiftness of the abuse dramatization became cartoon-like and "dangerously close to being played comedically."[118] Regardless of how spectators read this montage, the staging device allowed Hall to focus the second half of the musical on Turner's artistry and solo career.

In Hall's narrative, Tina moves beyond victimhood to the realization of her personal and artistic autonomy. This process begins by demanding her right to her stage name. When Rhonda chastises her for not asking for the financial compensation she "deserved" in the divorce, Tina responds, "I didn't want his money. All I wanted was my name, 'Tina Turner.' That was mine. I screamed for that name. I almost died for it." Turner reflects on the significance of the stage name in her 1986 autobiography:

> Ike explained: As a kid back in Clarksdale, he'd become fixated on the white jungle goddesses who romped through Saturday-matinee movie serials—revealingly rag-clad women with long flowing hair and names like Sheena, Queen of the Jungle, and Nyoka—particularly Nyoka. He still remembered *The Perils of Nyoka,* a fifteen-part Republic Picture serial from 1941, starring Kay Aldridge in the title role and featuring a villainess named Vultura, an ape named Satan, and Clayton Moore (later to be TV's Lone Ranger) as the love interest. Nyoka, Sheena—Tina! Tina Turner—Ike's own personal Wild Woman. He loved it.[119]

Clearly, Ike's choice of name greatly shaped her early public persona. hooks writes that "Ike's pornographic fantasy of the black female as wild sexual savage emerged from the impact of a white patriarchal controlled media, shaping his perceptions of reality. His decision to treat the wild black woman was perfectly compatible with prevailing representations of black female sexuality in a white supremacist society. Of course the Tina Turner story reveals that she was anything but a wild woman; she was fearful of sexuality, abused, humiliated, fucked, and fucked over."[120] Hall offers an explanation as to why Turner would choose to keep a stage name steeped in racism, sexism, and memories of her ex-husband's coercive control. "To keep it is to reclaim it. Reshape it. Refine it. Also, kind of like a 'fuck you' to Ike. 'Yeah, you gave me this name but watch what I build with it,'" remembers Hall.[121] In the musical, Tina uses the stage name as a stepping stone to refashion her self-image into a rock star, including a (now) iconic lion's wig and short skirts. When her new manager, Roger, tries to push her to sing more sexual songs, she refuses to do so. When Roger further presses her, noting that she already wears short skirts onstage, Tina responds, "I don't wear short skirts to be sexy. I wear short skirts so my legs can be free." With these words, Tina conceptualizes freedom as much more than sexual liberation, but as the fundamental right to shape her own appearance and move about the world free and uninhibited. She later asserts her creative autonomy when Roger suggests major changes to her performance before her showcase debut. Roger directs her to sing "sad" songs, not wear sequined costumes, and work with a choreographer to make her dance moves more current. Tina refuses, comparing his demands to her time with Ike. She stands up for herself, stating that she refuses to be a "rag doll" with a microphone "shoved" in her face or "some man's puppet." She asserts her artistic control by revealing: "Let's get this straight: *I* picked *you*!" Afterwards, a stunned Roger begins to realize that Tina is not a meek victim of circumstance but a creative artist in her own right. Tina then surrounds herself with managers and producers who *encourage* her, rather than *control* her. Her personal and artistic growth is evident when she performs her rendition of "What's Love Got To Do With It" and signs with Capitol Records after negotiating a contract that includes a $2 million salary, 30% in royalties, and a jaguar. In so doing, the musical elevates Turner's legacy from the patron saint of domestic violence to a savvy businesswoman and creative genius.

Rather than allow the character Ike and their toxic marriage to dominate the narrative, Hall emphasizes Tina's saving grace: her grandmother Georgeanna. When Zelma abandons Anna-Mae, her father ships her off to live with his mother. While living with her highly religious grandmother, Anna-Mae experiences her unconditional love and encouragement to pursue her passion for singing. After watching a teenage Anna-Mae (Warren) sing along to Elvis Presley's song "Heartbreak Hotel," Georgeanna suggests that she return to live with her mother and sister in Memphis and record her own album. She initially refuses, stating that "the one person who loves me just trying to get rid of me and throw me out like trash!" However, Georgeanna loves her so much that she lets her go to St. Louis, even though this means leaving her behind. This emotional scene reaches a peak as Georgeanna begins singing, "Don't Turn Around" with Anna-Mae. Singing the song as a duet about the love between a grandmother and granddaughter, the pain of their separation, and the desire to let the younger generation of Blackgirls achieve their dreams, the pair give the song new meaning. Georgeanna continues to positively influence Anna-Mae's life, even after she becomes an adult and takes the stage name Tina. In one particularly touching scene, Georgeanna and Young Anna-Mae appear in her dressing room right before her important showcase and sing a rendition of the solemn reggae-sounding song "Tonight" by David Bowie and Iggy Pop. "Everything will be alright / Tonight," the ghostly duo sings, and in so doing, provides the encouragement Tina needs before performing one of the most important concerts of her life. While their prediction does come true—Tina's showcase performance proves her worth as a solo artist—she has to first overcome insurmountable odds navigating a racist, sexist, and agist music industry.

Tina addresses how racism, sexism, and ageism within the music industry have harmed Black artists. For example, after the showcase, a white representative of Capitol Records named Carpenter tells Roger that while the showcase was good, they would not sign Tina without "a sure-fire hit." When Roger presses him to explain this decision, Carpenter finally reveals the real reason for their disinterest in signing Tina to a record deal. "There's no way Capitol is ever gonna give this old nigger douchebag a deal. Now it's time to pull the plug on your charity case. Time to pull it now!" Carpenter explains. Tina overhears this conversation which motivates her to finally agree to experiment with new technology and sound. She understands that the popularity of music videos means that spectators only want to see "a young, hot blonde." Even knowing that her physical appearance works against her, she remains determined to have a solo career in rock. She takes a risk by recording a song that relies heavily on a synthesizer—a decision that eventually catapults her career with the hit song "What's Love Got To Do With It." Unfortunately, many Black talented artists never achieve this level of success. Hall exposes this harsh truth early on in the musical when Tina, Ike, and their bandmates are denied hotel accommodations during their Mississippi tour because of their race. As they make due by sleeping in a car, Ike reveals that his authorship was removed from the first rock 'n roll hit record and how his father was denied medical treatment at a white hospital after being beaten by white men after sleeping with a white woman. His father eventually died prematurely from these long-term injuries.[122] Unfortunately, Ike only discloses the perils of show business and white vigilante justice to manipulate Tina into promising to marry him and never leave him. Immediately afterward, two white police officers come out and ask why they are sleeping in a car and not a motel. When they answer, one of the white police officers responds, "Well, you still got to pay your motel bill unless you wanna check out early, nigger." Having had experiential knowledge of anti-Black violence, Ike understands this as ritual violence and tries his best to protect Tina. After telling her to get in the car, he tells her he must "pay the Motel Mississippi," and the scene ends. Collectively, these brief moments offer spectators snapshots of how white-authored violence of the past continues to inform the present circumstances for Black America.

Finally, Tina's decision to ignore familial and societal pressures and take part in a socially taboo relationship might inspire Black queer spectators to also openly express their sexual desires. After Tina's showcase, she travels to London for three weeks to record a demo for Capitol Records. Once there, she meets German music marketer Erwin Bach, and the two experience an instant sexual attraction. Before she departs, Erwin reveals that he is in love with her, but Tina immediately rejects him. "This fairytale ends here. I am sixteen years older than you. We come from opposite sides of the world. I have my kids to get back home to. This would never work," states Tina. This talk of love and attraction leads Tina to express her true desires in the rock song, "What's Love Got to Do With It" (see Figure 6.10). In the song, Tina describes her initial excitement about her physical attraction to Erwin and ends with her fear of having her heart broken. She later expresses that her fear that their age, race, and cultural differences would tear them apart is not too far-fetched, considering the fact that the two met in 1985, less than two decades after the US Supreme Court repealed anti-miscegenation laws. In addition, Tina already receives little support from her sister Alline, who disapproves of her singing "white music" and having a white manager. Alline even states, "Hell, next thing you know you gonna have a white boyfriend." Even though Tina argues that "Music ain't got no color," it takes an abundance of courage for her to declare, "I don't care if the folks [back home] don't like my choices." Erwin returns at the end of the musical, kisses Tina right before she exits to perform her concert, and the two agree to continue

Figure 6.10 Adrienne Warren (Tina) in *Tina: The Tina Turner Musical* (2019), Theatre Box Office trailer. Still image courtesy of the author. https://www.youtube.com/watch?v=5sSfdjGyc8Q

their love affair. Spectators in the know will understand that against all the odds, Turner and Bach did continue their relationship, eventually getting married. The "fairytale" did not end until Turner's death on May 24, 2023, and even then, Bach remained at her side.

With all of the musical's merit, critics and scholars do acknowledge that *Tina* does hit a few sour notes. The theatre critic David Rooney praised Warren's "extraordinary" performance but noted the "poor characterization of minor characters."[123] "With Ike mostly out of the picture in these scenes, only sketchily developed characters are left to interact with Tina, including Erwin Bach (Ross Lekites), the German record exec who would become her second husband," writes Rooney.[124] Indeed, the character Erwin only exists in the world of *Tina* as an important plot point: to fall in love with Tina. Furthermore, Duncan Wheeler found Hall's characterization of record producer Phil Spector (Steven Booth) quite troubling. "Given his documented lifetime of abusing women, culminating with incarceration for murdering an ex-lover, the narrative of Phil Spector paving the way for Tina's rebirth is unsettling," writes Wheeler.[125] Indeed, to highlight both Spector and sexism/racism within the music industry while also ignoring his crimes against women may feel like a gut punch to socially conscious spectators.[126] Finally, Wheeler notes that the musical does not fully attend to sexual harassment and abuse accusations made against Ike and Tina Turner by their background singer, P. P. Arnold (b. Patricia Ann Cole), during the heyday of the Ike and Tina Turner Revue. While the accusation existed prior to her publication of *Soul Survivor: The Autobiography* (2023), Arnold's memoir provides vivid descriptions of Tina contributing to a culture of sexual harassment during her time as an Ikette. "Ike also had a habit of chasing us around the dressing room with his dick out. Everybody laughed, Tina most of all, but I thought this was just nasty. He and Tina were always talking about giving head. I would gag imagining her doing this, but they said it opened your throat to sing better."[127] Arnold later describes in painful detail being raped by Ike Turner. She alleges that afterward, Ike offered her money, but she refused. She also remembers feeling trapped in the situation, with nowhere to turn. "I took a bath and cried and cried. I didn't know what to do. If I told my family they would demand I come home. I couldn't tell Tina. I really didn't want her thinking I was after Ike. I was used to always defending myself with my father and [husband] David and whenever I tried explaining myself to Tina, I always sounded defensive. She always thought I was being argumentative. Most importantly, I didn't want to lose my job," remembers Arnold.[128] The next year, Arnold left the tour and relocated to London to start her solo career.[129] Arnold's perspective presents a more nuanced view of Tina Turner as both a victim of abuse and an enabler. However, knowing that Tina Turner and her second husband, Erwin Bach, co-produced the musical, it should come as no surprise that these types of accusations are completely excised from *Tina*. Despite these flaws, *Tina* remains an important musical, offering three-dimensional roles for talented Black actresses across the globe.

King Kong

King Kong (2018) tells the story of Ann Darrow (Christiani Pitts), an aspiring Black actress who, like Tina Turner, ventures from her family farm into the city with the dream of becoming a star (see Figure 6.11). However, she quickly discovers that the blight of the Great Depression (1929–1939) extends to the Broadway stage. She attends audition after audition but fails to land a role and secure a job. When not auditioning, she stands outside in a bread line for free food. After one particularly cold day, she's turned away from the bread line, finds warmth in a bar, and happens to meet film director Carl Denham (Eric Williams Morris). Unfortunately, the bar offers little sanctuary as the predatory bartender (Harley Jay) nearly tosses her out on the streets for

Figure 6.11 Christiani Pitts (Ann Darrow) in *King Kong* (2019), King Kong Broadway trailer. Still image courtesy of the author. https://www.youtube.com/watch?v=rT3omqgy-Vc

loitering. When Ann states, "It's cold," and pleads with the bartender to let her stay, he counters by stating, "Honey, make it worth my while, and I'll think about keeping you warm," and pulls her toward him.[130] Angered by his solicitation of sex work, she delivers a slow-motion push to the bartender's chest and smacks him soundly (and slowly) across the face. When the bartender tries to retaliate, Denham raises his fist to stop him, and the bartender retreats. Afterward, in real time, Ann politely states, "Thank you for the defense. I didn't ask for it or need it." Ann's spirit and grit in the face of danger capture Denham's interest. He then reveals that he's been looking for an actress with the courage to star in his latest film and travel on location to "a journey into the impossible." Without blinking an eye, she asks for a script or contract and Denham responds by vowing, "I promise I can make you a star... a queen." Having just performed her "I want" song, aptly titled "Queen of New York," Ann readily agrees without fully understanding the danger that awaits her on the prehistoric Skull Island. During the long voyage on the *SS Wanderer* to Skull Island, Ann meets Lumpy (Erik Lochtefeld), Denham's slow-witted assistant, who offers her company and friendship. Once on the island, Ann becomes separated from Denham, Lumpy, Captain Englehorn (Rory Donovan), and the dozen or so crew members, and is captured by

Kong (voiced by Jon Hoche). Rather than wait for rescue, Ann lures Kong to sleep by singing the ballad, "Full Moon Lullaby," and escapes. When Ann rejoins the company of men, Denham decides to capture Kong and convinces her to help him. After successfully securing Kong, Denham brings the oversized ape to New York and displays him in his new musical. Eventually, Kong breaks free of his chains, is shot down by the New York police, and falls to his death in midtown Manhattan.

King Kong's path to Broadway took about ten years of development, traveling the globe to finally reach its destination of New York, New York. Global Creatures, a live entertainment company owned by Gerry Ryan and Carmen Pavlovic, produced King Kong, their first traditional stage production, following a series of successful animatronic shows, including *Walking With Dinosaurs* and *How to Train Your Dragon*. Global Creatures originally mounted *King Kong* in Melbourne in 2013 after five years of preparation and five months of rehearsal. For this iteration of the musical, the openly gay writer Craig Lucas provided the book, with music by Marius de Vries, lyrics by Michael Mitnick and Lucas, and additional music and lyrics by 3D, Sarah McLachlan, Guy Garvey, Justice, and The Avalanches. The Melbourne production starred Esther Hannaford, a white blonde actress in the lead role of Ann Darrow. The Melbourne production received mixed reviews, with the *Guardian* reporting that "there were awe-struck descriptions of the 20-foot-tall Kong and the elaborate puppetry that brings him to life, but less enthusiasm for the book by Craig Lucas and the mix of original music and contemporary songs of the score."[131] In response to less-than-stellar reviews, the creative team brought lyricist Eddie Perfect and playwright Jack Thorne—known for his Tony Award-winning stage play *Harry Potter and the Cursed Child* and films *Wonder* and *Enola Holmes*—on board to revamp the songs and rewrite the book, respectively. The new songs and Thorne's book were then workshopped in 2016 with blonde actress Lora Lee Gayer and again in a 2017 workshop with Filipino and Mexican actress Eva Noblezada before officially opening in New York at Broadway Theatre on October 5, 2018, with Pitts as Ann Darrow.

All versions of the musical were based on Delos W. Lovelace's 1932 novelization of the film script and the 1933 film *King Kong*. Merian C. Cooper and Edgar Wallace provided the story for the 1933 film, with Ruth Rose and James Ashmore Creelman credited for the screenplay. Actress Fay Wray originated the role of Ann Darrow, replacing her naturally dark hair with a blonde wig to complete the iconic image of feminine white beauty.[132] The

Broadway version, however, radically departed from the original source material by casting a Black actress as the female lead role; eliminating the character Charley, a Chinese cook steeped in Asian stereotypes; and removing racist depictions of Black inhabitants of Skull Island and the corresponding theme of primitivism. In addition, the Broadway production made critical departures from the original film and previous Melbourne production by adding the character Lumpy and eliminating Ann Darrow's love interest, Jack Driscoll, from the narrative. The Broadway production team hoped these changes, coupled with the spectacular animatronic feat that is Kong, would strengthen the narrative and make the musical more palatable for contemporary audiences. Unfortunately, New York theatre critics also panned the Broadway adaptation, *King Kong* failed to draw in large audiences, and the musical has gone down in infamy as a box office failure.

The 2018 production of *King Kong* ran on Broadway for less than a year and received scathing reviews from theatre critics. For example, *The New York Times* critics Scott Heller and Nancy Coleman write that "the show eventually opened to stinging reviews, with most of the praise going to the towering title characters himself, a colossal marionette clocking in at 20 feet tall and 2,000 pounds. For the week ending June 23, it grossed just shy of $783,000 at the box office, only 53 percent of its potential take."[133] Furthermore, *The Guardian* reports that Thorne's book, de Vries's score, Perfect's songs, and Drew McOnie's direction, "provide a clumsy retread of the 1933 movie though now with a less coded racism, less coded rape and fewer anxieties about the tension between primitivism and modernity. What's left? A show that makes breathlessly little sense and is rarely even fun. The people who brought you *Walking with Dinosaurs* have now brought you *Lumbering with Primates*. This is less a musical than an amusement park ride perpetually needing repairs, a feat of projection design (Peter England) with occasional dance breaks."[134] In addition to terrible reviews, the production failed to capture the sustained attention of audiences, becoming a box office flop after failing to recoup the cost of the $30 million dollar production budget.[135] However, Pitts's performance as Ann did garner more positive reviews, with *The Guardian* noting, "If King Kong is an allegory of the havoc that ensues when you give a star subpar material, well done. Ann, who spends one night as Kong's prisoner before he's etherized and brought to New York, has to sing lines like 'You gave men an education / In how to be free. . . . Perfect can't be bothered to rhyme his songs."[136] In addition to the lack of "provocative or insightful songwriting," *The New York Times* critic Jesse Green argues that the problem with the *King Kong* adaption lies in its desire to tell two stories. "One is a morality tale about the evil of trapping a living being in a cheap entertainment scheme. [In addition,] a feminist angle is attempted, not very convincingly. [. . .] What is gained in bringing 'King Kong' to the stage?" asks Green.[137]

Despite this criticism, *King Kong* does provide meaning for Black queer feminist spectators living in the wake of the call to protect Black lives. There are moments in the production that allow Black queer feminist spectators to take pleasure in witnessing the "camp" production modes, the talent of a Blackgirl leading lady and her embodied feminism, and the musical's (albeit, unintentional) critique of racist casting practices. Perhaps most importantly, Black queer feminist spectators may draw meaning from Kong's new characterization and his painful death at the hands of the police. In other words, Black queer feminist spectators who witness the 2018 production of *King Kong* might understand the narrative as a metaphor for the ritual murder of Black men in America and Ann's loving embrace of Kong as a call to actively protect Black men.

To begin, Black queer feminist spectators might read the Broadway production—from the slow-motion action sequences to the visual representation of Skull Island, to the use of electronic dance music during Kong's "rampages"—as the embodiment of camp. By camp, I refer to filmmaker and activist Susan Sontag's conceptualization that "the essence of Camp is its love of the unnatural: of artifice and exaggeration."[138] This sensibility, which is often associated with gay male subculture, is not something that is universally shared or appreciated among spectators. Indeed, camp is a subjective, often solitary experience whereby spectators "convert the serious into the frivolous" by taking pleasure in the fantastic, androgyny, and outrageous spectacle.[139] Green writes that in the case of *King Kong*, "The camp here is all accidental. The Skull Island jungle looks like green spaghetti with phlegm balls. (The scenic and projection designer is Peter England.) But the oppressiveness of the music and the over-intensity of the staging never allow you to laugh at, and therefore enjoy, the ludicrousness of the story."[140] Perhaps Green could, as an openly gay white cis man, recognize the musical's camp aesthetic—but could not, as an arbiter of "taste," thoroughly enjoy the spectacle before him. Regardless of Green's authority on the matter, Black queer feminist spectators do have the capacity to take in and enjoy the campiness that is *King Kong*. Spectators are first introduced to a camp aesthetic when Ann delivers a slow-motion punch at the untoward barman and this aesthetic continues when she reaches Skull Island. As Ann reaches the jungles of Skull Island, spectators are greeted with a blast of an epic and intense-sounding score that could easily play during the emotional peak of *The Lord of the Rings* movie. Spectators are then visually assaulted as a dozen or so groups of green "vines" are revealed downstage, supplemented with additional vines projected from the sides of the stage. Ensemble members enter the stage wearing green full-body-covered spandex suits and dance between the said vines, weaving in and out as crewmen from the *SS Wanderer* move in slow motion through the jungle carrying rifles. Next, Ann appears onstage, delighted by the "jungle," and tells Denham, "You know, I could really like it here!" Spectators cannot help but chuckle at the disconnect between Ann's genuine excitement over what appears to many as "green spaghetti with phlegm balls."

Another major moment of camp aesthetics occurs during Kong's kidnapping of Ann. The action sequence begins with a flood of movement projections through a darkened jungle. Spectators hear Ann scream and Kong growl but can only see her white dress and his ultra-white teeth, as his body and her face are obscured in darkness. "The Ascent" score blasts, ending with a silhouette of Kong and a flash of fire behind him that fully reveals an upright Kong in all his splendor. For some spectators, this reveal—which includes two visible cords supporting Kong's upright "long-waisted baby body"—might prove laughable.[141] The "intensity" continues as Kong protects Ann from a new threat: a giant cobra. A new sweeping score, "The Cobra Fight," blasts as a silhouetted Kong grabs the cobra by the throat and squeezes it until spectators are hit with a projection of cobra blood spatter on a scrim. Kong and the cobra hold this position for several seconds—as if performing a climactic scene in a nineteenth-century melodrama—before concluding the fight. Later, when Kong wakes up and discovers Ann has escaped his lair, another intense action sequence begins. "The Descent," which features a techno dance beat, plays as a projection of the moon moves towards the audience before bursting into a thousand pieces as Kong roars his displeasure. During his pursuit, spectators see a profile of Kong running and roaring with gleaming white teeth agape as projections of firmament incircle him. These long, drawn-out action sequences were likely intended to be frightening, but for those with camp sensibilities, the "intense moments" come across as hilarious. However, appreciating camp allows spectators to experience joy, rather than displeasure, in witnessing these so-called creative "failures."[142] A Black queer feminist spectator's ability to experience pleasure becomes a particularly powerful contrast to the end of the musical, which concludes with the brutal murder of Kong.

While Black queer feminist spectators may revel in the production's camp aesthetics, the creative team took their production of *King Kong* seriously. Sontag writes that "in naïve, or pure, Camp, the essential element is seriousness, a seriousness that fails. Of course, not all seriousness that fails can be redeemed as Camp. Only that which has the proper mixture of the exaggerated, the fantastic, the passionate, and the naïve."[143] Regarding *King Kong*, the 30 million dollar production budget was no laughing matter to investors. The creative team understood that producers needed a return on their investment. As such, the creative team utilized an epic-sounding musical score and state-of-the-art technology—including animatronics, more than a dozen puppeteers, and dazzling projection designs—to create an extraordinary production for the ages. *The New York Times* theatre critics Jesse Green and Ben Brantley even note the production's unintentional use of camp, but then erroneously dismiss this as "accidental" and, therefore, a lower form of camp.[144] However, spectators in the know could argue that the creative team's serious and passionate embrace of the extraordinary through technological wonderment created a "pure" form of camp.[145] Sontag writes that "the pure examples of Camp are unintentional; they are dead serious."[146] Thus, rather than see *King Kong* as a box office failure, I argue that Black queer feminist spectators can read the production as a "success in certain passionate failures."[147] Additionally, spectators can take pleasure in the historic casting of Ann—not as a traditionally frightened blond beauty, but as a strong and talented Blackgirl fully capable of articulating her feminist beliefs.

In the Broadway production, Ann Darrow (Pitts) refuses to accept the life that many Blackgirls in the 1930s would take: that of forming a heteronormative union. The theatre critic Ben Brantley rightly suggests that "the equation of ape captivity with the oppression of women" is a major theme of the musical.[148] Indeed, Ann resonates with Kong's imprisonment because of her experiential knowledge of gender oppression. However, Ann uses her agency to fight the forces that would render her the property of a prospective husband. Instead, she moves to New York with nothing but a suitcase and dreams of stardom. She auditions for a role in a dancing/singing chorus and is quickly told "Next!" by a white male casting director. Facing rejection, Ann pleads for feedback to help her improve and is cut off by the casting director who gruffly yells, "Next!" Rather than internalize this rejection, Ann returns his dismissiveness with sass, stating: "Okay, then. I'll just dance, dance my way onto the street then." Despite this disrespectful treatment, Ann maintains a sense of self, declaring her resilience in the upbeat number, "Queen of New York." Ann sings: "Another arrow shoots an arrow through the chest / But every 'no' only brings me closer to 'yes' / New York drop me with a body shot, / But I'm not staying down / I'll fight like hell, so ring that bell, / Look who who's comin' out swingin' in the open rounds!" Likening herself to a boxer, Ann refuses to crumble, even when she experiences the pain of incivility and rejection. Her thoughts then shift to memories of the past, providing exposition for the audience. She sings/tells spectators that she has freshly arrived from a farm in the Midwest but is determined to become queen of New York by self-fashioning a new identity. She proudly boasts that she has given herself "a new name, a new accent, a new backstory, and a brand new walk." Ann then shares her innermost hope that by becoming a star, she can experience freedom. Ann sings: "The story ends when you're some man's wife, / I don't want to bend to fit some man's life / I can't give up til I'm up on stage, / Cause nobody's ever gonna put me back in that cage / So if poverty's how it's gotta be, / At least I'm not some man's property/ No one answers for Ann but me!" With these lyrics, Ann takes a critical departure from previous iterations of Ann Darrow, whose "story" typically ends with an engagement to misogynist John "Jack" Driscoll. In this new iteration, Ann views heteronormative marriage as another form of prison, a "cage" that will restrict her autonomy. A life in show business—even if she never becomes a star—offers a more viable alternative. Unfortunately, at no point does "Queen of New York" even hint at how being a *Blackgirl* informs her life choices or opportunities in show business.

While the *King Kong* script fails to mention Ann's blackness or how systemic racism impedes her growth within show business, Black queer feminist spectators might understand how her fictional story relates to a much larger (and very real) problem within the theatre industry. Teer exposed this system of oppression—specifically addressing racist casting practices in the television industry—in her *New York Times* article, "The Black Woman: She Does Exist" (1967). Teer writes that Black actresses have historically been confined to two basic character types: a domestic if she has "Negroid" features or a sex symbol if she is "Caucasoid."[149] Teer explains:

> This restriction has resulted from racist concepts created in the days of slavery which made the Negro woman either a work animal or a producing animal, consequently stripping her of any traits of intelligence and any

> attributes of femininity. [. . .] These antiquated concepts have greatly, if not completely, stifled the Negro actress' development as an entity in the industry. They determine what kind of roles she should or can apply for. She does not simply fight the battle of getting a job based on her talent as an actress; she must also fight the battle of being forced to conform to a Caucasian standard of beauty and she must fight the battle of racism which excludes the reality of her existence as a human being.[150]

Before audiences even meet Ann, she undergoes a transformation to make herself more appealing to casting directors. She now speaks with a standard American dialect; rejects her birth name, Anna Mae Darson, and assumes a new identity as "Ann Darrow"; and disavows her agrarian roots to better align her history with that of the New York elite. Despite her superb talent and best efforts to remove her cultural roots and present herself as an urbane leading lady, casting directors take only a few seconds to judge her appearance and dismiss her. Teer understood how stereotypes about Black people inform the casting system and wanted to completely reshape it for the betterment of the American public. "This system of casting is detrimental because it adds to the miseducation of the American public, which already knows that Negro women can clean a house, sing and dance. What the viewer does not know is that there are many Negro actresses capable of performing in ingenue, character, comedienne and leading lady roles," writes Teer.[151] While unintentional, Black queer feminist spectators might learn this important historical truth as they bear witness to the incredibly talented Pitts, performing as a 1930s Ann, face continual dismissal by white casting directors.

Despite the ongoing call to increase diversity, equity, and inclusion on theatre stages, it is still considered an exception to the rule for Black actresses to headline a Broadway show. Casting Pitts as the leading lady in a big-budget Broadway spectacle certainly defies the odds for most Black actresses. However, Pitts recalls needing to cultivate tremendous inner strength to endure her journey to Broadway. "There are some parts of this experience that are unique to me as a Black woman that, for a very long time, I contributed to, 'Oh, that's the business.' It's hard. You're going to get a thousand 'noes' and two 'yeses,' and that's just how it works. It wasn't until I actually got on Broadway and saw the opportunities that were presented to me that I said, 'Oh, okay, okay.' So, you do have to have a thick skin to say, 'I know you may only see me in this way, but I see myself as so much more,'" remembers Pitts.[152] In other words, Pitts's ability to eventually land the roles of Denise/

Jane (understudy) in *A Bronx Tale: The Musical* and Ann in *King Kong* should not serve as a narrative of "overcoming" racism. Rather, Pitts's story should provide a call for Black actresses and their allies to continue to wage personal and collective war against stereotypical roles and limited opportunities in show business. Pitts remembers:

> There's just so many stereotypes when it comes to what Black women are going to be on Broadway. What show can they sell? Who's going to come to see them do X, Y, and Z? I think there is this belief that they are only going to come to see us do one type of person, one type of character. And it can be really hard not to believe that. [. . .] I think my journey was just honestly trying my hardest to believe in myself enough to know that I'm not going to allow anybody to tell me I can only be one type of person or that people will only see me in one type of way—because we have a skillset. That's why we're all here. We all have the skillset to try and transform into other people and that doesn't stop at my blackness. That doesn't stop because I'm a Black woman.[153]

Pitts's refusal to accept limited roles has guided her career, motivating her to audition for the role of Ann, which a white and beautiful blond actress traditionally plays.

Fay Wray originated the role of the racially coded Ann Darrow, portraying her as a meek, fragile, and virginal damsel in distress in the 1933 film. Wray's Ann meets film director Carl Denham (Robert Armstrong) while on his quest to find a "beautiful" actress to play the lead in his upcoming picture. Unfortunately, Denham hits roadblocks due to being blacklisted by the Actors' Equity Association, politician Will H. Hays, and New York agents. Taking matters into his own hands, Denham searches the streets of New York for an attractive woman to accompany him to Skull Island. When his search seems futile, he stops for a cigarette and observes a starving Ann get caught stealing from a fruit stand. As the Greek proprietor grabs her, she can only weakly struggle to remove herself from his grasp. Denham intervenes, gives the fruit seller a dollar, and catches Ann as she stumbles back, half collapsing in his arms.[154] When she does regain her footing, the camera provides the first closeup of Ann, whose wide-eyed expression emphasizes her beauty and fright.[155] This opportune moment seals her fate with Denham, who supplies her with food and an offer to star in his newest film. While Wray's Ann describes herself as a "country gal" and seems unbothered by the thought of a long sea voyage to an unnamed locale, she does meekly hesitate about taking part in anything sexual. However, when Denham promises that his proposition is "strictly business," she quickly agrees to depart with him the next morning.[156] Once Kong, the king of the Black natives, lays his eyes on Wray's Ann, he desires to make her his newest "bride." Kong aggressively pursues, destroying native huts and killing white sailors and natives who get in his way. When Kong captures Ann, he plays cat and mouse with her, treats her like a rag doll, and tears off her clothes until she appears half-naked in what can only be described as a metaphorical rape. Throughout these action sequences, Wray's Ann does not speak or try to rescue herself. Instead, she screams, hides, and awaits the sailors to rescue her. Wray's characterization follows the *King Kong* shooting script, which only emphasizes Ann's subordinate role in the narrative, most often referring to her as "the girl," "the terrified girl," and "the screaming girl."[157] Throughout the film, sailor John "Jack" Driscoll (Bruce Cabot) rescues Ann a handful of times, including when he advises the white police officers to shoot Kong down without harming her while on top of the Empire State Building. When Kong finally dies, a tearful Ann is rescued off the ledge of the building and falls into Driscoll's passionate embrace as Denham summarizes the entire course of events, stating: "Oh no, 'twasn't the aviators. . . . It was Beauty killed the Beast."[158] In other words, Kong's obsession with capturing Ann, seen here as the exemplar of white beauty—blond, frail, virginal, and meek—ultimately cost him his life. Black queer feminist spectators who watch this film might find Wray's Ann a wholly unsatisfying leading lady and "read" Kong as the embodiment of the racist Mandingo or Black Brute stereotype, a beast ready and willing to insult and assault beautiful white women at every turn.

In addition to fostering a gendered and racialized dramatization of the beauty/beast metaphor, the original 1933 has also drawn contemporary criticism for utilizing the theme of primitivism to malign Black people (especially Blackgirls) and culture. In the 1933 film, the mostly Black inhabitants of Skull Island appear ignorant, superstitious, irrational, and sensual. In stark contrast, the white company (i.e., Ann, Driscoll, Denham, and sailors) appear as arbiters of knowledge, logic, reason, and civilization. These racial mores become most pronounced during a native ritual on Skull Island, witnessed by (uninvited) white guests. Appearing as if time has stood still, the Native Chief (Noble Johnson) stands tall, holding an ancient-looking spear in his hand while sporting an afro, a feathered crown, a large feather necklace, an assortment of bangle bracelets, a very short grass skirt, and white face paint of no cultural significance. Native Chief's warriors stand guard, wearing similar but less elaborate costumes, and watch the ritual unfold. Two groups of male dancers begin the ritual sacrifice by appearing as Kong, each wearing an ape costume (i.e., a jacket made of feathers). The dancers act as primates, beating their chests, chanting gibberish, and spinning around to the drum beat. Meanwhile, Sacrifice Victim (Etta McDaniel), a beautiful Blackgirl who appears scared and barely clothed kneels at the altar as two older Black women place white leis around her neck and dozens of tribal members look on. When Ann (Wray) expresses curiosity about the unfolding ceremony, Driscoll (Cabot) remains cautious, stating: "Up to some of their heathen tricks. Now don't go rushing out to see."[159] With these words, Driscoll performs linguistic acrobatics, positioning the natives as uncivilized and deceptive while simultaneously ignoring the fact that he and his company are intruding upon native land and spying on a *private* ceremony. When Native Chief does notice the presence of the white company, he orders them to leave until he lays eyes on Ann. Native Chief then points to Sacrifice Victim and speaking in a nonsense language, states: "Sani sita malem ati kow dia malem ma pakeno," meaning, "I will give six women like this for your woman of gold."[160] In other words, Native Chief perceives Ann and her golden beauty as having six times the value of one Blackgirl. When the white men refuse to sell Ann, Native Chief resorts to stealth and orders Witch King (Steve Clemente) to kidnap Ann and place her on the altar as a gift for Kong. These notoriously racist scenes not only present Black people as ignorant, deceitful, and superstitious savages but also as having no real culture. Perhaps even more alarming, Blackgirls appear voiceless, undervalued by Black communities, and mere pawns in a war between Black and white men. The film only reinforces the dominant society's perception of Blackgirls as unattractive, worthless, and undeserving of protection.

However, rather than confront the racism embedded within its source material head-on, Broadway creatives opted to eliminate Black native characters and cast Pitts in the role of Ann without regard for her race. Whether intentional or not, this decision gives the appearance of "color blindness" while also sidestepping the anti-Black rhetoric within the original film. According to Pitts, the New York agency Tara Rubin Casting saw her talent and without regard to her race, cast her in the role of a lifetime after months of strenuous auditioning. The entertainment lawyer Kristin Bria Hopkins, theatre historian Brandi Wilkins Catanese, and countless critics have discussed the inherent problems with "color-blind" or nontraditional casting in American commercial theatre.[161] Hopkins writes that "'color-blind,' or non-traditional casting is generally regarded as the best method for casting diverse theatre productions. Color-blind casting removes race from the casting process, and employs the best actor for the role."[162] However, we do not live in a "color-blind" society, nor should we want to. Ignoring minoritized bodies (i.e., "I don't see race") does not eliminate racism. Rather, doing so only allows the structures that harm the most vulnerable among us to continue unchecked. With these important truths in mind, Hopkins issues a call for casting directors to embrace "color-conscious" casting as a more viable way to foster a more diverse, equitable, and inclusive theatre industry. Writing in the wake of the musical smash hit, *Hamilton*, which includes a large cast of mostly brown and Black performers, Hopkins expressed dismay at the overall lack of opportunities afforded to minority performers. Hopkins writes:

> Minorities are still cast at lower rates in commercial theatre productions than White actors. There are productions where race is integral to a show, but, apart from those few circumstances, minorities do not enjoy an equal playing field under the color-blind casting method. [. . .] Instead of color-blind casting, race should be a factor taken into consideration during the casting process. This is called "color-consciousness." Color-conscious casting requires casting directors and producers to accept that the country is growing in diversity, and the stage should reflect the changing demographic make-up of the United States.[163]

If we want American stages to truly represent our tremendous diversity, casting directors must be included as an integral part of this change. Undoubtedly, Pitts understood the socio-political significance of casting her, a Blackgirl, to portray the beautiful and iconic Ann Darrow and used her agency to voice her concerns about Black representation within the musical.

While the all-white creatives were unprepared to consider the nuances of casting Black ensemble members in a historically racist storyline, Pitts was equipped to influence revisions of Jack Thorne's script. As a highly intelligent, deeply critical, and talented actress, Pitts was keenly aware of the problematic depictions of Black people within the original film and the lack of Black voices on the creative team. Knowing this, Pitts advocated for color-consciousness considerations within the musical's production modes. "I think they went into this wanting to cast someone who could portray strength. That was their thing. So, they didn't go into thinking or seeking a Black actress necessarily. They just wanted somebody who was going to not be your average ingenue. And so, with that being said, the script had no mention at all, no reference to what her experience would have been as a Black woman, no reference to any sort of anything," remembers Pitts.[164] Furthermore, the all-white creative team's lack of racial awareness of the historical period of the musical proved problematic during rehearsals with Black cast members.

> There were certain lines that we had to go in and ask, "Okay, it's 1930s America. You have a lot of Black sailors on this ship, and they are singing about being slaves. Now, I know that you all just mean hard-working (that the captain of the ship is working them like slaves). However, you have a lot of Black sailors singing about slavery in 1933. So, are these people channeling a legitimate fear? Are they really talking about something that their great-grandparents experienced?" We would have to constantly go through the script and say, "Let's keep in mind the legitimate historical context and figure out if we're turning a blind eye or if we're being realistic." So, we ended up cutting that line from the musical because they just wanted to focus on the relationship between Carl Denham and myself, remembers Pitts.[165]

Unfortunately, rather than truly confront the horrors of Jim Crow America, creatives chose to eliminate them altogether. Pitts remembers another revision involving Ann's characterization. Instead of Ann having roots in the South as was originally decided, creatives decided to have her come from the Midwest since they did not "feel capable of telling that specific story."[166] Pitts, however, remained cognizant of the racial climate of the past and current historical moment throughout rehearsals. In no way could she ignore the fact that for the first time, a Blackgirl would play the lead within the hugely popular *King Kong* franchise.

Pitts understood that although Thorne's book did not address her blackness within the world of the musical, spectators would nonetheless "read" her racialized and gendered body onstage.[167] Pitts was cognizant that by placing the creative team's vision of a "strong" Ann on a Black actress's body, the production ran the risk of (unintentionally) reproducing the strong Black woman archetype onstage. Rather than depict Ann as impervious to pain and suffering, Pitts found opportunities to depict her as having a spectrum of emotions. Pitts remembers:

> When we started working on this version of *King Kong*, Ann Darrow was written completely differently. We had a good time in the rehearsal process of me trying to ask the team and offer the team some insight into her moments of vulnerability. When can she be gentle? When can she be fragile? Is she trying to be gentle and fragile because that's what sells? What is that like for her? So, it was really nice to be able to create this character who is essentially really bold and courageous but only because she felt like she had to be. Not because she was naturally. So, it was really fun to find her natural softness and her natural ability to be an ingenue and then have to fight that because no one took her seriously and because no one would believe in her. That was a nuance that I don't think had been tapped into when it came to the franchise because that wasn't important. What was important was for Ann to be really soft and really beautiful and that was pretty much the extent of who she needed to be to progress the plot. So, it was nice that that wasn't the case for us.[168]

The creative team encouraged Pitts to fully embrace her creative impulses, which included drawing from her personal family history to give Ann a greater nuance. Pitts remembers: "I told them, 'You know, my grandmother was born in 1933. Her mother was around Ann Darrow's age at this time. What would she have been doing if she was able to follow her legitimate passions and move? She was a creative but didn't end up pursuing anything creative because she didn't have the means. It just wasn't possible for her. But what would that have been like?' I was able to bring that into the team, and then we were able to discuss what that would actually mean for this little Black girl chasing her dreams by herself."[169] The creative team liked Pitts's idea of channeling the past so much that they gave Ann the middle name "Mae" in honor of Pitts's great-grandmother, Cora Mae Cook. Portraying "Anna Mae" now had personal and professional meaning for Pitts.

> That was so much fun to pretend to be my great-grandmother on the Broadway stage. It was epic for me. I, myself, was doing something that was making history (that was a big deal for me, for sure), but then I was also thinking about my actual great-grandmother in that time who did not have the ability to pursue her dreams in that way. *What if*? Those were stakes and things that I was proud to be able to bring to the role that is unique to my Blackness. Again, the creatives didn't ask for that. That was just me asking

> them, "Hey, I had these ideas. This is what this means to me. Can we play around with this?" remembers Pitts.[170]

While Pitts was allowed to refine her character's emotional depth and influence the representation of blackness within the production modes, not every Black actress is afforded such opportunities.

Ultimately, Pitts's characterization of Ann as a gentle and courageous Blackgirl radically departs from Wray's performance in the original 1933 film. Spectators witness Pitts perform Ann's strength and vulnerability throughout the musical (see Figure 6.12). This duality is perhaps best reflected when Denham directs Ann in a test shoot aboard the *SS Wanderer*. Denham asks Ann, now draped in a lavish sequined white gown, to introduce herself to the crew while he films. Now the center of attention, Ann stands on a crate and awkwardly greets the sailors, fumbling over her words. By this moment, spectators have seen Ann find the courage to punch a barman for his attempted assault and then become somewhat self-conscious when asked to perform a simple introduction. Spectators further witness Ann's many layers when Denham orders the sailors to help him get her to scream. As the sailors sneak behind her and yell, "Boo!," she merely laughs at their antics. As a last resort, a now frustrated Denham tries to frighten Ann by describing the monster that awaits them on Skull Island. The two have the following exchange:

Figure 6.12 Christiani Pitts (Ann Darrow) in *King Kong* (2019), King Kong Broadway trailer. Still image courtesy of the author. https://www.youtube.com/watch?v=rT3omqgy-Vc

DENHAM: There is an eye looking at you. Can you see it? . . . He breathes and you can hear it, smell it, feel it. You're helpless. Yes. And there is no one around who can help you.

ANN: And I don't have a gun or a knife?

Ann moves into a fighting stance with an imaginary knife.

DENHAM: No, you're not armed. Why would you be armed? The beast gets closer still and you can smell the blood of kills that he's made. You know that you are trapped with him on Skull Island. He opens his mouth and he roars. And you, Ann, you scream like you have never screamed before.

Ann growls and throws her fists in the air.

ANN: I know what you want from me but I'm just not a damsel in distress. I'm sorry.[171]

In contrast to Wray, Pitts does not scream in fright or wait for a man to save her. Instead, she takes action just as she does in Denham's imaginary scenario. For example, when Captain Englehorn and his men pull their guns on Denham and try to throw him overboard for failing to give them coordinates, Ann threatens to use a "gas bomb detonator" if they don't release him. Captain Englehorn and his crew respond to Ann's order by pointing their guns towards her. Rather than show fear in the face of possible death, Ann continues her threat, warning them: "I came here to make a picture and that is what I intend to do. You ever hear it's bad luck to bring a dame onboard a ship? Well, you damn right it is. And I'll take you all down with me if you don't let me make my movie!" With Denham's encouragement, Ann roars and Captain Englehorn orders his crew to lower their weapons. It is only after Denham's release that she admits to using deception to save him (i.e., the "gas bomb detonator" is actually a curling iron). The street-smarts Ann acquired while living in New York—including finding a place to sleep in Central Park, scavenging for food, and making homemade "blush" by cutting herself and rubbing the blood on her cheeks for auditions—help her to assert herself and think quickly on her feet. Without mincing words, she tells Denham, "That stunt with the detonator, I did that for me, not you. You are, for better or worse my way out. . . . I came into this with my eyes open and open they still are." In contrast to Wray's portrayal of a naive, submissive, and voiceless Ann, Pitt's Ann becomes an icon of vulnerability and inner strength as she roars with defiance, outsmarts her more powerful adversaries, and uses her gift of song to rescue herself.

While Black queer feminist spectators might prefer Pitts's more physically demanding and feminist-leaning depiction than Wray's damsel-in-distress performance, theatre critics certainly did not. In his scathing review of the production, Ben Brantley includes unflattering comparisons between Pitts and Wray, even throwing pop singer Katy Perry into the mix. "Even the screams lacked eloquence. Fay Wray, the star of the original, is best remembered for her earsplitting howls of terror when she's in the big guy's clutches. But our intrepid Ann is incapable of screaming in fear. Instead, she roars, and that's what attracts her soul mate Kong to her. Unfortunately, I didn't hear a lot of Katy Perry power in Ms. Pitts's scream," remembers Brantley.[172] Clearly disappointed in Pitt's characterization of a fearless Ann, Brantley also finds her "roar" a poor imitation of the strength found in Perry's 2013 girl power anthem, "Roar." Released in the same year as the Melbourne production of *King Kong*, Perry's music video begins by mirroring the damsel-in-distress adventure narrative. Perry initially appears as a frightened ingenue who only narrowly survives a plane crash into a remote jungle. However, after witnessing a tiger maul her cis-male companion—an Indiana Jones-type adventurer—Perry casts aside her "damsel-in-distress" role and uses her inner strength and intellect to survive her harsh surroundings. She forms a spear out of her stiletto heel for protection, makes a garment out of leaves, and tames the aggressive tiger with her courageous roar. By the end of the video, Perry forms an unlikely community with the wild animals: a monkey sits on her shoulder, an elephant allows her to paint its nails pink, and the tiger sports a collar with the inscription, "Kitty Purry." While Pitts does not create a menagerie with her roar, Black queer feminist spectators may read her performance—including her incredible physicality—as the embodiment of Perry's hook: "I got the eye of a tiger, a fighter / Dancing through the fire / 'Cause I am a champion, and you're gonna hear me roar / Louder, louder than a lion / 'Cause I am a champion, and you're gonna hear me roar."[173] In addition to portraying Ann as a fighter who takes swings at predatory men, Pitts's performance also showcases her physical strength. During each performance, Pitts climbed up and down the gigantic Kong puppet, hung from "vines," danced her heart out, and hit incredible notes while suspended in a harness. To do this successfully and to ensure her own safety, Pitts underwent an intense workout regimen with a personal trainer to acquire the upper body strength needed to hold on to something for an extended period, should technology fail. "It felt like I was training for a really long race or prepping for a journey and that's what it ended up being. Every show was different, and every week, something new was happening because it was the first time that type of technology was being used so consistently.

So, things were constantly changing, but physically, I was ready for that," remembers Pitts.[174] Indeed, admiration for Pitts's physical strength is but one of the many reasons Black queer feminist spectators might find pleasure in witnessing a performance of *King Kong*.

Black queer feminist spectators may find *King Kong*'s thematical comparison between Kong's imprisonment and the second-class citizenship of women quite compelling. This theme becomes most overt as Denham makes plans to introduce Kong to New York audiences via a Vaudeville-style musical. After Ann refuses to follow Denham's direction to scream during rehearsals, a battle of wills ensues. Ann confronts Denham about his treatment of Kong—the morose, oversized gorilla refuses to eat—and demands he return Kong to Skull Island. Unmoved by Ann's change of heart, Denham puts her in her place, stating: "All I need you to do is stand in a dress, look pretty, and scream. There are thousands, thousands of other girls like you." When she does not back down, Denham continues to humiliate Ann, roughly grabbing her by the face and threatening to take away her new clothes, jewels, and career. "You're doing this. Because if you don't all your dreams—all of this—it won't happen and you will go back to begging for pocket change. So scream for him. Scream for me. Scream for the money. All that matters is that you will scream. I can destroy you as easily as I made you," states Denham. Ann responds to her conversation with Denham (who is now firmly entrenched in the role of melodramatic villain) and with the song, "Last of Our Kind." In this contemporary-sounding pop ballad, Ann sings about the pressure to perform her role in society and her desperation to break free. As she compares her captivity to Kong's, stars are projected on a scrim behind her, and lights slowly reveal a chained Kong. Ann sings: "I am just a woman / They say that's how I'm designed / Speak only when I'm asked / And pray that I'm the last so brutally designed." Ann also grieves the fact that people see Kong as "a monster with no soul" and treat her as a voiceless woman. In the next verse, Ann sings: "From birth we've both been playing / A game we cannot win / Never break the locks / Or ever leave the box / The world has put us in." She later adds: "A prisoner of history / Another wasted mind / But ain't we alike / Both you and I / We can survive this you know." This "radio-ready" ballad does more than any scream ever could. "Last of Our Kind" functions as a "girl power" musical anthem on the level of Perry's "Roar," inviting spectators to consider the historical plight of the "universal" woman. Yet, however powerful, "Last of Our Kind" only addresses Ann's gendered body and ignores the intersectional identity of the actress. However, Black queer feminist spectators cannot ignore the fact that Pitts, a Blackgirl actress, is singing about chains, prison, captivity, freedom, and history.

Black queer feminist spectators might read "Last of Our Kind" within the history of enslavement and mass incarceration of Black people and draw additional meaning. To begin, startling parallels exist between the capture, imprisonment, and display of Kong and the trafficking of millions of African people during the Transatlantic Slave Trade (1501–1867). The legacy of such crimes against humanity continues to haunt US society but has yet to be fully addressed by the federal government in any meaningful way. Kong's imprisonment and Ann's exploitation likewise resonate with the history of exploiting the bodies of Black people—whether for scientific experiments or entertainment for white audiences. For example, spectators might draw a comparison between Denham's manipulation and control of Ann and Kong with the infamous capture and exploitation of Saartjie Baartman (1789–1815), a Khoikhoi Blackgirl who was exhibited as a freakshow attraction across Europe during the nineteenth century. Kong's imprisonment also resonates with the prison industrial complex of today, as a generation of Black men, women, and children—cis, trans, queer, or otherwise—have been lost to incarceration. Furthermore, Pitt's love of a so-called "monster" and her struggle to be seen and heard would certainly resonate with spectators whose very identity (including who they choose to love) continues to be weaponized by politicians and demonized by religious organizations. In "Last of Our Kind," Ann describes her navigation of these trials as a "performance" and a "game" she and Kong have been forced to play. "From birth we've both been playing / A game we cannot win / Never break the locks / Or ever leave the box / The world has put us in," sings Ann. The "performance" that allows her and other marginalized subjects to survive could be understood in many ways, including the masking Black queer girls must do to safely navigate society or the code-switching Black professionals must do to traverse anti-Black spaces. Despite the harm that will surely befall her, Ann defies Denham and attempts to rescue Kong—an action in keeping with Black women's long history of resistance (see Figure 6.13).

Black queer feminist spectators might read Denham's characterization of Kong as a metaphor for racist America's perception of Black men. However, this reading reflects much of the *King Kong* franchise and is not unique to the musical. Indeed, many film scholars and theoreticians have provided similar readings of the 1933 film. The original shooting script describes Kong as angry, aggressive, and capable of "defying the whole civilized world."[175] As a

Figure 6.13 Christiani Pitts (Ann Darrow) in *King Kong* (2019), King Kong Broadway trailer. Still image courtesy of the author. https://www.youtube.com/watch?v=rT3omqgy-Vc

godlike "king" to an "uncivilized" tribe of Black natives, Kong is determined to have his way with Ann. As previously mentioned, he terrorizes her by constantly roaring, beating his chest, and manhandling her, even stripping her down to shredded undergarments. It does not take much of a jump to read Kong's uncouth behavior as a dramatization of the myth of the Black rapist, which arose out of white male fear of a newly freed Black population following emancipation. The sociologist Patricia Hill Collins writes that "according to this controlling image, Black men were naturally sexually violent, primarily through the potential use of the penis as a weapon of violence against White women. African American men were simultaneously accused of having a natural sexual desire for White women that grew in part from their now untamed buck status as sexual animals, and in part from ideas about White womanhood as beautiful, the most desirable and irresistible women, lacking agency in sexual matters, and in need of White male protection from dangerous 'free' Black men."[176] As such, spectators of the 1933 film could read Driscoll's saving Ann and Kong's eventual death as symbolically conquering the Black male threat. The film critic Ray Morton writes that "many found symbolic meanings and hidden subtext in the picture and identified Kong as everything from a symbol of oppressed workers striking back against their capitalist exploiters to a towering metaphor on race relations to a Freudian and nightmare of the first order. All of these interpretations were rejected by Merian Cooper, who maintained to the end that Kong was simply a gorilla and the film nothing more than a simple adventure story."[177]

While Cooper may have refused to read deeper subtext into his creation of Kong, spectators, artists, and critics certainly have. For example, when Pitts prepared to take on her role beside the pop-culture icon, she dove headfirst into researching the original film and the symbolic meaning of Kong. Pitts remembers:

> On the surface, I wanted to be able to focus on Kong being this incredible creature that Ann takes a liking to because he is so majestic and he's so beautiful and he should be protected at all costs. But another part of my creative process is research. I love researching, and I couldn't do any research on *King Kong* in 1930s America without it being shoved in my face what *King Kong* actually was supposed to be when it came out. The ways in which it was supposed to push this narrative of this aggressive Black man who needs to be put down to protect the sanctity of fragile white men. You couldn't work around it.[178]

Pitts and the creative team were aware of these stereotypes of Black men, as well as the history of racist imagery associating Black men with apes. However, if Kong represented Black men in America in the public imagination, Pitts and the creative team desired to humanize him and, in so doing, made his death all the more tragic.

The Broadway musical allows spectators to view Kong through the eyes of Ann, who sees him as a sad, beautiful, and intelligent wonder. Creatives created the seemingly "human" puppet by combining technology and human talent. The 2,000-pound animatronic ape was designed by Sonny Tilders and voiced by Jon Hoche, ten black-clad puppeteers operated the limbs, and the robotics (i.e., facial expressions) were controlled by three "voodoo operators" and an automation specialist off-stage.[179] Pitts worked with Hoche to establish a synergy between the human world and technology so that spectators would feel emotionally moved by Kong's humanity and saddened by his murder. Pitts remembers:

> In the rehearsal process, Jon and I established a relationship before I ever met the puppet. That was really beautiful. We would be in rehearsals doing that last scene [where Kong dies] and there wouldn't be a dry eye in the rehearsal studio. So, before we met the puppet, we talked about [the fact that] we don't want to lose that. We don't want to get into space, and all of a sudden, it's all about the technology of it. We want to make sure the relationship is still felt and the relationship is still real. I can confidently say that we did not lose that."[180]

In the Broadway production, Kong never goes on a blind rampage and Ann only initially fears him. After Kong saves her from the giant cobra and gives her water for her parched throat, Ann begins to listen to Kong's roars and understands them as his form of communication. As Kong and Ann roar at each other, the pair quickly establish a friendship like no other. Ann even recognizes the sadness in Kong's eyes as his need for friendship. She caresses Kong's face when he's upset, tends to his physical wounds, and, after helping him get captured, encourages him to break his chains and free himself from Denham's control. Kong, in turn, allows Ann to ride on his back to escape gunfire and protects her with his very life. Some critics, however, disliked the musical's characterization of Kong, noting that spectators might find his eventual death less meaningful. For example, a critic for *The Guardian* writes: "when he falls to his death, probably crushing a lot of midtown in the process, it doesn't much matter. Robbed of its terrible metaphors, the character is meaningless."[181] Pitts, however, remembers her moments with Kong onstage as not only thrilling for spectators to witness but also bringing personal joy. "Kong was the most beautiful scene partner I think I've ever had," remembers Pitts.[182] For Black queer feminist spectators, the dramatized murder of such a beautiful, intelligent, and human-like creature becomes all the more heartbreaking.

Black queer feminist spectators might read Kong's gruesome death at the hands of the New York Police Department as symbolic of contemporary extrajudicial violence against Black men. After Ann helps Kong escape his cage, the pair escape to the top of the Empire State Building. Spectators see projections of the New York skyline and the sound of wind with Kong and Ann standing on a metal platform enveloped in fog. Ann tries to comfort Kong during his hour of need, gently caressing his face, humming her lullaby, and encouraging him to keep fighting until she can return him to his island. "Anything is possible, you hear me? If we want to go to the stars, we can. You just have to hang on. You just have to stay with me, please. Because as strong as I am, as strong as you've made me, I can't hold you," Ann pleads. After her heartfelt monologue, projections of airplanes encircle them, and Ann waves her arms for them to stop, screaming "No! No! Please!" The stage lights immediately dim and spectators hear machine guns hammering shots near Kong's body. When the airplanes retreat, Ann again waves her arms for them to stop but the airplanes return, blasting bullets at Kong to the epic-sounding score, "Air War." When spectators think the barrage of death will conclude, Kong starts to fall in slow motion and pounds his chest as the airplanes fire on him. Spectators must then sit and witness a brutal death sequence, which takes about three agonizing minutes to complete until Kong finally succumbs to his injuries and "falls" to his death. Performing this emotional sequence night after night, against the backdrop of the Black Lives Matter movement proved taxing for Pitts, who remembers:

> It would really mess me up because I couldn't disassociate the two. I felt like Kong was more than just this majestic creature. He would literally be the physical personification of the beauty of Black men and it is just so beautiful and strong and multifaceted and capable of changing the world because that's what he did when he got to our world. He changed it. And it is just too much for people to handle so he must be put down. It was hard to watch the bullets and the gunshots at the end of the show because it felt a lot harder to deal with than thinking of him as just being this animal. When you think about—just on a greater scale—the ways in which Black men, Black people are being targeted specifically with bullets. It was just too much. It was honestly too much on some nights.[183]

While Black queer feminist spectators did not have the same level of intimacy as Pitts experienced performing beside Kong, they would understand how his death resonates with the disproportionate death rates of Black people killed by the police. All too often, Black women and girls are left to mourn the loss of their fathers, brothers, and sons as a result of anti-Black violence—whether through the extralegal actions of white police officers, the mass incarceration of a generation of Black men and boys, or other terrible means. For Ann, no amount of words can adequately describe this pain. All she can hope to do is capture her feelings with a song. Standing on the top of the Empire State Building, she solidifies this tremendous loss with the contemporary ballad "The Wonder." "This is the end / thank you, my friend / You taught me how to be free / how to be free / I can see another day coming," Ann sings. It is the hope that Black queer feminist spectators might also reach for their freedom and work hard to secure another day for the entire Black community.

The following conclusion issues a call for theatre artists to create more *opportunities* for BIPOC artists, including queer artists, so that we can realize the dream of a truly diverse, equitable, and inclusive theatre industry.

Conclusion

The summer of 2020 still feels like fever dream filled with both dread and possibility. As the COVID-19 pandemic raged on, many balked at following local "lockdown" mandates, grocery stores struggled to keep toilet paper on the shelves, and the theatre industry as we know it went completely "dark" across the globe. Yet, within this moment of political controversy, vitriol, and feelings of isolation, a community of Black, Indigenous, and People of Color (BIPOC) theatremakers gathered together remotely, in the legacy of August Wilson's 'Ground on White I Stand" (1996), to issue a call to alter the theatre industry for the better. While the sentiments of frustration, anger, and mental exhaustion expressed in the aptly titled "We See You White American Theater" are nothing new for many BIPOC theatre artists, the candidness and directness of the manifesto certainly shook the theatre industry. For a moment, with bated breath, I hoped that "We See You White American Theater" might inspire the US theatre industry to lead positive change. After all, for more than two decades I had taken Jill Dolan's words to heart that "theatre can move us toward understanding the possibility of something better, can train our imaginations, inspire our dreams and fuel our desires in ways that might lead to incremental cultural change."[1] My hope was that "We See You White American Theater" might serve as the first step to this much-needed cultural change.

Among other things, "We See You White American Theater" succinctly addresses how anti-Blackness, tokenism, white-dominated leadership, and white privilege lead to limited opportunities for BIPOC artists and harm the theatre industry as a whole. The manifesto concludes with the following call to action:

> We have watched you exploit us, shame us, diminish us, exclude us. We see you.
> We have always seen you.
> And now you will see us.

Black Queer Girlhood on the Musical Theatre Stage. La Donna L. Forsgren, Oxford University Press.
 DOI: 10.1093/9780197661444.003.0008

> We stand on this ground as BIPOC theatermakers, multi-generational, at varied stages in our careers, but fiercely in love with the Theater. Too much to continue it under abuse. We will wrap the least privileged among us and protection, and fearlessly share our many truths.
>
> About theaters, executive leaders, critics, casting directors, agents, unions, commercial producers, universities and training programs. You are all a part of this house of cards built on white fragility and supremacy. And this is a house that will not stand.
>
> This ends TODAY.
>
> We are about to introduce you . . . to yourself.[2]

As word of the manifesto traveled, the bold declarations sparked large-scale discussions about the importance of diversity, equity, and inclusion within Broadway, regional, and educational theatres nationwide. Many theatres responded to this challenge by issuing their own anti-racist statements, with some even promising targeted outcomes in the forthcoming years.

While "We See You White American Theatre" resulted in a moment of reflection across the industry, the manifesto has yet to realize the goal of long-term systemic change. Now living in the aftermath of the COVID-19 pandemic, when the call to actively foster anti-racist praxis have faded from our cultural memories, we have been left with little systemic change. As such, the anti-racist statements issued by theatres and corporations feel more like performative gestures of racial solidarity. In other words, business as usual has resumed. Professional and educational theatres, much like greater US society, continue to foster white supremacy.

Yet, under a second Trump administration, the need to create anti-racist systems within the theatre industry and society have never been so great. During his first one hundred days in office, President Trump has issued 103 Executive Orders, many of which have overturned the protections of the Civil Rights movement. The Leadership Conference on Civil and Human Rights reports that "Trump's executive actions have targeted immigration, employment, education, technology, justice reform, and other civil rights areas, as well as the federal workforce itself—all of which are likely to attempt to unravel much of the progress made toward building a more diverse, equitable, inclusive, accessible society. Much of what we are seeing was described in Project 2025, the wildly unpopular and radical blueprint that Trump disavowed but—as we now see—was the Trump agenda all along."[3] In the first few months alone, Trump's executive orders have prioritized discriminatory policies and executive overreach. For example, Trump's Executive Order 14160 would threaten birthright citizenship as outlined in the 14th Amendment to the Constitution of the United States.[4] In addition to this order, the Trump administration has deported thousands of people without due process, or adhering to the procedures that protect every person's life, liberty, and property. Programs that promote diversity, equity, and inclusion have also been targeted by the Trump Administration. For example, Executive Order 14151 "Ending Radical and Wasteful Government DEI Programs and Preferencing" and Executive Order14173 "Ending Illegal Discrimination and Restoring Merit-Based Opportunity" attempt to dismantle federal programs that foster diversity, equity, and inclusion, as well as pressure corporations, nonprofits, schools, and professional organizations to follow suit.[5] In addition to these internally focused directives, many more international-focused executive orders have damaged the United States's reputation on a global scale, leading to both economic uncertainty and alienation from historical allies. In other words, the Trump administration has created chaos within the federal government, within private and public sectors, and around the globe in the hopes of advancing a conservative, white-supremacist agenda.

Within this current political climate, "diversity, equity, and inclusion" has become a catch-all phrase to target the most vulnerable within society (including transgender, nonbinary, and intersex folx) and weaken their legal protections. As theatremakers, we must double our efforts to foster diversity, equity, and inclusion within our society and on our stages. We must dismantle all systems of white oppression and create spaces wherein BIPOC theatremakers can *lead* at every level of theatre production, *share* their creative talent with the world, and *thrive*.

Creating a more just and equitable theatre will allow BIPOC theatremakers to amplify the importance of theatre within our society. The COVID-19 global pandemic taught us that theatremakers are not perceived as "essential workers." The second Trump administration has taught us how fragile our democracy truly is. Can we envision a society wherein theatre is an essential component of our lives? A space that cultivates the musical talents of Blackgirls—queer, trans, or otherwise—at every level of production? A space where heretofore marginalized spectators can see their hopes, dreams, and desires represented on the stage? Can theatre act as "ground zero" of the cultural change that is so desperately needed in this country? Jill Dolan believes that it is possible for theatre to move society toward the understanding of something better. I believe this to be true. I just don't think that the large-scale cultural change that is needed will happen in my lifetime. However, it is my hope that BIPOC artists and their allies can work together to create the foundation for something better for future generations to build upon.

Future generations of BIPOC artists and their allies *can* and *should* learn from our mistakes. I want to conclude by sharing the thoughts expressed by two current artists to benefit future artists who desire a career in the professional theatre industry. When asked what advice he would offer emerging BIPOC designers and students, the Tony-nominated designer Jeff Suggs stressed the importance of withstanding opposition. "Don't give up. It's the thing that everybody gets told by some theater professor in school but make sure this is what you think you can do. Don't just go into the theater because you think it will be fun. It won't last, I promise. I'm one of the three dozen. I'm very fortunate to have made a career out of this and even more fortunate to have been part of a show like *Tina*—that has such an immense amount of success—to actually feel some financial benefits through my career. But that is insanely rare. I would encourage up-and-coming BIPOC designers or students to reach out, reach out, reach out," advises Sugg.[6] Christiani Pitts also stresses the pitfalls of navigating the theatre industry but also encourages Black actresses to express themselves across artistic mediums. Pitts states:

> Believe in yourself beyond the sort of boundaries that have been put up in front of you. Believe you are greater than that and that is going to be difficult. Man, that is going to be difficult but for anyone else to buy into what you are trying to portray, you honestly have to believe in it and yourself first. That sounds so cliché but I found it to be true. And never stop creating. I was recording music before I started doing plays and I was dancing. I was doing all these other things but I felt like I had to just do this one thing and be really good at it so I could make it on Broadway. And then I stopped creating in other spaces. I stopped writing music, I stopped doing things like that. So, I would also say keep your creative life going in every aspect if you can. Definitely stay focused, but don't feel like you have to put all of your eggs in one basket per se. Feel free to express yourself creatively in all the ways that make you happy and all the ways that make you feel fulfilled because that will also make you a better performer.[7]

Collectively, Dolan, Sugg, and Pitt's words are an important reminder to continue to dream, create, form communities with like-minded artists/activists, and fight for cultural change.

Notes

Introduction

1. Lorraine Hansberry, *Lorraine Hansberry in Her Own Words: To Be Young, Gifted and Black* (New York: Vintage Books, 1995 [1969]), 256.
2. Kirsten Childs, interview with author, February 3, 2021.
3. Laura Alexandra Harris, "Queer Black Feminism: The Pleasure Principle," *Feminist Review* 54 (1996), 21.
4. Harris, "Queer Black Feminism," 28.
5. Harris, "Queer Black Feminism," 7.
6. Liesl Tommy's production of *Eclipsed* received a 2016 Tony Award nomination for Best Direction of a Play.
7. Colin Larkin, *The Guinness Encyclopedia of Popular Music: Lincoln, Abe-Primettes* (Middlesex: Guinness Publishing, 1995), 2680.
8. Allen Woll, *Black Musical Theatre: From Coontown to Dreamgirls* (Baton Rouge: Louisiana State University Press, 1989), xiv.
9. Stacy Wolf, *Beyond Broadway: The Pleasure and Promise of Musical Theatre Across America* (New York: Oxford University Press, 2020), 32.
10. Rashida Z. Shaw McMahon, *The Black Circuit: Race, Performance, and Spectatorship in Black Popular Theatre* (New York: Routledge, 2020), 7.
11. McMahon, *The Black Circuit*, 4.
12. Sara Whitfield, "Introduction," in *Reframing the Musical: Race, Culture and Identity*, ed. Sara Whitfield (London: Red Globe Press, 2019), xix.
13. Whitfield, "Introduction," xiv.
14. Ryan Donovan, *Queer Approaches in Musical Theatre* (London: Methuen Drama, 2023), 3.
15. Ruth Nicole Brown, *Black Girlhood Celebration: Toward a Hip-Hop Feminist Pedagogy* (New York: Peter Lang Publishing, Inc., 2009), 1.
16. Dominique C. Hill, "Blackgirl, One Word: Necessary Transgressions in the Name of Imagining Black Girlhood," *Cultural Studies, Critical Methodologies* 19, no. 4 (2016): 276.
17. Hill, "Blackgirl, One Word," 276.
18. For more information about political and scientific research that pathologizes Black girlhood, see Monique W. Morris, *Pushout: The Criminalization of Black Girls in Schools.* Foreword by Mankaprr and Melissa Harris-Perry (New York: The New Press, 2016).
19. Kirsten Childs, interview with author, February 3, 2021.
20. Nazera Sadiq Wright, *Black Girlhood in the Nineteenth Century* (Urbana: University of Illinois Press, 2016), 3.
21. bell hooks, "Oppositional Gaze: Black Female Spectators," in *Black American Cinema*, ed. Manthia Diawara (New York: Routledge, 1993), 288–289.
22. hooks, "Oppositional Gaze," 288.
23. Charlene A. Carruthers, *Unapologetic: A Black, Queer, and Feminist Mandate For Radical Movements* (Boston: Beacon Press, 2018), 5–6.
24. Mignon R. Moore, "Color Us Invisible: In the Shadows of Communities Black and Gay, Black Lesbians Forge Lives, Loves, and Family," *Huffpost*, November 4, 2011 (updated February 2, 2016), *www.huffingtonpost.com/mignon-r-moore/black-lesbians_b_1075251.html* (accessed January 19, 2018).
25. For example, the names of important Black women musical theatre artists such as Vy Higginsen, Vinnette Carroll, and Micki Grant are not included in Ethan Mordden's *Broadway Babies: The People Who Made the American Musical* (New York: Oxford University Press, 1983), nor in his more recent book, *Anything Goes: A History of American Musical Theatre* (New York: Oxford University Press, 2013). Black women artists receive cursory acknowledgement in older collections such as Lehman Engel's *The American Musical Theatre* (New York: Macmillan

Publishing Co., Inc., 1975) and *Musical Comedy in America* (New York: Theatre Arts Books, 1981). When American musical theatre histories do include Black musical or Off-Broadway productions, they are often confined to one chapter of a collection. For example, see Denny Martin Flinn, *Musical! A Grand Tour: The Rise, Glory, and Fall of an American Institution* (New York: Schirmer Books, 1997).
26. Grace Barnes, *Her Time on Stage: The Role of Women in Musical Theatre* (Jefferson, North Carolina: McFarland, 2015), 109.
27. Barnes, *Her Time on Stage*, 109.
28. David Savran, *A Queer Sort of Materialism: Recontextualizing American Theater* (Ann Arbor: University of Michigan Press, 2003), 59.
29. Stacy Wolf, *A Problem Like Maria: Gender and Sexuality in the American Musical* (Ann Arbor: University of Michigan Press, 2002), 20.
30. Wolf, *A Problem,* 19.
31. Wolf, *A Problem,* 21.
32. Wolf, *A Problem,* 21; emphasis added.
33. Judith Fetterly, *The Resisting Reader: A Feminist Approach to American Fiction* (Bloomington: Indiana University Press, 1978), xxii–xxiii.
34. Fetterly, *The Resisting Reader*, xxiii.
35. Jill Dolan, *The Feminist Spectator as Critic* (Ann Arbor: University of Michigan Press, 2012), 2.
36. Dolan, *The Feminist Spectator*, 2.
37. bell hooks, *Bone Black: Memories of Girlhood* (New York: Henry Holt and Company, 1996), xii.
38. Patricia Hill Collins, *Black Sexual Politics: African Americans, Gender, and the New Racism* (New York: Routledge, 2005), 107.
39. Collins, *Black Sexual Politics*, 7; original emphasis.
40. Carruthers, *Unapologetic*, 39.
41. Schele Williams, interview with author, December 19, 2019.

Chapter 1

1. Marybeth Gasman, "Hand in Hand: Black Women in Pursuit of the Ph.D," *Forbes*, August 9, 2021, https://www.forbes.com/sites/marybethgasman/2021/08/09/hand-in-hand-black-women-in-pursuit-of-the-phd/?sh = 57b47ec766a2
2. American Psychological Association. "The road to resilience," https://www.apa.org/search?query = resilence (accessed November 25, 2025).
3. Sara Goodkind, Britney G. Brinkman, and Kathi Elliott, "Redefining Resilience and Reframing Resistance: Empowerment Programming with Black Girls to Address Societal Inequities," *Behavioral Medicine* 46, no. 3–4 (2020): 318.
4. Goodkind et al., 318.
5. Goodkind et al., 317.
6. Goodkind et al., 317.
7. Goodkind et al., 318.
8. Goodkind et al., 319.
9. Venus E. Evans-Winters, *Teaching Black Girls: Resiliency in Urban Classrooms* (New York: Peter Lang Publishing, Inc., 2011), 12.
10. Bennefield Zinobia and Jackson Taylor, "The Girls Are Alright: Examining Protective Factors of US Black Culture and Its Impact on the Resilience of Black Girls and Women," *Open Cultural Studies* 6 (2002): 218.
11. Zinobia and Taylor, "The Girls Are Alright," 218.
12. Zinobia and Taylor, "The Girls Are Alright," 218–219.
13. Schele Williams, interview with author, December 19, 2019.
14. For more information about honey bees, see Thomas D. Seeley, *The Lives of Bees: The Untold Story of the Honey Bee in the Wild* (Princeton, NJ: Princeton University Press, 2019).
15. Judy Juanita, interview with author, August 14, 2018.
16. E. Patrick Johnson, *Honeypot: Black Southern Women Who Love Women* (Durham, NC: Duke University Press, 2019), xiv.
17. Lorde, "Uses," 55.
18. Charlie Duncan, "The Color Purple Star Calls out Film for Queer Erasure: 'It's a story about Black lesbians. Period,'" *The Pink News*, February 22, 2023, https://www.thepinknews.com/2024/02/22/the-color-purple-star-queer-erasure-aunjanue-ellis-taylor/ (accessed November 24, 2025).

19. Alice Walker, *In Search of Our Mothers' Gardens: Womanist Prose* (San Diego: Harvest Books, 1984), xi.
20. Walker, *In Search*, xii.
21. Alice Walker, *The Same River Twice: Honoring the Difficult* (New York: Scribner, 1996), 170.
22. Ashley Lee, "The 40-year Fight Over 'The Color Purple's' Queer Love Story," *Los Angeles Times*, Dec 21, 2023, https://www.latimes.com/entertainment-arts/movies/story/2023-12-21/the-color-purple-celie-shug-queerness-musical-movie-alice-walker (accessed November 24, 2025).
23. Patricia Hill Collins, *Black Sexual Politics: African Americans, Gender, and the New Racism* (New York: Routledge, 2005), 225.
24. Monique W. Morris, *Pushout: The Criminalization of Black Girls in Schools.* Foreword by Mankaprr and Melissa Harris-Perry (New York: The New Press, 2016), 183.
25. Anthony Breznican, "Steven Spielberg: The EW Interview," *Entertainment Weekly*, December 2, 2011, https://ew.com/article/2011/12/02/steven-spielberg-ew-interview/
26. Breznican, "Steven Spielberg."
27. Walker, *The Same*, 35.
28. Walker, *The Same*, 35–36.
29. Lee, "The 40-year Fight."
30. Walker, *The Same*, 30.
31. Walker, *The Same*, 30.
32. Walker, *The Same*, 30.
33. Walker, *The Same*, 41.
34. Walker, *The Same*, 41.
35. Walker, *The Same*, 41.
36. Salamishah Tillet, "The Great Experiment That Is 'The Color Purple,'" *The New York Times*, December 24, 2023.
37. For more information about the critical reception of the 1985 *The Color Purple* film and Walker's reaction to the media storm, see Alice Walker, *The Same River Twice: Honoring the Difficult* (New York: Scribner, 1996).
38. *The Color Purple Original Broadway Cast Recording*, liner notes, Angel Records (New York, 2006), 9, CD.
39. *The Color Purple*, liner notes, 9–10.
40. Hand clapping has always been a major source of musical creativity and empowerment for Blackgirls. For more information on this subject, see Kyra D. Gaunt, *The Games Black Girls Play: Learning the Ropes from Double-Dutch to Hip-Hop* (New York University Press, 2006).
41. *The Color Purple: The Musical*, book by Marsha Norman, music and lyrics by Brenda Russell, Allee Willis, and Stephen Bray, directed by Gary Griffin, Broadway Theatre, New York, NY, April 12, 2006. The New York Public Library Theatre on Film and Tape Archive, (DVD). Subsequent citations are from this production.
42. Ben Brantley, "One Woman's Awakening, in Double Time," *The New York Times*, December 2, 2005.
43. Katie Clonan-Roy, Charlotte E. Jacobs, and Michael J. Nakkula, "Towards a Model of Positive Youth Development Specific to Girls of Color: Perspectives on Development, Resilience, and Empowerment," *Gender Issues* 33 (2016), 104.
44. Walker, *The Same*, 170.
45. "The Church Ladies," in *The Color Purple: A Memory Book of the Broadway Musical*, ed. Lise Funderburg (New York: Carroll & Graf, 2006), 107.
46. Marsha Norman et al., "The Libretto," in *The Color Purple: A Memory Book of the Broadway Musical*, ed. Lise Funderburg (New York: Carroll & Graf, 2006), 113.
47. "The Church Ladies," 107.
48. Walker, *The Same*, 42.
49. Angela Y. Davis, *Blues Legacy and Black Feminism: Gertrude "Ma" Rainey, Bessie Smith, and Billy Holiday* (New York: Pantheon Books, 1998), 123–124.
50. Johnson, *Honeypot*, xiii.
51. "The Songs," in *The Color Purple: A Memory Book of the Broadway Musical*, ed. Lise Funderburg (New York: Carroll & Graf, 2006), 50.
52. Alice Walker, *The Color Purple* (New York: Pocket Books, 1982), 81; original emphasis.
53. Audre Lorde, "Uses of the Erotic: The Erotic as Power" in *Sister Outsider: Essays and Speeches by Audre Lorde* (Berkeley: Crossing Press, 2007 [rpt. 1984]), 53.

54. "The Songs," in *The Color Purple: A Memory Book of the Broadway Musical*, ed. Lise Funderburg (New York: Carroll & Graf, 2006), 49.
55. "The Songs," 51.
56. "The Songs," 51.
57. Akasha Gloria Hull, *Soul Talk: The New Spirituality of African American Women* (Rochester, Vt: Inner Traditions International, 2001), 2.
58. In the novel, Alice Walker's Celie provides a more scathing critique of God. Celie admits: "He gave me a lynched daddy, a crazy mana, and a lowdown dog of a step pa and a sister I probably won't ever see again. Anyhow, I say that God I been praying and writing to is a man. And act just like all the other mens I know. Trifling, forgitful and lowdown" (Walker, *The Color Purple*, 99).
59. "The Journey," in *The Color Purple: A Memory Book of the Broadway Musical*, ed. Lise Funderburg (New York: Carroll & Graf, 2006), 11.
60. Porshé R. Garner, "What We Know and How We Know It: Defining, Black Girlhood Spirituality," in *Black Girl Magic Beyond the Hashtag: Twenty-First-Century Acts of Self-Definition*, eds. Julia S. Jordan-Zachery and Duchess Harris (Tucson: The University of Arizona Press, 2019), 117.
61. Ashley McDonough, "Why Black Sisterhood is The Unshakable Bond that Keeps Us Going," *Elite Daily*, October 11, 2017, https://www.elitedaily.com/p/what-is-black-sisterhood-you-ask-why-its-the-unshakeable-bond-that-keeps-us-going-2807361#:~:text=Black%20sisterhood%20is%20an%20unexplainable,been%20passed%20down%20throughout%20generations.
62. Janell Hobson, *Black Girl Magic Beyond the Hashtag: Twenty-First-Century Acts of Self-Definition* (Tucson: University of Arizona Press, 2019), ix–x.
63. Hobson, *Black Girl Magic*, x.
64. David Rooney, "Walker's Message a 'Purple' People Pleasure," *Variety*, December 5–11, 2005, 59.
65. Rooney, "Walker's Message," 59.
66. Jeremy McCarter, "Metropolitan Oprah," *New York Magazine*, December 1, 2005, https://nymag.com/nymetro/arts/theater/reviews/15230/
67. Ben Brantley, "One Woman's Awakening, In Double Time," *The New York Times*, December 2, 2005.
68. Brantley, "One Woman's Awakening."
69. Brantley, "One Woman's Awakening."
70. Aaron Brown, "Hallelujah and Amen: The Revival of *the Color Purple* as African-American Church," *Ecumenica: Performance and Religion* 11, no. 1 (2018): 64.
71. Brown, "Hallelujah and Amen," 65.
72. Brown, "Hallelujah and Amen," 63.
73. "'Color Purple' Musical on Broadway Has a Divine, Moving Spirit," *The Los Angeles Times*, December 10, 2015.
74. Mey Rude, "The Queer Love Story At the Heart of *The Color Purple* Has Been Restored," *Out*, November 28, 2023, https://www.out.com/film/the-color-purple-lesbian
75. Rude, "The Queer Love Story."
76. Ashley Lee, "The 40-year Fight Over 'The Color Purple's' Queer Love Story," *Los Angeles Times*, December 21, 2023, https://www.latimes.com/entertainment-arts/movies/story/2023-12-21/the-color-purple-celie-shug-queerness-musical-movie-alice-walker
77. *The Color Purple*, directed by Blitz Bazawule (Burbank, CA: Warner Bros. Pictures, 2023; DVD).
78. Lee, "The 40-year Fight."
79. Charlie Duncan, "The Color Purple Star Calls out Film for Queer Erasure: 'It's a story about Black lesbians. Period,'" *The Pink News*, February 22, 2023, https://www.thepinknews.com/2024/02/22/the-color-purple-star-queer-erasure-aunjanue-ellis-taylor/
80. Carmen Phillips, "If Only 'The Color Purple' Had Loved Us All," *Autostraddle*, December 19, 2023, https://www.autostraddle.com/the-color-purple-review/
81. Jacquelyn Dowd Hall argues that the Civil Rights movement began in the late 1930s and continued past the 1960s. See Jacquelyn Dowd Hall, "The Long Civil Rights Movement and Political Uses of the Past," *Journal of American History* 91, no. 4 (2005): 1233–1263.
82. Frank Rizzo, "Off Broadway Review: 'The Secret Life of Bees," *Variety*, June 13, 2019, https://variety.com/2019/legit/reviews/secret-life-of-bees-review-musical-atlantic-theater-1203242056/
83. Sue Monk Kidd, *The Secret Life of Bees* (New York: Penguin Books, 2002), 54.
84. Kidd, *The Secret Life*, 55.
85. Kidd, *The Secret Life*, 2.

86. Kidd, *The Secret Life*, 2.
87. Patricia Hill Collins, *Black Feminist Thought: Knowledge, Consciousness, and the Politics of Empowerment* (New York: Routledge, 1990), 125.
88. Jocelyn Frye, "Rejecting Business As Usual: Improving Employment Outcomes and Economic Security for Black Women," National Partnership for Women & Families, July 2023, https://nationalpartnership.org/report/improving-employment-outcomes-economic-security-for-black-women/
89. Frye, "Rejecting Business As Usual."
90. *The Secret Life of Bees*, book by Lynn Nottage, music by Duncan Sheik, lyrics by Susan Birkenhead, directed by Sam Gold, Atlantic Theatre Company, New York, NY, July 19, 2019. The New York Public Library Theatre on Film and Tape Archive (DVD). Subsequent citations are from this production.
91. Stacey Abrams, *Minority Leader: How to Lead from the Outside and Make Real Change* (New York: Henry Holt and Company, 2018), xx.
92. Nottage, *The Secret Life of Bees*, 54.
93. Darlene Clark Hine, *Hine Sight: Black Women and the Re-Construction of American History* (New York: Carlson Publishing, 1994), 41.
94. The "de mule uh de world" refers to the derogatory image of Black women and girls which is critiqued in Zora Neal Hurston's novel, *Their Eyes Were Watching God* (1937).
95. Lynn Nottage, Duncan Sheik, and Susan Birkenhead, *The Secret Life of Bees* (2019), Unpublished Manuscript, New York Public Library for the Performing Arts, Billy Rose Theatre Division (NCOF + 20-564).
96. Beverly J. Robinson, "The Sense of Self in Ritualizing New Performance Spaces for Survival," in *Black Theatre: Ritual Performance in the African Diaspora*, eds. Paul Carter Harrison, Victor Leo Walker, and Gus Edwards (Philadelphia: Temple University Press, 2002), 332–344, 332.
97. Robinson, "The Sense of Self," 332.
98. Robinson, "The Sense of Self," 332.
99. Kidd, *The Secret Life*, 90.
100. Johnson, *Honeypot* xiii.
101. Nottage, *The Secret Life of Bees*, Unpublished Manuscript, 61.
102. Nottage, *The Secret Life of Bees*, 30.
103. Lynn Nottage's story of April's death varies from Sue Monk Kidd's novel. In the novel, an eleven-year-old April and May go to the market to buy ice cream. They had seen white kids eat ice cream cones and sift through cartoon books. However, after their purchase, the store owner made them go outside and eat. August tells Lily that May argued with the store owner, who "took her arm and pulled her to the door, and her ice cream dropped on the floor." When May tells her father, a dentist, what happened, he tells her "'Nothing's fair in this world. You might as well get that straight right now" (Kidd 96). August shares that after this incident, May "got deflated about life" and experienced "terrible depressions" until one day, when she was fifteen, she took their father's shotgun and killed herself (Kidd 97).
104. Nottage, 42.
105. Collins, *Black Feminist Thought*, 147.
106. Asha DuMonthier, Chandra Childers, and Jessica Milli, "The Status of Black Women in the United States," The Institute for Women's Policy Research (2017), 1, https://iwpr.org/wp-content/uploads/2020/08/The-Status-of-Black-Women-6.26.17.pdf
107. "About," Black Lives Matter, https://blacklivesmatter.com/about/ (accessed January 3, 2020).
108. Patrisse Khan-Cullors and Asha Bandele, *When They Call You a Terrorist: A Black Lives Matter Memoir* (New York: St. Martin's Griffin, 2020), 205.
109. "About."
110. Audre Lorde, "Poetry is Not Luxury" in *Sister Outsider: Essays and Speeches* (Berkeley: Crossing Press, 1984), 32–35.
111. Abrams, *Minority Leader*, xxii.

Chapter 2

1. Theresa W. Tobin and Dawne Moon, "Sacramental Shame in Black Churches: How Racism and Respectability Politics Shape the Experiences of Black LGBTQ and Same-Gender-Loving Christians," in *Voices from the Edge: Centering Marginalized Perspectives in Analytic Theology*, eds. Michelle Panchuk and Michael Rea (Oxford: Oxford University Press, 2020), 140–165, 140.

2. Patricia Hill Collins, *Black Sexual Politics: African Americans, Gender, and the New Racism* (New York: Routledge, 2005), 107.
3. Patricia Hill Collins writes that Black women make up close to 70% of churchgoing members of the Black Church (45).
4. Evelyn Brooks Higginbotham, *Righteous Discontent: The Women's Movement in the Black Baptist Church, 1880–1920* (Cambridge: Harvard University Press, 1993), 187.
5. Higginbotham, *Righteous Discontent*, 204.
6. Higginbotham, *Righteous Discontent*, 193.
7. Collins, *Black Sexual Politics*, 107.
8. Collins, *Black Sexual Politics*, 107.
9. Collins, *Black Sexual Politics*, 108.
10. Besheer Mohamed, Kiana Cox, Jeff Diamant, and Claire Gecewicz, "Faith Among Black Americans," Pew Research Center, February 16, 2021,109. https://www.pewresearch.org/religion/2021/02/16/faith-among-black-americans/
11. Mohamed et al., 109.
12. Mohamed et al., 109.
13. Mohamed et al., 109.
14. Mohamed et al., 139.
15. E. Patrick Johnson, *Sweet Tea: Black Gay Men of the South* (Chapel Hill: University of North Carolina Press, 2008), 183.
16. Johnson, *Sweet Tea*, 183.
17. E. Patrick Johnson, *Black. Queer. Southern. Women* (Chapel Hill: University of North Carolina Press, 2018), 165.
18. Williams, xiv.
19. Williams, xiv.
20. Micki Grant, interview with author, August 16, 2018.
21. Nora Cole, interview with author, August 16, 2018.
22. Described by J. e. Franklin as "a chorus of three or four Young Girls (around 16 or 17 years old)," the DoWahs function as backup singers to the musical numbers and provide commentary on the action of the play. In so doing, the DoWahs emphasize Jackie's interior life and provide comic relief for the audience. See J. e. Franklin and Micki Grant, *The Prodigal Sister*, Alexander Street Press, 1974, https://search.alexanderstreet.com/view/work/bibliographic_entity%7Cbibliographic_details%7C3606936.
23. *The Prodigal Sister* premiered the same year as two other important all-Black Broadway musicals: *The Wiz* and Carroll's *The Ups and Downs of Theophilus Maitland.*
24. Jack Gaver, "Music and Lyrics Make 'The Prodigal Sister' Shine," *Los Angeles Times*, December 2, 1974.
25. Jessica B. Harris, "'Prodigal Sister' Rises Above Its Weaknesses," *New York Amsterdam News*, December 7, 1974.
26. Harris, "'Prodigal Sister' Rises."
27. Mel Gussow, "Stage: 'Prodigal Sister,'" *New York Times*, July 16, 1974.
28. Gussow, "Stage."
29. Harris, "'Prodigal Sister' Rises."
30. Angela E. Smith, "Bright Cast, Lively Music in New Play," *New York Amsterdam News*, July 27, 1974.
31. Smith, "Bright Cast."
32. Harris, "'Prodigal Sister' Rises."
33. Gussow, 'Stage."
34. Ed Bullins, "A Playwright Lauds Prodigal Sister," *New York Amsterdam News*, December 21, 1974.
35. Bullins, "A Playwright."
36. Ed Bullins writes that his Aunt Bea is a member of the church choir at The Williams Institutional Baptist Church of West Philly which she helped found in 1944 ("A Playwright").
37. J. e. Franklin and Micki Grant, *The Prodigal Sister* (New York: Samuel French, Inc., 1974), 5. Subsequent citations of this script are given parenthetically in the text.
38. Tobin and Moon, "Sacramental Shame," 141–142.
39. Tobin and Moon, "Sacramental Shame," 143.
40. Tobin and Moon, "Sacramental Shame," 144.
41. Tobin and Moon, "Sacramental Shame," 144.

42. Tobin and Moon, "Sacramental Shame," 144.
43. Tobin and Moon, "Sacramental Shame," 160.
44. Cheryl Clarke, "Lesbianism: An Act of Resistance," in *This Bridge Called My Back: Writings by Radical Women of Color*, eds. Cherrie Morago and Gloria E. Anzaldúa (New York: SUNY Press, 1981), 126–135, 126.
45. Julian Honkasalo, "Genderqueer," *lambda nordica* 25, no.1 (2020): 59.
46. Honkasalo, "Genderqueer," 61.
47. Matthew Morton, Amy Dworsky, and Sonali Patel, "Missed Opportunities: LGBTQ Youth Homelessness in America" (Chicago, IL: Chapin Hall at the University of Chicago, 2018), https://www.chapinhall.org/research/lgbtq-young-adults-experience-homelessness-at-more-than-twice-the-rate-of-peers/
48. Morton et al, "Missed Opportunities."
49. Franklin and Grant, *The Prodigal Sister*.
50. Clarke, "Lesbianism," 135.
51. James Weldon Johnson, *The Autobiography of an Ex-Colored Man* (New York: Library of America Paperback Classics, 2011 [1912]), 107.
52. Juanita Karpf, "Vinnette Carroll," *Notable Women in the American Theatre: A Biographical Dictionary* (Westport, CT: Greenwood Press, 1989), 81–82.
53. For more information about Vinnette Carroll's work as a director and theatre founder, see Henry Bial and Chase Bringardner's edited collection, *Great North American Stage Directors Volume 4: George Abbott, Vinnette Carroll, Harold Prince* (London: Methuen Drama, 2024).
54. Vinnette Carroll is often erroneously cited as the first African American woman to direct on Broadway, but that honor goes to Evelyn Ellis, a Lafayette Players actress who directed *Tabacco Road* on Broadway in 1950. Carroll holds the distinction as the first African American woman to direct a *musical* on Broadway and third African American to direct on Broadway, following Lloyd Richard's 1959 production of *A Raisin in the Sun*.
55. Clinton Turner Davis, "Preface," in *The Work of Vinnette Carroll: An African American Theatre Artist* by Calvin A. McClinton (Woodstock, IL: Dramatic Publishing, 2000), 2.
56. Calvin A. McClinton, *The Work of Vinnette Carroll: An African American Theatre Artist* (Woodstock, IL: Dramatic Publishing, 2000), 75.
57. Davis, "Preface," 2.
58. Emory Lewis, "Hallelujah for Gospel Show," *Bergen Record*, December 23, 1976.
59. Lewis, "Hallelujah."
60. Davis, "Preface," 1.
61. Vinnette Carroll, Alex Bradford, and Micki Grant, *Your Arm's Too Short to Box With God* (1975), New York Public Library for the Performing Arts, Billy Rose Theatre Division (NCOF + 11-3204). Subsequent citations are to this unpublished manuscript.
62. John Beaufort, "Gospel Music to George Abbitt to Lincoln," *The Christian Science Monitor*, December 27, 1976.
63. Lucile M. Scott, "Too Short to Box With God Gets to Audience," *Atlantic Daily World*, May 13, 1979.
64. Scott, "Too Short."
65. Following Jesus's death, His resurrection is noted in the traditional gospel number, "Can't No Grave Hold My Body Down," attributed to songwriter and preacher Claude Ely (later recorded by Sister Rosetta Tharpe [1946–1947] and others). The gospel number was performed by Clinton Derricks-Carroll, and company (prod. 1976), Derek Williams; Ray Stephens and company (prod. 1980); Al Green, Quincella, Elijah Gill and company (prod. 1982).
66. Calvin A. McClinton, *The Work of Vinnette Carroll: An African American Theatre Artist* (Lewiston, NY: Edwin Mellen Press, 2000), 278.
67. Brian Granger, "An Architect of Feeling: Vinnette Carroll and Her Broadway Gospel Musicals," in *Great North American Stage Directors Volume 4: George Abbott, Vinnette Carroll, Harold Prince*, eds. Henry Bial and Chase Bringardner (London: Methuen Drama, 2024), 98–118, 114.
68. Beaufort, "Gospel Music," 29.
69. Scott, "Too Short."
70. Janel Cubbage and Leslie Adams, "Still Ringing the Alarm: An Enduring Call to Action for Black Youth Suicide Prevention," Johns Hopkins Center for Gun Violence Solutions, 2023. https://publichealth.jhu.edu/sites/default/files/2023-08/2023-august-still-ringing-alarm.pdf, 1–52, 9.
71. For more information on the history of gospel music and Black women gospel singers, see Robert Darden, *People Get Ready! A New History of Black Gospel* (New York: Continuum,

2004); Robert M. Marovich, *A City Called Heaven: Chicago and the Birth of Gospel Music* (Urbana: University of Illinois Press, 2015); *The Mahalia Jackson Reader* ed. Mark Burford (New York: Oxford University Press, 2020); and Cheryl Wills, *Isn't Her Grace Amazing!: The Women Who Changed Gospel Music* (New York: Amistad, 2022).

72. Darden, *People Get Ready!*, 197.
73. Scott, "Too Short."
74. Peter Bailey, "'Mama I Want to Sing' Celebrates Fifth Smash Year at Heckscher Theatre" *New York Amsterdam News*, March 12, 1988.
75. Bailey, "'Mama I Want to Sing' Celebrates."
76. Bailey, "'Mama I Want to Sing' Celebrates."
77. Bailey, "'Mama I Want to Sing' Celebrates."
78. Mel Tapley, "Is City Forcing 'Mama' to Close?: Is City Forcing 'Mama, I Want to Sing' to Cry?" *New York Amsterdam News*, February 16, 1991.
79. Bailey, "'Mama I Want to Sing' Celebrates."
80. Colin Larkin, "Mama, I Want To Sing," *The Encyclopedia of Popular Music* 4 ed. (Oxford University Press, 2006), https://www-oxfordreference-com.proxy.library.nd.edu/display/10.1093/acref/9780195313734.001.0001/acref-9780195313734-e-56660?rskey=8XO1x1&result
81. Bailey, "'Mama I Want to Sing' Celebrates."
82. Bailey, "'Mama I Want to Sing' Celebrates."
83. Richard Harrington, "Gotta Sing, and Very Charmingly," *The Washington Post*, March 27, 1986.
84. Bailey, "'Mama I Want to Sing' Celebrates."
85. Kalia Richardson, "'Mama, I Want to Sing!' Returns for 40th Anniversary" *The New York Times*, Feb 24, 2023, https://www.nytimes.com/2023/02/24/theater/mama-i-want-to-sing-40th-anniversary.html
86. Richardson, "Mama, I Want to Sing! Returns."
87. Ken Wydro directed the November 16, 2020 production of *Mama, I Want to Sing* at the El Teatro (formerly Heckscher Theatre). Costumes were designed by Theda Dennis. The cast included: Vy Higginsen (Narrator/DJ), Ahmaya Knoelle Higginson (Doris Winter), Tara Bramble (Mama Winter), Tyrone Flowers (Reverend Winter), Sandra Huff (Sister Carrie), and Elijah Ahmad Lewis (Minister of Music). Ensemble members, who functioned as choir members, dancers, and early blueswomen, included Dorothy Colon, Dominique Coppin, Carlton Ellen, Thomas Gatling, Barry Manderson, David Moses, Tiffany Obi, Michael Reid, Kareda Robinson, Yvette Rogers, Damion Triston, Alanna Underwood. A live house band included Kevin McKoy (D/Keyboards), Greg Kelly (keyboards), Andre Cleghorn (bass), and David McKoy (drums).
88. *Mama, I Want to Sing*, script by Vy Higginsen and Ken Wydro, directed by Ken Wydro, El Teatro (formerly Heckscher Theatre), New York, NY, November 16, 2020. Subsequent citations are from this production.
89. V. Williams, 'Mama I want to sing': Play Delivers Powerful Performances," *Afro-American*, April 5, 1986.
90. Linda Armstrong, "'Mama I Want to Sing,'" *New York Amsterdam News*, October 30, 2003.
91. Bailey, "Mama I Want to Sing! Celebrates."
92. The italicized portion of the block quote is the author's description of the stage action.
93. Civilla D. Martin, "His Eye Is on the Sparrow," (1905) https://hymnary.org/text/why_should_i_feel_discouraged_why_should
94. Harrington, "Gotta Sing."
95. For more in-depth information about R. Kelly's sexual crimes committed against Blackgirls, see the explosive Lifetime documentary series, *Surviving R. Kelly* (2019), written and directed by Nigel Bellis and Astral Finnie.
96. For more information about the life of Doris Troy, see Amelia McDonell-Parry, "Doris Troy" in *Rollingstone* issue 944 (Mar 18, 2004), 26; David Nathan, *The Soulful Divas: Personal Portraits of Over a Dozen Divine Divas, from Nina Simone, Aretha Franklin & Diana Ross to Patti LaBelle, Whitney Houston & Janet Jackson* (New York: Billboard Books, 1999).
97. Harrington, "Gotta Sing."
98. Interview with Vy Higginsen and Ahmaya Knoelle Higginson, Spectrum News NY1, February 25, 2023, https://www.facebook.com/search/posts?q = vy%20higginsen%20photos
99. For more information about the novel's depiction of Doris's loss, see Vy Higginsen with Tonya Bolden, *Mama, I Want To Sing* (New York: Scholastic, 1992), 58–61.

100. Higginsen and Bolden, *Mama*, 113.
101. Higginsen and Bolden, *Mama*, 132.
102. The 2012 film adaptation of *Mama, I Want to Sing* also stars actor Billy Zane (Amara's Manager); Tony Award-winning actor Ben Vereen (Horace Payne); actor and politician Hill Harper (Jeff Andrews); and prominent televangelist and gospel singer, Juanita Byrum (Beverly).
103. Samuel A. Hay, *African American Theatre: An Historical and Critical Analysis* (Cambridge: Cambridge University Press, 1994), 54.
104. Rashida Z. Shaw McMahon, *The Black Circuit: Race, Performance, and Spectatorship in Black Popular Theatre* (New York: Routledge, 2020), 4.
105. McMahon, 4.
106. Mohamed et al., 9.
107. Mohamed et al. define the Silent Generation as those born prior to 1946, Baby Booms as those born from 1946 to 1964, Generation X as those born from 1965 to 1980, Millennials born between 1981–1996, and Generation Z adult respondents (born between1997–2002) (9–10).
108. Jazmine Steele, "New Plays Reveal Women's Stories," *The Michigan Citizen*, March 21, 2010.
109. "Direct to DVD Film of Angela Barrow-Dunlap's Hit Stage Play 'Church Girl' Starring Robin Givens Will Hit Retail Stores on January 31, 2012," *Columbus Times*, Jan 25–Jan 31, 2012.
110. "National Hit Musical Stage Play 'Church Girl' Brings All-Star Cast to Houston," Press Release, April 30, 2010, https://www.newswire.com/news/national-hit-musical-stage-play-church-girl-brings-all-star-cast-to-148346
111. "Direct to DVD."
112. "National Hit Musical Stage."
113. Dwain Wellington, "'Church Girl'- - A Theatrical Review," September 3, 2011, https://dwainwellington.wordpress.com/2011/09/03/%E2%80%9Cchurch-girl%E2%80%9D-a-theatrical-review/
114. *Church Girl*, written by Angela Barrow-Dunlap and directed by Reuben Yabuku (Culver City, CA: Sony Pictures Home Entertainment, 2011). Subsequent citations of this production are to this DVD.

Chapter 3

1. Charlene A. Carruthers, *Unapologetic: A Black, Queer, and Feminist Mandate for Radical Movements* (Boston: Beacon Press, 2018), 33.
2. Carruthers, *Unapologetic*, 33.
3. Patricia Hill Collins, *Black Sexual Politics: African Americans, Gender, and the New Racism* (New York: Routledge, 2005), 186.
4. Carruthers, *Unapologetic*, 39.
5. Harriet Jacobs, *Incidents in the Life of a Slave Girl* (New York: Dover Publications, 2001; 1861 repr.), 27.
6. Nazera Sadiq Wright, *Black Girlhood in the Nineteenth Century* (Urbana: University of Illinois Press, 2016), 3.
7. Kirsten Childs, interview with author, February 3, 2021.
8. Mel Gussow, "Stage: 'Madame Zora,' A Biographical Musical," *New York Times*, March 2, 1986.
9. Sexual Assault Support Center Inc., "Statistics: African-American & Black Communities," https://www.thecenterat909.org/africanamerican (accessed May 3, 2021).
10. Katelyn Burns, "A Brutal Video Shows a Black Trans Woman Getting Beat Up by Dozens of Men," *Vox*, June 3, 2020, https://www.vox.com/identities/2020/6/3/21279407/video-black-trans-woman-iyanna-dior-beaten.
11. For more information on the death of Black imagination, see Carruthers, *Unapologetic*, 33.
12. Childs, interview.
13. *Bella: An American Tale*, book, music, and lyrics by Kirsten Childs, directed by Robert O'Hara, Playwrights Horizons, New York, NY, June 21, 2017. The New York Public Library Theatre on Film and Tape Archive (DVD). Subsequent citations are from this production.
14. Childs, interview.
15. Childs, interview.
16. Kirsten Childs, *Bella: An American Tale* (New York: Samuel French, 2019), 7.
17. The Exoduster movement (1870–1880) was the first major migration of African Americans following emancipation. More than 21,000 African Americans, called "Exodusters," migrated from states near the Mississippi River to Kansas to pursue land opportunity and escape racial oppression. For more information, see Mike Meacham, "The Exoduster Movement," *Western*

Journal of Black Studies 27, no. 2 (2003): 108–117; Lisa M. Frehill-Rowe, "Postbellum Race Relations and Rural Land Tenure: Migration of Blacks and Whites to Kansas and Nebraska, 1870–1890," *Social Forces* 72, no. 1 (1993): 77–92.
18. Jeff Sugg, interview with author, March 26, 2021.
19. "National Assessment of Adult Literacy," National Center for Education Statistics, https://nces.ed.gov/naal/lit_history.asp#:~:text = In%201870%2C%2020%20percent%20of,percent%20of%20blacks%20remained%20illiterate.
20. Monique W. Morris, *Pushout: The Criminalization of Black Girls in Schools.* Foreword by Mankaprr and Melissa Harris-Perry (New York: The New Press, 2016), 5.
21. Despite its importance in the lives of Blackgirls, Black dance has not always served a core function within American musical theatre. Richard A. Long writes that before the 1970s, "black dance, stance, and gesture, while usually integrated with the action, were often made so by the will of the actor/dancer, rather than be the design of the director or choreographer" (329). Indeed, the pioneering efforts of choreographers such as Katherine Dunham, Pearl Primus, Dianne McIntyre, Alvin Ailey, Geoffrey Holder, George Faison, Billy Wilson, Talley Beatty, Louis Johnson, and Donald McKayle paved the way for contemporary Black women choreographers such as Camille A. Brown to enter the musical theatre stage.
22. "Camille A. Brown," 2018, https://www.camilleabrown.org/camille (accessed March 2, 2021).
23. Camille A. Brown has also crafted her own Blackgirl-centered theatrical pieces. For example, *Black Girl: Linguistic Play* (2015) uses Black vernacular dance, including double Dutch and steppin', to celebrate memories of Black girlhood.
24. Although the dance known as twerking began in the 1980s, the term "twerking" was not used until the early 1990s. DJ Jubilee (Jerome Temple) first used the term in the song "Do the Jubilee All" in 1992. Thus, the style of dance predates the term.
25. Kyra D. Gaunt, "YouTube, Twerking & You: Context Collapse and the Handheld Co-Presence of Black Girls and Miley Cyrus," *Journal of Popular Music Studies* 27, no. 3 (2015): 248.
26. Gaunt, "YouTube, Twerking & You," 252.
27. Beyoncé's "Single Ladies (Put a Ring on It)" dance routine was choreographed by Frank Gatson Jr. and JaQuel Knight.
28. "Camille A. Brown."
29. Tim Sanford and Robert O' Hara, "Artist Interview with Robert O' Hara," Playwrights Horizons, October 21, 2014, https://www.playwrightshorizons.org/shows/trailers/artist-interview-robert-ohara/
30. Childs, interview.
31. Sugg, interview.
32. Patricia A. Young, "Acts of Terrorism, or, Violence on 'Sunday Morning in the South,'" *MELUS* 26, no. 4 (Winter 2001): 33.
33. Young, "Acts of Terrorism," 34.
34. "Anti-Lynching Legislation Renewed," *United States House of Representatives: History, Art & Archives*, https://history.house.gov/Exhibitions-and-Publications/BAIC/Historical-Essays/Temporary-Farewell/Anti-Lynching-Legislation/.
35. Sander L. Gilman, "Black Bodies, White Bodies: Toward an Iconography of Female Sexuality in Late Nineteenth-Century Art, Medicine, and Literature," *Critical Inquiry* 12, no. 1 (1985): 213.
36. Aishah Rahman, *Tale of Madame Zora*, Alexander Street, 1985, https://search.alexanderstreet.com/view/work/bibliographic_entity%7Cdocument%7C3876691. Subsequent citations are to this script.
37. Thadious M. Davis, "Aishah Rahman's Writing in the Dark: The Presence of an Absence," *Obsidian III* 1, no. 1 (1999): 56.
38. Davis, "Aishah Rahman's Writing," 56–57.
39. Davis, "Aishah Rahman's Writing," 66.
40. Davis, "Aishah Rahman's Writing," 66.
41. Larry Neal, "The Black Arts Movement," *The Drama Review* 12,no. 4 (1968): 30.
42. Aishah Rahman, "Living in the Black Arts Movement," in *SOS—Calling All Black People: A Black Arts Movement Reader*, eds. John H. Bracey Jr, Sonia Sanchez, and James Smethurst (Amherst: University of Massachusetts Press, 2014), 440–441.
43. Glenda Dickerson, "The Cult of True Womanhood: Toward a Womanist Attitude in African-American Theatre," *Theatre Journal* 40, no. 2 (1988): 179.
44. Dickerson, "The Cult," 180.

45. Zora Neale Hurston, "Dust Tracks on a Road" in *Zora Neale Hurston: Folklore, Memoirs, and Other Writings* (New York: The Library of America, 1995 [1942]), 599–601.
46. Gussow, "Stage: 'Madame Zora.'"
47. Gussow, "Stage: 'Madame Zora.'"
48. Gussow, "Stage: 'Madame Zora.'"
49. Zora Neale Hurston, "Characteristics of Negro Expression" in *Zora Neale Hurston: Folklore, Memoirs, and Other Writings* (New York: The Library of America, 1995 [1934]), 836.
50. Hurston, "Characteristics," 837.
51. Alice Walker, "In Search of Zora Neal Hurston," *Ms.* 3, no. 9 (March 1, 1975), 74–89.
52. Narrator Cora Mae speculates that Zora Neal Hurston may have secretly married or nearly died during the "lost" or undocumented decade of her life.
53. Hurston, "Characteristics," 830.
54. Hurston, "Characteristics," 831.
55. Alice Walker, *In Search of Our Mothers' Gardens: Womanist Prose* (San Diego: Harcourt Brace Jovanovich, 1983), xi.
56. Aishah Rahman, *Chewed Water: A Memoir* (Lebanon: University Press of New England, 2001), 3.
57. Rahman, *Chewed*, 7.
58. Rahman, *Chewed*, 8–9.
59. Rahman, *Chewed*, 92.
60. "When Zora Neale Hurston Was Falsely Accused of Child Molestation," Prison Culture: How the PIC Structures Our World, March 31, 2013, https://www.usprisonculture.com/blog/2013/03/31/when-zora-neale-hurston-was-falsely-accused-of-child-molestation/.
61. James F. Wilson, *Bulldaggers, Pansies, and Chocolate Babies: Performance, Race, and Sexuality in the Harlem Renaissance* (Ann Arbor: University of Michigan Press, 2010), 31.
62. Wilson, *Bulldaggers*, 31.
63. Gussow, "Stage: 'Madame Zora.'"
64. Kirsten Childs, *The Bubbly Black Girl Sheds Her Chameleon Skin* (New York: Dramatists Play Service, 2003), 7.
65. *The Bubbly Black Girl Sheds Her Chameleon Skin*, book, music, and lyrics by Kirsten Childs, directed by Wilfredo Medina, Playwrights Horizons, New York, NY, July 15, 2000. The New York Public Library Theatre on Film and Tape Archive, 2000 (VHS). Subsequent citations are from this production.
66. Childs, interview.
67. Toni Cade Bambara, "Salvation is the Issue," in *Black Women Writers (1950-1980): A Critical Evaluation*, ed. Mari Evans (New York: Anchor Press, 1984), 41.

Chapter 4

1. Irene Visser, "Fairy Tale and Trauma in Toni Morrison's 'Home,'" *Negotiating Trauma and Affect* 41, no. 1 (2016): 149–150.
2. For more information about early feminist fairy tale debates, see Alison Lurie, "Fairy Tale Liberation," *New York Review of Books*, December 17, 1970: 42–44; Alison Lurie, "Witches and Fairies: Fitzgerald to Updike," *New York Review of Books*, December 2, 1971:6–11; Marcia R. Lieberman, "'Some Day My Prince Will Come': Female Acculturation through the Fairy Tale," *College English*, 34 (1972): 383–395; and Karen E. Rowe, "Feminism and Fairy Tales," *Women's Studies*, 6 (1979): 237–257.
3. Donald Hasse, "Preface," in *Fairy Tales and Feminism: New Approaches*, ed. Donald Hasse (Detroit: Wayne State University Press, 2004), x–xi.
4. Donald Hasse, "Feminist Fairy-Tale Scholarship," in *Fairy Tales and Feminism: New Approaches*, ed. Donald Hasse (Detroit: Wayne State University Press, 2004), 1–36, 28–29.
5. Laretta Henderson, "Black Aesthetic in Revised African American Fairy Tales," in *Fairy Tales With Black Consciousness: Essays on Adaptations of Familiar Stories*, eds. Vivian Yenika-Agbaw, Ruth McKoy Lowery, and Laretta Henderson (Jefferson, NC: McFarland & Company, 2013), 206.
6. Jack Zipes, *When Dreams Came True: Classical Fairy Tales and Their Tradition* (New York: Routledge, 2007), 37.
7. For more information on the Brothers Grimm editorial changes, see Ruth B. Bottigheimer, *Grimms' Bad Girls and Bold Boys: The Moral and Social Vision of the Tales* (New Haven: Yale University Press, 1987).

8. Haase, "Feminist," 11.
9. Jack Zipes, "The Evolution of Folk-and Fairy Tales in Europe and North America," in *Teaching Fairy Tales*, ed. Nancy L. Canepa et al. (Detroit: Wayne State University Press, 2019), 34–53, 47.
10. Jemimah L. Young, Marquita D. Foster, and Dorothy Hines, "Even Cinderella is White," *The English Journal* 107, no. 6 (2018): 103.
11. Young et al., "Even Cinderella," 103.
12. Young et al., "Even Cinderella," 104.
13. Patricia Ann Spencer, "The Harlem Children's Theatre Company: No Longer a 'Crazy Idea' Cover . . . ," *New York Amsterdam News*, December 13, 1975.
14. The number of Harlem Children's Theatre Company members varied throughout the years. Productions of The Liberation of Mother Goose ranged from 60 to 85 cast members.
15. Spencer, "The Harlem Children's Theatre Company."
16. Aduke Aremu, interview with author, October 13, 2017.
17. Aremu, interview.
18. The Harlem Children's Theatre Company performed *The Liberation of Mother Goose* in Lagos, Nigeria, for the Second International Black Arts Festival (FESTAC) in 1978. The company also toured the production on Frankfurt, London, Rome, Zurich, and against the backdrop of the Eiffel Tower in Paris, before an audience of 75,000 Parisians who applauded the production. For more information, see Mel Tapley, "Harlem's Children's Group Tops Black Arts Festival," *New York Amsterdam News*, November 25, 1978.
19. Aduke Aremu, "The Liberation of Mother Goose" (1972), Unpublished Manuscript, Courtesy of Aduke Aremu. Subsequent citations are from this manuscript.
20. Christina Phillips Mattson and Maria Tatar, "Fairy Tales, Myth, and Fantasy," in *New Approaches to Teaching Folk and Fairy Tales*, eds. Claudia Schwabe and Christa Jones (Logan, UT: Utah State University Press, 2016), 21–34, 23.
21. Author emphasis.
22. Dawn Alli, interview with author, October 14, 2017.
23. Patricia Ann Spencer, "'The Liberation of Mother Goose' A Heavy Satire for Children," *New York Amsterdam News*, December 13, 1975; the 1975 Negro Ensemble Company Children's Festival production of "The Liberation of Mother Goose" was directed by Mical Whitaker and included musical director Robert Williams, costume designer Pat Cummings, choreographer Lilias White, voice teacher Mimi Locadi, set designer Mynra Lee, and lighting designer Sandra Ross.
24. Julia L. Mickenberg, "Radical Children's Literature for Adults in *The Inner City Mother Goose*," *Journal of Children's Literature Research* 42 (2019):14.
25. Spencer, "'The Liberation.'"
26. "I Am Black and Comely" was written by Jimmy Justice for *The Liberation of Mother Goose.*
27. "Each One Teach One" was written by Michele Fields with music by Jimmy Justice for *The Liberation of Mother Goose.*
28. Aremu, interview.
29. Aremu, interview.
30. While tales of girls in red encountering wolves date back to the early eleventh century, the modern story of "Little Red Riding Hood," as we know it, first appears through the hands of Charles Perrault's "Le Petit Chaperon rouge" in *The Tales of Mother Goose* (1696). Little Red Riding Hood later appears in the Brothers Grimms' tale, "Rotkäppchen" (1812). For more information on Little Red Riding Hood variants, see: Francisco Vaz da Silva, "Charles Perrault and the Evolution of 'Little Red Riding Hood'" *Marvels & Tales* 30, no. 2 (2016): 167–190.
31. Charles Perrault, *The Tales of Mother Goose*, trans. Charles Welsh (Boston: D.C. Heath & Co., Publishers, 1901[1696]), 84, https://www.gutenberg.org/cache/epub/17208/pg17208-images.html.
32. Sandra L. Beckett, "Introduction: A Global Fairy-Tale Icon," in *Provisioning Red Riding Hood Around the World in Anthology of International Retellings*, ed. Sandra L Beckett (Detroit: Wayne State University Press, 2014), 1–12.
33. Beckett, "Introduction," 5.
34. Jack Zipes, *The Trials and Tribulations of Little Red Riding Hood* (New York: Routledge, 1993), xi.
35. Aremu, interview.
36. Spencer, "'The Liberation.'"
37. Aremu, "Mother Goose," 68.

38. Deborah L. Thompson, "Not All Cinderellas Wear Glass Slippers: A Critical Analysis of Selected Cinderella Variants from the Black Perspective," in *Fairy Tales with a Black Consciousness: Essays on Adaptations of Familiar Stories*, eds. Vivian Yenika-Agbaw, Ruth McKoy Lowery, and Laretta Henderson (Jefferson, NC: McFarland & Company, Inc., 2013), 74.
39. Thompson, "Not All Cinderellas Wear Glass Slippers," 75.
40. Thompson, "Not All Cinderellas Wear Glass Slippers," 74.
41. Marian Roalfe Cox includes the South African Xhosa tale, "Story of the Wonderful Horns" in her compilation. For more information, see Marian Roalfe Cox, *Cinderella: Three Hundred and Forty-five Variants of Cinderella, Catskin and Cap O'Rushes* (London: Forgotten Books, 2015 [1893]).
42. Zipes, "The Evolution," 52.
43. Jackie Taylor, interview with author, February 6, 2020.
44. Jackie Taylor, "Message From the Writer/Director," *The Other Cinderella* program, Black Ensemble Theater, 2019.
45. Taylor, interview.
46. Zipes, "The Evolution," 52.
47. Thompson, "Not All Cinderellas Wear Glass Slippers," 76.
48. For a complete view of Deborah L. Thompson's "Table 2. Important Motifs Across All Cinderella Tale Types," see Thompson, "Not All Cinderellas Wear Glass Slippers," 77.
49. Thompson, "Not All Cinderellas Wear Glass Slippers," 77.
50. Thompson, "Not All Cinderellas Wear Glass Slippers," 77.
51. Taylor, interview.
52. Jackie Taylor directed, produced, and designed costumes for the Black Ensemble Theatre production of *The Other Cinderella* on November 15, 2019. The production included sixteen musical numbers composed by Taylor and collaborator Michael Ward.
53. Taylor, Interview.
54. *The Other Cinderella*, book, music, and lyrics by Jackie Taylor, directed by Jackie Taylor, Black Ensemble Theatre, Chicago, November 15, 2019. Subsequent citations are from this production.
55. Maryam M. Jernigan and Jessica Henderson Daniel, "Racial Trauma in the Lives of Black Children and Adolescents: Challenges and Clinical Implications," *Journal of Child and Adolescent Trauma* 4 (2011): 133.
56. Jernigan and Daniel, "Racial Trauma," 133.
57. Jernigan and Daniel, "Racial Trauma," 132.
58. Jernigan and Daniel, "Racial Trauma," 132.
59. Jernigan and Daniel, "Racial Trauma," 131.
60. Taylor, interview.
61. Taylor, interview.
62. Chardée A. Galán et al., "An Intersectional-Contextual Approach to Racial Trauma Exposure Risk, and Coping Among Black Youth," *Journal of Research on Adolescence* 32, no. 2 (2022): 584.
63. Janel Cubbage and Leslie Adams, "Still Ringing the Alarm: An Enduring Call to Action for Black Youth Suicide Prevention," Johns Hopkins Center for Gun Violence Solutions, 2023, https://publichealth.jhu.edu/sites/default/files/2023-08/2023-august-still-ringing-alarm.pdf, 4.
64. Cubbage and Adams, "Still Ringing the Alarm," 9.
65. Cubbage and Adams, "Still Ringing the Alarm," 37–39.
66. Cubbage and Adams, "Still Ringing the Alarm," 29.
67. Taylor, interview.
68. Taylor, interview.
69. Taylor, interview.
70. Taylor, interview.
71. Taylor, interview.
72. Taylor, interview.
73. Taylor, interview.
74. *Once on this Island*, book and lyrics by Lynn Ahrens, music by Stephen Flaherty, directed by Graciela Daniele, Playwrights Horizons, New York, NY, May 13, 1990. The New York Public Library Theatre on Film and Tape Archive (DVD). Subsequent citations are from this production.
75. Ken Mondschein, "Introduction," in *Hans Christian Andersen's Complete Fairy Tales*, trans. Jean Hersholt (San Diego: Canterbury Classics, 2014 [1837]), xi–xvii, xii.
76. Mondschein, "Introduction," xii.

77. Hans Christian Andersen, "The Little Mermaid," in *Hans Christian Andersen's Complete Fairy Tales*, trans. Jean Hersholt (San Diego: Canterbury Classics, 2014 [1837]), 41–55, 42.
78. Andersen, "Mermaid," 42.
79. Andersen, "Mermaid," 48.
80. Andersen, "Mermaid," 49.
81. Andersen, "Mermaid," 49–50.
82. Andersen, "Mermaid," 51.
83. Andersen, "Mermaid," 51.
84. Andersen, "Mermaid," 51.
85. Andersen, "Mermaid," 52.
86. Mondschein, "Introduction," xiii.
87. Mondschein, "Introduction," xiii.
88. Andersen, "Mermaid," 54.
89. Rosa Guy, *My Love, My Love, or, the Peasant Girl* (Minneapolis: Coffee House Press, 2001), 24.
90. Guy, *My Love*, 25.
91. Guy, *My Love*, 44.
92. Guy, *My Love*, 45.
93. Guy, *My Love*, 68, 73.
94. Guy, *My Love*, 77.
95. Guy, *My Love*, 131–132.
96. Guy, *My Love*, 142.
97. Guy, *My Love*, 142.
98. Guy, *My Love*, 149.
99. Guy, *My Love*, 150.
100. Guy, *My Love*, 155.
101. Guy, *My Love*, 142.
102. "Rosa Guy papers," New York Public Library. Schomburg Center for Research in Black Culture, Manuscripts, Archives and Rare Books Division (ScMG 903).
103. Brinsley Samaroo, "The February Revolution (1970) as a Catalyst for Change in Trinidad and Tobago," in *Black Power in the Caribbean*, ed. Kate Quinn (Gainesville, FL: University Press of Florida, 2014), 97–116, 97.
104. Imamu Baraka, "Black Literature and the Afro-American Nation: The Urban Voice," in *Literature and the Urban Experience: Essays on the City and Literature*, eds. Michael C. Jaye and Ann Chalmers Watts (New Brunswick, NJ: Rutgers University Press, 1981), 139–159, 153–154; Original emphasis.
105. I have previously argued that the rise of the Black feminist drama was an outgrowth from the Black Arts Movement theatre. See, La Donna L. Forsgren, *In Search of Our Warrior Mothers: Women Dramatists of the Black Arts Movement* (Evanston: Northwestern University Press, 2018).
106. Jerrie Norris, *Presenting Rosa Guy* (Boston: Twayne Publishers, 1988), 33.
107. Norris, *Presenting*, 19.
108. Margalit Fox, "Rosa Guy, 89, Author of Forthright Novels for Young People," *New York Times*, June 7, 2012.
109. Norris, *Presenting*, 31.
110. Fox, "Rosa Guy."
111. Prizgar R. Gonzales, "A Conversation with Rosa Guy," *Quarterly Black Review of Books* 1, no. 3 (Feb 28, 1994), 33.
112. Norris, *Presenting*, 11.
113. Bill Rosenfield, Untitled, *Once on This Island* liner notes. 1990 BMG Music, New York, CD, 4–5.
114. Rosenfield, Untitled, 4–5.
115. Julia Eklund Koza, "Unhappy Happy Endings: Cultural Politics in the Broadway Musical Hit 'Once on This Island,'" *The Review of Education/Pedagogy/Cultural Studies* 19, no. 4 (1997): 396.
116. Michael Kilian, "Caribbean Tales: The Gods Make 'Island' a Simple But Profound Hit," *Chicago Tribune*, March 29, 1992.
117. Koza, "Unhappy Happy Endings," 377.
118. Lynn Ahrens and Stephen Flaherty, Untitled, *Once on This Island* liner notes. 1990 BMG Music, New York, CD, 7.

119. Ahrens and Flaherty, Untitled, 10.
120. Ahrens and Flaherty, Untitled, 10.
121. Saidiya Hartman, *Lose Your Mother: A Journey Along the Atlantic Slave Route* (New York: Farrar, Straus and Giroux, 2007), 6.
122. Koza, "Unhappy Happy Endings," 373.
123. Lynn Ahrens and Stephen Flaherty, *Once on This Island, Libretto/Vocal Book* (New York: Music Theatre International, 1991), 50.
124. Ahrens and Flaherty, *Once*, 52.
125. Ahrens and Flaherty, *Once*, 53.
126. Ahrens and Flaherty, *Once*, 54.
127. Ahrens and Flaherty, *Once*, 54.
128. Guy, *My Love*, 163.
129. Guy, *My Love*, 167.
130. Guy, *My Love*, 168.
131. Judith Weinraub, "The Writer's Happily Ever After: Rosa Guy and the Musical With a Fairy Tale Ending," *The Washington Post*, May 26, 1992.
132. Michael Feingold, "Island-Hopping," *The Village Voice*, October 30, 1990.
133. For more information about the marking of *Once on This Island* as "family entertainment," see Koza, "Unhappy Happy Endings," 367–407.

Chapter 5

1. Jill Dolan, *The Feminist Spectator as Critic*, 2nd ed. (Ann Arbor: University of Michigan Press, 2012 [1988]), 2.
2. For more information on *The Wiz*–themed vogue balls, see Ryan Crawford, "Ball Culture Hitting Seattle with 'Return of the Wiz' Black Pride Event," *Seattle Gay Scene*, August 10, 2018, http://seattlegayscene.com/2018/08/ball-culture-hitting-seattle-with-return-of-the-wiz-black-pride-event/ (accessed January 15, 2018).
3. Kenyon Farrow, "Stephanie Mills' 'Home': So Black and So Gay!" *Kenyon Farrow Blog*, October 9, 2018, https://kenyonfarrow.com/2008/10/09/stephanie-mills-home-so-black-and-so-gay/ (accessed December 20, 2018).
4. Farrow, "Stephanie Mills' 'Home.'"
5. Tommy J. Curry, "When the Wiz Goes Black, Does It Ever Go Back?" in *The Wizard of Oz and Philosophy: Wicked Wisdom of the West*, eds. Randall E. Auxier and Phillip S. Seng, (Chicago and La Salle, IL: Open Court, 2008), 63–78.
6. Ryan Bunch, "Oz and the Musical: The American Art Form and the Reinvention of the American Fairy Tale," *Studies in Musical Theatre* 9, no. 1 (2015): 63.
7. Stacy Wolf, *Changed for Good: A Feminist History of the Broadway Musical* (Oxford and New York: Oxford University Press, 2011), 112.
8. Wolf, *Changed for Good*, 115.
9. Rhonda Williams, "*The Wiz*: American Culture at Its Best," in *The Universe of Oz: Essays on Baum's Series and Its Progeny*, ed. Kevin K. Durand and Mary K. Leigh (Jefferson, NC: McFarland, 2010), 191–199.
10. Laura Alexandra Harris, "Queer Black Feminism: The Pleasure Principle," *Feminist Review* 54 (1996): 3.
11. L. Harris, "Queer Black Feminism," 7.
12. Jessica B. Harris, "Harper a Show Biz 'Wiz,'" *New York Amsterdam News*, March 29, 1975.
13. Alexander Doty, *Flaming Classics: Queering the Film Canon* (New York: Routledge, 2000), 50.
14. Doty, *Flaming Classics*, 53–71.
15. Larry Neal, "The Black Arts Movement," *The Drama Review* 12, no. 4 (1968): 29.
16. For more information about the "Negro" to "Black" conversion and revolutionary drama of Martie Evans-Charles, see La Donna L. Forsgren, *In Search of Our Warrior Mothers: Women Dramatists of the Black Arts Movement* (Evanston, IL: Northwestern University Press, 2018).
17. W. E. B. Du Bois Papers, "Krigwa Players Little Negro Theater" (1926), MS 312, Special Collections and University Archives, University of Massachusetts Amherst Libraries.
18. Mance Williams, *Black Theatre in the 1960s and 1970s: A Historical-Critical Analysis of the Movement* (Westport, CT: Greenwood Press, 1985), 101.
19. W. E. B. Du Bois, Amiri Baraka, Allen Woll, and many theatre artists, critics, and scholars have engaged with the question of what constitutes Black theatre or the Black musical.

20. Judith Cummings, "Blacks Gain on Broadway; Lag in 2 Other Arts," *New York Times*, June 6, 1975.
21. Cummings, "Blacks Gain on Broadway."
22. Tim Stack, "*The Wiz Live:* On the Set of NBC's Latest Musical Event," interview with Queen Latifah, *Entertainment Weekly*, December 2, 2015, www.ew.com/article/2015/12/02/wiz-live-production-set/ (accessed July 7, 2017).
23. Bryant Rollins, "Does *The Wiz* Say Something Extra to Blacks?" *New York Times*, December 28, 1975.
24. Allen Woll, *Black Musical Theatre: From "Coontown" to "Dreamgirls"* (Baton Rouge: Louisiana State University Press, 1989), 265.
25. Woll, *Black Musical Theatre*, 263.
26. Rollins, "Does *The Wiz* Say Something."
27. James V. Hatch, "From Hansberry to Shange," in *A History of African American Theatre*, eds. Errol G. Hill and James V. Hatch (Cambridge: Cambridge University Press, 2003), 375–429, esp. 379–380.
28. Woll, *Black Musical Theatre*, 60.
29. M. Williams, *Black Theatre in the 1960s and 1970s*, 103.
30. Mel Gussow, "Casting by Race Can Be Touchy," *New York Times*, August 1, 1976.
31. Concern with the double standard of casting practices recently resurfaced with the Broadway success of *Hamilton*. For an in-depth analysis of the politics of casting and race, see Brandi Wilkins Catanese, *The Problem of the Color[blind]: Racial Transgression and the Politics of Black Performance* (Ann Arbor: University of Michigan, 2011).
32. Quoted in Hatty Lee, "Three Black Female Playwrights Debut New York on Broadway," *Colorlines*, September 21, 2011, *www.colorlines.com/articles/3-black-female-playwrights-debut-new-work-broadway* (accessed January 16, 2019).
33. Gary Anderson, "Black Theatre Survey 2016–2017: A Report on the Health of Black Theatre in America," *Black Theatre Matters*, June 14, 2018, https://blacktheatrematters.files.wordpress.com/2018/06/black-theatre-survey-2016-20173.pdf (accessed January 16, 2019), 17.
34. William F. Brown and Charlie Smalls, *The Wiz* (New York: Samuel French, 1979), 9. Subsequent citations of this script are given parenthetically in the text.
35. Janet Staiger, *Media Reception Studies* (New York: New York University Press, 2005), 150.
36. Patricia Hill Collins, *Black Sexual Politics: African Americans, Gender, and the New Racism* (New York: Routledge, 2005), 109.
37. Collins, *Black Sexual Politics*, 109.
38. Collins, *Black Sexual Politics*, 108.
39. Collins, *Black Sexual Politics*, 108.
40. Mignon R. Moore, "Color Us Invisible: In the Shadows of Communities Black and Gay, Black Lesbians Forge Lives, Loves, and Family," *Huffpost*, November 4, 2011 (updated February 2, 2016), *www.huffingtonpost.com/mignon-r-moore/black-lesbians_b_1075251.html* (accessed January 19, 2018).
41. Tiffany Thomas, "The Legacy of Women in the Black Church," *Christianity Today*, February 11, 2016, *www.christianitytoday.com/women-leaders/2016/february/legacy-of-women-in-black-church.html* (accessed July 19, 2017).
42. Thomas, "Legacy."
43. Collins, *Black Sexual Politics*, 108.
44. For more information, see Daniel Patrick Moynihan et al., *The Negro Family: The Case for National Action* (Washington, DC: GPO, 1965), 30–4; Michele Wallace, *Black Macho and the Myth of the Superwoman* (New York: Dial Press, 1978), 31–32.
45. Wallace, *Black Macho*, 32.
46. Mychal Denzel Smith, "The Dangerous Myth of the 'Missing Black Father,'" *Washington Post*, January 10, 2017, *www.washingtonpost.com/posteverything/wp/2017/01/10/the-dangerous-myth-of-the-missing-black-father/?noredirect = on&utm_term=.9f2391d55e87* (accessed January 19, 2018).
47. Daphne Duval Harrison, *Black Pearls: Blues Queens of the 1920s* (New Brunswick and London: Rutgers University Press, 1988), 287.
48. Angela Y. Davis, *Blues Legacies and Black Feminism: Gertrude "Ma" Rainey, Bessie Smith, and Billy Holiday* (New York: Pantheon Books, 1998), 66–67.
49. Davis, *Blues Legacies and Black Feminism*, 67.

50. Housing covenants were legally enforceable mandates for future buyers of property. Racially restrictive covenants were used to prevent African Americans and other minorities from purchasing, leasing, or occupying property in whites-only neighborhoods.
51. Tim Lawrence, "Disco and Queering the Dance Floor," *Cultural Studies* 25, no. 2 (2011), 232.
52. Lawrence, "Disco," 240.
53. Amy Abugo Ongiri, *Spectacular Blackness: The Cultural Politics of the Black Power Movement and the Search for a Black Aesthetic* (Charlottesville: University of Virginia Press, 2010), 160.
54. Gerald Posner, *Motown: Music, Money, Sex, and Power* (New York: Random House, 2002), 293.
55. Wendy S. Watters, "Blackness in Present Future Tense: Broadside Press, Motown Records, and Detroit Techno," in *New Thoughts on the Black Arts Movement*, eds. Lisa Gail Collins and Margo Natalie Crawford, 117–133 (New Brunswick: Rutgers University Press, 2006), 123.
56. Watters, "Blackness in Present Future Tense," 124–125, quote at 124.
57. Quoted in Alvin Klein, "Dorothy and Wiz Hip-Hop into the 90's," *New York Times*, February 7, 1993. Brown noted that, in the revamped stage version, "Dorothy has more depth, Dorothy is less passive."
58. Klein, "Dorothy."
59. Posner, *Motown*, 294.
60. *The Wiz*, directed by Sidney Lumet (prod. Motown Productions, dist. Universal Pictures, 1978; DVD, Universal City, CA: Universal Pictures Home Entertainment, 2009). Subsequent citations of this film are to this DVD.
61. Bunch, "Oz and the Musical," 62.
62. R. Williams, *The Wiz*, 196–197.
63. Lawrence, "Disco," 231.
64. Lawrence, "Disco," 236, 231.
65. Susan Sontag, "Notes on 'Camp,'" in *Against Interpretation and Other Essays* (London: Penguin Books, 2009 [rpt. 1966]), 275–292, 275.
66. Sontag, "Notes," 276.
67. Pamela Robertson, "What Makes the Feminist Camp?" in *Camp: Queer Aesthetics and the Performing Subject: A Reader*, ed. Fabio Cleto, (Ann Arbor: University of Michigan Press, 1999), 266–282, 267.
68. In 2015, more than one hundred or 36% of unarmed people killed by police were Black. Yet, Black people constitute only 13% of the US population; "Mapping Police Violence: Unarmed Victims" at https://mappingpoliceviolence.org/unarmed (accessed August 25, 2017). These numbers continue to rise, with more than three hundred reported cases in 2016. For more information, visit "Mapping Police Violence" at https://mappingpoliceviolence.org/ (accessed August 25, 2017).
69. The White Lives Matter movement argues that the US government's immigration and integration policies effectively undermine the proliferation of the white race. For more information, visit https://vk.com/whitelivesmatter (accessed April 18, 2019).
70. Bonnie Faller, "*The Wiz* Racist? Twitter Explodes in Furious Argument Over Show's All Black Cast," *Hollywood Life*, December 3, 2015, *http://hollywoodlife.com/2015/12/03/the-wiz-live-racist-all-black-cast-nbc-twitter/* (accessed July 10, 2017).
71. Quoted in Stack, "*The Wiz Live*."
72. Melena Ryzik, "The Story Behind the Return of *The Wiz*," *New York Times*, November 30, 2015, *www.nytimes.com/2015/12/01/arts/television/the-wiz-with-added-street-cred-heads-for-tv-and-broadway.html?mcubz = 3* (accessed July 24, 2017).
73. Rick Kissell, "*The Wiz Live* Ratings Strong: NBC Musical Draws 11.5 Million Viewers," *Variety*, December 4, 2015, http://variety.com/2015/tv/news/the-wiz-live-ratings-nbc-musical-1201653402/(accessed July 7, 2017).
74. Rob Smith, "Five Reasons *The Wiz Live* Was the Gayest Thing on TV This Year," *Queerty**, December 4, 2015, www.queerty.com/five-reasons-the-wiz-live-was-the-gayest-thing-on-tv-this-year-20151204 (accessed July 9, 2017).
75. Robertson, "What Makes," 278.
76. *The Wiz Live!*, directed by Kenny Leon and Matthew Diamond (Universal City, CA: Universal Studios Home Entertainment, 2015). Subsequent citations of this production are to this DVD.
77. Emphasis added.
78. Adam Liptak, "Supreme Court Revives Transgender Ban for Military Service," *New York Times*, January 22, 2019, *www.nytimes.com/2019/01/22/us/politics/transgender-ban-military-supreme-court.html* (accessed January 22, 2019).

79. Zach Laws, "Mary J. Blige on Playing the Wicked Witch Evillene in *The Wiz Live!*" interview with Mary J. Blige, YouTube, June 19, 2016, www.youtube.com/watch?v=eIiwtZfL7nk (accessed August 3, 2017).
80. "Mary J. Blige Talks 'Wiz' Critics' Choice Nomination," *E! News*, YouTube, January 20, 2016, *www.youtube.com/watch?v=9XDY-ZvAta0* (accessed August 3, 2017).
81. Laws, "Mary J. Blige."
82. Laws, "Mary J. Blige."
83. Collins, *Black Sexual Politics*, 123.
84. For information on the black cultural expression of signifyin', see Henry Louis Gates Jr., *The Signifying Monkey: A Theory of African-American Literary Criticism* (Oxford and New York: Oxford University Press, 1988).
85. "The Wiz Broadway Grosses," https://www.broadwayworld.com/grosses/THE-WIZ, (accessed September 10, 2024).
86. "The Broadway Show: Schele Williams on Directing the Return of THE WIZ," Broadwaycom, uploaded August 29, 2023, https://www.youtube.com/watch?v=xDRYeLT1L9I&t=4s
87. Schele Williams, interview with author, December 19, 2019.
88. S. Williams, interview.
89. "The Broadway Show."
90. "The Broadway Show."
91. "Avery Wilson Reveals Scarecrow is Bisexual & Lion is Queer in 'The Wiz' (Exclusive)," PRIDE, April 15, 2024, https://www.youtube.com/watch?v=YnjG-Te-ets.
92. "Avery Wilson."
93. *The Wiz*, book by William F. Brown, music and lyrics by Charlie Smalls, additional material by Amber Ruffin, and directed by Schele Williams. Marquis Theatre, New York, April 2, 2024. All subsequent citations are from this production.
94. "The Broadway Show."
95. In *The Wiz* 2024 Broadway revival, the Poppies are portrayed by actresses Maya Bowles, Allyson Kaye Daniel, Shayla Caldwell, Judith Franklin, Amber Jackson, Olivia Jackson, Christina Jones, and Cristina Raé. Christina Jones and Judith Franklin also portray *The Wiz*'s backup singers.
96. "The Broadway Show."
97. "The Broadway Show."

Chapter 6

1. Barbara Ann Teer, "Needed: A New Image," in *The Black Power Revolt: A Collection of Essays*, ed. Floyd B. Barbour (Boston: Porter Sargent Publisher, 1968), 219–223, 219–220.
2. Teer, "Needed," 220.
3. Teer, "Needed," 221.
4. Eddie Shapiro, *Nothing Like A Dame: Conversations with the Great Women of Musical Theatre* (New York: Oxford University Press, 2014), 267.
5. Shapiro, *Nothing*, 268–269.
6. Shapiro, *Nothing*, 271.
7. Shapiro, *Nothing*, 270.
8. Shapiro, *Nothing*, 275.
9. "Audra McDonald Is A Tornado On Stage As Mama Rose," *The Late Show with Stephen Colbert*, YouTube, February 4, 2025, *https://www.youtube.com/watch?v=RL4quHtcN2Y* (accessed April 1, 2025).
10. Viola Davis, *Finding Me: A Memoir* (San Francisco: HarperOne, 2022), 177.
11. V. Davis, 189.
12. Jayla Williams-Craig, interview with author, July 9, 2020.
13. Williams-Craig, interview.
14. Williams-Craig, interview.
15. Christiani Pitts, interview with author, January 17, 2020.
16. Pitts, interview.
17. Olivia Clement, "Sign Up Now for BAC's Broadway for Black Lives Matter Again," *Playbill*, June 4, 2020, https://playbill.com/article/sign-up-now-for-bacs-broadway-for-black-lives-matter-again
18. Casey Mink, "Just Try and Stop Her," *Backstage*, July 23, 2020, 16.
19. Schele Williams, interview with author, December 19, 2019.

20. Mark Brown, "Katori Hall, writer of Tina Turner musical, on #MeToo, diversity and inclusion," *The Guardian*, March 4, 2018. https://www.theguardian.com/music/2018/mar/04/katori-hall-writer-of-tina-turner-musical-on-metoo-diversity-and-inclusion (accessed August 3, 2024).
21. Tarana Burke, "History & Inception," Me Too, https://metoomvmt.org/get-to-know-us/history-inception/ (accessed August 3, 2024).
22. Burke, "History."
23. While sexual predators of every kind should stand accountable for their actions, including the rich and famous, I do worry that social media has shifted the focus away from helping everyday survivors—Black women, Blackgirls, and other vulnerable populations—to merely sensationalizing celebrity crimes for easy consumption.
24. Burke, "History."
25. Aishah Rahman, *Lady Day*, Alexander Street, 1972, https://search-alexanderstreet-com.proxy.library.nd.edu/view/work/bibliographic_entity%7Cbibliographic_details%7C3607299#search/lady + day. Subsequent citations are from this script.
26. Thadious M. Davis, "Aishah Rahman's Writing In the Dark: The Presence of An Absence," *Obsidian III* 1, no. 1 (1999): 57–58.
27. Billie Holiday and William Duffy, *Lady Sings the Blues* (New York: Penguin Books, 1992 [rpt. 1956]), 61.
28. T. Davis, "Aishah Rahman," 57–58.
29. T. Davis, "Aishah Rahman," 57.
30. Aishah Rahman, "Living in the Black Arts Movement" in *SOS—Calling All Black People: A Black Arts Movement Reader*, eds. John H. Bracey Jr., Sonia Sanchez, and James Smethurst (Amherst: University of Massachusetts Press, 2014), 441.
31. Angela Y. Davis, *Blues Legacy and Black Feminism: Gertrude "Ma" Rainey, Bessie Smith, and Billie Holiday* (New York: Vintage Books, 1998), 184.
32. A. Davis, *Blues Legacies*, 184.
33. Davi Napoleon, *Chelsea on the Edge: The Adventures of an American Theater* (Ames, Iowa: Iowa State University Press, 1991), 99.
34. Napolean, *Chelsea*, 99.
35. Napolean, *Chelsea*, 99.
36. Roger Robinson would later appear in six of August Wilson's cycle plays, which chronicle the history of African Americans throughout the 20th century, and win a Tony Award for Best Performance by a Featured Actor in a Play for the 2009 revival of August Wilson's *Joe Turner's Come and Gone.*
37. Martin Gottfried, "Lady Day: A Musical Tragedy," *Women's Wear Daily*, October 27, 1972.
38. Clive Barnes, "Stage: Chelsea Players' Tragedy of Billie Holiday," *The New York Times*, October 26, 1972.
39. Napoleon, *Chelsea*, 100.
40. T. Davis, "Aishah Rahman," 60.
41. Napoleon, *Chelsea*, 100.
42. Richard Nixon, "Remarks About an Intensified Program for Drug Abuse Prevention and Control," June 17, 1971, The American Presidency Project, https://www.presidency.ucsb.edu/documents/remarks-about-intensified-program-for-drug-abuse-prevention-and-control (accessed June 26, 2024).
43. Nixon, "Remarks."
44. E. Ann Carson, "Prisoners in 2018," April 2020, U.S. Department of Justice, Office of Justice Programs, Bureau of Justice Statistics, https://bjs.ojp.gov/content/pub/pdf/p18.pdf (accessed March 9, 2026).
45. Brian Mann, "After 50 Years Of The War On Drugs, 'What Good Is It Doing For Us'?" NPR, June 17, 2021, https://www.npr.org/2021/06/17/1006495476/after-50-years-of-the-war-on-drugs-what-good-is-it-doing-for-us
46. Mann, "After 50 Years."
47. Wendy Sawyer and Peter Wagner, "Mass Incarceration: The Whole Pie 2024," *Prison Policy Initiative*, March 14, 2024, https://www.prisonpolicy.org/reports/pie2024.html#:~:text=Together%2C%20these%20systems%20hold%20over,centers%2C%20state%20psychiatric%20hospitals%2C%20and
48. Sawyer and Wagner, "Mass Incarceration."
49. Mann, "After 50 Years."

50. Holiday and Dufty, 132.
51. Holiday and Dufty, 16.
52. Holiday and Dufty, 103–104.
53. Seanna Leath et al. "Raising Resilient Black Women: A Study of Superwoman Mothering and Strength as a Form of Gendered Racial Socialization in Black Mother–Daughter Relationships," *Sex Roles* 89 (2023): 626.
54. Original emphasis.
55. A. Davis, *Blues Legacies*, 173.
56. Holiday and Dufty, 84.
57. Holiday and Dufty, 68–69.
58. Holiday and Dufty, 84.
59. Holiday and Dufty, 114.
60. Billie Holiday, "Strange Fruit," written by Abel Meeropol, produced by Milton Gabler, Commodore Records, 1939.
61. For more information on health, educational, and economic disparities, see Bryana H. French, Jioni A. Lewis, and Helen A. Neville, "Naming and Reclaiming: An Interdisciplinary Analysis of Black Girls' and Women's Resistance Strategies," *Journal of African American Studies* 17, no. 1 (2013): 1–6.
62. Michelle Parkerson, *Stormé: The Lady in the Jewel Box*, 21 min., color, 16mm/video, 1987.
63. Bud Coleman, "The Jewel Box Revue: America's Longest-Running, Touring Drag Show," *Theatre History Studies* 17 (1997): 81.
64. Coleman, "The Jewel Box Revue," 88.
65. Ted Fox, *Showtime at the Apollo: The Epic Tale of Harlem's Legendary Theater* (New York: Holt, Rinehart and Winston, 1983), 282.
66. Coleman, "The Jewel Box Revue," 87.
67. A. Davis, *Blues Legacies*, 171.
68. Even *Lady Day*'s harshest theatre critic, Clive Barnes, describes Roger Robinson's drag performance as a "clever" imitation of Billie Holiday's voice and style. See Clive Barnes, "Stage: Chelsea Players' Tragedy of Billie Holiday," *The New York Times*, October 26, 1972.
69. Angela Bassett's and Laurence Fishburne's performance as Tina Turner and Ike Turner, respectively, in the 1993 film *What's Love Got to Do With It* garnered Academy Award nominations for Best Actress and Best Actor. Bassett also won a Golden Globe Award for Best Actress—Motion Picture Comedy or Musical for her outstanding performance.
70. King Charles III met Tina Turner when she performed in London at his Prince's Trust All-Star Rock Concert at Wembley Stadium in 1986. Days after her May 23, 2023, death, King Charles had the Band of Welsh guards play Turner's "The Best" at Buckingham Palace.
71. Nate Woodall, "Tina Turner, Queen of Rock 'N' Roll, dies at 83," *Q News*, May 25, 2023, https://qnews.com.au/tina-turner-queen-of-rock-n-roll-dies-at-83/
72. Maureen Mahon, *Black Diamond Queens: African American Women and Rock and Roll* (Durham: Duke University Press, 2020), 270.
73. Mark Brown, "Katori Hall, Writer of Tina Turner Musical, on #MeToo, diversity and inclusion," *The Guardian*, March 4, 2018. https://www.theguardian.com/music/2018/mar/04/katori-hall-writer-of-tina-turner-musical-on-metoo-diversity-and-inclusion
74. Bobby Hankinson, "Gay Iconography: Tina Turner Is Simply The Best," *Towleroad Gay News*, August 22, 2015, https://www.towleroad.com/2015/08/gay-iconography-tina-turner/
75. Marcus Wratten, "Tina Turner Was a Fearless LGBTQ+ Ally – Long Before it Was Popular to Be One," *PinkNews*, May 25, 2023, https://www.thepinknews.com/2023/05/25/tina-turner-lgbtq-ally-legacy/
76. Wratten, "Fearless LGBTQ+ Ally."
77. Woodall, "Queen of Rock 'N' Roll."
78. Tina Turner with Kurt Loder, *I, Tina: My Life Story* (New York: William Morrow, 2010 [rpt. 1986]), 204.
79. Ike Turner with Nigel Cawthorne, *Takin' Back My Name: The Confessions of Ike Turner* (CreateSpace Independent Publishing Platform, 2015 [rpt. 1999]), 61.
80. Joshua S. Mackey, "5 Ways Tina Turner Proved She Was a Gay Icon," *Into*, May 25, 2023, https://www.intomore.com/entertainment/music/5-ways-tina-turner-proved-she-was-a-gay-icon/.
81. Charles Passy, "Tina Turner Musical Is Rollin' at the Box Office," *Wall Street Journal*, October 29, 2019.

82. "Tina-The Tina Turner Musical Broadway Grosses," https://www.broadwayworld.com/grosses/TINA-THE-TINA-TURNER-MUSICAL (accessed August 21, 2024).
83. Millie Taylor, *Musical Theatre, Realism, Entertainment* (Burlington, VT: Ashgate Publishing Limited, 2012), 162.
84. George Rodosthenous, "*Mamma Mia!* and the Aesthetics of the Twenty-First-Century Jukebox Musical," in *The Oxford Handbook of the British Musical*, eds. Robert Gordon and Olaf Jubin, (Oxford: Oxford University Press, 2016), 613–632, 614.
85. *Tina: The Tina Turner Musical Original Cast Recording*, liner notes, Sh-K-Boom Records, LLC, New York, NY, 2019, CD.
86. *Tina*, liner notes.
87. *Tina*, liner notes.
88. For more information about jukebox musical controversy, see Michael John LaChiusa, "The Great Gray Way: Is Prognosis Negative for the Broadway Musical?" *Opera News* 1 (August 2005): 30–35; George Rodosthenous, "*Mamma Mia!* and the Aesthetics of the Twenty-First-Century Jukebox Musical," in *The Oxford Handbook of the British Musical*, eds. Robert Gordon and Olaf Jubin (Oxford: Oxford University Press, 2016), 613–632; and Barbara Ellen, "I Want to Break Free . . . Now," *The Observer*, April 16, 2006.
89. LaChiusa, "The Great," 32.
90. LaChiusa, "The Great," 32.
91. LaChiusa, "The Great," 35.
92. Michael John LaChiusa, "Open Season," *Opera News* 79, no. 2 (August 2014): 15.
93. Ellen, "I Want to Break Free."
94. Ellen, "I Want to Break Free."
95. Rodosthenous, "Aesthetics," 623.
96. Jeff Sugg, interview with author, March 26, 2021.
97. Mark Kennedy, "Broadway's Tony Nominations in for Tina Turner Musical," *Miami Times*, March 3–9, 2021.
98. *Tina*, liner notes.
99. *Tina*, liner notes.
100. Kennedy, "Broadway's Tony Nominations."
101. Kennedy, "Broadway's Tony Nominations."
102. Kennedy, "Broadway's Tony Nominations."
103. Katori Hall, "A Note From the Playwright," in *Tina: The Tina Turner Musical Original Cast Recording*, liner notes, Sh-K-Boom Records, LLC, New York, NY, 2019, CD.
104. Memuna Forna, "What's Race Got to Do with It,' *Guardian*, September 13, 1993; HBO's release of *Tina* (2021) provides a third major artistic examination of Tina Turner's life and legacy. Rather than allow others to speak for her, Turner recounts her own life story, including her roots in Black gospel and the blues traditions. The three-time Primetime Emmy-nominated documentary includes commentary from her family, friends, and artistic collaborators, including Katori Hall.
105. bell hooks, *Reel to Real: Race, Sex, and Class at the Movies* (New York: Routledge, 1996), 112.
106. Duncan Wheeler, "The Rock Musical: From Creation to Curation (2015–2020)," *New Theatre Quarterly* 39, no. 2 (May 2023): 166.
107. hooks, *Reel to Real*, 112.
108. Wheeler, "The Rock Musical," 164.
109. Wheeler, "The Rock Musical," 165.
110. Rodosthenous, "Aesthetics," 615.
111. Rodosthenous, "Aesthetics," 615.
112. Natalie de la Garza, "*Tina: The Tina Turner Musical* a Rocking Ode to Resilience," *Houston Press*, January 3, 2024, https://www.houstonpress.com/arts/things-to-do-a-review-of-tina-the-tina-turner-musical-17186985; see also Chris Jones, "'Tina Turner Musical' Has a Fabulous Tina: Warren Nails Every Note in Role as the Overworked Diva," *Chicago Tribune*, November 8, 2019.
113. de la Garza, "Rocking Ode to Resilience."
114. Marilyn Stasio, "Tina: The Tina Turner Musical," *Variety*, November 12, 2019, 213.
115. Sugg, interview.
116. Sugg, interview.
117. *Tina: The Tina Turner Musical*, book by Katori Hall, with Frank Ketelaar and Kees Prins, directed by Phyllida Lloyd, Lunt-Fontanne Theatre, New York, NY, November 23, 2019.

Subsequent citations are from this production. All stage direction notations are from the author.

118. de la Garza, "Rocking Ode to Resilience."
119. Turner and Loder, *I, Tina*, 77–78.
120. hooks, *Reel to Real*, 67.
121. *Tina*, directed Dan Lindsay and TJ Martin, HBO Documentary Films, 2021, DVD.
122. Ike and his Kings of Rhythm band recorded "Rockett 88" (1951), the first rock and roll album. Unfortunately, the single was credited to his saxophone player, "Jackie Brenston and his Delta Cats." For more information about Ike Turner's father, see Turner and Cawthorne, *Takin' Back My Name*, 6.
123. David Rooney, "Tina: The Tina Turner Musical," *The Hollywood Reporter*, November 13, 2019, 87.
124. Rooney, "Musical," 87.
125. Wheeler, "The Rock Musical," 166.
126. Record producer Phil Spector was convicted of murdering actress Lana Clarkson (after two trials) on April 13, 2009, and sentenced to nineteen years to life in state prison. Spector then died in a prison hospital on January 16, 2021.
127. P. P. Arnold, *Soul Survivor: The Autobiography* (London: Blink Publishing, 2023), 50.
128. Arnold, *Soul Survivor*, 51.
129. P. P. Arnold eventually forged a successful solo singing career in the UK with singles "The First Cut Is the Deepest" (1967) and "Angel of the Morning" (1968).
130. *King Kong*, book by Jack Thorne, score by Marius de Vries, songs by Eddie Perfect, directed by Drew McOnie, Broadway Theatre, New York, July 31, 2019. Subsequent citations are from this production.
131. "'King Kong' Musical, With Eye on Broadway, Opens in Australia," *The Guardian*, June 17, 2013.
132. Ray Morton, *King Kong the History of a Movie Icon: From Fay Wray to Peter Jackson* (New York: Applause Theatre & Cinema Books, 2005), 31. For more information about the casting of the 1933 film *King Kong*, see Fay Wray, *On the Other Hand: A Life Story* (New York: St. Martin's Press, 1989).
133. Scott Heller and Nancy Coleman, "'King Kong' and 'Cher Show' Musicals Announce Closings," *The New York Times*, June 25, 2019.
134. "King Kong Review-Broadway Kills the Beast in Monstrously Bad Musical," *The Guardian*, https://www.theguardian.com/stage/2018/nov/08/king-kong-review-braodway-musical (accessed July 24, 2024).
135. Heller and Coleman, "Announce Closings."
136. "King Kong Review-Broadway."
137. "King Kong Review-Broadway."
138. Susan Sontag, "Notes on 'Camp,'" in *Against Interpretation and Other Essays* (London: Penguin Books, 2009 [rpt. 1966]), 275–292, 275.
139. Sontag, "Notes," 276.
140. Jesse Green and Ben Brantley, "Review: 'King Kong' Is the Mess that Roared," *New York Times*, November 8, 2018, https://www.nytimes.com/2018/11/08/theater/king-kong-review.html.
141. Green and Brantley, "Review."
142. Sontag, "Notes," 285.
143. Sontag, "Notes," 283.
144. Green and Brantley, "Review."
145. Sontag, "Notes," 283.
146. Sontag, "Notes," 282.
147. Sontag, "Notes," 292.
148. "King Kong Review-Broadway."
149. Barbara Ann Teer, "The Black Woman: She Does Exist," *The New York Times*, May 14, 1967.
150. Teer, "The Black."
151. Teer, "The Black."
152. Pitts, interview.
153. Pitts, interview.
154. Merian C. Cooper, Ernest B. Schoedsack, Edgar Wallace, Ruth Rose, and James Ashmore Creelman, *King Kong (1933): Shooting Script*, eds. Marian C. Cooper and Ernest B. Schoedsack

(Alexandria, VA: Alexander Street, 2009), https://search-alexanderstreet-com.proxy.library.nd.edu/view/work/bibliographic_entity/bibliographic_details,3070368.

155. Cooper et al, *Script.*
156. Cooper et al, *Script.*
157. Cooper et al, *Script.*
158. Cooper et al, *Script.*
159. Cooper et al, *Script.*
160. Cooper et al, *Script.*
161. See Brandi Wilkins Catanese, *The Problem of the Color[blind]: Racial Transgression and the Politics of Black Performance* (Ann Arbor: University of Michigan Press, 2011) for an excellent discussion of societal casting, cross-cultural casting, conceptual casting, blind casting, and color conscious casting within American commercial theatre and film.
162. Kristin Bria Hopkins, "There's No Business Like Show Business: Abandoning Color-Blind Casting and Embracing Color-Conscious Casting in American Theatre," *Journal of Sports and Entertainment Law* (2018):133–134.
163. Hopkins, "No Business," 133–134.
164. Pitts, interview.
165. Pitts, interview.
166. Pitts, interview.
167. Jack Thorne's book for the 2018 Broadway version of *King Kong* is a re-working of Craig Lucas's 2013 book for the Melbourne production.
168. Pitts, interview.
169. Pitts, interview.
170. Pitts, interview.
171. Italicized stage directions are author's notations.
172. Green and Brantley, "Review."
173. Katy Perry, "Roar," *Prism* (2013), https://www.youtube.com/watch?v = CevxZvSJLk8.
174. Pitts, interview.
175. Cooper et al, *Script.*
176. Patricia Hill Collins, *Black Sexual Politics: African Americans, Gender, and the New Racism* (New York, Routledge, 2005), 64.
177. Morton, *History of a Movie Icon*, 84.
178. Pitts, interview.
179. Nick Romano, "The New King of Broadway: Meet the King Kong Musical's 2,000-pound Puppet," *Entertainment Weekly*, November 5, 2018, https://ew.com/theater/2018/11/05/king-kong-musical-broadway-puppet/.
180. Pitts, interview.
181. "King Kong Review-Broadway."
182. Pitts, interview.
183. Pitts, interview.

Conclusion

1. Jill Dolan, "Performance, Utopia, and the 'Utopian Performative,'" *Theatre Journal* 53 (2001): 460.
2. "We See You White American Theatre," https://www.weseeyouwat.com/statement (accessed March 9, 2026).
3. "Chaos, Confusion, & Abuse of Power: Trump's First Week Back in Office," *The Leadership Conference on Civil and Human Rights*, January 30, 2025, https://civilrights.org/blog/chaos-confusion-abuse-of-power-trumps-first-week-back-in-office/.
4. "Executive Order on Birthright Citizenship," *American Immigration Lawyers Association*, January 1, 2025, https://www.aila.org/library/president-trump-signs-executive-order-protecting-the-meaning-and-value-of-american-citizenship.
5. "Chaos."
6. Jeff Sugg, interview with author, March 26, 2021.
7. Christiani Pitts, interview with author, January 17, 2020.

Bibliography

Archival Materials

Aremu, Aduke. "The Liberation of Mother Goose" (1972), Unpublished Manuscript, Courtesy of Aduke Aremu.

Bella: An American Tale, book, music, and lyrics by Kirsten Childs, directed by Robert O'Hara, Playwrights Horizons, New York, NY, June 21, 2017. The New York Public Library Theatre on Film and Tape Archive (DVD).

Carroll, Vinnette, Alex Bradford, and Micki Grant. *Your Arm's Too Short to Box With God* (1975), New York Public Library for the Performing Arts, Billy Rose Theatre Division (NCOF + 11-3204).

Nottage, Lynn, Duncan Sheik, and Susan Birkenhead, *The Secret Life of Bees* (2019), Unpublished Manuscript, New York Public Library for the Performing Arts, Billy Rose Theatre Division (NCOF + 20-564).

Once on this Island, book and lyrics by Lynn Ahrens, music by Stephen Flaherty, directed by Graciela Daniele, Playwrights Horizons, New York, NY, May 13, 1990. The New York Public Library Theatre on Film and Tape Archive (DVD).

"Rosa Guy papers," New York Public Library. Schomburg Center for Research in Black Culture, Manuscripts, Archives and Rare Books Division (ScMG 903).

The Bubbly Black Girl Sheds Her Chameleon Skin, book, music, and lyrics by Kirsten Childs, directed by Wilfredo Medina, Playwrights Horizons, New York, NY, July 15, 2000. The New York Public Library Theatre on Film and Tape Archive, 2000 (VHS).

The Color Purple: The Musical, book by Marsha Norman, music and lyrics by Brenda Russell, Allee Willis, and Stephen Bray, directed by Gary Griffin, Broadway Theatre, New York, NY, April 12, 2006. The New York Public Library Theatre on Film and Tape Archive (VHS).

The Color Purple, book by Marsha Norman, music and lyrics by Brenda Russell, Allee Willis, and Stephen Bray, directed by John Doyle, Bernard B. Jacobs Theatre, New York, NY, November 9, 2016. The New York Public Library Theatre on Film and Tape Archive, 2016, Videodiscs (DVD), 120 min.

The Secret Life of Bees, book by Lynn Nottage, music by Duncan Sheik, lyrics by Susan Birkenhead, directed by Sam Gold, Atlantic Theatre Company, New York, NY, July 19, 2019. The New York Public Library Theatre on Film and Tape Archive (DVD).

W. E. B. Du Bois Papers, "Krigwa Players Little Negro Theater" (1926), MS 312, Special Collections and University Archives, University of Massachusetts Amherst Libraries.

Works Cited

"About," Black Lives Matter, https://blacklivesmatter.com/about/ (accessed January 3, 2020).

Abrams, Stacey. *Minority Leader: How to Lead from the Outside and Make Real Change.* New York: Henry Holt and Company, 2018.

Ahrens, Lynn and Stephen Flaherty. *Once on This Island, Libretto/Vocal Book.* New York: Music Theatre International, 1991.

American Psychological Association. "The road to resilience." https://www.apa.org/search?query = resilence (accessed March 9, 2026).

Andersen, Hans Christian. *Hans Christian Andersen's Complete Fairy Tales*, trans. by Jean Hersholt. San Diego: Canterbury Classics, 2014 [1837].

Anderson, Gary. "Black Theatre Survey 2016–2017: A Report on the Health of Black Theatre in America," *Black Theatre Matters*, June 14, 2018, *https://blacktheatrematters.files.wordpress.com/2018/06/black-theatre-survey-2016-20173.pdf* (accessed January 16, 2019).

"Anti-Lynching Legislation Renewed," *United States House of Representatives: History, Art & Archives*, https://history.house.gov/Exhibitions-and-Publications/BAIC/Historical-Essays/Temporary-Farewell/Anti-Lynching-Legislation/ (accessed November 24, 2025).

Armstrong, Linda. "'Mama I Want to Sing,'" *New York Amsterdam News*, Oct 30, 2003.

Arnold, P. P. *Soul Survivor: The Autobiography*. London: Blink Publishing, 2023.

"Audra McDonald Is a Tornado on Stage As Mama Rose," *The Late Show with Stephen Colbert*, YouTube, February 4, 2025, *https://www.youtube.com/watch?v = RL4quHtcN2Y* (accessed April 1, 2025).

Auxier, Randall E. and Phillip S. Seng, eds. *The Wizard of Oz and Philosophy: Wicked Wisdom of the West*. Chicago and La Salle, IL: Open Court, 2008.

"Avery Wilson Reveals Scarecrow is Bisexual & Lion is Queer in 'The Wiz' (Exclusive)," PRIDE, April 15, 2024, https://www.youtube.com/watch?v = YnjG-Te-ets.

Bailey, Peter. "'Mama I Want to Sing' Celebrates Fifth Smash Year at Heckscher Theatre," *New York Amsterdam News*, March 12, 1988.

Barbour, Floyd B., ed. *The Black Power Revolt: A Collection of Essays*. Boston: Porter Sargent Publisher, 1968.

Barnes, Clive. "Stage: Chelsea Players' Tragedy of Billie Holiday," *The New York Times*, October 26, 1972.

Barnes, Grace. *Her Time on Stage: The Role of Women in Musical Theatre*. Jefferson, NC: McFarland, 2015.

Beaufort, John. "Gospel Music to George Abbitt to Lincoln," *The Christian Science Monitor*, December 27, 1976.

Beckett, Sandra L., ed. *Provisioning Red Riding Hood Around the World in Anthology of International Retellings*. Detroit: Wayne State University Press, 2014.

Bernard, Emily. *Black is the Body: Stories from My Grandmother's Time, My Mother's Time, and Mine*. New York: Vintage, 2019.

Bial, Henry and Chase Bringardner, eds. *Great North American Stage Directors Volume 4: George Abbott, Vinnette Carroll, Harold Prince*. London: Methuen Drama, 2024.

Bottigheimer, Ruth B. *Grimms' Bad Girls and Bold Boys: The Moral and Social Vision of the Tales*. New Haven: Yale University Press, 1987.

Bracey Jr, John H., Sonia Sanchez, and James Smethurst, eds. *SOS—Calling All Black People: A Black Arts Movement Reader*. Amherst: University of Massachusetts Press, 2014.

Brantley, Ben. "One Woman's Awakening, in Double Time," *The New York Times*, December 2, 2005.

Breznican, Anthony. "Steven Spielberg: The EW Interview," *Entertainment Weekly*, December 2, 2011, https://ew.com/article/2011/12/02/steven-spielberg-ew-interview/.

Brown, Aaron. "Hallelujah and Amen: The Revival of *the Color Purple* As African-American Church," *Ecumenica: Performance and Religion* 11, no. 1 (2018): 63–71.

Brown, Mark. "Katori Hall, Writer of Tina Turner Musical, on #MeToo, diversity and inclusion," *The Guardian*, March 4, 2018, https://www.theguardian.com/music/2018/mar/04/katori-hall-writer-of-tina-turner-musical-on-metoo-diversity-and-inclusion (accessed August 3, 2024).

Brown, Ruth Nicole. *Black Girlhood Celebration: Toward a Hip-Hop Feminist Pedagogy*. New York: Peter Lang Publishing, 2009.

Brown, William F. and Charlie Smalls. *The Wiz*. New York: Samuel French, 1979.

Bullins, Ed. "A Playwright Lauds Prodigal Sister," *New York Amsterdam News*, December 21, 1974.

Bunch, Ryan. "Oz and the Musical: The American Art Form and the Reinvention of the American Fairy Tale," *Studies in Musical Theatre* 9, no. 1 (2015): 53–69.

Burford, Mark, ed. *The Mahalia Jackson Reader*. New York: Oxford University Press, 2020.
Burke, Tarana. "History & Inception," Me Too, https://metoomvmt.org/get-to-know-us/history-inception/ (accessed 3 August 2024).
Burns, Katelyn. "A Brutal Video Shows a Black Trans Woman Getting Beat up by Dozens of Men," *Vox*, June 3, 2020, https://www.vox.com/identities/2020/6/3/21279407/video-black-trans-woman-iyanna-dior-beaten.
"Camille A. Brown," 2018, https://www.camilleabrown.org/camille (accessed March 2, 2021).
Canepa, Nancy L. et al., ed. *Teaching Fairy Tales*. Detroit: Wayne State University Press, 2019.
Carby, Hazel V. *Reconstructing Womanhood: The Emergence of the Afro-American Woman Novelist*. New York: Oxford University Press, 1987.
Carruthers, Charlene A. *Unapologetic: A Black, Queer, and Feminist Mandate For Radical Movements*. Boston: Beacon Press, 2018.
Carson, E. Ann. "Prisoners in 2018," U.S. Department of Justice, Office of Justice Programs, Bureau of Justice Statistics, https://bjs.ojp.gov/content/pub/pdf/p18.pdf (accessed March 6, 2026).
Catanese, Brandi Wilkins. *The Problem of the Color[blind]: Racial Transgression and the Politics of Black Performance*. Ann Arbor: University of Michigan, 2011.
Childs, Kirsten. *Bella: An American Tale*. New York: Samuel French, 2019.
Childs, Kirsten. *The Bubbly Black Girl Sheds Her Chameleon Skin*. New York: Dramatists Play Service, 2003.
Church Girl, written by Angela Barrow-Dunlap and directed by Reuben Yabuku. Culver City, CA: Sony Pictures Home Entertainment, 2011, DVD.
Clement, Olivia. "Sign Up Now for BAC's Broadway for Black Lives Matter Again," *Playbill*, June 4, 2020, https://playbill.com/article/sign-up-now-for-bacs-broadway-for-black-lives-matter-again
Cleto, Fabio, ed. *Camp: Queer Aesthetics and the Performing Subject: A Reader*. Ann Arbor: University of Michigan Press, 1999.
Clonan-Roy, Katie, Charlotte E. Jacobs, and Michael J. Nakkula. "Towards a Model of Positive Youth Development Specific to Girls of Color: Perspectives on Development, Resilience, and Empowerment," *Gender Issues* 33 (2016): 96–121.
Coleman, Bud. "The Jewel Box Revue: America's Longest-Running, Touring Drag Show," *Theatre History Studies*, 17 (1997): 80–92.
Coleman, Bud and Judith A. Sebesta, eds. *Women in American Musical Theatre: Essays on Composers, Lyricists, Librettists, Arrangers, Choreographers, Designers, Directors, Producers and Performance Artists*. Jefferson, NC: McFarland, 2008.
Collins, Lisa Gail and Margo Natalie Crawford, eds. *New Thoughts on the Black Arts Movement*. New Brunswick: Rutgers University Press, 2006.
Collins, Patricia Hill. *Black Sexual Politics: African Americans, Gender, and the New Racism*. New York: Routledge, 2005.
Collins, Patricia Hill. *Black Feminist Thought: Knowledge, Consciousness, and the Politics of Empowerment*. New York: Routledge, 1990.
"'Color Purple' Musical on Broadway Has a Divine, Moving Spirit," *The Los Angeles Times*, December 10, 2015.
Cooper, Merian C., Ernest B. Schoedsack, Edgar Wallace, Ruth Rose, and James Ashmore Creelman. *King Kong (1933): Shooting Script*, edited by Marian C. Cooper and Ernest B. Schoedsack. Alexander Street, 2009. https://search-alexanderstreet-com.proxy.library.nd.edu/view/work/bibliographic_entity/bibliographic_details,3070368.
Cox, Marian Roalfe. *Cinderella: Three Hundred and Forty-five Variants of Cinderella, Catskin and Cap O'Rushes*. London: Forgotten Books, 2015 [1893].
Crawford, Ryan. "Ball Culture Hitting Seattle with 'Return of the Wiz' Black Pride Event," *Seattle Gay Scene*, August 10, 2018, http://seattlegayscene.com/2018/08/ball-culture-hitting-seattle-with-return-of-the-wiz-black-pride-event/(accessed January 15, 2018).
Cubbage, Janel and Leslie Adams. "Still Ringing the Alarm: An Enduring Call to Action for Black Youth Suicide Prevention," Johns Hopkins Center for Gun Violence Solutions

(2023), 1–52, https://publichealth.jhu.edu/sites/default/files/2023-08/2023-august-still-ringing-alarm.pdf

Cummings, Judith. "Blacks Gain on Broadway; Lag in 2 Other Arts," *The New York Times*, 6 June 1975.

Darden, Robert. *People Get Ready! A New History of Black Gospel*. New York: Continuum, 2004.

Davis, Angela Y. *Blues Legacy and Black Feminism: Gertrude "Ma" Rainey, Bessie Smith, and Billy Holiday*. New York: Pantheon Books, 1998.

Davis, Thadious M. "Aishah Rahman's Writing In the Dark: The Presence of An Absence," *Obsidian III* 1, no. 1 (1999): 56–72.

Davis, Viola. *Finding Me: A Memoir*. San Francisco: HarperOne, 2022.

de la Garza, Natalie. "*Tina: The Tina Turner Musical* a Rocking Ode to Resilience," *Houston Press*, January 3, 2024, https://www.houstonpress.com/arts/things-to-do-a-review-of-tina-the-tina-turner-musical-17186985.

Diawara, Manthia, ed. *Black American Cinema*. New York: Routledge, 1993.

Dickerson, Glenda. "The Cult of True Womanhood: Toward a Womanist Attitude in African-American Theatre." *Theatre Journal* 40, no. 2 (1988): 178–187.

"Direct to DVD Film of Angela Barrow-Dunlap's Hit Stage Play 'Church Girl' Starring Robin Givens Will Hit Retail Stores on January 31, 2012," *Columbus Times*, January 25–January 31, 2012.

Dolan, Jill. *The Feminist Spectator as Critic*. Ann Arbor: University of Michigan Press, 2012 [1988].

Dolan, Jill. "Performance, Utopia, and the 'Utopian Performative,' *Theatre Journal*, 53 (2001): 455–479.

Donovan, Ryan. *Queer Approaches in Musical Theatre*. London: Methuen Drama, 2023.

Doty, Alexander. *Flaming Classics: Queering the Film Canon*. New York: Routledge, 2000.

DuMonthier, Asha, Chandra Childers, and Jessica Milli. "The Status of Black Women in the United States," The Institute for Women's Policy Research (2017), 1, https://iwpr.org/wp-content/uploads/2020/08/The-Status-of-Black-Women-6.26.17.pdf.

Duncan, Charlie. "The Color Purple Star Calls out Film for Queer Erasure: 'It's a story about Black lesbians. Period," *The Pink News*, February 22, 2023, https://www.thepinknews.com/2024/02/22/the-color-purple-star-queer-erasure-aunjanue-ellis-taylor/

Durand, Kevin K. and Mary K. Leigh, eds. *The Universe of Oz: Essays on Baum's Series and Its Progeny*. Jefferson, NC: McFarland, 2010.

Ellen, Barbara. "I Want to Break Free . . . Now," *The Observer*, April 16, 2006.

Engel, Lehman. *Musical Comedy in America*. New York: Theatre Arts Books, 1981.

Engel, Lehman. *The American Musical Theatre*. New York: Macmillan Publishing Co. Inc: 1975.

Evans, Mari, ed. *Black Women Writers (1950–1980): A Critical Evaluation*. New York: Anchor Press, 1984.

Evans-Winters, Venus E. *Teaching Black Girls: Resiliency in Urban Classrooms*. New York: Peter Lang Publishing, Inc., 2011.

Faller, Bonnie. "*The Wiz* Racist? Twitter Explodes in Furious Argument Over Show's All Black Cast," *Hollywood Life*, December 3, 2015, http://hollywoodlife.com/2015/12/03/the-wiz-live-racist-all-black-cast-nbc-twitter/ (accessed July 10, 2017).

Farrow, Kenyon. "Stephanie Mills' 'Home': So Black and So Gay!" *Kenyon Farrow Blog*, October 9, 2018, https://kenyonfarrow.com/2008/10/09/stephanie-mills-home-so-black-and-so-gay/ (accessed December 20, 2018).

Feingold, Michael. "Island-Hopping," *The Village Voice*, October 30, 1990.

Fetterly, Judith. *The Resisting Reader: A Feminist Approach to American Fiction*. Bloomington: Indiana University Press, 1978.

Flinn, Denny Martin. *Musical! A Grand Tour: The Rise, Glory, and Fall of An American Institution*. New York: Schirmer Books, 1997.

Forna, Memuna. "What's Race Got to Do With It," *Guardian*, September 13, 1993.

Forsgren, La Donna L. *In Search of Our Warrior Mothers: Women Dramatists of the Black Arts Movement.* Evanston: Northwestern University Press, 2018.

Fox, Margalit. "Rosa Guy, 89, Author of Forthright Novels for Young People," *The New York Times*, June 7, 2012.

Fox, Ted. *Showtime at the Apollo: The Epic Tale of Harlem's Legendary Theater.* New York: Holt, Rinehart and Winston, 1983.

Franklin, J. e. and Micki Grant. *The Prodigal Sister*, Alexander Street Press, 1974, https://search.alexanderstreet.com/view/work/bibliographic_entity%7Cbibliographic_details%7C3606936.

Franklin, J. e. and Micki Grant. *The Prodigal Sister: A New Black Musical.* New York: Samuel French, 1974.

Frehill-Rowe, Lisa M. "Postbellum Race Relations and Rural Land Tenure: Migration of Blacks and Whites to Kansas and Nebraska, 1870–1890," *Social Forces*, 7 (1993): 77–92.

French, Bryana H., Jioni A. Lewis, and Helen A. Neville's "Naming and Reclaiming: An Interdisciplinary Analysis of Black Girls' and Women's Resistance Strategies," *Journal of African American Studies* 17, no. 1 (2013): 1–6.

Frye, Jocelyn. "Rejecting Business As Usual: Improving Employment Outcomes and Economic Security for Black Women," National Partnership for Women & Families (July 2023), https://nationalpartnership.org/report/improving-employment-outcomes-economic-security-for-black-women/.

Funderburg, Lise, ed. *The Color Purple: A Memory Book of the Broadway Musical.* Foreword by Oprah Winfrey. New York: Carroll & Graf Publishers, 2006.

Galán, Chardée A. et al. "An Intersectional-Contextual Approach to Racial Trauma Exposure Risk, and Coping Among Black Youth," *Journal of Research on Adolescence* 32, no. 2 (2022): 583–595.

Garner, Porshé R. "What We Know and How We Know It: Defining, Black Girlhood Spirituality," in *Black Girl Magic Beyond the Hashtag: Twenty-First-Century Acts of Self-Definition*, eds. Julia S. Jordan-Zachery and Duchess Harris (Tucson: The University of Arizona Press, 2019), 105–125.

Gasman, Marybeth. "Hans in Hand: Black Women in Pursuit of the Ph.D," *Forbes*, August 9, 2021, https://www.forbes.com/sites/marybethgasman/2021/08/09/hand-in-hand-black-women-in-pursuit-of-the-phd/?sh = 57b47ec766a2

Gates Jr., Henry Louis. *The Signifying Monkey: A Theory of African-American Literary Criticism.* Oxford and New York: Oxford University Press, 1988.

Gaunt, Kyra D. *The Games Black Girls Play: Learning the Ropes From Double-Dutch to Hip-Hop.* New York: New York University Press, 2006.

Gaunt, Kyra D. "YouTube, Twerking & You: Context Collapse and the Handheld Co-Presence of Black Girls and Miley Cyrus," *Journal of Popular Music Studies* 27, no. 3 (2015): 244–273.

Gaver, Jack. "Music and Lyrics Make 'The Prodigal Sister' Shine," *Los Angeles Times*, December 2, 1974.

Gilman, Sander L. "Black Bodies, White Bodies: Toward an Iconography of Female Sexuality in Late Nineteenth-Century Art, Medicine, and Literature," *Critical Inquiry* 12, no. 1 (1985): 204–242.

Gonzales, Prizgar R. "A Conversation with Rosa Guy," *Quarterly Black Review of Books* 1, no. 3 (February 28, 1994): 33.

Goodkind, Sara, Britney G. Brinkman, and Kathi Elliott. "Redefining Resilience and Reframing Resistance: Empowerment Programming with Black Girls to Address Societal Inequities," *Behavioral Medicine* 46, no. 3–4 (2020): 317–329.

Gordon, Robert and Olaf Jubin, eds. *The Oxford Handbook of the British Musical.* Oxford: Oxford University Press, 2016.

Gottfried, Martin. "Lady Day: A Musical Tragedy," *Women's Wear Daily*, October 27, 1972.

Green, Jesse and Ben Brantley. "Review: 'King Kong' Is the Mess that Roared," *The New York Times*, November 8, 2018, https://www.nytimes.com/2018/11/08/theater/king-kong-review.html

Gussow, Mel. "Casting by Race Can Be Touchy," *The New York Times*, August 1, 1976.

Gussow, Mel. "Stage: 'Madame Zora,' A Biographical Musical," *The New York Times*, March 2, 1986.

Gussow, Mel. "Stage: 'Prodigal Sister,'" *The New York Times*, July 16, 1974.

Guy, Rosa. *My Love, My Love, or, the Peasant Girl*. Minneapolis: Coffee House Press, 2001.

Hall, Jacquelyn Dowd. "The Long Civil Rights Movement and Political Uses of the Past," *Journal of American History* 91, no. 4 (2005): 1233–1263.

Hankinson, Bobby. "Gay Iconography: Tina Turner Is Simply The Best," *Towleroad Gay News*, August 22, 2015, https://www.towleroad.com/2015/08/gay-iconography-tina-turner/

Hansberry, Lorraine. *Lorraine Hansberry in Her Own Words: To Be Young, Gifted and Black*. New York: Vintage Books, 1995 [1969].

Harrington, Richard. "Gotta Sing, and Very Charmingly," *The Washington Post*, March 27, 1986.

Harris, Jessica B. "Harper a Show Biz 'Wiz,'" *New York Amsterdam News*, March 29, 1975.

Harris, Jessica B. "'Prodigal Sister' Rises Above Its Weaknesses," *New York Amsterdam News*, December 7, 1974.

Harris, Laura Alexandra. "Queer Black Feminism: The Pleasure Principle," *Feminist Review*, 54 (1996): 3–30.

Harrison, Daphne Duval. *Black Pearls: Blues Queens of the 1920s*. New Brunswick and London: Rutgers University Press, 1988.

Harrison, Paul Carter, Victor Leo Walker, and Gus Edwards, eds. *Black Theatre: Ritual Performance in the African Diaspora*. Philadelphia: Temple University Press, 2002.

Hartman, Saidiya. *Lose Your Mother: A Journey Along the Atlantic Slave Route*. New York: Farrar, Straus and Giroux, 2007.

Hasse, Donald, ed. *Fairy Tales and Feminism: New Approaches*. Detroit: Wayne State University Press, 2004.

Hay, Samuel A. *African American Theatre: An Historical and Critical Analysis*. Cambridge: Cambridge University Press, 1994.

Heller, Scott and Nancy Coleman. "'King Kong' and 'Cher Show' Musicals Announce Closings," *The New York Times*, June 25, 2019.

Higginbotham, Evelyn Brooks. *Righteous Discontent: The Women's Movement in the Black Baptist Church, 1880–1920*. Cambridge: Harvard University Press, 1993.

Higginsen, Vy with Tonya Bolden. *Mama, I Want To Sing*. New York: Scholastic, 1992.

Hill, Dominique C. "Blackgirl, One Word: Necessary Transgressions in the Name of Imagining Black Girlhood," *Cultural Studies, Critical Methodologies* 19, no. 4 (2016): 1–9.

Hill, Errol G. and James V. Hatch, eds. *A History of African American Theatre*. Cambridge: Cambridge University Press, 2003.

Hine, Darlene Clark. *Hine Sight: Black Women and the Re-Construction of American History*. New York: Carlson Publishing, 1994.

Hobson, Janell. *Black Girl Magic Beyond the Hashtag: Twenty-First-Century Acts of Self-Definition*. Tucson: University of Arizona Press, 2019.

Holiday, Billie and William Duffy. *Lady Sings the Blues*. New York: Penguin Books, 1992 [rpt. 1956].

Honkasalo, Julian. "Genderqueer," *lambda nordica* 25, no. 1 (2020): 57–63.

hooks, bell. *Bone Black: Memories of Girlhood*. New York: Henry Holt and Company, 1996.

hooks, bell. *Reel to Real: Race, Sex, and Class at the Movies*. New York: Routledge, 1996.

Hopkins, Kristin Bria. "There's No Business Like Show Business: Abandoning Color-Blind Casting and Embracing Color-Conscious Casting in American Theatre," *Journal of Sports and Entertainment Law* 9, no. 2 (2018): 131–155.

Hull, Akasha Gloria. *Soul Talk: The New Spirituality of African American Women*. Rochester, VT: Inner Traditions International, 2001.

Hurston, Zora Neale, ed. *Zora Neale Hurston: Folklore, Memoirs, and Other Writings*. New York: The Library of America, 1995 [1934].

Hurston, Zora Neale. *Their Eyes Were Watching God.* New York: Amistad, 2006 [1937].

Jacobs, Harriet. *Incidents in the Life of a Slave Girl.* New York: Dover Publications, 2001[rpt. 1861].

Jaye, Michael C. and Ann Chalmers Watts, eds. *Literature and the Urban Experience: Essays on the City and Literature.* New Brunswick, N.J.: Rutgers University Press, 1981.

Jernigan, Maryam M. and Jessica Henderson Daniel. "Racial Trauma in the Lives of Black Children and Adolescents: Challenges and Clinical Implications," *Journal of Child and Adolescent Trauma,* 4 (2011): 123–141.

Johnson, E. Patrick. *Black. Queer. Southern. Women.* Chapel Hill: University of North Carolina Press, 2018.

Johnson, E. Patrick. *Honeypot: Black Southern Women Who Love Women.* Durham, NC: Duke University Press, 2019.

Johnson, E. Patrick. *Sweet Tea: Black Gay Men of the South.* Chapel Hill: University of North Carolina Press, 2008.

Johnson, James Weldon. *The Autobiography of an Ex-Colored Man.* New York: Library of America Paperback Classics, 2011 [1912].

Karpf, Juanita. "Vinnette Carroll," *Notable Women in the American Theatre: A Biographical Dictionary.* Westport, CT: Greenwood Press, 1989.

Kennedy, Mark. "Broadway's Tony Nominations in for Tina Turner musical," *Miami Times,* March 3–9, 2021.

Khan-Cullors, Patrisse and Asha Bandele, *When They Call You a Terrorist: A Black Lives Matter Memoir.* New York: St. Martin's Griffin, 2020.

Kidd, Sue Monk. *The Secret Life of Bees.* New York: Penguin Books, 2002.

Kilian, Michael. "Caribbean Tales: The Gods Make 'Island' a Simple But Profound Hit," *Chicago Tribune,* March 29, 1992.

King Kong, book by Jack Thorne, score by Marius de Vries, songs by Eddie Perfect, directed by Drew McOnie, Broadway Theatre, New York, July 31, 2019.

"'King Kong' Musical, With Eye on Broadway, Opens in Australia," *The Guardian,* June 17, 2013.

"King Kong Review-Broadway Kills the Beast in Monstrously Bad Musical," *The Guardian,* https://www.theguardian.com/stage/2018/nov/08/king-kong-review-braodway-musical (accessed July 24, 2024).

Kissell, Rick. "*The Wiz Live* Ratings Strong: NBC Musical Draws 11.5 Million Viewers," *Variety,* December 4, 2015, http://variety.com/2015/tv/news/the-wiz-live-ratings-nbc-musical-1201653402/ (accessed July 7, 2017).

Klein, Alvin. "Dorothy and Wiz Hip-Hop into the 90's," *The New York Times,* February 7, 1993.

Koza, Julia Eklund. "Unhappy Happy Endings: Cultural Politics in the Broadway Musical Hit 'Once on This Island,'" *The Review of Education/Pedagogy/Cultural Studies* 19, no. 4 (1997): 367–407.

LaChiusa, Michael John. "Open Season," *Opera News* 79, no. 2 (August 2014): 14–15.

LaChiusa, Michael John. "The Great Gray Way: Is Prognosis Negative for the Broadway Musical?" *Opera News,* 1 (August 2005): 30–35.

Larkin, Colin. *The Guinness Encyclopedia of Popular Music: Lincoln, Abe-Primettes.* Middlesex: Guinness Publishing, 1995.

Larkin, Colin. *The Encyclopedia of Popular Music,* 4 ed. Oxford: Oxford University Press, 2006.

Lawrence, Tim. "Disco and Queering the Dance Floor." *Cultural Studies* 25, no. 2 (2011): 230–243.

Laws, Zach. "Mary J. Blige on Playing the Wicked Witch Evillene in *The Wiz Live!*" interview with Mary J. Blige, YouTube, June 19, 2016, www.youtube.com/watch?v = eIiwtZfL7nk (accessed August 3, 2017).

Leath, Seanna et al. "Raising Resilient Black Women: A Study of Superwoman Mothering and Strength as a Form of Gendered Racial Socialization in Black Mother-Daughter Relationships," *Sex Roles,* 89 (2023): 625–642.

Lee, Ashley. "The 40-year Fight Over 'The Color Purple's' Queer Love Story," *Los Angeles Times*, December 21, 2023, https://www.latimes.com/entertainment-arts/movies/story/2023-12-21/the-color-purple-celie-shug-queerness-musical-movie-alice-walker.

Lee, Hatty. "Three Black Female Playwrights Debut New York on Broadway," *Colorlines*, September 21, 2011, www.colorlines.com/articles/3-black-female-playwrights-debut-new-work-broadway(accessed January 16, 2019).

Lewis, Emory. "Hallelujah for Gospel Show," *Bergen Record*, December 23, 1976.

Lieberman, Marcia R. "'Some Day My Prince Will Come': Female Acculturation through the Fairy Tale," *College English*, 34 (1972): 383–395.

Liptak, Adam. "Supreme Court Revives Transgender Ban for Military Service," *New York Times*, January 22, 2019, *www.nytimes.com/2019/01/22/us/politics/transgender-ban-military-supreme-court.html* (accessed January 22, 2019).

Loney, Glenn. *Musical Theatre in America: Papers and Proceedings of the Conference on the Musical Theatre in America*. Westport: Greenwood Press, 1984.

Lorde, Audre. *Sister Outsider: Essays and Speeches by Audre Lorde*. Berkeley: Crossing Press, 2007 [rpt. 1984].

Lurie, Alison. "Fairy Tale Liberation," *New York Review of Books*, December 17, 1970: 42–44.

Lurie, Alison. "Witches and Fairies: Fitzgerald to Updike," *New York Review of Books*, December 2, 1971: 6–11.

Mackey, Joshua S. "5 Ways Tina Turner Proved She Was a Gay Icon," *Into*, May 25, 2023, https://www.intomore.com/entertainment/music/5-ways-tina-turner-proved-she-was-a-gay-icon/.

Mahon, Maureen. *Black Diamond Queens: African American Women and Rock and Roll*. Durham: Duke University Press, 2020.

Mama, I Want to Sing, written and directed by Charles Randolph-Wright, adapted from the 1983, stage musical, Universal City, CA: CodeBlack Entertainment, 2012, DVD.

Mama, I Want to Sing, script by Vy Higginsen and Ken Wydro, directed by Ken Wydro, El Teatro (formerly Heckscher Theatre), New York, NY, November 16, 2020.

Mann, Brian. "After 50 Years Of The War On Drugs, 'What Good Is It Doing For Us'?" *NPR*, June 17, 2021, https://www.npr.org/2021/06/17/1006495476/after-50-years-of-the-war-on-drugs-what-good-is-it-doing-for-us.

"Mapping Police Violence: Unarmed Victims" at https://mappingpoliceviolence.org/unarmed (accessed August 25, 2017).

Marovich, Robert M. *A City Called Heaven: Chicago and the Birth of Gospel Music*. Urbana: University of Illinois Press, 2015.

Martin, Civilla D. "His Eye Is on the Sparrow" (1905) https://hymnary.org/text/why_should_i_feel_discouraged_why_should.

"Mary J. Blige Talks 'Wiz' Critics' Choice Nomination," *E! News*, YouTube, January 20, 2016, www.youtube.com/watch?v = 9XDY-ZvAta0 (accessed August 3, 2017).

Mattson, Christina Phillips and Maria Tatar, "Fairy Tales, Myth, and Fantasy," in *New Approaches to Teaching Folk and Fairy Tales*, eds. Claudia Schwabe and Christa Jones (Logan, UT: Utah State University Press, 2016), 21–34, 23.

Meacham, Mike. "The Exoduster Movement," *Western Journal of Black Studies* 27, no. 2 (2003): 108–117.

McCarter, Jeremy. "Metropolitan Oprah," *New York Magazine*, December 1, 2005, https://nymag.com/nymetro/arts/theater/reviews/15230/.

McClinton, Calvin A. *The Work of Vinnette Carroll: An African American Theatre*. Woodstock, IL: Edwin Mellen Press, 2000.

McDonell-Parry, Amelia. "Doris Troy," *Rollingstone*, issue 944, March 18, 2004.

McDonough, Ashley. "Why Black Sisterhood is The Unshakable Bond that Keeps Us Going," *Elite Daily*, October 11, 2017, https://www.elitedaily.com/p/what-is-black-sisterhood-you-ask-why-its-the-unshakeable-bond-that-keeps-us-going-2807361#:~:text=Black%20sisterhood%20is%20an%20unexplainable,been%20passed%20down%20throughout%20generations.

McMahon, Rashida Z. Shaw. *The Black Circuit: Race, Performance, and Spectatorship in Black Popular Theatre*. New York: Routledge, 2020.

Mickenberg, Julia L. "Radical Children's Literature for Adults in *The Inner City Mother Goose*," *Journal of Children's Literature Research*, 42 (2019): 1–29.

Mink, Casey. "Just Try and Stop Her," *Backstage*, July 23, 2020: 12–16.

Mohamed, Besheer, Kiana Cox, Jeff Diamant, and Claire Gecewicz. "Faith Among Black Americans," Pew Research Center, February 16, 2021, 109, https://www.pewresearch.org/religion/2021/02/16/faith-among-black-americans/.

Moore, Mignon R. "Color Us Invisible: In the Shadows of Communities Black and Gay, Black Lesbians Forge Lives, Loves, and Family," Huffpost, November 4, 2011 (updated 2 February 2016), www.huffingtonpost.com/mignon-r-moore/black-lesbians_b_1075251.html (accessed January 19, 2018).

Morago, Cherrie and Gloria E. Anzaldúa, eds. *This Bridge Called My Back: Writings By Radical Women of Color*. New York: SUNY Press, 1981.

Mordden, Ethan. *Anything Goes: A History of American Musical Theatre*. New York: Oxford University Press, 2013.

Mordden, Ethan. *Broadway Babies: The People Who Made the American Musical*. New York: Oxford University Press, 1983.

Morris, Monique W. *Pushout: The Criminalization of Black Girls in Schools*. Foreword by Mankaprr and Melissa Harris-Perry. New York: The New Press, 2016.

Morton, Matthew, Amy Dworsky, and Sonali Patel, "Missed Opportunities: LGBTQ youth Homelessness in America," Chicago, IL: Chapin Hall at the University of Chicago, 2018. https://www.chapinhall.org/research/lgbtq-young-adults-experience-homelessness-at-more-than-twice-the-rate-of-peers/

Morton, Ray. *King Kong the History of a Movie Icon: From Fay Wray to Peter Jackson*. New York: Applause Theatre & Cinema Books, 2005.

Moynihan, Daniel Patrick et al. *The Negro Family: The Case for National Action*. Washington, DC: GPO, 1965.

Napoleon, Davi. *Chelsea on the Edge: The Adventures of an American Theater*. Ames, Iowa: Iowa State University Press, 1991.

Nathan, David. *The Soulful Divas: Personal Portraits of Over a Dozen Divine Divas, from Nina Simone, Aretha Franklin & Diana Ross to Patti LaBelle, Whitney Houston & Janet Jackson*. New York: Billboard Books, 1999.

"National Assessment of Adult Literacy," National Center for Education Statistics, 2026, https://nces.ed.gov/naal/lit_history.asp#:~:text = In%201870%2C%2020%20percent%20of,percent%20of%20blacks%20remained%20illiterate(accessed March 10, 2026).

"National Hit Musical Stage Play 'Church Girl' Brings All-Star Cast to Houston," Press Release, April 30, 2010, https://www.newswire.com/news/national-hit-musical-stage-play-church-girl-brings-all-star-cast-to-148346.

Neal, Larry. "The Black Arts Movement," *The Drama Review* 12, no.4 (1968): 29–39.

Nixon, Richard. "Remarks About an Intensified Program for Drug Abuse Prevention and Control" The American Presidency Project, June 17, 1971, https://www.presidency.ucsb.edu/documents/remarks-about-intensified-program-for-drug-abuse-prevention-and-control (accessed June 26, 2024).

Norris, Jerrie. *Presenting Rosa Guy*. Boston: Twayne Publishers, 1988.

Once on This Island, cast album, New York: BMG Music, 1990, CD.

Ongiri, Amy Abugo. *Spectacular Blackness: The Cultural Politics of the Black Power Movement and the Search for a Black Aesthetic*. Charlottesville: University of Virginia Press, 2010.

Panchuk, Michelle and Michael Rea, eds. *Voices from the Edge: Centering Marginalized Perspectives in Analytic Theology*. Oxford: Oxford University Press, 2020.

Parkerson, Michelle. *Stormé: The Lady in the Jewel Box*, 21 min., color, 16mm/video. Eye of the Storm Productions, Inc., 1987.

Passy, Charles. "Tina Turner Musical Is Rollin' at the Box Office," *Wall Street Journal*, October 29, 2019.

Perrault, Charles. *The Tales of Mother Goose*, trans. Charles Welsh. Boston: D.C. Heath & Co., Publishers, 1901[1696], https://www.gutenberg.org/cache/epub/17208/pg17208-images.html.

Perry, Katy. "Roar," *Prism* (2013), https://www.youtube.com/watch?v = CevxZvSJLk8.

Phillips, Carmen. "If Only 'The Color Purple' Had Loved Us All," Autostraddle, December 19, 2023, https://www.autostraddle.com/the-color-purple-review/.

Posner, Gerald. *Motown: Music, Money, Sex, and Power*. New York: Random House, 2002.

Quinn, Kate, ed. *Black Power in the Caribbean*. Gainesville, FL: University Press of Florida, 2014.

Rahman, Aishah. *Chewed Water: A Memoir*. Lebanon: University Press of New England, 2001.

Rahman, Aishah. *Lady Day*, Alexander Street, 1972, https://search-alexanderstreet-com.proxy.library.nd.edu/view/work/bibliographic_entity%7Cbibliographic_details%7C3607299#search/lady + day.

Rahman, Aishah. *Tale of Madame Zora*, Alexander Street, 1985, https://search.alexanderstreet.com/view/work/bibliographic_entity%7Cdocument%7C3876691.

Richardson, Kalia. "'Mama, I Want to Sing!' Returns for 40th Anniversary," *The New York Times*, February 24, 2023, https://www.nytimes.com/2023/02/24/theater/mama-i-want-to-sing-40th-anniversary.html.

Rizzo, Frank. "Off Broadway Review: 'The Secret Life of Bees," *Variety*, June 13, 2019, https://variety.com/2019/legit/reviews/secret-life-of-bees-review-musical-atlantic-theater-1203242056/.

Rollins, Bryant. "Does *The Wiz* Say Something Extra to Blacks?" *The New York Times*, December 28, 1975.

Romano, Nick. "The New King of Broadway: Meet the King Kong Musical's 2,000-pound Puppet," *Entertainment Weekly*, November 5, 2018, https://ew.com/theater/2018/11/05/king-kong-musical-broadway-puppet/.

Rooney, David. "Tina: The Tina Turner Musical," *The Hollywood Reporter*, November 13, 2019: 87.

Rooney, David. "Walker's Message a 'Purple' People Pleasure," *Variety*, December 5–11, 2005: 42, 59.

Rosenfield, Bill. Untitled, *Once on This Island*, liner notes, New York: BMG Music, 1990, CD, 4–5.

Rowe, Karen E. "Feminism and Fairy Tales," *Women's Studies*, 6 (1979): 237–257.

Rude, Mey. "The Queer Love Story at the Heart of *The Color Purple* Has Been Restored," *Out*, November 28, 2023, https://www.out.com/film/the-color-purple-lesbian.

Ryzik, Melena. "The Story Behind the Return of The Wiz," *New York Times*, November 30, 2015, www.nytimes.com/2015/12/01/arts/television/the-wiz-with-added-street-cred-heads-for-tv-and-broadway.html?mcubz = 3 (accessed July 24, 2017).

Sanford, Tim and Robert O' Hara. "Artist Interview with Robert O' Hara," Playwrights Horizons, October 21, 2014, https://www.playwrightshorizons.org/shows/trailers/artist-interview-robert-ohara/.

Savran, David. *A Queer Sort of Materialism: Recontextualizing American Theater*. Ann Arbor, University of Michigan Press, 2003.

Sawyer, Wendy and Peter Wagner. "Mass Incarceration: The Whole Pie 2024," *Prison Policy Initiative*, March 14, 2024, https://www.prisonpolicy.org/reports/pie2024.html#:~:text=Together%2C%20these%20systems%20hold%20over,centers%2C%20state%20psychiatric%20hospitals%2C%20and

Schwabe, Claudia and Christa Jones, eds. *New Approaches to Teaching Folk and Fairy Tales*. Logan, UT: Utah State University Press, 2016.

Scott, Lucile M. "Too Short to Box With God Gets to Audience," *Atlantic Daily World*, May 13, 1979.

Seeley, Thomas D. *The Lives of Bees: The Untold Story of the Honey Bee in the Wild*. Princeton, NJ: Princeton University Press, 2019.

Sexual Assault Support Center Inc. "Statistics: African-American & Black Communities," https://www.thecenterat909.org/africanamerican (accessed May 3, 2021).

Shapiro, Eddie. *Nothing Like a Dame: Conversations With the Great Women of Musical Theatre.* New York: Oxford University Press, 2014.

Spencer, Patricia Ann. "The Harlem Children's Theatre Company: No Longer a 'Crazy Idea' Cover . . . ," *New York Amsterdam News*, December 13, 1975.

Spencer, Patricia Ann. "'The Liberation of Mother Goose' A Heavy Satire for Children," *New York Amsterdam News*, December 13, 1975.

Smith, Angela E. "Bright Cast, Lively Music in New Play," *New York Amsterdam News*, July 27, 1974.

Smith, Mychal Denzel. "The Dangerous Myth of the 'Missing Black Father,'" *Washington Post*, January 10, 2017, www.washingtonpost.com/posteverything/wp/2017/01/10/the-dangerous-myth-of-the-missing-black-father/?noredirect = on&utm_term=.9f2391d55e87 (accessed January 19, 2018).

Smith, Rob. "Five Reasons *the Wiz Live* Was the Gayest Thing on TV This Year," *Queerty**, December 4, 2015, www.queerty.com/five-reasons-the-wiz-live-was-the-gayest-thing-on-tv-this-year-20151204(accessed July 9, 2017).

Sontag, Susan. *Against Interpretation and Other Essays.* London: Penguin Books, 2009 [rpt. 1966].

Stack, Tim. "*The Wiz Live*: On the Set of NBC's Latest Musical Event," interview with Queen Latifah, *Entertainment Weekly*, December 2, 2015, www.ew.com/article/2015/12/02/wiz-live-production-set/ (accessed July 7, 2017).

Staiger, Janet. *Media Reception Studies.* New York: New York University Press, 2005.

Stasio, Marilyn. "Tina: The Tina Turner Musical," *Variety*, November 12, 2019: 213.

Steele, Jazmine. "New Plays Reveal Women's Stories," *The Michigan Citizen*, March 21, 2010.

Surviving R. Kelly, written and directed by Nigel Bellis and Astral Finnie. New York: Lifetime, 2019.

Tapley, Mel. "Harlem's Children's Group Tops Black Arts Festival," *New York Amsterdam News*, November 25, 1978.

Tapley, Mel. "Is City Forcing 'Mama' to Close?: Is City Forcing 'Mama, I Want to Sing' to Cry?" *New York Amsterdam News*, February 16, 1991.

Taylor, Millie. *Musical Theatre, Realism, Entertainment.* Burlington, VT: Ashgate Publishing Limited, 2012.

Teer, Barbara Ann. "The Black Woman: She Does Exist," *The New York Times*, May 14, 1967.

"The Broadway Show: Schele Williams on Directing the Return of THE WIZ," Broadwaycom, uploaded August 29, 2023, https://www.youtube.com/watch?v = xDRYeLT1L9I&t = 4s.

The Color Purple, directed by Stephen Spielberg. Burbank: Warner Brother Pictures, 1985, DVD.

The Color Purple: A Memory Book of the Broadway Musical. New York: Carroll & Graf, 2006.

The Color Purple Original Broadway Cast Recording, New York: Angel Records, 2006, CD.

The Color Purple, directed by Blitz Bazawule. Burbank, CA: Warner Bros. Pictures, 2023, DVD.

The Other Cinderella, book, music, and lyrics by Jackie Taylor, directed by Jackie Taylor, Black Ensemble Theatre, Chicago, November 15, 2019.

"The Wiz Broadway Grosses," https://www.broadwayworld.com/grosses/THE-WIZ (accessed September 10, 2024).

The Wiz, book by William F. Brown, music and lyrics by Charlie Smalls, additional material by Amber Ruffin, and directed by Schele Williams, Marquis Theatre, New York, April 2, 2024.

The Wiz, directed by Sidney Lumet, prod. Motown Productions, dist. Universal Pictures, 1978; Universal City, CA: Universal Pictures Home Entertainment, 2009, DVD.

The Wiz Live!, directed by Kenny Leon and Matthew Diamond. Universal City, CA: Universal Studios Home Entertainment, 2015, DVD.

Thomas, Tiffany. "The Legacy of Women in the Black Church," *Christianity Today*, February 11, 2016, www.christianitytoday.com/women-leaders/2016/february/legacy-of-women-in-black-church.html (accessed July 19, 2017).

Tillet, Salamishah. "The Great Experiment That Is 'The Color Purple,'" *The New York Times*, December 24, 2023.

Tina, directed by Dan Lindsay and TJ Martin, HBO Documentary Films, Santa Monica, CA, 2021, DVD.

Tina: The Tina Turner Musical, book by Katori Hall, with Frank Ketelaar and Kees Prins, directed by Phyllida Lloyd, Lunt-Fontanne Theatre, New York, NY, November 23, 2019.

Tina: The Tina Turner Musical Original Cast Recording, liner notes, New York, NY: Sh-K-Boom Records, LLC, 2019, CD.

"Tina-The Tina Turner Musical Broadway Grosses," 2026, https://www.broadwayworld.com/grosses/TINA-THE-TINA-TURNER-MUSICAL (accessed August 21, 2024).

Turner, Ike with Nigel Cawthorne. *Takin' Back My Name: The Confessions of Ike Turner*. Scotts Valley, CA: CreateSpace Independent Publishing Platform, 2015 [rpt. 1999].

Turner, Tina with Kurt Loder. *I, Tina: My Life Story*. New York: William Morrow, 2010 [rpt. 1986].

Vaz da Silva, Francisco. "Charles Perrault and the Evolution of 'Little Red Riding Hood,'" *Marvels & Tales* 30, no. 2 (2016): 167–190.

Visser, Irene. "Fairy Tale and Trauma in Toni Morrison's 'Home,'" *Negotiating Trauma and Affect* 41, no. 1 (2016): 148–164.

Walker, Alice. *In Search of Our Mothers' Gardens: Womanist Prose*. San Diego: Harcourt Brace Jovanovich, 1983.

Walker, Alice. "In Search of Zora Neal Hurston," *Ms.* 3, no. 9 (March 1, 1975), 74–89.

Walker, Alice. *The Color Purple*. New York: Pocket Books, 1982.

Walker, Alice. *The Same River Twice: Honoring the Difficult*. New York: Scribner, 1996.

Wallace, Michele. *Black Macho and the Myth of the Superwoman*. New York: Dial Press, 1978.

Weinraub, Judith. "The Writer's Happily Ever After: Rosa Guy and the Musical With a Fairy Tale Ending," *The Washington Post*, May 26, 1992.

Wellington, Dwain. "'Church Girl'- - A Theatrical Review," September 3, 2011, https://dwainwellington.wordpress.com/2011/09/03/%E2%80%9Cchurch-girl%E2%80%9D-a-theatrical-review/.

"We See You White American Theatre," https://www.weseeyouwat.com/statement (accessed March 9, 2026).

Wheeler, Duncan. "The Rock Musical: From Creation to Curation (2015–2020)," *New Theatre Quarterly* 39, no. 2 (May 2023): 159–180.

"When Zora Neale Hurston Was Falsely Accused of Child Molestation," Prison Culture: How the PIC Structures Our World (March 31, 2013), https://www.usprisonculture.com/blog/2013/03/31/when-zora-neale-hurston-was-falsely-accused-of-child-molestation/.

Whitfield, Sara, ed. *Reframing the Musical: Race, Culture and Identity*. London: Red Globe Press, 2019.

Williams, Delores S. *Sisters in the Wilderness: The Challenge of Womanist God-Talk*. Maryknoll, NY: Orbis Books, 1993.

Williams, Mance. *Black Theatre in the 1960s and 1970s: A Historical-Critical Analysis of the Movement*. Westport, CT: Greenwood Press, 1985.

Williams, V. 'Mama I want to sing': Play Delivers Powerful Performances," *Afro-American*, April 5, 1986.

Wills, Cheryl. *Isn't Her Grace Amazing!: The Women Who Changed Gospel Music*. New York: Amistad, 2022.

Wilson, James F. *Bulldaggers, Pansies, and Chocolate Babies: Performance, Race, and Sexuality in the Harlem Renaissance*. Ann Arbor: University of Michigan Press, 2010.

Wolf, Stacy. *A Problem Like Maria: Gender and Sexuality in the American Musical*. Ann Arbor: University of Michigan Press, 2002.

Wolf, Stacy. *Beyond Broadway: The Pleasure and Promise of Musical Theatre Across America.* New York: Oxford University Press, 2020.

Wolf, Stacy. *Changed for Good: A Feminist History of the Broadway Musical.* Oxford: Oxford University Press, 2011.

Woll, Allen. *Black Musical Theatre: From Coontown to Dreamgirls.* Baton Rouge: Louisiana State University Press, 1989.

Woodall, Nate. "Tina Turner, Queen of Rock 'N' Roll, Dies at 83," *Q News*, May 25, 2023, https://qnews.com.au/tina-turner-queen-of-rock-n-roll-dies-at-83/.

Wratten, Marcus. "Tina Turner Was a Fearless LGBTQ+ Ally – Long Before it Was Popular to Be One," *PinkNews*, May 25, 2023, https://www.thepinknews.com/2023/05/25/tina-turner-lgbtq-ally-legacy/.

Wray, Fay. *On the Other Hand: A Life Story.* New York: St. Martin's Press, 1989.

Wright, Nazera Sadiq. *Black Girlhood in the Nineteenth Century.* Urbana: University of Illinois Press, 2016.

Yenika-Agbaw, Vivian, Ruth McKoy Lowery, and Laretta Henderson, eds. *Fairy Tales with Black Consciousness: Essays on Adaptations of Familiar Stories.* Jefferson, NC: McFarland & Company, 2013.

Young, Jemimah L., Marquita D. Foster, and Dorothy Hines. "Even Cinderella Is White," *The English Journal* 107, no. 6 (2018): 102–108.

Young, Patricia A. "Acts of Terrorism, or, Violence on 'Sunday Morning in the South,'" *MELUS* 26, no. 4 (Winter 2001): 25–39.

Zinobia, Bennefield and Jackson Taylor, "The Girls Are Alright: Examining Protective Factors of US Black Culture and Its Impact on the Resilience of Black Girls and Women," *Open Cultural Studies*, 6 (2002): 218–227.

Zipes, Jack. *The Trials and Tribulations of Little Red Riding Hood.* New York: Routledge, 1993.

Zipes, Jack. *When Dreams Came True: Classical Fairy Tales and Their Tradition.* New York: Routledge, 2007.

Index

For the benefit of digital users, indexed terms that span two pages (e.g., 52–53) may, on occasion, appear on only one of those pages.